Luxury in the Eighteenth Century

Frontispiece, Bernard Mandeville, *The Fable of the Bees: or, Private Vices, Publick Benefits*, first edition, 1714 (courtesy of the British Library, London).

Luxury in the Eighteenth Century

Debates, Desires and Delectable Goods

Edited by

Maxine Berg
Professor of History and Director of the Warwick Eighteenth Century Centre
University of Warwick

and

Elizabeth Eger
Lecturer
Department of English
King's College London

macmillan

First published in hardback 2003
First published in paperback 2007 by
PALGRAVE MACMILLAN
Houndmills, Basingstoke, Hampshire RG21 6XS and
175 Fifth Avenue, New York, N.Y. 10010
Companies and representatives throughout the world

PALGRAVE MACMILLAN is the global academic imprint of the Palgrave
Macmillan division of St. Martin's Press, LLC and of Palgrave Macmillan Ltd.
Macmillan® is a registered trademark in the United States, United Kingdom
and other countries. Palgrave is a registered trademark in the European
Union and other countries.

ISBN-13: 978-0-333-96382-1 hardback
ISBN-10: 0-333-96382-2 hardback
ISBN-13: 978-0-230-51779-0 paperback
ISBN-10: 0-230-51779-X paperback

This book is printed on paper suitable for recycling and made from fully managed and
sustained forest sources.

A catalogue record for this book is available from the British Library.

Library of Congress Cataloging-in-Publication Data
Luxury in the eighteenth century : debates, desires and delectable goods / edited by
Maxine Berg and Elizabeth Eger.
      p. cm.
   Includes bibliographical references and index.
   ISBN 0-333-96382-2
      1. Luxury – History – 18th century.   2. Wealth – History – 18th century.
   3. Economic history – 1600–1750.   4. Economic history – 1750–1918.   I. Berg,
   Maxine, 1950–   II. Eger, Elizabeth.

   HC52.5 .L89 2002
   306.3–dc21   2002075805

10   9   8   7   6   5   4   3   2
16   15   14   13   12   11   10   09   08   07

Printed and bound in Great Britain by
Antony Rowe Ltd, Chippenham and Eastbourne

Contents

List of Plates

List of Contributors

Ros Ballaster is Fellow and Tutor in English Literature, Mansfield College, Oxford. She is the author of *Seductive Forms: Women's Amatory Fiction 1684–1740* (1989) and *Women's Worlds: Ideology, Femininity and the Women's Magazine* (1991).

Maxine Berg is Professor of History and Director of the Warwick Eighteenth-Century Centre at the University of Warwick. She directed the Luxury Project 1997–2001, and is now director of the Leverhulme Art and Industry Project. She is the co-editor with Helen Clifford of *Consumers and Luxury: Consumer Culture in Europe 1650–1850* (1999), and author of *The Age of Manufactures 1700–1820* (1994). She is completing a book entitled *Consumer Delight: Modern Luxury in Eighteenth-Century England*.

John Crowley is George Munro Professor of History at Dalhousie University, Halifax, Nova Scotia. He is the author of *The Invention of Comfort: Sensibilities and Design in Early Modern Britain and Early America* (2001) and *The Privileges of Independence: Neo-Mercantilism and the American Revolution*. He is now researching the development of a global landscape in British visual culture 1750–1820.

Rebecca Earle is Lecturer in Comparative American Studies, University of Warwick. She has recently completed a book on New Granada in the late colonial period, and has edited a volume on *Epistolary Selves: Letter Writers, 1600–1945*. She is currently researching gender and race in late eighteenth and early nineteenth-century Spanish America.

Elizabeth Eger is a Lecturer in the Department of English, Kings College London. She has been Research Fellow in the Department of English, University of Liverpool. She was the Luxury Research Fellow in the Warwick Eighteenth-Century Centre. She is co-editor of *Women and the Public Sphere* (2000), and editor of *The Selected Writings of Elizabeth Montagu* (1999). She completed a thesis, now being revised for publication, on '*The Nine Living Muses of Great Britain*: Women, Reason and Literary Community in Eighteenth-Century England'.

Laurence Fontaine is Professor of History, The European University Institute, and CNRS, Paris. She is the author of *A History of Pedlars in Europe* (1996).

Dena Goodman is Professor of History at the University of Michigan, Ann Arbor, and author of *The Republic of Letters* (1994).

Edward Hundert is Professor of History, University of British Columbia and author of *The Enlightenment's Fable: Bernard Mandeville and the Discovery of Society* (1994).

Vivien Jones is Senior Lecturer in English, University of Leeds and author of *How to Study a Jane Austen Novel* (second edition 1997), and *Women in the Eighteenth Century: Constructions of Femininity* (1990).

Michael McKeon is Professor of English at Rutgers University, New York. His research interests include the prehistory of domestic fiction, the theory of the novel and the nature of the early modern 'division of knowledge'. His publications include *Politics and Poetry in Restoration England: The Case of Dryden's 'Annus Mirabilis'* (1975), *The Origins of the English Novel* (1987) and *Theory of the Novel: A Historical Approach* (editor, 2000). He is completing a new book, *The Secret History of Domesticity: Public, Private, and the Division of Knowledge.*

Annie Richardson is a lecturer in the History of Art and Design at the University of Southampton. Publications on Hogarth's aesthetic theory include 'Framing One's Own Fortune: the Country Dance in Hogarth's Analysis of Beauty', DHDS Conference Proceedings, 2001, and 'An Aesthetics of Performance: Dance in Hogarth's Analysis of Beauty', forthcoming in *Dance Research.*

John Styles is Director of the MA in the History of Design, V&A/Royal College of Art. He is the co-author of *Design and the Decorative Arts. Britain 1500–1900* (2001), and the author of 'Manufacturing, Consumption and Design in Eighteenth-Century England' in John Brewer and Roy Porter, eds., *Consumption and the World of Goods* (1993) and 'Product Innovation in Early Modern London', *Past and Present*, 168, 2000, pp 124–69.

Jenny Uglow is Honorary Professor of the Department of English, University of Warwick, editor at Chatto and Windus, and author of *Hogarth a Life*, as well as biographies of Elizabeth Gaskell and George Eliot. She has recently published a new book on the Lunar Society, *The Lunar Men.*

Shelagh Vainker is curator of Eastern Arts at the Ashmolean Museum Oxford and Fellow of St Hugh's College, Oxford. She is the author of *Chinese Pottery and Porcelain from Pre-History to the Present* (British Museum, 1991).

Jan de Vries is Professor of History and Economics, University of California, Berkeley, and co-author of *The First Modern Economy. The Dutch Economy 1500–1815* (1997) and author of *European Urbanisation 1500–1800* (1984) and 'Between Purchasing Power and the World of Goods: Understanding the Household Economy of Early Modern Europe' in John Brewer and Roy Porter, eds. *Consumption and the World of Goods* (1993).

Acknowledgements

Luxury in the Eighteenth Century arises out of the Luxury Project, funded by the University of Warwick, 1997–2001. We are particularly grateful to Professor Anne Janowitz, now Professor of English Literature at Queen Mary Westfield College, who was the Co-Director of the Project from 1997 to 1999 for her creative inspiration and organisational initiative in helping to shape this as an interdisciplinary project.

Most of the essays in this volume are developed from contributions to three major conferences, three workshops and a three-year seminar series, and we would like to thank all those who participated in these.

We are grateful to the University of Warwick for the research and development grant which started both the Project and the Warwick Eighteenth-Century Centre and to the British Academy for a small grant for picture reproductions for the volume.

We thank Dr Claire Walsh who did the picture searches and Dr Matt Adams for editorial assistance.

Introduction

Maxine Berg and Elizabeth Eger

This volume provides the first interdisciplinary treatment of the history of luxury. It departs from the now well-worked theme of consumer culture to explore the power of luxury as a concept and a cultural phenomenon. In 1711, John Dennis wrote *An Essay upon Publick Spirit; being a Satyr in Prose upon the Manners and Luxury of the Times*, in which he described London as 'a visible, palpable Proof of the Growth of the *British* Luxury'.[1] He paints a vivid picture of a town bursting with luxury goods, brimming with excessive and extravagant gestures, teetering on the brink of lascivious chaos and ruinous debauchery. According to Dennis, 'Luxury . . . has not only chang'd our Natures, but transform'd our Sexes'.[2] His virulent critique betrays a fascination with his subject. Luxury was irresistible, if only as a topic of debate, and provided the focus for hundreds of political and satirical pamphlets like Dennis's over the course of the eighteenth century. Particularly in Europe's rising capital cities, luxury was no less than the keyword of the period, a central term in the language of cultural transformation.

Critiques of luxury, of course, have existed since the time of Ancient Greece and Rome.[3] Classical writing on luxury reflected fears over maintaining social hierarchies and a strong military state. In the medieval and Renaissance periods luxury was associated with the iconography of sin, and in the early modern period with the excess expenditure of the very rich: kings, aristocrats and the court. In the eighteenth century, however, the trappings of luxury began to reach a wider section of society and took on new forms. Northern Europe imported manufactured goods from the East on a wider scale than ever before – porcelain, silk and colourful printed cotton goods. New foods and raw materials were drawn in from around the world: sugar; coffee, chocolate and tea; dyestuffs such as indigo; and exotic woods such as mahogany. The appearance of these goods coincided with a new civility in middling and upper class society which was conveyed in new ways of eating and socialising. Domestic dining and tea-drinking complemented public leisure in coffee-houses, shops, pleasure gardens, assemblies and the theatre. It was such material novelties that stimulated contemporary debates about luxury, contributing to its emergence as a catalyst and signpost of social and intellectual change.

From the early years of the century, argument over the moral implications of the new presence of luxury was fierce. For the first time, the notion of luxury sometimes carried positive connotations. The lively social satire of doctor and philosopher Bernard Mandeville prompted a lively pamphlet war in the European press. His acute vision of human avarice was first conveyed in the form of an energetic poem, 'The Grumbling Hive', in which he emphasised the power of luxury to support and transform society at the same time:

> ... Luxury
> Employ'd a Million of the Poor
> And odious Pride a Million more.
> Envy it self, and Vanity
> Were Ministers of Industry;
> Their darling Folly, Fickleness
> In Diet, Furniture, and Dress,
> That strange ridic'lous Vice, was made
> The very Wheel, that turn'd the Trade.
> Their Laws and Cloaths were equally
> Objects of Mutability.[4]

Here Mandeville links the legal and material fabric of society in a piercing vision of the moral texture of his age. He concludes with the amoral assertion that 'Fraud, Luxury, and Pride must live / Whilst we the Benefits receive.'[5] His later *Fable of the Bees* (1714), in which he defined luxury as 'a refinement in the gratification of the senses', a form of sociability, was widely read throughout Europe, a realist defence of luxury's improving forces, which provided an important challenge to traditional assumptions of luxury's power to corrupt.

This volume provides a history of the many responses, both positive and negative, to the ideas captured in Mandeville's provocative and transformative text.[6] While deeply indebted to recent studies of the history of consumer society, particularly John Brewer and Roy Porter's path-breaking *Consumption and the World of Goods* (1993), our book provides a new outlook. Our focus on luxury has moved the discussion away from social-scientific preoccupations with the origins of consumer society, towards a recognition of the integral relation between material and intellectual culture. On the one hand, Enlightenment culture adapted itself to luxury as a positive social force, viewing it with confidence as an instrument (and indication) of the progress of civilisation. On the other hand, it feared luxury as a debilitating and corrosive social evil, clinging to classical critiques of excessive indulgence and wanton profligacy, urban chaos and plebeian idleness. The diverse range of essays included here demonstrates, however, that there was no simple progression from disapprobation to endorsement of luxury, but rather an ongoing contest over the concept and the phenomena it might cover.

This book is divided into five parts. Here we will briefly sketch the prevailing themes before providing fuller summaries of the contents of the essays in the head-notes to each part. First, *Debates* opens with our survey chapter

'The Rise and Fall of the Luxury Debates', in which the divergent strands of eighteenth-century arguments about luxury are discussed in more depth than possible in this brief introduction. We consider a wide range of political, philosophical and economic writings, setting these in their contemporary context and considering their importance in the longer history of modern consumer societies. Further contributors provide compelling new discussions of the philosophical ideas of Mandeville, Smith and Rousseau, as well as those of the Dutch moralists and the British novelist Tobias Smollett.

From a focus on theory, we move to more practical considerations in Part II, *Delectable Goods*. Here our contributors combine their analysis of past values and beliefs with that of specific material goods.[7] Essays on the various topics of fashionable writing desks, the taxonomy of metropolitan trade and plebeian fashionable clothing share a preoccupation with issues of class in relation to the consumption of domestic luxuries.

Our third part, *Beauty, Taste and Sensibility*, explores the relationship between luxury and aesthetics through the mediating concept of taste in its real and metaphorical senses. The contributors reveal the close relation between a history of material improvement and broader histories of education, taste and desire, tracing the important relationship between visual and literary culture in the development of an aesthetic of luxury. Discussions of Hogarth on beauty, British 'vase mania' and the history of the fashionable cottage suggest that attempts to analyse and define taste in positive terms contributed to a new aesthetic of the senses, an aesthetic that was closely tied to a sense of national identity.

Part IV, *The Female Vice?*, addresses the gender politics of the luxury debates, in which interest in luxury was often associated with the dangers of effeminisation and perilous female desire. Conversely, women were linked to a move to remoralise luxury as a socially progressive force. The contributors investigate the representation of oriental femininity, the iconography of Lady Luxury in relation to the figure of the prostitute, and the reforming role of salon culture.

Finally, *Luxury and the Exotic* investigates luxury's association with other places and other cultures, as depicted here in chapters on China and South America, and the impact of Asian luxury in stimulating Europe's consumer revolutions. Eighteenth-century discourse on luxury was inextricably linked to responses to the expansion of global trade and the still relatively recent contact of European populations with goods from Asia and the New World.

This volume sets out a wide spectrum of historical and literary treatments of luxury in the eighteenth century, shedding new light on the West's first extended debate on consumer desires and practices. Readers will encounter a broad range of individual yet interlinked approaches to the history of a term that, from its first widespread use in the eighteenth century, provided a hermeneutical challenge for philosophers and economists, moralists and poets, traders and artists. The phenomenon of luxury connected a number of different discourses, exposing the links between reason and feeling, and posing a set of problems relating to epistemology, politics, aesthetics, morality and bodily sensation. By tracing the ways in which the concept of luxury was altered, redefined, influenced, modified, confused and reinforced in different social, geographical and literary contexts, it is possible to grasp the conjunction of culture and economics embodied by the concept itself. Above all, the presence and perception of luxury in eighteenth-century society required new engagements with the links between material and intellectual culture. Only through interdisciplinary work of the type gathered here can one comprehend the full richness and significance of a topic that, then and now, crosses conventional intellectual boundaries.

Notes

1. John Dennis, *An Essay upon Publick Spirit; being a Satyr in Prose upon the Manners and Luxury of the Times, The Chief Sources of our present Parties and Divisions* (London, 1711), p. 11. See also, John Dennis, *Vice & Luxury: Public Mischiefs: or, Remarks on a Book Intituled, The Fable of the Bees; or Private Vices Publick Benefits* (London, 1724).
2. Dennis, *Essay upon Publick Spirit*, p. 15. For an interesting collection of essays dealing with the connections between luxury and sexuality in this period, see Vincent Quinn and Mary Peace, eds., 'Luxurious Sexualities', *Textual Practice* 11 (3) (1997).
3. See John Sekora, *Luxury: the Concept in Western Thought, Eden to Smollett* (Baltimore, 1977), and Christopher Berry, *The Idea of Luxury: a Conceptual and Historical Investigation* (Cambridge, 1994).
4. F.B. Kaye, ed., *The Fable of the Bees: or Private Vices, Publick Benefits by Bernard Mandeville, With a Commentary, Historical and Explanatory* (Oxford, 1924), vol. I, p. 25.
5. Kaye, ed., *Fable of the Bees*, vol. I, p. 36.
6. For a useful anthology of the primary texts related to the debate surrounding Mandeville's work, see J. Martin Stafford, ed., *Private Vices, Publick Benefits? The Contemporary Reception of Bernard Mandeville* (Solihull, 1997).
7. Our contributors bring to life the texture and colour of an era that has fascinated us in recent best-sellers such as Stella Tillyard's *Aristocrats* (London, 1996); Amanda Foreman's *Georgiana, Duchess of Devonshire* (London, 1998); Isobel Grundy's *Comet of the Enlightenment: The life of Mary Wortley Montagu* (Oxford, 1999) and John Brewer's *The Pleasures of the Imagination* (London, 1998).

Part I
Debates

Luxury was a key issue at the heart of intellectual discourse in political economy, moral philosophy, literary culture and aesthetics throughout the eighteenth century. But the debate drew on traditions of discourse reaching back to the ancient world, and continued to affect social and political discourse in various periods up to the present. In Chapter 1, 'The Rise and Fall of the Luxury Debates', Maxine Berg and Elizabeth Eger provide an overview of the debates, comparing mercantilist and enlightenment economic and commercial ideas with a long literary tradition of moral critique and satire in novels such as Smollett's *Humphry Clinker* and poems such as Gay's *Trivia*. At the turn of the nineteenth century, luxury's focus diminished to issues of income distribution, its social and psychological dimensions not to re-emerge until the turn of the twentieth century, and now once again at the turn of the current century.

Edward Hundert, in Chapter 2, 'Mandeville, Rousseau and the Political Economy of Fantasy', opens with Mandeville's paradox. 'Private vice and public virtue' challenges the meaning of the concept of luxury in a modern commercial society, where luxury was anything that was not a necessity. Where social status was conveyed by conspicuous displays of consumer goods, fashion and women's vanity prevailed over political virtue in the economic progress of nations. Hundert connects Mandeville's commercial world of the self-interested to Rousseau's critique of modernity. The vice at the heart of modernity makes the history of commercial society a history of increasing inequality. Rousseau traces the impact of possessions to the definition of the self; Mandeville's vice becomes the alienation of the self. As Hundert argues, Mandeville projects the voice of modernity; we have rejected Rousseau's sumptuary disciplines, and embraced consumer citizenship.

Luxury, the keynote debate of the Enlightenment, was experienced and remarked upon in the century before in the context of the unprecedented expansion of wealth during the Dutch Republic. In Chapter 3, 'Luxury in the Dutch Golden Age in Theory and Practice', Jan de Vries identifies a turning in the luxury debates from a critique of 'old luxury' to an endorsement of 'new luxury'. The Dutch developed a new luxury in a context where a large part of the society could take part in consumer culture, but faced no oppositional politics or culture.

They developed no vocabulary or theory to discuss and to defend a republican socialised luxury. New cultural forms of court and aristocratic luxury spreading through Europe from the later seventeenth century were to displace the Dutch practice until the revival once again of new luxury in theory and in practice mid eighteenth-century Britain.

The celebration of commerce, trade and new luxury in eighteenth-century Britain was conducted, however, against a continuing tradition of anti-luxury argument, an argument traced by John Sekora in his classic *Luxury: The Concept in Western Thought*. Sekora's sets the anti-luxury debate in literature, especially in Henry Fielding and Smollett in a long tradition of moral philosophy. Michael McKeon's Chapter 4, 'Aestheticising the Critique of Luxury: Smollett's *Humphry Clinker*', reassesses Smollett's novel. Apparently a conservative attack on the luxury of metropolitan and city life, and an endorsement of the stable values of the English countryside, the novel in fact provides a link between luxury and sensibility. Michael McKeon reveals Smollett's use of images of the 'man of feeling', his use of the language of sensibility, and his early appeal to romantic tropes.

1
The Rise and Fall of the Luxury Debates

Maxine Berg and Elizabeth Eger

I

Luxury is no novelty of our own times. The shifting divide between need and desire, necessities and luxuries, was a guiding preoccupation of statesmen and intellectuals at the birth of consumer society in the later seventeenth and eighteenth centuries. Luxury was the defining issue of the early modern period. A newly experienced and perceived world economy brought greater access to Asian consumer societies and to the exotic foods and raw materials of the New World. This new trade in luxuries was to stimulate innovation in technologies, products, marketing strategies and commercial and financial institutions. Asian consumer goods – cottons, especially muslins and printed calicoes, silk, porcelain, ornamental brass and ironware, lacquer and paper goods – became imported luxuries in Europe, and were later to become indigenous European consumer goods. The widespread trade in these goods coincided with a new civility in middling and upper-class society, which was conveyed in new ways of eating and socialising. Domestic dining and tea-drinking complemented public leisure in coffee houses, shops, pleasure gardens, assemblies and the theatre.

The definition of luxury was also central to Enlightenment debates over the nature and progress of society. Luxury gradually lost its former associations with corruption and vice, and came to include production, trade and the civilising impact of superfluous commodities. Writers and governments across Europe debated their specific national responses to luxury, and the capacity of their economies and social structures to produce and absorb this new phenomenon. While the terms of the discussion shifted away from a focus on the vices of luxurious excess to embrace modern comfort and convenience, enjoyment and sociability, taste, aesthetics and refinement, there was no simple progression from disapprobation to endorsement of luxury, but rather a dialectical debate which centred on questions of individual and national virtue, economic expansion and canons of taste, definitions of the self and the social redistribution of wealth.

II

Anxieties over the morality of luxury extended from the ancient world to the modern, and were central to Asian as much as to Western moral and economic debate.[1] Aristotle, in Book IV of the *Nicomachean Ethics* of 355 BC, developed the concept of 'liberalità', as a virtue with an objective of moral beauty in contrast to the vices of prodigality and avarice. Debate in Rome in the century before Christ turned to praise for the more public 'munificencia'. Luxury continued to find its virtues in Renaissance Florentine 'splendour' and the 'magnificencia' of Philip IV's Spain in the 1630s which prevailed against counsel for a little 'modestia'.[2] Luxury was thus integral to emerging definitions of state and civic power.

From the earliest times the concept of luxury was associated with 'foreignness'. Archaeologists and anthropologists have explored the connection between luxuries and foreign goods and their traders in ancient and primitive societies. Rare and precious objects were the stimulus of long-distance trade in the ancient world. Particular materials were singled out: obsidian and shell in Stone Age societies, precious metals in the Bronze and Iron Ages. Amber, ivory, incense, pepper and silk were the priorities of Roman trade.[3] But there was also a fundamental antagonism between traders in foreign goods and local sumptuary structures. In primitive societies trade was frequently restricted to a few commodities, and those who dealt in such trade were strangers rather than kinsmen or friends.[4] During the first decades of colonial contact tensions grew between popular demand for fashionable new western and eastern products and the sumptuary regulations that controlled their consumption. This tension developed into a struggle between indigenous and alien production systems.

Eastern or oriental imports were part of the classical, western definition of luxury. Livy argued that Rome had been contaminated with 'Asiatic' luxuries, imported from Greece and the East. The close contact of Europeans with eastern manufactured goods went back to a longstanding ancient trade with the East through Constantinople and the Byzantine Empire. The trade with China was also well established during the Roman Empire, via the silk route through Samarkand and sea-borne trade from China to the Indian Ocean. Not just silks, but mirrors, paper, pottery and some porcelain were exported to the Persian Gulf from the seventh to the tenth centuries. From Pliny onwards, arguments made against eastern luxuries were based on a fear of financial ruin in the West, as silver and gold flowed east to purchase the treasures of the Indies.[5]

Sumptuary legislation was invoked in various societies in the ancient, medieval and early modern periods to confine the consumption of specific commodities to the elites, and thus to enforce rigid status structures. This legislation in practice became centred on protectionist regulation, import and export regulations and quality controls. The first English sumptuary laws were about food and excess in meeting bodily satisfaction. Later legislation focused on clothing and imported cloth. Legislation of 1363 proscribed all but the royal family wearing imported cloth. An Act of 1510 forbade the wearing of foreign woollens, and other legislation debarred the wearing of velvets, especially in red and purple, fine silks, furs and embroideries for all but the highest ranks. The lower ranks were limited to clothing in local, heavy fabrics, dyed in natural colours. Though most such regulations were repealed in England in the seventeenth century, the attempt by the state to control luxury expenditure was continued in protectionist and fiscal measures.[6] The close association between luxury and foreign imports continued into the eighteenth century. In Britain the dangers posed by French and Chinese manufactures were frequently deployed in mercantilist debates and protectionist legislation enacted during the mid-eighteenth century.[7]

Economic and social theorists during the late seventeenth century and throughout the eighteenth century debated the implications of the luxury trades. Aspects of this debate have been treated by historians as problems in the history of political thought, or as literary and moral issues.[8] However, contemporaries were perhaps most interested in the changing definitions of luxury goods, and the problems of separating these from necessaries. Concerns over the economic dislocation and moral danger posed by foreign and exotic goods turned to a more open debate on the advantages of trade and the more cosmopolitan development of the senses. Nicholas Barbon, in a classic passage, identified the incentive provided by rare and luxurious commodities. 'The wants of the Mind are infinite, Man naturally Aspires, and as his Mind is elevated, his Senses grow more refined, and more capable of Delight; his Desires are inlarged, and his Wants increase with his Wishes, which is for everything that is rare, can gratifie his Senses, adorn his Body and promote the Ease, Pleasure and Pomp of Life.'[9] Observers increasingly associated a broadening of the world of luxury commodities with the expansion of trade and commerce, and both with a new consumerism among the middling classes.

Commercial writers, even in the seventeenth century, were well ahead of the intellectuals in the close connections they drew between commerce and luxury. Jacques Savary, the Comptroller of the French customs, and editor of France's first major commercial dictionary, wrote in *Le parfait negociant*, a textbook for businessmen:

> [Divine Providence] has not willed for everything that is needed for life to be found in the same spot. It has dispersed its gifts so that men would trade together and so that the mutual need which they have to help one another would establish ties of friendship among them. This continuous exchange of all the comforts of life constitutes commerce and this commerce makes for all the gentleness (douceur) of life.[10]

Over the course of the eighteenth century the luxury debates moved far beyond their traditional concerns with the corruption of wealthy elites. The sumptuary laws which had previously proscribed the wearing of specific types of cloth and of gold and silver lace to all but the elites were repealed or withered away. There was increasingly a distinction made between 'new' and 'old' luxury, or between 'modern' and 'ancient' luxury. New luxuries were created out of the division of labour and the expansion of commerce, in contrast to old luxuries, which relied on excessive displays of large bodies of retainers. The luxury of aristocratic profligacy and associations with wealth, status and power shifted to a discussion of commerce, utility, taste and comfort. The language of luxury evolved to redefine 'excess' as 'surplus', 'vanity' as 'refinement'.

Bernard Mandeville, doctor and wide-ranging social and political essayist, a Dutchman who had made his home in London, provoked a turning point in the discussion of luxury. He accepted traditional associations of luxury with vice. But in contrast to religious and moral campaigners who disparaged the influence of luxury, as well as many intellectuals and political thinkers who sought to define the virtuous citizen, Mandeville declared luxury to be a public benefit. Furthermore he challenged the defining boundaries between luxuries and necessities. Claims to moral virtue in the 'needs' for cleanliness, comforts, decencies and conveniences were no greater than those for luxury housing and furnishings. Men and women, in Mandeville's view, are by nature self-interested, pleasure-seeking and vain, and they seek luxuries to fulfil these psychological attributes. By acting on their self-interest and indulging their desires for luxuries, the rich and others who could afford it, paradoxically, contributed to the expansion of commerce and the wider employment of the poor. This paradox was based in Mandeville's acceptance of the position that human behaviour is motivated by the passions to seek pleasure and to avoid pain. He also accepted the Christian divide between virtue and vice, associating vice with luxury and virtue with self-denial.[11] He claimed that we all respond to the vice of luxury, masking our vanity and avarice with hypocrisy. As Hundert has argued in his aptly titled *The Enlightenment's Fable*, hypocrisy in commercial nations masks the emulative striving arising from envy. Such hypocrisy accounts for the spread of modern manners, those 'socially useful methods of making ourselves acceptable to others'. This difference between being and appearing becomes the 'most psychologically significant characteristic of public life in commercial societies'.[12] In Mandeville's words: 'whilst thus Men study their own private Interest, in assisting each other to promote and encrease the pleasures of life in general, they find by experience that to compass those Ends, everything ought to be banish'd from Conversation, that can have the least Tendency of making others uneasy.'[13]

Luxury goods took on a new significance as marks of esteem. The primitive powers of the elites to compel approbation by 'looks and gestures' backed by force were replaced by material acquisitions from coaches to buildings. A newly mobile world of goods accompanied the anonymity of commercial society and city life. In the company of strangers, individuals were accorded honour and status according to the clothes they wore.[14] Mandeville shifted the discussion of luxury to psychological motivation and a self identity through fantasy, possessions and the restless pursuit of change and novelty. His challenge to the definition of luxury set the framework for the subsequent debate and, more significantly, the association of luxury and trade opened a much broader discussion of commercial expansion and consumer society. After Mandeville, luxury was increasingly seen in terms of economic advantage.

The debate, which was conducted among several hundred writers at all levels of eighteenth-century discourse from polemical pamphlets to political theory, popular ballads to epic poetry, political journalism to novels, fundamentally turned on problems of defining the term. Hume described luxury as 'a word of uncertain significance', calling for greater precision in contemporary usage of the word. In France, Melon and Montesquieu devoted chapters of their treatises on political economy and government to luxury. They distinguished its meaning as a subject of moral discourse from that of political economy.[15] Diderot challenged contributors to and readers of the *Encyclopédie*: 'But what is this luxury that we so infallibly attribute to so many objects? This question can only be answered with any accuracy on the basis of discussion among those who show the most discrimination in their use of the term luxury: a discussion which has yet to take place, and which even they may be incapable of bringing to a satisfactory conclusion.'[16] Saint-Lambert in his article in the *Encyclopédie* dealt with this by summarising the many definitions. Galiani also put the point: 'no one knows or dares to say what luxury might properly be. This spectre, as it must be called, wanders among us, never seen in its true light, or recognized for its efficacy; and it, perhaps never occurs to the virtuous.' Such anxiety over the problem of definition suggests the central role of luxury in provoking contemporary social and intellectual transformations.

The subject of how to define luxury was now treated within a wider discussion of commerce. In Britain, Sir James Steuart, in the preface to his *Inquiry into the Principles of Political Economy* (1767), warned against the 'imperfection of language' which 'engages us frequently in disputes merely verbal'. He tried to define his terms more precisely: 'I shall set out by distinguishing *luxury*, as it affects our different interest, by producing hurtful consequences; from *luxury*, as it regards the moderate gratification of our natural or rational desires.' He separated out the effects of luxury into moral, physical, domestic and political categories, and defined the immoderate gratification of natural desires as excess. He argued the importance of distinguishing the meanings of luxury, sensuality and excess: 'Luxury consists in providing the objects of sensuality, so far as they are superfluous. Sensuality consists in the actual enjoyment of them and excess implies an abuse of enjoyment. A person, therefore, according to these definitions, may be very luxurious from vanity, pride, ostentation, or with a political view of encouraging consumption, without having a turn for sensuality, or a tendency to fall into excess.'[17]

The provision of luxury objects, Steuart argued, encouraged 'emulation, industry and agriculture'.[18] This emerging pride in national industry was shared by philosophers on the continent. Montesquieu compared Persian and Parisian luxury and went on to praise English luxury as the epitome of modern luxury. The abbé Raynal in the 1770s compared the commercial Arabs of the Middle Ages who cultivated the arts and literature with the 'barbaric ostentation' of the French nobility under feudalism; their excessive table was indicative of 'savage luxury'.[19] Analysis of luxury's role in building or destroying a society was central to a new comparative approach to history.

The philosophers of the Scottish Enlightenment were particularly keen to establish new definitions of luxury as a progressive social force. David Hume and Adam Smith associated luxury almost entirely with commerce, convenience and consumption. Hume separated out 'philosophical' from economic questions. Luxury was a 'refinement in the gratification of the senses', and an incentive to the expansion of commerce. The expansion of commerce would make available to all persons not just the necessaries of life, but its 'conveniences'.[20] The consumer incentives offered by world trade provided the impetus to domestic economic development. Hume set out these connections in felicitous terms, not in his essay on 'Luxury', later entitled 'Of the Refinement of the Arts', but in his essay 'Of Commerce':

> If we consult history, we shall find, that in most nations foreign trade has pre-ceded any refinement in home manufactures, and given birth to domestic luxury . . . Thus men become acquainted with the *pleasures* of luxury, and the *profits* of commerce; and their *delicacy* and *industry* being once awakened, carry them on to further improvements in every branch of domestic as well as foreign trade; and this perhaps is the chief advantage which arises from a commerce with strangers.[21]

Adam Smith was similarly proud of national industry, arguing that the wealth of a nation lay in its ability to increase the quantity of 'necessaries and conveniences' which its labour could produce or exchange relative to its population. The divi-sion of labour yielded a 'multiplication of the productions of all the different arts', and in 'a well-governed society' a 'universal opulence which extends itself to the lowest ranks of the people'.[22] This universal opulence could provide for these lower ranks at a relatively simple level in comparison with the 'extravagant luxury' of the great, 'and yet it may be true, perhaps, that the accommodation of a European prince does not always so much exceed that of an industrious and frugal peasant, as the accommodation of the latter exceeds that of many an African king, the absolute master of the lives and liberties of ten thousand naked savages.'[23] Smith thus contrasted opulence and luxury, the one the result of economic growth founded in the division of labour, the other the expenditure of revenue on un-productive labour. The proportion of labour fixed in durable commodities and produced in mercantile and manufacturing towns promoted such growth; the labour supporting retainers and fine eating by elites in courtly cities was supported by revenue which could only diminish. Thus the people in mercantile and man-ufacturing towns were 'industrious, sober and thriving'; those in cities supported by revenue were 'idle, dissolute and poor'.[24] The goods produced in these manu-facturing towns were 'new luxuries' made from the steel and iron that Hume saw as replacing the gold and rubies of the Indies. Behind their production lay a shift in consumer practices associated with the decline of feudalism. Landowners gave up their feudal privileges and large bodies of retainers to 'gratify their childish vanity' to possess durable consumer goods, goods which might be 'fitter to be the playthings of children than the serious pursuits of men'.[25] New luxuries, however frivolous, were durable consumer goods, and their production generated eco-nomic growth.

Thus we see that the debate on the moral and economic effects of luxury turned on the definition of the luxury good. Contemporary perceptions of the category of 'luxury object' changed over the course of the eighteenth century. Mandeville referred to buildings, furniture, equipages and clothes. Melon mentioned food-stuffs and raw materials – sugar, coffee, tobacco and silk – but also wrote else-where of rich stuffs, works of gold and silver and foreign laces, and diamonds.[26] It seems that it was not until Adam Smith that we see luxury goods distinguished in analytical terms – ornamental building, furniture, collections of books, pictures, frivolous jewels and baubles – and separated from expenditure on retainers, a fine table, horses and dogs.[27] But luxuries and other non-essential goods were also widely written about by commercial writers. Daniel Defoe provided classic descrip-tions of a new kind of consumer good which met the demands of the middling and trading people, and extended far beyond the imported luxuries of the wealthy. The rich, he argued, might take the top quality wines, spices, coffee and tea, but the coarser varieties and the overall bulk of trade in all of these were taken by the middling groups – 'these are the people that are the life of trade'. The gentry might take the finest hollands, cambricks and muslins, but the tradespeople took vast quantities of linens of other kinds from Ireland, France, Russia, Poland and Germany. They, like their wealthy superiors, imported any number of drugs and dyestuffs, including 'brasil and brasiletta wood, fustic, logwood, sumach, red-wood, red earth, gauls, madder, woad, indigo, tumerick, cocheneal, cantharides, bark peru, gums of many kinds, civet, aloes, cassia, turkey drugs, african drugs, east India drugs, rhubarb, sassafras, cum allis'.[28] To this abundance of imported foreign luxuries, the British now added their own desirable commodities, ranging from bone lace to wrought iron and brass, toys and locks, instruments, clocks and watches for their own domestic as well as foreign customers.[29]

Other commercial writers, such as Malachy Postlethwayt (1707–67), distin-guished different classes of consumer, and singled out the capacity to provide the widest variety and range of qualities of commodities, that 'art of seducing, or pleasing to a higher degree the consumer of every kind'. 'To tempt and please them all, it is proper to offer them assortments of every kind proportioned to their different abilities in point of purchase.' Luxuries meeting the test of 'look', 'ele-gance' and price were now within the reach of the tradespeople. 'The mechanic's wife will not buy a damask of fifteen shillings a yard; but will have one of eight or nine; she does not trouble herself much about the quality of the silk; but is satisfied with making as fine a shew as a person of higher rank or fortune.'[30]

Commercial writers such as Defoe and Postlethwayt realised that luxury goods might exist at many levels of quality and expense; their definition as luxuries was dictated by the responses of different classes of consumer. Luxury was thus not just about goods, but about social behaviour. It was increasingly perceived as a sociable activity, generated by cities and participated in by the middling as well as the upper classes. Mandeville celebrated the pleasure of the city, its commer-cial exchange, its shopping and its anonymity. Merchants, in the course of strik-ing a deal, exchanged civility, entertainment, the use of country houses and coaches, conversation and humour.[31] Shopping was a display of fashion, and the actions of gesture and conversation which established an emotional relationship between the shopkeeper and female customer. The young lady and the mercer both held a certain power in this relationship – he the knowledge of the price, she the choice over which shop she would patronise. The mercer is 'a Man in whom consummate Patience is one of the mysteries of his Trade . . . By Precept, Example and great Application he has learn'd unobserv'd to slide into the inmost recesses of the Soul, sound the Capacity of his Customers, and find out their Blind Side unknown to them.' But whatever his skill in deploying the arts of conversation and fashion, he can lose her custom through such trifles as insufficient flattery, some fault in behaviour or the tying of his neckcloth, or gain it by no more than a handsome demeanour or fashion. The 'reasons some of the Fair Sex have for their choice are often very Whimsical and kept as a great Secret.'[32]

The sociability of commerce and shopping was no longer the preserve of great merchants and young ladies. It was also the pleasure of manufacturers, tradesmen and the middle ranks. Defoe in 1731 claimed 'tis for these your markets are kept open late on Saturday nights; because they usually receive their week's wages late . . . these are the life of our whole commerce . . .'[33] The Scottish social thinker John Millar was to give a special place by the end of the eighteenth century to 'the middle rank of men' who dealt with a large number of customers instead of being dependent on the favours of a single person.[34]

This new, eighteenth-century economic endorsement of luxury developed in continuing dialogue with critics of luxury who feared that it was at the root of national social problems. Powerful moral, political and aesthetic critiques of luxury drew on arguments about the social distribution of income and the consumer behaviour of the poor. In France, Rousseau emphasised aristocratic profligacy and the negative effects of consumerism in destabilising the social order. French critics associated luxury with France's humiliation by England during the Seven Years' War.[35] In England the Seven Years' War also provided a platform for a denunciation of French luxury. A print entitled 'The Imports of Great Britain from France' (1758), dedicated to the Anti-Gallican Society and the Society for the Encouragement of Arts, Manufactures and Commerce, showed a ship unloading French luxuries and retainers at a London dock. These were represented by goods such as fine fabrics, wines, brandies, cheeses, gloves, beauty washes, toilet waters and pomades; and as aristocratic retainers and luxury occupations such as fops, cooks, dancers, priests, milliners, mantua-makers, tailors, tutoresses and *valets de chambre*. The print in its representation of the dangers of trade with France depicted all the tropes of luxury associated with vanity, desire and the corruption of national customs and spirit.[36] Journalism during the war years rehabilitated classical condemnations of luxury in defence of Britishness. Pamphlets such as Rev. John Brown's *Estimate of the Manners and Principles of the Times* (1757) were extracted and reprinted many times, and articles penned by pseudonyms such as 'Britannicus' pronounced in *The London Magazine* that 'the time of War . . . seems the fittest to suppress Luxury'. The themes of plays such as 'The Tryal of the Lady Allurea Luxury' (1757) were to be repeated in later decades, reappearing in those such as Lady Eglantine Wallace's, 'The Ton: or, Follies of Fashion' (1788).[37] Thus the advocates of luxury as a progressive social force did not achieve an easy ascendance during the eighteenth century, but were continually challenged by their detractors. Tension between those who disapproved and those who supported the influence of luxury can be seen clearly in the ongoing literary debate surrounding the term.

III

The moral critique of luxury was a key theme in a long literary tradition set out by John Sekora in his *Luxury: the Concept in Western Thought, Eden to Smollett* (1977). For Sekora, apologists for luxury such as Hume and Smith augur the modern world. He argues that Smollett's *Humphry Clinker* represents the last major English literary work to be informed by the older, classical sense of luxury, demonstrating what he terms 'an eloquence of horror'.[38] He describes luxury as 'one of the oldest, most important and most pervasive negative principles for organising society that western history has known'.[39] In his inspirational exploration of the early context and vocabulary of luxury, he aims to retrieve what he termed a 'lost system of discourse', 'a network of suppositions'. Following in the footsteps of Foucault, he creates an archaeology of the term, arguing the conservative perceptions of eighteenth-century English critics of luxury were influenced by an intellectual tradition whose taproots lay deep in the soil of antiquity.

In Sekora's view, luxury was named to be abhorred, and in his story of the concept's changing meanings he emphasises the sense in which the hierarchy of necessity and luxury became ever stricter, evolving into a means of drawing fixed social distinctions. He argues for the pre-eminence of one central idea: while all men could be guilty of luxury, the vice belonged primarily to the poor and downtrodden, the labouring classes. Sumptuary laws, through their long history, were designed to maintain social distinctions, to allow luxurious man to be controlled by the 'naturally superior', 'the natural legislator', who is in fact the 'man of the land whose birth, wealth, and intellect had elevated him to independence of other persons'.[40] Several eighteenth-century writers focused on the impact of luxury on the lives and behaviour of the labouring poor. Fielding denounced indolence and crime; Goldsmith regretted the loss of the simple communal pleasures of rural life in his famous poem, *The Deserted Village*. On the broader front of political and social commentary, fears were continually expressed over the impact of luxurious and addictive expenditure on the poor's incentives to labour. Debates on high and low wages, on the consumption of sugar, tea and gin, turned to those on the consumption of fashionable clothing.[41]

Having provided a compelling history of the concept, Sekora goes on to use luxury as a frame for his readings of Smollett's prose. He observes that, like any comprehensive social concept, 'luxury gave Smollett the habit and ability to think in terms of types of people, classes of events and patterns of behaviour'.[42] He argues that in Smollett's work luxury is a tool, a reflexive instrument to simplify and clarify his work. This approach provides the key to some acute readings of Smollett's journalism, history and novels. Sekora highlights the power of the novel as a genre of cultural critique, arguing that *Humphry Clinker* is most vigorous as a tract against the times, demonstrating its author's ability to transform matters of accidental taste into urgent moral issues. *Humphry Clinker* depicts a fluid culture of exchange, a culture bursting at the seams with new, foreign luxury goods. Ironically, his catalogue of aversion forms one of the most meticulous and alluring records of the material culture he condemns, from Lydia's tortoise-shell 'heart-housewife' to ephemeral Bath souvenirs, Belgian lace to pineapples. Smollett's language of distaste for luxury is endlessly expansive, obsessed with notions of chaos and excess. His prose raises pressing questions regarding the nature of boundaries in a commercial society: his precarious metaphors of contagion and pollution seem to be poised nervously against his sense of contemporary social and political instability.

Smollett contributes to a long tradition of moral satire in which disgust and incredulity inform a radical vision of human greed. From Juvenal to Johnson, poets as well as novelists have criticised corruption in compelling terms. This tradition can be seen continuing into the nineteenth and twentieth centuries, as for example in Thackeray's portrait of conspicuous consumption.[43] The domestic interiors of Georgian novels work in a similar way. The careful catalogues of spatial and decorative detail that we find in the work of Burney, Austen and Edgeworth, for example, convey a world in which social distinction is achieved through luxury objects, a world in which the moral drama is often derived from the characters' relation to objects and places. The complex relationships between desires for material and moral improvement are told in scenes that are both tenderly precise and harshly accurate in their depiction of quotidian life.

Smollett was 'not a deep or systematic writer', according to Sekora, who argues that the concept of luxury gives his novels a cohesion they would otherwise lack. However, it could be argued that Sekora is sometimes in danger of granting the concept of luxury a coherence which it does not have. By investing so much in a particular reading of luxury, and by casting a long view over the history of critiques of luxury, Sekora assimilates the concept into his own 'irresistible tide' of meaning. He often equates very different times and texts within his overarching view of a transhistorical, classical tradition of luxury as a literary mode, writing that luxury 'has been expressed in many genres. Because it seeks to reveal the (often hidden) dimension of causes, relations and devolutions, it is primarily a heuristic, narrative mode, usually found in those forms which express developing awareness or expanding experience: quest, journey, psychomania, imaginary voyage, retrospective elegy, nostalgic pastoral, panoramic survey, or moral history.'[44]

Sekora argues that luxury, while a traditional concept, accommodated and absorbed change. His position, however, elides enormous national and historical differences,[45] and also fails to acknowledge the ambivalence inherent in attacks on luxury, the double-edged nature of any continual iteration of luxury's evils. Luxury attracts and repels. It has been figured as both plague and medicine, friend and foe of social progress.

Sekora raises important questions regarding the nature of satire as a medium of social critique. However, his focus on the negative reaction to luxury neglects a strand of satire that is less clearly poised in a position of moral outrage, but rather suggests the complexity and confusion of modern experience. Mandeville, the arch-catalyst and defender of the luxury debates, also chose this as his critical medium.[46] If used as a neutral index of the effect of increasing affluence in portions of society, then the idea of luxury could be brilliantly suggestive, as in Mandeville's sparkling satire. Mandeville was deeply immersed in London literary culture at the beginning of the eighteenth century, contributing articles to *The Female Tatler*, for example.[47] Here he took on the Tatler's editor, Isaac Bickerstaff, challenging his claims to instil public virtue and disagreeing with his support for introducing sumptuary laws in Britain. Few critics have yet analysed Mandeville's journalism or poetry in literary terms, or considered the implications of his choice of medium for distilling his political message. He himself described his *Fable of the Bees* as 'a rhapsody, void of order or method' and later as 'an incoherent rhapsody', terms more suited to a poet than a political philosopher.[48] It is worth briefly setting him alongside one of his contemporary poets, John Gay, who came to London at about the same time as Mandeville, initially to work as an apprentice to a silk-mercer who had a shop above the New Exchange.[49] Gay's knowledge of London was from underneath. In trying to elevate his status to that of a professional writer, he depended upon the burgeoning commercial economy for success.

In his vivid poem *Trivia, or the Art of Walking the Streets of London*, first published in 1715, Gay both satirised and depended upon commercial culture, creating an unrivalled picture of the British capital as it came to terms with new luxuries.[50] Gay's multilayered description of London is of a society brimming with implements, accoutrements and consumable goods, from amber-tipped canes to flaxen wigs, shoes of Morocco leather to collars of spongy nap and coats of Kersey cloth. Critics have often interpreted Gay's poem as a documentary, a bracingly realistic and lightly ironic commentary on a city on the cusp of modernity. However, it is arguably a far more complex and contradictory poem than such an approach allows. *Trivia* does far more than merely represent the city. Gay's closely observed details are both significant and insignificant, oscillating between, rather than fixing upon, meaning. The architecture of the poem, like that of London itself, multiplies perspectives, revelling in confusion. Gay's contradictory impulse is found in both the literary structure and the vivid descriptive energy of his poem. His appetite for detail embraces both the elaborate trinkets and the cruder tools of society, from lace cuffs and snuff-boxes to butcher's greasy trays and the chandler's basket. In creating a bold catalogue of the city's various material goods, he makes use of an eclectic assortment of literary sources and rhetorical devices. This is 'Trivia *or the Art of Walking the Streets of London*'. Gay dramatises the distinction between sheer display and solid function, parading his work as both useless and useful at one and the same time. Gay's reluctance to attribute worth to his own text is perhaps suggestive of his ambivalent relation to contemporary debate about the relation between labour and society, morality and economy.

Gay's poem shows a strong affinity with Mandeville's ideas, particularly in its acknowledgement of the interdependent relationship between wealth and waste in forming the urban economy. His fanciful myth of Cloacina, goddess of Fleet

Ditch, London's notorious open sewer, articulates a strand of thought otherwise only hinted at in the poem, suggesting that there is something energetic and life-giving about the currents of filth that course beneath the streets of London. The outcome of Cloacina's assignation with a 'mortal scavenger' is the birth of a boy who grows up on the streets of London as a shoe-shine in a stall in the vicinity of the Fleet. Cloacina pities her deserted child, and obtains help from the other deities in preparing a new japanning oil which will easily bring a fine polish to the most heavily besmeared shoes (III, 155–69). In hymning the humble street trader, Gay draws attention to the literal polish needed in a society that creates dirt at the same rate that it displays refinement. This implicit connection between prosperity and waste is made far more explicitly and forcefully by Bernard Mandeville in his writings on the economy. The two writers share a cynical and witty mode of detachment that is very different from the strict code of moral reform suggested by Smollett's prose.

While Sekora may ignore the complexity and richness of alternative modes of satire in relation to the luxury debates, none the less, in casting the eighteenth-century attack on luxury in terms of a literary mode, he makes important links between language and political change, acknowledging his debt to John Pocock's work on the interdependent relationship between rhetoric and history, language and culture. Sekora's work was published only a year after Raymond Williams' influential *Keywords, A Vocabulary of Culture and Society*.[51] Williams describes his Keywords in two connected senses, as 'significant, binding words in certain activities and their interpretation', and as 'significant, indicative words in certain forms of thought'.[52] His stress on interdependent and interlocking networks of signification has proved to be transformative of the field of cultural history. By tracing the ways in which the word luxury has been altered, redefined, influenced, modified, confused and reinforced in different historical, professional and literary contexts, we can realise the conjunction of culture and economics embodied by the concept itself. Close attention to the vocabulary of luxury in the eighteenth century can, then, reveal shifts in attitude. An obvious example would be Hume's decision to change the title of his essay 'Of Luxury' (1752) to 'Of Refinement in the Arts' (1760). For Hume, politeness and civility, refinement and polish were the beneficial forces and effects of luxury. In choosing the term 'refinement' over luxury, he was arguably trying to counterbalance the vivid and impermeable language of Mandeville. Close analysis of the language and literature of luxury, then, is vital in building a cultural history of the concept.

Just as the term luxury attracted positive and negative definitions, the category of 'woman' was associated with both virtue and vice over the course of the eighteenth century, frequently oscillating between the two moral extremes. The classical debate on luxury associated women with excess and female desire. Luxury was identified with effeminacy and weakness. Writers from Mandeville to Mercier argued that vanity, fashion and sexuality stimulated consumer demand. The association between luxury and femininity came to inform the representation of commerce and the market. Women were depicted as capricious, inconstant, the slaves to fashion. Fears over female desire were elided with those over the instability of market demand. Concepts of 'commerce', 'intercourse' and 'conversation' were adopted to describe both the market and social and sexual exchange. In Defoe's words of 1706, 'Trade is a mystery which will never be completely discovered or understood. It suffers convulsive fits, hysterical disorders, and the most unaccountable emotions.'[53] In the period which many historians have identified with the confinement of women to private, domestic space, that most public of spheres, the market, was depicted as a woman.

The female vice continued to shape the depiction of luxury in the classic accounts of Sombart and Simmel at the turn of the twentieth century. Sensuality and sexual appetite, fashion and emulation drove courtesans and female domestic servants to an endless quest for novelties that was seen to have a devastating impact on the wider society.[54] However, women's contribution to the economy could also be seen in a more constructive sense, as something to be wooed and appreciated. Mandeville depicted women in a more positive light in his defence of luxury's role in forming human sociability. In the *Fable of the Bees*, he described women as 'quicker of Invention and more ready at Repartee'.[55] As moral and political philosophers such as Hume and Smith sought new defences of commercial culture, they began to acknowledge women's important role in carrying out the civilising process. In the second half of the century it is arguable that women dominated the luxury markets as powerful consumers of luxury objects. Sombart described this historical period as the moment of 'objectification', a time in which there is 'a greater expenditure of human labour on a specific object, provided the refinement is not restricted to the use of more costly materials. The result is a widening of the scope of capitalist industry and, because of the necessity of securing rare materials from foreign countries, also of capitalist commerce.'[56] In the hands of the cultivated salon hostess and patron of the arts, for example, luxury, like taste and refinement, could become a female virtue.

IV

The commerce and sociability of luxury were debated within a wider moral debate on taste and aesthetics. From the mid- to the later eighteenth century Britain became the leading producer of distinctive luxury and new consumer goods, so desirable as to generate a contemporary Anglomania in Europe. Inventors created new goods for a heterogeneous urban environment which valued individuality, variety and accessibility of a range of qualities. Delight in ingenuity went with a desire for difference, and the new commercial economy circulated accessible luxuries.

Contemporary artists and intellectuals, from Hogarth and Reynolds to Smith and Hume, sought to understand these new luxuries through their theoretical writings on aesthetics and taste. They emphasised the pleasures people took in variety and novelty, in ingenuity and utility. Manufacturers such as Josiah Wedgwood and Matthew Boulton used this aesthetic debate to design their products and sell them, appealing to contemporary ideas about the cultivation of masculine virtue and the superiority of women's taste.[57]

The luxury debates also turned on the development of a secular aesthetic culture in the eighteenth century. The language of taste was rooted in Shaftesbury's aristocratic language of civility and politeness, as has been argued by Pocock and Barell, but the eighteenth century also witnessed an attempt by various writers, thinkers and painters to reformulate the civic discourse on virtue to promote a new account which might sanction the actions, desires and pleasures of the middle classes, as long as they were accomplished with prudence, industry and compassion.[58] The concept of taste acts to crystallise the complex dynamic between economic and cultural history, providing a focus for problems of representation in a consumer society in which new desires for emulation, distinction and solidarity emerge.

One significant development of eighteenth-century culture was the extent to which aesthetic appreciation became a shared, public activity in newly founded museums, theatres and gardens. Alexander Gerard wrote in his *Essay on Taste* in 1756: 'A man, who devotes a considerable part of his time to the gratification of the senses, is an object of contempt or indignation: but a person who can fill up those parts of life, that afford no opportunities for social offices, with pleasures of taste, who can find entertainment for many hours in a gallery of pictures, or in a collection of poems, is esteemed on this very account.'[59] This argument was also made by Kames, who believed that the Fine Arts could transform wealth into virtue. Like Hume, he celebrated the positive link between commerce and culture in this period, arguing that culture itself made the leisure of wealth more virtuous. Here we see an intriguing relation between the material presence of luxury and the development of a public and national culture – a culture that defined itself at least in part, in positive relation to luxury and the advances of commerce, rather than against them.

Parallel debates in France on luxury and taste also centred on commercial aspirations and new wealth. In France the *gout moderne*, or the rococo, was associated with new wealth. Rich objects in old regime France were no longer representations of royal and aristocratic political power. Commerce and taste became associated with the new fashion trade. A backlash against commercial and speculative wealth provoked a turn to antiquity. Classicism was equated with aristocracy, and modernity with plutocracy. But this modernity came with a slavish imitation of the material culture of the nobility – an obsessive determination of the new men to 'grasp the full encyclopaedic range of noble cultural signs'.[60] The nobility took on the moral language of the critique of luxury as a resistance to the power of commerce and finance. There were renewed proposals for sumptuary legislation and for confining all offices in the king's household and the armed forces to gentlemen.[61] The debate on luxury moved into the salons as a debate on taste, and noble virtues were upheld in the values of the ancients. Those hostile to the *gout moderne* deplored the vulgar preference for costly materials – glittering azure and gold. The comte de Caylus criticised the gilding of rococo interiors – gold lost its symbolism. Mirrors, it was argued, had displaced history paintings. Technology, through the production of plate glass at Saint Gobain, had put mirrors into locations previously beyond reach. The sparkle of widely polished surfaces, and new goods, finishes, surfaces in glass, wood, varnish, gilt, stucco, cloth, could not hide the corruption at the heart of modern luxury. This aesthetic critique became part of the wider social critique of speculation and the new financial and commercial classes of Louis XV's France.[62] De Caylus helped to lead the change in French taste towards classical themes and models. Mercier wrote of him: 'Count Caylus has revived Greek taste amongst us and we have at last renounced our Gothic [rococo] forms.' From a similar perspective, the Baron d'Hancarville wrote the text for Hamilton's four-volume *Collection of Etruscan, Greek and Roman Antiquities from the Cabinet of the Hon. W. Hamilton – 1766–1776*. He devoted the first 58 pages of Hamilton's volume I to a discourse on the role of the artist in society, praising Greek pottery as a valuable commodity to be displayed by the *cognoscenti*. Greek vases appealed to a 'taste for simplicity', and provided models of proportion and elegance. The clash between ancient and modern attitudes to luxury can be found even in such self-conscious attention to, and elevation of, individual decorative objects.

V

The young Rousseau, in his *Discourse on the Arts and Sciences* and *Discourse on the Origin of Inequality*, repudiated the cultural and moral optimism of his elders. He asked whether luxury had helped to refine the arts and sciences and the manners of men, and replied it had not: luxury and the arts were the products of inequality. Luxury, furthermore, brought about a continuous process of moral corruption. It ruined taste, substituted effeminacy for courage, and drew the population from the countryside to capital cities. He advocated withdrawal to the country and a new standard of civic virtue. Rousseau's aspirations had their widest appeal in the later part of the century. His association of commerce and luxury with moral displacement penetrated deep into the psychology of the self. Luxury increased the dependency of the self on the opinion of others. Objects of luxury acquired a new dominion and the power to promote fantasies of identity.[63]

As we have seen, Rousseau's critique was followed by Smith's solution to the riddle of luxury, that is, that it was not consumption that made wealth grow, but frugality and capital accumulation. The distribution of labour over productive and unproductive activities determined the generation of a surplus.[64] Adam Smith's solution did not, however, completely displace luxury from later eighteenth-century debate. He himself, in the last edition of the *Theory of Moral Sentiments* in 1790, pointed out that the disposition to admire the rich and neglect the poor caused corruption of our moral sentiments. The paradox of luxury, he argued, in both *The Theory of Moral Sentiments* and *The Wealth of Nations*, was also about the unintended public benefits that derived from morally indefensible private behaviour – behaviour he describes as desire for objects of 'frivolous utility', the disposal of the social surplus by the 'proud and unfeeling landlord', who spent this surplus on 'trinkets and baubles', the 'deception' which 'keeps in continual motion the industry of mankind'.[65] Smith's chapter 'Of the origin of Ambition, and of the distinction of Ranks' in *The Theory of Moral Sentiments* analysed the 'parade' and 'pursuit of riches'. This was based, he argued, in man's desire 'to be observed, to be attended to, to be taken notice of with sympathy, complacency, and approbation . . . It is the vanity, not the ease, or the pleasure, which interests us. The rich man glories in his riches, because he feels that they naturally draw upon him the attention of the world'.[66] This vanity was expressed in laying out riches on luxury commodities. 'How many people ruin themselves,' Smith asks, 'by laying out money on trinkets of frivolous utility?' It is not the ease and pleasure of the rich that others admire, Smith argues, but 'the numberless artificial and elegant contrivances for promoting this ease or pleasure'. In profoundly bleak terms, Smith set out the ultimate meaninglessness of the luxury goods and riches we strive for: 'Power and riches appear then to be, what they are, enormous and operose machines contrived to produce a few trifling conveniencies to the body . . . They . . . can protect him from none of the severer inclemencies of the season. They keep off the summer shower, not the winter storm, but leave him always as much, and sometimes more exposed than before, to anxiety, to fear, and to sorrow; to diseases, to danger and to death.'[67] Smith's philosophical reservations were echoed in the writings of Adam Ferguson, who condemned the spread of luxury amongst the poor and the corruption of manners in commercial society.[68] Ferguson expressed reservations about the 'polished' society of expanding commerce in England, the social feelings of relative deprivation and the psychological effects of fears of losing wealth.[69]

At the beginning of the nineteenth century, Malthus and Sismondi debated luxury and underconsumption, and took the luxury debates much more explicitly into the framework of the distribution of income. Malthus also expressed a widespread concern over the balance of the population between agriculture, manufacturing and commerce, arguing for the instability of urban occupations. Rousseau's critique was applied in a new moral framework which re-emerged with the food shortages of the 1790s – writing turned to the social divide between luxury and poverty. Radicals in Britain reintroduced a language of sumptuary legislation, and an association of vice and the landed aristocracy. Moral and agricultural fundamentalism reappeared in the writings of Thomas Spence and William Godwin as well as Mary Wollstonecraft. Godwin argued that luxury and inequality had been necessary to build up civilisation, but society in the future would be simple, refusing to pursue superfluities. Richard Price argued against the concentration of the poor and the lower orders in cities. Luxury was associated with manufactures and machinery – these were sources of inequality. Thelwall argued for a love of virtuous poverty as against tinsel ornaments. Charles Hall, in *The Effects of Civilisation on the People in European States* (1805), argued that the progress of manufactures had generated inequality, and civilisation and the luxuries of life were not justifiable from the viewpoint of the majority.[70]

VI

The luxury debates, both as contemporary issue and as historical subject, reappear at the turn of the twentieth century when they are picked up by Sombart and Simmel in Germany and Veblen in America. Mandeville first appeared in translation in Germany in 1914. And in Veblen's America, F.B. Kaye completed his great edition of *The Fable*. The return to the luxury of the eighteenth century was prompted by writing on singular patterns of consumption and display in the advanced capitalist societies of late nineteenth- and early twentieth-century Germany and America.

Sombart explained luxury in psychological terms; it arose from purely sensuous pleasure, fostered especially in the court and the salon. He conveyed a sense of the powerful roles of disgust and desire through his extensive use of the writings of Sebastien Mercier. Drawing on Mercier's descriptions of eighteenth-century Paris, Sombart focused on the role of salons and sexuality in advancing luxury. He argued that mistresses and courtesans sensualised and refined luxury. They drew opulence into the confines of the domestic sphere; they 'objectified' it, replacing the feasts and entertainments of the feudal age with a preference for rich dresses, comfortable houses and precious jewels.[71] Simmel and Veblen both returned to Mandeville, the one to look at the culture of fashion and style in distinguishing individuals from social groups; the other to denounce the status-seeking and ostentatious lifestyles of the super-rich.[72]

The beginning of a new century is an ideal time to reconsider the history of luxury, for luxury is an obsession of today's consumer society. There has been an upscaling of consumer aspirations associated with luxury and designer goods, with the branding revolution described by Naomi Klein in *No Logo*, and with this a decline of the High Street chains and the mass consumerism which once underpinned these. The lifestyle choices of affluence are associated with distinction, diversity and individuality. Luxury has become a commonplace of advertising slogans – luxury holidays, luxury housing and luxury cars complement designer labels in clothing. Luxury is now seen not as something extra or excessive to everyday life, but something attainable and desirable. Just as consumption displaced labour and production as the defining entity of post-1970s society, so too do concepts of luxury, fashion, fantasy and desire define cultures of consumption.

The enormous literature on consumerism which has dominated social theory since the 1980s has only recently turned to this aspect of commercial culture.[73] It was, however, anticipated in Colin Campbell's pioneering *The Romantic Ethic and the Spirit of Modern Consumerism* (1987), which sought to explain the origins of the desire for new goods, their rapid multiplication and their equally rapid demise. He set his explanation in the framework of 'hedonism', and looked to pleasure, anticipation and disappointment. He identified a turning point in the eighteenth century, and like the many theorists of luxury of this period, he too distinguished the 'traditional' from the 'modern'. Traditional hedonism referred to the material aspects of objects, whereas modern hedonism referred to fantasy, anticipation and the emotion of desire. He turned Max Weber's innerworldly asceticism on its head, finding alongside it the emergence of a history of sentiment, the romantic personality and affective self-indulgence which, he argues, underlay the consumption of the eighteenth century. The demand for new consumer goods, and especially for luxuries was rooted in delayed gratification and hedonistic longing, in an addictive anticipation of a continuing stream of novelties.[74] These emotional states of fantasy, anticipation and desire were directed not to consumption in general, but to the consumption of luxuries.

The widespread use of the word in recent years may be an indication of greater prosperity, but it also reveals greater social division. The moral choices associated with the consumption of luxury goods have been highlighted by individuals who choose to boycott certain brands associated with the exploitation of cheap, third World labour, as well as by large-scale political action surrounding recent world trade summits. A critique of luxury has emerged with increasing social division at home between the rich and the poor, and with a newly prominent global division between countries mainly in the northern hemisphere consuming luxuries, and those of the southern hemisphere producing them. Consumption has become a key marker of inclusion and exclusion in recent Human Development Reports. Books such as Juliet Schor's *The Overspent American* (1998) and Robert Frank's *Luxury Fever* (1999) mark our anxiety over the excesses of consumerism combined with the extremes of social division. Not even the most prescient eighteenth-century critic anticipated a world in which the individual and collective uses of luxury had such disquieting implications for the future of civilisation.

Notes

1. On the luxury debates in China and Japan, see Craig Clunas, 'Anxieties about Things', in Craig Clunas, *Superfluous Things. Material Culture and Social Status in Early Modern China* (Cambridge, 1991), pp. 141–65; Peter Burke, 'Res et verba: Conspicuous Consumption in the Early Modern World', in John Brewer and Roy Porter, eds, *Consumption and the World of Goods* (London, 1993), pp. 148–62; Kenneth Pomeranz, *The Great Divergence. China, Europe and the Making of the Modern World Economy* (Princeton, 2000), pp. 127–51.
2. For a fine discussion of the development of these concepts, see Guido Guerzoni, 'Liberalitas, Magnificentia, Splendor: the Classic Origins of Italian Renaissance Lifestyles', in Neil De Marchi and Craufurd D.W. Goodwin, eds, *Economic Engagements with Art* (Durham, NC and London, 1999), pp. 332–78.
3. Andrew Sherratt, 'Reviving the Grand Narrative: Archaeology and Long-term Change', *Journal of European Archaeology*, vol. 3 (1995), pp. 1–32, pp. 12–14.
4. A. Appadurai, ed., *The Social Life of Things. Commodities in Cultural Perspective*, p. 33.
5. C.J. Berry, *The Idea of Luxury* (Cambridge, 1994), pp. 74–84.
6. On sumptuary law, see Alan Hunt, *Governance of the Consuming Passions: a History of Sumptuary Law* (London, 1996); Negley Harte, 'State Control of Dress and Social Change in Pre-industrial England', in D.C. Coleman and A.H. John, eds, *Trade, Government and Economy in Pre-industrial England* (London, 1976), pp. 132–65.
7. Hunt, *Governance of the Consuming Passions*, p. 371; Harte, 'State Control of Dress', pp. 132–65.
8. See Berry, *The Idea of Luxury*; John Sekora, *Luxury: the Concept in Western Thought, Eden to Smollett* (Baltimore, 1977).
9. [Nicholas Barbon], *A Discourse of Trade* (London, 1690).
10. Cited in A.O. Hirschman, *The Passions and the Interests, Political Arguments for Capitalism before Its Triumph* (Princeton NJ, 1977), p. 60.

11. The philosophical and theological framework of Mandeville's thought is discussed in John Robertson, 'Epicurean Origins of Enlightenment in Naples and Scotland: Vico, Mandeville and Hume', unpublished paper, 2002.
12. Edward Hundert, *The Enlightenment's Fable. Bernard Mandeville and the Discovery of Society* (Cambridge, 1994), p. 181.
13. Cited in, *ibid.*, p. 181.
14. Bernard Mandeville, *The Fable of the Bees* (1714), ed. Phillip Harth (Harmondsworth, 1970), Remark M, p. 150.
15. See F. Melon, *Essai politique sur le commerce* (Paris, 1734), and Montesquieu, *Esprit des Lois* (Paris, 1748).
16. (Saint-Lambert), 'Luxe', D. Diderot and J. d'Alembert, eds. *Encyclopédie, ou Dictionnaire raisonné des sciences, des arts, et des métiers* (Paris, 1751–65), Vol. 5.
17. James Steuart, *An Inquiry into the Principles of Political Oeconomy* [1767], ed. Andrew S. Skinner (Edinburgh and London, 1966), I, p. 266.
18. See Jan de Vries, 'Were Eighteenth-century People Aspiring Consumers or Oppressed Workers?' Unpublished Paper to History Seminar, 5 February 1998; cf. Berry, *The Idea of Luxury*, pp. 138–9 and de Vries, 'Luxury in the Dutch Golden Age', this volume.
19. See Dena Goodman, 'Furnishing Discourses: Readings of a Writing Desk in Eighteenth-century France', this volume.
20. David Hume, *Essays Moral, Political and Literary* (1741, 1742), London, 1903 Part II, Essay 1, 'Of Commerce' pp. 259–75; Essay 2, 'Of Refinement in the Arts', pp. 275–89.
21. David Hume, 'Of Commerce', in Hume, *Essays, Moral Political and Literary* (1752) (Oxford, 1963), pp. 259–75, p. 270.
22. Adam Smith, *The Wealth of Nations* (1776), ed. R.H. Campbell and A.S. Skinner (Oxford, 1976), Book I, ch. 1, p. 22.
23. *Ibid.*, p. 24.
24. *Ibid.*, Book I, ch. 3, sec. 12.
25. Smith discusses this shift in elite consumption and in urban production as a part of the 'natural progress of opulence' in Book III. For discussion of this, see Maxine Berg, 'Political Economy and the Principles of Manufacture', in M. Berg, P. Hudson and M. Sonenscher, eds, *Manufacture in Town and Country before the Factory* (Cambridge, 1983), pp. 33–58, at 45–50; and Neil De Marchi, 'Adam Smith's Accommodation of "altogether endless" Desires', in Maxine Berg and Helen Clifford, eds, *Consumers and Luxury* (Manchester, 1999), pp. 18–36, at 23–5.
26. Mandeville, *The Fable of the Bees*, Remark L, p. 144; Jean-François Melon, *Of Luxury, in A Political Essay upon Commerce, written in French by Monsieur M***. Translated with some Annotations, and remarks by David Bindon, Esq.* (Dublin, 1739), pp. 1, 3–8.
27. See De Marchi, 'Adam Smith's Accommodation'.
28. Daniel Defoe, *A Plan for the English Commerce* (London, 1731), p. 166; also p. 78.
29. *Ibid.*, p. 218.
30. Malachy Postlethwayt, *Britain's Interest Explained and Improved*, 2 vols. (London, 1757), vol. 2, p. 395.
31. Mandeville, *The Fable of the Bees*, Remark B, pp. 96–7.
32. Bernard Mandeville, 'A Search into the Nature of Society', in *The Fable of the Bees*, p. 353.
33. Defoe, *A Plan for the English Commerce*, p. 77.
34. John Millar, *Origins of the Distinction of Ranks*, cited in Hirschman, *The Passions and the Interests*, p. 105.
35. See Sarah Maza, 'Luxury, Morality and Social Change: Why there was no Middle-Class Consciousness in Pre-revolutionary France', *Journal of Modern History* 69 (June 1997), p. 217.
36. See Kathleen Wilson, *The Sense of the People. Politics, Culture and Imperialism in England, 1715–1785* (Cambridge, 1998), pp. 191–2.
37. See James Raven, 'Defending Conduct and Property. The London Press and the Luxury

Debate', in John Brewer and Susan Staves, ed., *Early Modern Conceptions of Property* (London, 1995), pp. 301–19, p. 304.

38. Vincent Quinn and Mary Peace, eds, *Luxurious Sexualities, Textual Practice* 11 (3), 1997, 405–16.

39. Sekora, *Luxury*, pp. 1–2.

40. *Ibid.*, p. 32.

41. See Jonathan White, 'Representations of the Consumption of the Labouring Poor in Eighteenth-Century England', PhD Dissertation, University of Warwick, 2001. Also see John Styles, 'Custom or Consumption', this volume.

42. Sekora, *Luxury*, p. 12.

43. See Barbara Hardy, *The Exposure of Luxury: Radical Themes in Thackeray* (London, 1972), pp. 20–1.

44. Sekora, *Luxury*, p. 32.

45. See introduction to Vincent Quinn and Mary Peace, eds, *Luxurious Sexualities, Textual Practice* 11 (3), 1997.

46. Edward Hundert, *The Enlightenment's Fable: Bernard Mandeville and the Discovery of Society* (Cambridge, 1994), p. 13.

47. See Bernard Mandeville, *By a Society of Ladies: Essays in The Female Tatler*, ed. M.M. Goldsmith (Bristol, 1999).

48. See J. Martin Stafford, ed., *Private Vices, Publick Benefits? The Contemporary Reception of Bernard Mandeville* (Hull, 1997), p. xii.

49. See David Nokes, *John Gay. A Profession of Friendship* (Oxford, 1995).

50. See Stephen Copley and Ian Haywood, 'Luxury, Refuse and Poetry: John Gay's *Trivia*', in Peter Lewis and Nigel Wood, eds, *John Gay and the Scriblerians* (London, 1988), pp. 62–83.

51. Raymond Williams, *Keywords. A Vocabulary of Culture and Society* (London: Fontana/Croom Helm, 1976; revised edition 1984).

52. Williams, *Keywords*, p. 13.

53. Cited in Hundert, *The Enlightenment's Fable*, p. 209. See his broader discussion in 'Homo economica and her Double', pp. 205–18.

54. Werner Sombart, *Luxury and Capitalism* (1913), p. 105; David Frisby and Mike Featherstone, eds, *Simmel on Culture* (London, 1997), pp. 187–90.

55. Bernard Mandeville, *Fable of the Bees*, ed. Kaye, vol. 2, pp. 30–41.

56. Sombart, *Luxury and Capitalism*, p. 96.

57. See Neil De Marchi and Hans J. Van Miegroet, 'Ingenuity, Preference and the Pricing of Pictures: The Smith–Reynolds Connection', in De Marchi and Goodwin, eds, *Economic Engagements with Art* , pp. 379–412; Maxine Berg, 'New Commodities, Luxuries and their Consumers in Eighteenth-Century England', in Berg and Clifford, eds, *Consumers and Luxury*, pp. 63–87.

58. Robert Jones, *Gender and the Formation of Taste in Eighteenth-Century Britain: The Analysis of Beauty* (Cambridge, 1998).

59. Alexander Gerard, *Essay on Taste* (London, 1756), p. 194.

60. Katie Scott, *The Rococo Interior* (Yale, 1995), p. 216.

61. *Ibid.*, p. 226.

62. *Ibid.*, pp. 234–8.

63. See Hundert, *The Enlightenment's Fable*, pp. 178–9.

64. See Berry, *The Idea of Luxury*, pp. 162–77; Istvan Hont, 'Luxury', forthcoming in *The Cambridge History of Political Thought*; also see Istvan Hont and Michael Ignatieff, 'Needs and Justice in the *Wealth of Nations*: an Introductory Essay' in *Wealth and Virtue* (Cambridge, 1993).

65. Donald Winch, *Riches and Poverty. An Intellectual History of Political Economy in Britain 1750–1834* (Cambridge, 1996), pp. 76–80, 106–9.

66. Adam Smith, *The Theory of Moral Sentiments* (1759), revised 1790, eds D.D. Raphael and L.L. McFie (Oxford, 1976), Book I, iii, ch. 2, pp. 50–2.

67. Smith, *ibid.*, Book IV, ch. 1, pp. 180–3.
68. Winch, *Riches and Poverty*, pp. 333–8, 366–9. Joyce Appleby, 'Consumption in Early-Modern Social Thought', in Brewer and Porter, eds, *Consumption and the World of Goods*, pp. 162–77.
69. Hirschman, *The Passions and the Interests*, pp. 107–21.
70. Gregory Claeys, 'The Origins of the Rights of Labor: Republicanism, Commerce and the Construction of Modern Social Theory in Britain, 1796–1805', *Journal of Modern History*, 66 (1994), pp. 249–90; Noel Thompson, 'Social Opulence, Private Asceticism: Ideas of Consumption in Early Socialist Thought', in Martin Daunton and Matthew Hilton, eds, *The Politics of Consumption. Material Culture and Citizenship in Europe and America* (Oxford, 2001), pp. 51–68.
71. Sombart, *Luxury and Capitalism*, pp. 61, 105.
72. See David Frisby and Mike Featherstone, eds, *Simmel on Culture*; Thorstein Veblen, *The Theory of the Leisure Class* (New York, 1899).
73. See Daniel Miller, ed., *Acknowledging Consumption* (London, 1995).
74. Colin Campbell, *The Romantic Ethic and the Spirit of Modern Consumerism* (London, 1987); also see Jean-Christophe Agnew, 'Coming up for Air: Consumer Culture in Historical Perspective', in John Brewer and Roy Porter, eds, *Consumption and the World of Goods* (London, 1993), pp. 19–39, pp. 25–6.

2
Mandeville, Rousseau and the Political Economy of Fantasy

Edward Hundert

Denis Diderot, setting out to explain the purposes of the Enlightenment's greatest monument, said that the *Encyclopédie* would expose the abuses to which words have commonly been put.[1] In offering 'luxury' as the term which best exemplified contemporary conceptual confusion, Diderot counted on his readers' familiarity with a continuing controversy about the consequences of massively increased consumption in Europe's Atlantic rim since the beginning of the seventeenth century. Voltaire, Montesquieu, Hutcheson and Hume had already contributed to this body of argument, which would further be enriched by many entries in the *Encyclopédie* itself and, most notably, by Adam Smith's account in Book III of *The Wealth of Nations* of the role of 'baubles and trinkets' in the demise of feudalism.[2]

Whatever their understanding of the issue, all participants in the eighteenth century's luxury debate were obliged to come to terms with Bernard Mandeville's *Fable of the Bees* (1723 and 1728), the text which initiated the controversy by arguing that 'luxury' denoted a cluster of concepts revealed as empty in the context of commercial modernity, and that, in reality, heightened expectations of affluence had become constituent features of the modern polity.[3] No eighteenth-century writer sought to expose contemporary society's diminished stock of moral capital more forcefully than Jean-Jacques Rousseau, and in what follows I shall suggest both that his critique of modernity emerged from his encounter with *The Fable of the Bees*, and that Rousseau's deepest insights into the fantasies inherent in cultures of consumption bear upon our own historical understanding.[4]

Mandeville achieved great notoriety throughout the eighteenth century, but not because of any supposed economic doctrines buried in *The Fable*'s dialogues and polemical essays. Responsible, rather, was his claim that Christian ethics were psychologically implausible and that the traditions of moral philosophy derived from Christianity served the ideological and socialising purpose of keeping the self-regarding sources of human desire hidden from view. According to Mandeville, contemporary ethical reasoning falsely moralised social processes. By displacing impulse as the primary unit from which to comprehend human action, his contemporaries were prevented from understanding the novel conditions under which personalities had recently come to be formed. *The Fable*'s radical analysis of luxury gained its conceptual force within the framework of this larger consideration of the dynamics of Western history.

Modern commercial societies differ from others – in Mandeville's view – not only because of their unprecedented affluence but because the difference between being and appearing is for commercial moderns the most psychologically signifi-cant characteristic of public life. Envy and the emulative propensities to which, through envy, opulence gives rise had become defining features of the modern moral subject, whose heightened propensities for display and dissimulation could not be comprehended within the terms provided by the inherited moral tradition.

Mandeville sought to show that the forms of domination characteristic of pre-vious social formations had been rendered obsolete. Persons now derived their social power not from an ability to subdue competitors by force, but from the attention and deference conspicuous displays of articles of consumption in an expanding world of goods engendered amongst social actors. The primitive powers that once enabled governing elites to compel approbation and obedience no longer applied. Now, 'costly Equipages, Buildings, Titles of Honour, and every-thing that Men can acquire' are the primary 'Marks and Tokens' of esteem from which social power derives.[5] In modern conditions, persons are obliged to orient their public performances to the imperatives of a world of mobile property, in which relations with others are rarely elemental, but are instead mediated by the unstable values embodied in possessions themselves. Nowhere was this more apparent than in the commercial metropolis. In a passage which Montesquieu cited in his own discussion of luxury, Mandeville wrote that

> people, where they are not known, are generally honoured according to their clothes and other accoutrements they have about them. From the richness of them we judge of their wealth, and by their ordering of them we guess at their understanding. It is this which encourages everybody who is conscious of his little merit, if he is anyways able, to wear clothes above his rank, especially in large and populous cities, where obscure men may hourly meet with fifty strangers to one acquaintance, and consequently have the pleasure of being esteemed by a vast majority, not as what they are, but what they appear to be . . .[6]

Mandeville injected into public consciousness the question of what happens when large numbers of individuals are required to engage with, and are power-fully moved by, the imagery produced by the display and manipulation of com-modities. He showed how fantasy had become an integral feature of worlds transformed by a surfeit of goods. Rather than disciplined attention to work and duty, the frivolous pursuits of leisure, decisively shaped by the inconstancy and whimsy of women, had become the energising forces of contemporary prosperity and, moreover, permanent features of the culture of opulence. These were trou-bling thoughts indeed at a time when Britain's most important philosopher could ask 'whether a woman of fashion ought not to be declared a public enemy' and republics of the ancient world as well as contemporary Venice were seen to have been corrupted and made effeminate by luxury.[7] Mandeville's argument was even more disturbing when placed in the context of his thesis about the role of fashion in modern European history. 'The Reformation,' he wrote, 'has scarce been more instrumental in rendering the Kingdoms and states that have embraced it, flourishing beyond other Nations, than the silly and capricious invention of Hoop'd and Quilted Petticoats.'[8]

When conceived as driven by fashion industries catering primarily to female tastes and women's liberated incomes, commercial exchange could appear radically transfigured. In Britain particularly, Protestant, especially 'vulgar Whig', associations of commerce with liberty were fed by complementary misogynist fears that were themselves exacerbated in the early eighteenth century by the explosion of the European luxury trades. In reducing to self-serving cant the attempt to moralise economic expansion by associating it with the frugal virtues of pious, independent citizens, Mandeville challenged his readers to confront the sheer power of their now unadorned avarice. As he put it, 'nothing could make amends for the Detriment Trade would sustain, if all those of that Sex, who enjoy the happy State of Matrimony, should act and behave themselves as a sober wise Man could wish them'.[9] Indeed,

> a considerable Portion of what the Prosperity of London and Trade in general and all the worldly Interest of the Nation consists in, depends entirely on the Deceit and vile Stratagems of Women; and that Humility, Content, Meekness, Obedience to reasonable Husbands, Frugality, and all the Virtues together, if they were possess'd of them in the most eminent Degree, could not possibly be a thousandth Part so serviceable, to make an opulent, powerful, and what we call a flourishing Kingdom, than their most hateful Qualities.[10]

Mandeville transformed the notion of female desire from a localised force driving recent economic advance into a general principle of social explanation. His acid observation that a great society depends upon 'the abominable improvement of Female Luxury' was meant to and succeeded in challenging one of his audience's deepest assumptions about the moral integrity of its own aspirations.[11] He forced this audience to confront the possibility that an environment had arisen in which features of one's identity previously thought to be essential and enduring had become mere markers distinguishing practices of display and role distance that could be altered or discarded when they came into conflict with contemporary forms of economic opportunity. Under these conditions, the desire of persons activated by vanity, 'pride's ornamental and vestimentary embodiment', to have their self-image acknowledged by others could account for social interaction in a commercial world inhabited by self-interested egoists.

Private Vices, Publick Benefits, *The Fable*'s sub-title, was thus a paradoxical thesis about the contemporary functions of self-regard, supported by an inquiry into moral psychology both meant and taken by Mandeville's audience as a threat to contemporary self-understanding. Mandeville claimed that, from the perspective of the dramatically altered intersubjective conditions which had come to characterise commercial modernity, an enormous range of social actions could be understood without any reference to outworn moral categories. They were, rather, purely instrumental attempts to satisfy pride through the promotion of one's status.

Mandeville recognised that his audience was comprised of persons who possessed a subjectivity at a considerable remove from any available alternative account of the person in terms of which he could be said to assent to society's norms as an autonomous and self-reflecting member. He put it to his readers that commerce, rather than being just one sector of the economy, was the environment within which all other sectors of society exist, and that the polity in which they lived had insensibly given birth to a semi-autonomous region of civil society sustained by private fantasies and driven by future prospects of wealth. In this world, personality is discontinuous with Christian moral commitment, social standing and identity are distributed through the mechanisms of the market, and character is nothing more than an artifact crafted by role-players within theatrical forms of social exchange. All would have to remain so, moreover, to ensure that commercial society would survive and flourish. Mandeville, in other words, showed how the modern polity could best be understood, not as the context required for the citizen's self-realisation, nor as the guardian of his rights, but rather as the habitat of his desire conceived in terms of consumer satisfaction.

Although Mandeville's contemporaries were often scandalised by the licentious premises of these assertions, some thinking that *The Fable* signalled the imminent 'destruction' of 'the desire of rational esteem', they would not have been surprised by the economic content of his arguments.[12] From the time of Mun and Sully, writers on economic subjects had focused on the ability of modern states to generate a surplus derived from the demand of a restricted class of luxury consumers. In England particularly, intellectuals during the first decades of the Restoration – most notably Nicholas Barbon and Dudley North – began to understand that material possessions beyond those necessary to sustain a frugal existence 'have their value', as Barbon put it, 'from supplying the wants of the mind'.[13]

Luxuries were seen to be desired more for their aesthetic effects and power to compel admiration than for the actual material needs they satisfied. These writers reasoned that the aggregate demand for economic goods would be intensified in wealthy trading nations primarily because of the esteem they attracted. Once the implications of such observations were understood, a process of burgeoning consumption could be seen as normal under appropriate legal and political conditions, since goods in the economic realm, emptied of lasting psychological satisfaction, would quickly lose their lustre in the face of other novelties supplied by trade and manufacture.

Mandeville's primary economic insight – wealth creation in commercial society depended upon the 'emulation and continual striving to out-do one another' – extended these discoveries. While he concentrated on the spending habits of monied elites, Mandeville recognised that persons throughout the social hierarchy could now participate in patterns of conspicuous consumption, beginning, as he put it, with 'the poorest Labourer's Wife', and extending through the several degrees of Quality to an incredible Expence, till at last the Prince's great Favourites and those of the first Rank of all, having nothing else left to outstrip some of their Inferiors, are forc'd to lay out vast Estates in pompous Equipages, magnificent Furniture, sumptuous Gardens and Princely Palaces . . .[14]

It was this claim about the social significance of hyper-consumption and luxury spending that *The Fable*'s readers found both socially shocking and morally suspect, since the unbridled emulative propensities Mandeville had identified posed a threat to social stability. In such a society, Henry Fielding warned,

while the Nobleman will emulate the Grandeur of a Prince and the Gentleman will aspire to the proper state of a Nobleman, the Tradesman steps from behind his Counter into the vacant place of the Gentleman. Nor doth the confusion end there: It reaches the very Dregs of the People, who aspire still to a degree beyond that which belongs to them.[15]

In the course of these wider arguments, Mandeville made two particularly unsettling claims about luxury and its connection with these destabilising social processes. Luxury consumption, first of all, enriches a nation through the promotion of avarice, the particular vice which has as its unintended consequence encouragement for the manufacture and circulation of goods. He argued that the fundamental psychological reality of opulent societies is that they are populated by egoists responding to opportunities for consumption and display, that they are driven by excess rather than moderation, and that they are characterised by extravagance masquerading as refinement. Not only did all 'great societies' rest upon 'increased wants', but the satisfaction of these wants and the consequent creation of others in their stead constitute the propulsive mechanism for change in the interdependent domains of fashion and morals. In so pointing to an intimate connection between ethical standards and prevailing tastes, Mandeville arrived at his most radical thesis: the history of the civilising process offered conclusive evidence that moral reasoning itself was a species of fashion and, like changing habits of dress, a dependent feature of the universal search for esteem.[16] If true, this claim would demolish arguments within the natural law tradition that, as Locke put it, conceived of the 'habits of fashion' as distinct from and as the enemy of morality, since they produce a 'fantastical uneasiness' that gives rise to a desire for unmerited honour, power and riches.[17]

Mandeville's second disturbing point about luxury is that the conventional moral condemnation of superfluous material indulgence trades upon the impossibility of arriving at any strict definition of luxury, and thus of moderation, in which consumption above the level of subsistence could be considered an indulgence, and therefore vicious. In conventional usage, he wrote, luxury is 'that not immediately necessary to make Man subsist'.[18] 'It increases Avarice and Rapine: And where they are reigning Vices, Offices of the greatest Trust are bought and sold; the Ministers that should serve the Publick . . . corrupted, and the Countries every Moment in danger of being betray'd to the highest Bidders: And lastly, that it effeminates and enervates the people, by which the Nations become an easy Prey to the first Invaders.'[19] But, he added,

> If you tell me, that Men may make use of all . . . things with Moderation, and consequently that the Desire after them is no Vice, then I answer, that either no Degree of Luxury ought to be called a Vice, or that it is impossible to give a definition of Luxury, which Everybody will allow to be a just one . . . [for] if once we depart from calling every thing Luxury that is not absolutely necessary to keep a Man alive, then there is no Luxury at all.[20]

The term 'luxury', Mandeville sought to show, effectively captures the behaviour of individuals who, by virtue of their command of monied wealth, possess the ability to satisfy the desires they share with others. In commercial societies these desires are decisively shaped by newly liberated emulative propensities which may be (temporarily) satisfied through the acquisition of socially esteemed goods. The intemperance of the great, as well as those who ape their habits of living, in no way threatens public security, Mandeville argued. On the contrary, he claimed that the historical record provided incontrovertible evidence that modern states like Britain, recently made great by growing opulence, were in fact more stable and better able to defend themselves than were the Mediterranean primitives populating the ancient republics whose supposed virtue and frugality inspired many of his critics. If correct, Mandeville saw, his understanding of the dynamics of consumption would immediately throw into question the semantic force of 'luxury' as conventionally understood. For in asserting that there is no natural limit to desire, he denied that there was any objective standard of self-sufficiency appropriate to humans, any *telos* or *summum bonum* which individuals or communities naturally seek – a point which so revolted Francis Hutcheson that he spent much of the rest of his career in a vain attempt to refute it. Indeed, even a looser definition of luxury than the one inherited from classical and Christian ethics, Mandeville maintained, would offer no conceptual advantage in understanding the moral implications of persons living in societies characterised by rapidly increasing levels of consumption. The mobility of modern property had amplified natural acquisitive propensities, which governing classes were powerless to eliminate and were now required to manage. Commercial moderns had, largely unknowingly, traversed an unbridgeable gulf, separating themselves irrevocably from an antique or Christian ethic of private restraint.

The depth of this rupture, with its attendant sense of loss, made *The Fable of the Bees* compelling reading for Rousseau. Repelled by what he took to be the ethical distortions of modernity, Rousseau's reflections on the economy were usually second-hand and bore an unwitting resemblance to the discomfort expressed by members of the nobility at the increasing social power of wealthy commoners.[21] He accepted as obvious the already suspect claim that increased urban consumption would impoverish and depopulate the countryside, and that, as the physiocrat Baudeau put it, the production of domestic superfluities threatened agriculture through an 'inversion of the natural order'.[22]

Virtually alone amongst the *philosophes*, Rousseau argued in the *Discourse on Political Economy* (1755) that the proper task of government is to institute sumptuary legislation so that 'the arts of pleasure and pure invention' would not be 'favoured at the expense of useful and difficult trades'.[23] Indeed, the Parisian intellectuals whose polished sociability he so despised paid considerably less attention to Rousseau's economic views than to his rejection of fashionable dress when he adopted the rustic 'Corsican' costume which came to serve as his public emblem.

Rousseau's engagement with the problem of luxury profoundly shaped his thinking on virtually all social questions. It brought to the forefront of his critique of modernity precisely those issues of moral psychology that Mandeville had insisted were commercial society's defining features. Mandeville was decisive for Rousseau because he believed *The Fable* to be the unembarrassed expression of modernity's immoral voice, proclaiming that luxury is the 'paradox so worthy of our time', in which 'a man is worth no more to the state than the value of his domestic consumption'.[24]

Rousseau agreed with Mandeville that luxury spending was a constitutive feature of the progress of the arts and sciences and of the polite and polished habits of living which characterised the modern commercial metropolis. Here especially social understanding itself had been transformed, and the Mandevillian maxim, as Rousseau called it, that 'men have all the same passions, above all [that] self-love and interest lead them, [and] in this they are all alike', was now taken to be self-evident.[25]

Rousseau further agreed with Mandeville that an ethic of self-display, dependent on the encouragement of vanity in successive regimes of fashion, had come to shape modern morals, producing in its wake a transformation in the conception of the self. Just as Mandeville had claimed, we 'now seek our happiness in the opinion of others'.[26]

These views achieved international prominence in Rousseau's enormously influential *Discourse on the Origins of Inequality* (1755), which elevated the question of luxury into the wider Enlightenment discussion about the moral implications of the progress of civilisation. Rousseau's conjectural history of the emergence of culture was modelled, like Mandeville's, on a secular, Lucretian account of the evolution of human nature. Its purpose was to offer an anthropologically informed analysis of the discontinuities between any scientifically plausible description of aboriginal, asocial human capacities and the insatiable desires of socialised men. Rousseau explicitly distanced his imagined savages in the state of nature from the pre-political primitives described in *The Fable* by emphasising the power of pity in their hearts. Still, the amoral endowments of the brutes Rousseau described bore a striking resemblance to Mandeville's primitives, whose physical impulses and self-love conditioned their behaviour.[27]

Like Mandeville, Rousseau tied the problem of the foundation of society to the ability of cunning minorities to tame and discipline their fellows. Mandeville had argued that polities originated in acts of ideological duplicity as elites laid claim to virtue by disguising their own self-seeking, thereby commanding the respect and acquiescence of subordinates.[28] Similarly, Rousseau described the first society as founded by the 'trick of the rich man' who, assuming 'the mask of benevolence', wrested from the weak their consent to agreements sanctifying property rights, and thereby their own subordination.[29] Where they disagreed was that, for Mandeville, the history of the blessings of civilisation was initiated in this founding moment; for Rousseau, by contrast, the momentous transition to civil life marked instead a decisive break between a benign human nature and the deformations of the 'artificial men' who had come to populate civil societies. Adam Smith caught just this difference when he reviewed the *Discourse of the Origins of Inequality* for *The Edinburgh Review*: through a feat of 'philosophical chemistry', he wrote, Rousseau had transformed 'the principles and ideas of the profligate Mandeville' into a critique of modernity.[30]

Once torn from the natural order, Rousseau argued, socialised men were destined to live within regimes of ever-increasing complexity and interdependence. Commercial society, the most recent expression of what is in essence a history of increasing inequality, was distinguished by the rise of the 'liberal and mechanical arts', themselves dependent for their flourishing upon a widening class of consumers of the luxury items these arts supply. For Rousseau, the processes of socialisation themselves establish the intersubjective conditions in which 'the sociable man knows how to live in the opinion of others; and it is . . . from their judgement alone that he draws the sentiment of his existence'.[31]

But in truth, commercial moderns, in sharp contrast to their predecessors, have at their disposal a hitherto unimagined armoury of goods whose display functions as the primary vehicle for the construction of a self that has the opinion of others as an indelible part of its content. In this way, 'luxury, impossible to prevent among men greedy for their own commodities and the esteem of others, soon completes the evil that societies began'.[32]

Rousseau grasped the deepest implications of Mandeville's insight that opportunities for hyper-consumption would intensify the role of vanity as a spur to economic expansion, and at the same time encourage and be dependent upon a theatricised public sphere. As in the theatre, so in modern society, 'everything being reduced to appearances, all becomes fractious and deceptive: honour, friendship, virtue, and often even vices themselves, about which men finally discover the secret of boasting . . .'[33]

Rapidly changing fashions of dress were the most ubiquitous expressions of cultures of consumption, as Rousseau was vividly reminded when his decision to adopt modest attire inspired a fashion craze in Parisian society, soon extending to Versailles, where the Queen would don peasant costume to play at being a milkmaid. Such displays only confirmed for Rousseau the association, celebrated by Mandeville, of feminine power with the arts of excess, and excited his already developed misogyny – although they did not prevent him from wearing fashionable clothing when opportunities for seduction seemed to demand it. (I cannot resist adding that on one of these occasions Rousseau failed to win the attentions of Elisabeth d'Houdetot, the mistress of Saint-Lambert, who wrote the article

'Luxe' for Diderot's *Encyclopédie*.) In women's dress we can discern two distinct moral economies, he claimed: one represented by Paris where women adopt fashions to conceal those faults the fashion industries themselves define, the other by rustic communities like that of Clarens in *La Nouvelle Héloïse*, where, by contrast, the rejection of superfluities secures material abundance, and dress conforms to need alone. Rousseau longed for, but certainly did not expect, a transparent social order in which persons would wear clothing appropriate to their ages and stations. Here 'the sign [would] say everything before one speaks' and, as he fantasised in his polemic against the stage, luxurious adornment would vanish while, as in ancient Sparta and republican Rome, persons would be on permanent public view.[34]

Rousseau's refusal to accept as legitimate societies in which 'the less natural and urgent the needs, the more the passions augment . . . the power to satisfy them' derived from his adherence to the ideals of those antique polities which Mandeville dismissed as absurd, mythic or simply impractical.[35] But this utopian commitment, fuelled by an unstable compound of rage and fascination, also afforded Rousseau the conceptual distance from which to assess the habits of his contemporaries. Mandeville had argued that commercial moderns, confronting one another in societies transformed into markets for marks of esteem, were obliged to learn the arts of managing impressions in order to establish their public identities. Regimes of fashion dependent upon a wide circulation of goods were indelible features of these societies, and Mandeville sought to show that in them social actors would perforce calculate the symbolic value of these tokens of status, and then, moved by a desire to emulate the great, acquire and display those items whose possession one's credit or disposable income made possible.

Rousseau agreed with Mandeville that the 'furor to distinguish oneself' was a defining feature of modernity. The prosperity brought by commerce and manufacture did not signal independence, but rather a permanent preoccupation with the opinions of others. His critique of these habits, however, went far beyond the insight that possessions can become morally exhausting. For Rousseau understood that the rich, as he put it, are 'vulnerable in every part of their goods'.[36]

Mandeville had described a social actor who responds to opportunities for consumption through purely instrumental attempts to promote his standing. Rousseau, by contrast, was perhaps the first to grasp that the symbolic power of superfluous possessions extends beyond their intended audience so as to define, if not even to dominate, the very persons who possess them. He understood that individuals in commercial societies could not be expected simply to delight in their own plasticity and maintain a spectatorial distance from their own practices of consumption and display. Luxury goods, he saw, have as one of their greatest powers the self-endorsement of their possessors. Emulation and the envy from which it springs might account for the first impulses to consume superfluities, but no examination of its power could by itself explain the dramatic, and for Rousseau distorting, transformations of the self promoted in consumer societies. Commercial moderns crafted their public identities through the ostentatious display of frivolities inaccessible to the majority. But also, and in Rousseau's view crucially, luxuries themselves had come to acquire the symbolic power to shape the self-understanding of the private man behind the public mask, of the actor-consumer upon whose escalating needs the progress of commercial society depends. Rousseau was probably right in thinking that his attempts to counter Mandeville had failed.[37]

By the 1780s, as the abbé Pluquet conceded in a review of the luxury debate, Mandeville's ideas had effectively dissolved the moral and theological connotations of the term, while in Britain, Bentham said, *The Fable of the Bees* had 'broken the chains of ordinary language in the minds of educated persons'.[38]

In cultures whose middle and upper ranks had largely accepted Mandeville's view that the modern economy is founded upon the satisfaction of desire and that 'the wants of Man are innumerable', 'luxury' would lose many of its previous associations with decadence and immorality. In my judgement, Rousseau was also correct in believing that fashion, once commercialised to become the concern of more than a few, and hyper-consumption, once generalised to include a vast range of persons, do not merely increase one's dependence upon the opinion of others, but endow objects themselves with the power to promote fantasies of identity, fantasies that even Mandeville, 'the most excessive detractor of human virtues', could have barely imagined.[39] In another discourse, as we have learned to say, these fantasies would be called alienation on the one hand, and on the other, the fetishism of commodities.

We are all Mandevillians now, however, although not simply because of the decomposition of Marxism, nor because more than a few still subscribe to Mandeville's cynical appraisal of the possibility of leading a genuinely moral life in conditions of abundance. As its publishing history demonstrates, *The Fable of the Bees* began to gain a modern readership only during the first decades of the twentieth century, just after Simmel and Veblen detected singular patterns of consumption and display in advanced capitalist societies, particularly in Simmel's Germany, where Mandeville first appeared in translation in 1914, and in Veblen's America, where, in 1924, F.B. Kaye completed his great edition of *The Fable*.[40] Shortly before publication, the historian Arthur Lovejoy wrote to encourage Kaye, telling him that Mandeville's masterpiece contained all the main ideas of Veblen's *Theory of the Leisure Class*.[41] After the first postwar boom, when Friedrich von Hayek proposed that Mandeville was a 'master mind', Mandeville's reputation rose, and has continued to rise, in proportion to an awareness that the fashion systems first analysed in *The Fable* have metastasised into dominant elements of Western consumer societies, access to whose goods voters expect their governments to protect and sustain.[42]

Mandeville's first readers may have thought it not only perverse but ridiculous to describe the modern citizen as above all a consumer. Today, we have considerably fewer grounds for such scepticism. We are Mandevillians now not only in accepting the larger implications of the 'petticoat thesis' that the history of consumption is an inextricable element in the history of our selves – but in acknowledging that the management of escalating desire is an unavoidable responsibility of the modern state.

As Mandeville's significance has grown, Rousseau's has diminished, so that he is now regarded as a decidedly past master, even in the face of recently revived communitarian sentiments. Rousseau's idealisation of peoples free of excess, of Corsican primitives and Swiss mountain villagers, may evoke nostalgic longings in some; but these desires, as he would have bitterly recognised, seem as often as not to be indulged through the purchase of goods that the fashion industries happily confect for the purpose. Beyond fleeting cravings somehow to re-inhabit a simpler, less luxurious past through the conversion of its symbols into elements of decor, the career of Jacobin and Leninist sumptuary regimes have made most of us more than a little wary of any actually existing Spartan manifestation of the General Will.

Situated as we are, it is understandable that we have become attentive to the social functions of opulence in the Renaissance, the Dutch Golden Age, pre-revolutionary France and, of more immediate interest, to the birth of the first consumer society in eighteenth-century Britain and its attendant pleasures of the imagination.[43]

These issues, and the distinguished scholarship to which they have given rise, speak to us more directly than would have been thought possible even one generation ago. But this very immediacy, as some of the scholars to whom I have alluded might have reminded us, may threaten to compromise our attempts to achieve the historical distance necessary for a full appreciation of the eighteenth-century world of goods. To the degree that we seek to capture, and not merely to register, the sense of bewilderment and moral displacement which accompanied feelings of exhilaration and exuberance in the passage to commercial modernity, Rousseau's self-confessed failure may serve as a more useful point of departure than Mandeville's surprising triumph.

Notes

1. Denis Diderot, *Encyclopédie*, in Diderot *et al.*, *Encyclopédie, ou Dictionnaire raisonée des sciences, des arts et des matiers, par une société des gens des lettres* (New York, 1984), pp. 635–6.
2. Daniel Roche, *The Culture of Clothing* (Cambridge, 1989), pp. 435–69; Adam Smith, *An Inquiry Into the Nature and Causes of the Wealth of Nations*, 2 vols., ed. A.S. Skinner, W.B. Todd and R.H. Campbell (Oxford, 1976), pt III, ch. iv. See also Donald Winch, *Riches and Poverty. An Intellectual History of Political Economy in Britain, 1750–1834* (Cambridge, 1996), pp. 57–89, and M.J.D. Roberts, 'The Concept of Luxury in British Political Economy: Adam Smith to Alfred Marshall', *History of the Human Sciences* 11.1 (1998), pp. 23–47.
3. Citations to Bernard Mandeville, *The Fable of the Bees*, or *Private Vices, Public Benefits: The Fable of the Bees*, will refer to the volume and page number of the edition of F.B. Kaye, 2 vols. (Oxford, 1924).
4. For useful discussions of the theme of luxury, see Mary Douglas and Baron Isherwood, *The World of Goods* (New York, 1979); Christopher J. Berry, *The Idea of Luxury. A Conceptual and Historical Investigation* (Cambridge, 1994); and John Sekora, *Luxury. The Concept in Western Thought, Eden to Smollett* (Baltimore, 1977). See, too, Peter Stearns, 'Stages of Consumerism: Recent Work on the Issues of Periodization', *The Journal of Modern History* 69 (March, 1997), pp. 102–17.
5. Mandeville, *The Fable*, II, p. 126.

6. Charles Secondat, baron de Montesquieu, *The Spirit of the Laws* (1748), A.M. Cohler, B.C. Miller and H.S. Stone, eds. (Cambridge, 1989), Bk VII, ch. 1; Mandeville, *The Fable*, I, pp. 127–8.
7. George Berkeley, *The Querist*, in *The Works of George Berkeley*, ed. T.E. Jessop (London, 1948), II, p. 117. For related contemporary opinion, see Erin Mackie, *Market à la mode. Fashion, Commodity and Gender in The Tatler and The Spectator* (Baltimore, 1977).
8. Mandeville, *The Fable*, I, p. 356.
9. *Ibid.*
10. *Ibid.*, I, p. 228.
11. *Ibid.*, I, p. 356.
12. John Brown, *Estimate of the Manners and Principles of the Times*, 2 vols. (London, 1757), I, p. 173.
13. Nicholas Barbon, *A Discourse Concerning the Coining of New Money Lighter in Answer to Mr Lock's Consideration about raising the Value of Money* (London, 1696), p. 14.
14. Mandeville, *The Fable*, I, pp. 129–30.
15. Henry Fielding, *An Enquiry Into the . . . Recent Causes . . . of the Increase in Robbers* [1751], in *Complete Works of Henry Fielding*, W.B. Henley, ed. (London, 1903), II, p. 783.
16. Mandeville, *The Fable*, I, pp. 330–1 and pp. 323–70.
17. John Locke, *An Essay Concerning Human Understanding*, Peter Niddich, ed. (Oxford, 1975), Book 2, ch. 21, para. 45.
18. Mandeville, *The Fable*, I, p. 107.
19. *Ibid.*, I, p. 135.
20. *Ibid.*, I, p. 108.
21. R. Galliani, 'Rousseau, le luxe et l'ideologie nobilière', in *Studies in Voltaire and the Eighteenth Century*, no. 268 (Oxford, 1989).
22. Jean-Jacques Rousseau, *A Discourse on Inequality*, in *The First and Second Discourses*, Roger Masters, ed. (New York, 1964), pp. 199–200; Nicolas Baudeau, *Principles de la science morale et politique sur le luxe et les lois sumptuaires* (1767), in A. Dubois, ed., *Collection des Economistes* (Paris, 1912), p. 14.
23. Jean-Jacques Rousseau, *Discourse on Political Economy*, in Roger Masters and Christopher Kelly, eds. and trans., *The Collected Writings of Rousseau* (Hanover, New Hampshire, 1992), III, p. 154.
24. Jean-Jacques Rousseau, *Discourse on the Arts and Sciences*, in *The First and Second Discourses*, Roger Masters, ed. and trans. (New York, 1964), p. 51.
25. Jean-Jacques Rousseau, *Narcisse ou l'amant de lui-même*, in *Oeuvres Complètes*, II, Jean Starobinski, ed. (Paris, 1964), Preface, p. 969n.
26. Rousseau, *Discourse on the Arts and Sciences*, p. 64.
27. Rousseau, *Inequality*, p. 131.
28. Mandeville, *The Fable*, I, pp. 41–57.
29. Rousseau, *Inequality*, p. 159.
30. Adam Smith, 'A Letter to the Editors of the Edinburgh Review', in W.P.D. Wightman and J.C. Bryce eds., *Essays on Philosophical Subjects* (Indianapolis, 1982), p. 251.
31. Rousseau, *Inequality*, p. 179.
32. *Ibid.*, p. 199.
33. Rousseau, *Inequality*, p. 180; Rousseau, *A Letter to M. D'Alembert on the Theatre*, in Allan Bloom, trans., *Politics and the Arts* (Glencoe, 1960), pp. 17–25.
34. Jean-Jacques Rousseau, *Emile*, trans. Allan Bloom (Harmondsworth, 1991), pp. 322 and 348; Rousseau, *Letter to D'Alembert*, pp. 127–8.
35. Rousseau, *Inequality*, p. 195.
36. *Ibid.*, p. 162.
37. Rousseau, *Narcisse*, p. 966.
38. F.A. Pluquet, *Traité philosophique*, cited in Ellen Ross, 'Mandeville, Melon and Voltaire: The Origins of the Luxury Controversy in France', *Studies in Voltaire and the Eighteenth Century* 155 (1976), pp. 1897–1912, p. 1906; Jeremy Bentham, *Introduction to the Princi-*

ples of Morals and Legislation (1800), J.H. Burns and H.L.A. Hart, eds., (London, 1970), ch. 10, XIII.

39. Rousseau, *Inequality*, p. 130.
40. George Simmel, *The Philosophy of Money* [1900], trans. Tom Bottomore and David Frisby (London, 1990); Thorstein Veblen, *Theory of the Leisure Class* [1899] (New York, 1967).
41. Mandeville, *The Fable*, II, p. 452.
42. Friedrich von Hayek, 'Dr Bernard Mandeville', *Proceedings of the British Academy* 52 (1966), pp. 125–41.
43. Lisa Jardine, *Worldly Goods* (London, 1996); Simon Schama, *The Embarrassment of Riches: An Interpretation of Dutch Culture in the Golden Age* (London, 1988); Daniel Roche, *A History of Everyday Things. The Birth of Consumption in France, 1600–1800* (Cambridge, 2000); Neil McKendrick, John Brewer and J.H. Plumb, *The Birth of a Consumer Society. The Commercialization of Eighteenth-Century England* (London, 1982); John Brewer and Roy Porter eds., *Consumption and the World of Goods* (London, 1993); John Brewer, *The Pleasures of the Imagination* (New York, 1997).

3
Luxury in the Dutch Golden Age in Theory and Practice

Jan de Vries

Locating the origins of modern consumerism within the seemingly timeless pool of luxury consumption is becoming for modern historians something akin to the search for the Holy Grail. At least three bodies of literature now exist each proclaiming to have located the wellspring of modern materialism in as many eras stretching from the eighteenth century to the present day.[1] This essay proposes that modern consumer behaviour made a decisive advance earlier still, in the seventeenth-century Dutch Republic. In order to make this argument, I find it necessary to work backward from the eighteenth century to the seventeenth, and from British theory to Dutch practice. My thesis, put simply, is that theory followed practice with long and curious delays: that a modern form of consumer culture emerged before a means to describe and defend it existed.

The Old Luxury

Pre-commercial societies deployed a discourse of 'luxury' to discuss consumer behaviour, and luxury consumption was generally a prerogative of the privileged classes of rulers, warriors, churchmen and landowners. Their desire for luxury was by far the most important source of support for the craftsmen, artists and performers who produced society's non-quotidian goods and services. It was luxury production that supplied the elites with the markers of their status and authority, and that embodied the definitions of refinement of taste, elegance of design and power of expression. In short, luxury production was the material embodiment of high culture. Its production depended on the appropriation of surplus resources by elites whose fitness for rule was visibly justified by their patronage of the suppliers of luxurious goods and services. Luxury consumption in this context was profoundly conservative, in the sense that it reinforced the prevailing society and culture.

Luxury was an essential prop upholding the established order, yet at the same time luxury was universally understood to be fraught with moral danger. The seven deadly sins and all the vices of concern to us were implicated in it: gluttony, lust, avarice, malice, anger, greed, vanity, sloth, pride. Only a thin line separated the noble patron of the arts from the vain, prideful self-aggrandiser; the refined palate merged effortlessly with gluttony; the admiration of a fine garment easily turned to lust. The pursuit of luxury could bankrupt one's family, undermine one's health and submerge a healthy personality in debauchery.

Nor were the dangers of luxury purely personal. The individuals whose vanity, pride and gluttony drove them to an arbitrary and limitless pursuit of the sensations of pleasure formed an elite that could become so incapacitated in character (effeminate) and depleted in purse as to bring about the downfall of the state. The comforts and pleasures of a luxurious life left men unfit for military service and averse to taking the hard decisions needed to defend the state. The study of ancient history made these lessons accessible to every educated European. A 'Dance to the Music of Time' led society through a seemingly unavoidable cycle leading from poverty via hard work to riches, and from the luxury supplied by riches to decadence and back to poverty.

This rich complex of associations, between luxury and high culture and between luxury, personal decadence and societal ruin drew upon both the Christian and classical traditions. It took shape in the pre-capitalist societies of feudal Europe, when luxury was associated with – indeed, largely defined by – princely and episcopal courts. But even in later centuries, as a far more complex society, with large commercialised and urbanised sectors, emerged in western Europe, court cultures long exercised a dominant role in defining 'civilisation' via their cultivation of luxury.

Norbert Elias's *The Process of Civilization* explored this phenomenon, arguing that 'civilisation' (polite manners, elevated tastes, etc.) flowed via emulation from the princely courts to the aristocracy and gentry, and so to the bourgeoisie. Later, the concept of emulation was implanted into British historiography via the influential thesis of Harold Perkins (in *The Origin of Modern English Society*) that the aim of English trading people was to leave their bourgeois origins behind. There was, he argued, no authentic commercial culture in the eighteenth century. Emulation of the aristocracy, rather than an autonomous bourgeois materialism, must have been the prime mover of consumer behaviour.[2]

Earlier, in 1913, Werner Sombart, in his *Luxury and Capitalism*, had also denied bourgeois origins to the rise of consumer cultures. Indeed, he saw capitalism more generally, as emerging not from frugality, savings and investment (as Max Weber had had it), but from luxury spending – a spending incited by the example of the court and by the 'rule of women' in such environments, which led men into the reckless pursuit of sensuous pleasure: all those things which 'charm the eye, the ear, the nose, the palate, or the touch'.[3]

Earlier still, Montesquieu had also emphasised the strategic position of women, although he assessed their role quite positively. They functioned as the intermediaries between the luxury of the old nobility and the more frugal culture of the new commercial classes. Competition for their favours created the emulative link, triggering consumption among those endowed with a work ethic, and setting the stage for a temperate, moderate progress.

All these interpretations focus on the power and influence of an 'Old Luxury' of the pre-capitalist society living on to influence – perhaps even to shape – the more commercial society of the eighteenth and nineteenth centuries. This type of luxury lives on today, most obviously in the high-fashion apparel and accessories of designers whose authority and influence is secured by the patronage of elites – preferably non-bourgeois elites. It remains associated with ruinous expense and moral questions. It would not impress us so much if these dangerous associations were absent.

The New Luxury

There is another kind of luxury, let me call it the 'New Luxury', for which there was no established place in the pre-capitalist economy, but which is dominant today. In making this crude distinction I appropriate a rhetorical device deployed repeatedly by eighteenth-century writers seeking to identify that which required a re-examination of the old moral strictures concerning luxury consumption. Sir James Steuart, in 1767, distinguished Ancient Luxury (arbitrary and limitless) from Modern Luxury (systematical and beneficial); Montesquieu distinguished Persian Luxury (wasteful and degenerate) from what, ironically, I am forced to call Parisian Luxury (where the influence of women meets the work ethic).[4] Adam Smith had it, more generally, over the savage state of 'baubles' and lavish hospitality and the higher state of commercial society, and, among modern commentators, Colin Campbell distinguished the Traditional Consumer (whose utility derived from the immediate sensation of [corporal] pleasure) from the modern consumer – new to the eighteenth century – who substitutes illusory for real stimuli, and depends therefore on a never ending stream of new products to sustain the illusions.[5] If the Old Luxury satisfied a natural appetite, the new depended upon the cultivation of an addiction.

My New Luxury, rather than being defined by a royal court, is generated by urban society. Rather than presenting a coherent style and hegemonic cultural message, it consists of heterogeneous elements. The Old Luxury, striving for grandeur or exquisite refinement, could be emulated, if at all, only by burlesque or parody – obvious falsifications. The New Luxury, striving more for comfort and enjoyment, lends itself to multiplication and diffusion. Where the Old Luxury served primarily as a marker, a means of discriminating between people, times and places, the New Luxury served more to communicate cultural meaning, permitting reciprocal relations – a kind of sociability – among participants in consumption.[6]

The New Luxury was a product of the commercial and urban societies that Europe possessed by the sixteenth century, and which grew in size and influence in the following centuries. Its promise and its dangers differed from the Old Luxury. It was accessible to a much larger portion of society, which raised new dangers of social confusion and the erosion of established hierarchies as diffusion and emulation subverted the marker function of luxury consumption. Sumptuary laws regulating dress were promulgated more frequently, but could not restore the old patterns. Moreover, because the New Luxuries had a broader reach, their aggregate consumption supported larger groups of producers who came to form significant industries. In many cases, the luxury products were imported, and on such a scale that they visibly affected the balance of trade. This attracted the attention of the state and the development of Mercantilist doctrines, which linked luxury with imports, and imports with the shipment of gold and silver abroad, to pay for the luxuries. A drain of coin abroad to pay for needless luxury, the theory went, struck directly at the economic health of the state. Thus, in the seventeenth century, the old arguments about the moral and social dangers of luxury came to be joined by new, political ones.

The luxury debate

Luxury consumption had much to answer for, and yet the experience of the most advanced economies of the time spurred a succession of philosophers from the 1690s to the 1770s to raise up a fundamental challenge to the arguments against luxury that I have just rehearsed, with their ancient pedigrees and godly endorsements.

The 'great luxury debate' of the eighteenth century exercised some of the best minds of the time and led to the fundamental new insights in political economy of Adam Smith. At its heart was the new understanding, based on experience rather than theory, that consumer aspirations – the desire for luxury – formed a powerful wellspring of economic improvement. In fact, it led to what we would come to call economic development.

In 1691 Sir Dudley North wrote, in his pamphlet *Discourses upon trade*,

> The main spur to trade, or rather to industry and ingenuity, is the exorbitant appetites of men, which they will take pains to gratify, and so be disposed to work, when nothing else will incline them to it; for did men content themselves with bare necessities, we should have a poor world.[7]

Steuart, over 70 years later, claimed that:

> The moment a person begins to live by his industry, let his livelihood be ever so poor, he immediately forms little objects of ambition. [He] compares his situation with that of his fellows who are a degree above him ...[8]

Between these two observers are any number of others who noted the recent appearance of some combination of new desire and new incitements to desire.

David Hume, beginning with the axiom that 'everything in the world is purchased by labour', and asserting further that our passions are the only cause of labour – that is, motivation to action – concluded that a society of sufficient specialist producers causes all to apply themselves since, 'the superfluity which arises from their labour is not lost; but is exchanged ... for those commodities which men's luxury now makes them covet'.[9]

The appetites of men, the little objects of ambition, the coveting of luxuries: aren't these the seat of the vices – of lust and gluttony, pride and vanity? Could the unashamed indulgence in these vices lead to the social good of economic prosperity and growth? Bernard Mandeville, the Dutch emigrant to England, affirmed precisely this in his scandalous poem of 1705, *The Fable of the Bees*.[10] He describes there a human society disguised as a beehive, in which the self-seeking, vain, envious, lustful behaviour of individuals has the net effect of producing a productive, prosperous society.

> The Root of evil Avarice
> That damn'd ill-natured baneful Vice,
> Was slave to Prodigality,
> That Noble Sin; whilst Luxury
> Employed a million of the poor
> and odious Pride a million more.

He concludes:

> Thus every part was full of Vice,
> Yet the whole Mass a Paradise.

With this challenge to conventional wisdom, a sustained debate of consumer behaviour and its relationships to society and morality was well and truly launched. But the social and economic reality to which the debate referred – the development of a New Luxury – had taken shape earlier, and had developed most fully not in England, but across the North Sea in the Dutch Republic. Thus, rather than pursue in greater detail the English debate launched in the generation after the Glorious Revolution, this essay will turn backward, to inquire into the society that pioneered the New Luxury in the seventeenth century. Did it also develop a discourse on luxury that corresponded to the new consumer behaviour of this society? Or do we have here a situation in which practice outpaced theory, where what people said about Dutch consumer behaviour was outmoded and misleading, being based on antiquated social categories.

Dutch luxury in theory

Did the Dutch develop a body of theory about luxury consumption? To answer this question, we might turn first to the social thought of Calvin and of the Reformed Church, which laboured to put its stamp on Dutch society in the wake of the Revolt and Reformation of religion.

For most people today, access to Calvin's thought is mediated by Max Weber, or by a potted version of Weber's argument in the *Protestant Ethic*. So it may not hurt to go directly to the source. However, diligent readers of Calvin's *Institutes* and his several *Commentaries* will be disappointed in what they find. Rather, they will be disappointed in what they do not find, for Calvin's views on the material world did not really differ from those found more generally in sixteenth-century humanism. With Erasmus and Aristotle he recommended the *via media* – moderation in the use of God's gifts – rather than abstinence. For example, in his explication of the Lord's Prayer, Calvin writes about the request 'Give us this day our daily bread':

> By this petition we ask of God all things in general that our bodies have need to use under the elements of this world, not only for food and clothing but also for everything God foresees to be beneficial to us, that we may eat our bread in peace.

In his discourse on Christian freedom, Calvin gives evidence that the range of goods 'God foresees to be beneficial to us' might be quite broad: 'Let every man live in his station, whether slenderly, or moderately, or plentifully, so that all may remember God nourishes them to live, not to luxuriate.'

The message is clear, but without specific guidance about practical implementation. As our means increase, more of what God foresees to be beneficial is available to us. We are not forbidden to use and enjoy these things. But, Calvin goes on to warn:

> those who, not content with daily bread but panting after countless things with unbridled desire, or sated with their abundance, or carefree in their piled-up riches, nonetheless supplicated God with this prayer [give us this day our daily bread] are but mocking him.

'Unbridled desire' turns one's attention away from the source of one's material comforts. That is the line one cannot cross, and Calvin did not think most people were capable of detecting and honouring that line:

> There is almost no one whose resources permit him to be extravagant who does not delight in lavish and ostentatious banquets, bodily apparel, and domestic architecture; who does not outstrip his neighbor in all sorts of elegance . . .[11]

Calvin did not counsel otherworldliness, an escape from the temptations of prosperity. Nor did he demand what we would call 'Puritan abstemiousness'. Such a course was playing it safe – staying far away from the line. Calvin actually recommends something much more difficult to implement: station or income-specific moderation – i.e. keeping material goods in a proper perspective.[12]

Calvin's views on luxury were not really exceptional. It is more likely that the indirect impact of Calvinism, rather than its specific teachings on luxury, had the greater impact on consumer behaviour, and perhaps the best place to look is in Calvin's emphasis on what we might today call the examined life. The beginning of Christian knowledge was to know one's true self – that is, one's own sinfulness and one's dependence on God's grace. It is here where the Heidelberg Catechism – the introduction to the faith used by the Reformed Churches – began with its first questions and answers. The Christian was to possess authenticity, in the psychological sense, and this raised a vigorous objection to a 'culture of appearances' such as would be fostered by a fashion industry, or even to the theatre, where the declared intention was to pretend to be what you are not. The use of luxury goods to project a power, wealth or status one does not possess – to exploit the anonymity of urban society to deceive strangers through theatrics and the grand gesture, as an actor fools a (willing) audience – was anathema.

A second intellectual tradition capable of giving shape to a Dutch posture towards luxury is Republican theory. The most influential – indeed, almost the only – developed argument in the seventeenth century is found in the work of the De la Court brothers, Johan and Pieter.[13] Their argument, presented in the 1660s, is premised on the belief that all persons seek their own interest, motivated by the passion of self-love. In monarchies this pursuit is unbridled, uninspected and unresisted, leading inevitably to decadent luxury – the Old Luxury. In republics, they reasoned, the human passions are checked by the evident need for cooperation with others. Consequently, they are subject to self-examination and therefore they are more likely to be governed and directed towards virtuous, moderate consumption and prudent frugality.

Just how self-love is channelled in a republic is not developed in their work, but not long thereafter Jansenist thinkers developed more fully the concept of a non-vicious self-love channelled by commercial society to become a civilising agent. Jansenism, a Catholic theology based on the Augustinian tradition that also shaped Calvinism, emerged first in the Netherlands, North and South, and attained its greatest influence via the scholars associated with Port Royal, a female monastery near Paris. *Amour-propre*, or self-love, they defined as a desire for the recognition of others. Rather than being a 'pre-social' passion of natural man – base and uncontrollable – self-love in Port Royal philosophy was viewed as a passion that emerges (providentially, they would say) at a certain stage in societal development. Only in a commercial society could self-love be directed, via the civilising mechanisms of reputation and opinion, and by mirroring one's needs through the eyes of others.[14] Material goods had a new and honourable role in this new context (and Port Royal philosophy had become familiar to Mandeville before he moved to England in the 1690s).[15]

Two conclusions may be drawn from these observations. The first is that one should not be too quick to align Calvinist teachings with abstemiousness. Like all Christian theologies, it denounced hedonism, but unlike some it could accommodate readily to the material world of a commercial society so long as this did not undermine 'authenticity'. Second, republican theory and the Jansenist concept of self-love combined to lead to an early recognition that some societies could harness otherwise sinful and harmful human passions to the support of a healthy polity and dynamic economy. The Dutch Republic appeared to be such a society, and its hallmark was a self-examined, sociable consumerism.

The religious and the secular strands of this discussion had much in common, but it cannot be said that they mingled to activate a fruitful, public debate. One notable exception emerged in the 1730s as Dutch republican thought theorised a concept of the virtuous citizen that was entirely compatible with, indeed predicated on the existence of, a commercial society. Classical republicanism viewed commerce, luxury and economic specialisation (i.e. dependence on others) as destructive of virtue, and republican states as inherently unstable and short-lived. Even late in the eighteenth century Rousseau continued to uphold such views. In Holland, Justus van Effen, publisher of the *Hollandsche Spectator* (1731–35), argued that free and commercial societies were the necessary basis for civilised communication and sociability (what we might call an information-rich society). In monarchies, such as France, sociability led too easily to *politesse* ('a refined and elegant form of behaviour that was pleasing to others, a capacity for smooth and cultured conversation, a stylish presentation of self'). To Van Effen such a 'culture of appearances', with its hypocrisy, deceptions and dependence on the whims of fashion, was far removed from the true (republican) politeness based on reason, virtue and sociability.[16] In sum, *amour-propre* led to a theatricised public sphere in monarchical societies, such as France, but it could also lead to the establishment of a new foundation for republican virtue – reasonable and sociable – in commercial societies such as the Netherlands.

Still, the two strands of thought I have identified did not develop into a full-blown body of theory capable of defending and explaining the 'real existing' commercial society that was the Netherlands of the seventeenth century. This may be because of the conspicuous absence of a third strand: a determined opposition. Across the North Sea, in England, the re-examination of obsolete social prescriptions concerning luxury got underway later than in the Netherlands, after the Glorious Revolution. It led almost immediately to a vigorous debate because of the strength of the conservative opposition. Joyce Appleby speculates that this debate was triggered by a practical political struggle focused on the East India Company's importation of cotton textiles. The defenders of the Company – and of the consumption of imported luxuries more generally – had to attack the balance of trade doctrines. In doing so, according to Appleby, they stumbled upon a defence of domestic consumption as a positive and vital force.[17]

Nothing like this happened in the Netherlands. There, too, Indian calicoes were imported on a large scale. The VOC was only slightly behind the English company in the volume of its imports, and, since a large portion of the cotton goods landed at London were re-exported to Holland, their impact on Dutch society must have been great.[18] Dutch textile producers duly protested this new competition, to be sure, but the Republic did nothing to intervene in the importation of cotton goods. In the absence of a body of theory or state policy to argue against there was no need to develop an explicit theory in defence of innovative consumption. What became explicit in England long remained implicit in Holland.

Dutch luxury in practice

A vocabulary to describe adequately the consumer behaviour of a commercial society shaped by the 'New Luxury' took time to develop. Consequently, the contemporary commentaries on the material culture of seventeenth-century Holland – whether written or visual in form – require a careful interrogation on the part of the modern reader and viewer.

The written records are primarily the observations of foreign visitors, and these are nearly unanimous in their verdict. But, in interpreting these documents we must be mindful of the heavy ideological baggage that attached to this subject, and the propagandistic purposes for which the 'Dutch Example' was paraded before foreign readers.

Visual images appear to offer a rich alternative source of information about this society. Indeed, Dutch paintings easily seduce us into believing that they offer framed views of society, where we employ a historian's gaze, poking about the paintings for evidence as an amateur sociologist today might by walking down a Dutch street and glancing into the uncurtained front windows of the houses. This, too, is a temptation to be resisted, for the new material world revealed in many of these paintings is typically enveloped in moral and iconographic conventions steeped in the vocabulary of the Old Luxury.[19]

The writings of contemporary visitors were unanimous in celebrating what Constantijn Huygens called 'Holland's glorious simplicity'. The English ambassador in the years 1668–70, Sir William Temple, wrote *Observations upon the United Provinces*, a book that has long been accepted as an authoritative account of Golden Age society, if for no other reason than the fact that so many later writers corroborated, or simply appropriated, his views.[20] Temple was concerned to explain the amazing economic power and prosperity of the Republic to his envious English readers, and he placed great emphasis on

> The simplicity and modesty of their magistrates in their way of living, which is so general, that I never knew one among them exceed the common frugal popular air.

He described every social class in turn, and except for the small corps of noblemen, whom he regarded as poor imitations (of French fashion) rather than good originals, he concluded with the observation:

> There are some customs and dispositions that seem to run generally through all these degrees of men among them; as great frugality and order in their expense. Their common riches lye in every man's having more then he spends; or to say it more properly, in every man's spending less than he has coming in, be that what it will.

Of course, a rich person could save a good deal and still have plenty left to indulge in extravagance, but Temple thought that such luxury expenditure in the Republic

> ... is laid out in the fabrick, adornment, or furniture of their houses; things not so transitory, or so prejudicial to Health and to Business as the constant excesses and luxury of tables; nor perhaps altogether so vain as the extravagant expenses of clothes and attendance.

Here is an observation – insightful, in my opinion, of the character of the New Luxury relative to the Old – to which we will return.

But, for the most part, Temple stressed frugality to the point of self-denial.

> By this we find out the foundation of the Riches of Holland . . . For never any Country traded so much and consumed so little. They buy infinitely, but this to sell again . . .
>
> They are the great masters of the Indian spices, and of the Persian silks; but wear plain woollens and feed upon their own fish and roots. Nay, they sell the finest of their own cloath to France, and buy coarse out of England for their own wear. They send abroad the best of their butter . . . and buy the cheapest out of Ireland . . . for their own use.
>
> In short, they furnish infinite Luxury, which they never practice, and traffique in Pleasures which they never taste.[21]

Now, no one who has spent an afternoon viewing Dutch genre paintings or still-lifes can lend full credence to Temple's observations. Did they really 'traffique in Pleasures which they never taste', and then, for added measure, hang on their walls paintings of those very pleasures – just to remind themselves of what they were missing? (See Plates 1a and b.)

Temple's words alert us to a special feature of Dutch society – it was more than ordinarily frugal and sober in the face of more than ordinary access to all the world's luxuries and pleasures. As Dutch trade expanded, her ports filled with the precious cargoes brought from the Levant, Russia, Africa, Asia and the New World. Amsterdam, the foremost port, could be described by 1648 as: 'The warehouse of the world, the seat of opulence, the rendezvous of riches, and the darling of the gods.'[22]

This unique accessibility to the goods of the world was paired with a growth in the productivity of domestic agriculture and industry to raise the purchasing power of broad segments of society as well as make many merchants, investors, property owners, and industrialists very, very rich. Here, for the first time – on such a scale and on so enduring a basis – was a society in which the potential to purchase luxuries extended well beyond a small, traditional elite. A substantial tranche of society was now in a position to exercise choice – to enter the market and spend money to fashion a consumer culture.

Interpreting Dutch consumer behaviour

Choice gives freedom, and freedom exposes one to moral dilemmas. Now these dilemmas were faced by large numbers who earlier, and in other societies still, had had their consumer choices constrained by the heavy hand of scarcity and custom, and whose extravagances were channelled narrowly into well-choreographed displays of excessive eating and drinking.

Simon Schama, in his celebrated book *The Embarrassment of Riches*, draws with relish on the venerable arguments about the moral pitfalls that surround luxury consumption – which he (wrongly, in my view) ascribes to Calvinist preaching – to evoke a society caught on the horns of a dilemma: its own singular virtues, producing prosperity, lead inexorably to the vices of luxury. He relies heavily on paintings and other visual images in making his evocation, and these, I believe, relied in turn on the ancient themes of luxury's dangers that derived from pre-capitalist, pre-market societies – the Old Luxury.

An ally in his project was the view of many historians of earlier generations that the Republic's decline after the 1670s was closely associated with, if not caused by, the onset of a cultural over-ripeness which befell a decadent genera-tion accustomed to luxury and, therefore, without the character and determina-tion of their forefathers. On their watch, French fashion overwhelms Calvinist simplicity, classicism pollutes the fresh spring of Dutch artistic genius and the burgher families succumb to the blandishments of aristocratic life-styles. This argument, owing far more to the contemplation of the fall of Rome than to the reality of seventeenth-century Dutch society, was once uncritically embraced by historians eager for simple explanations of a difficult subject. (See Plates 2a and b.)

Rather than succumbing to the seductive vision of republican society in the grip of the Old Luxury, we should set this venerable, but derivative, imagery aside and attempt to see the new consumer culture being constructed by the innu-merable choices of an enlarged population newly endowed with discretionary income. In discussing their choices, the old discourse remained influential for the simple reason that it was the only vocabulary available, but the reality of their behaviour brought into being a distinctive material culture in which the luxuries were directed towards the home more than the body, and adorned the interior – of both home and body – more than the exterior. They tended to achieve comfort more than refinement.[23]

Mandeville, that notorious champion of prodigality as the road to prosperity, rejected the conventional wisdom about the sources of Dutch prosperity, as he also rejected the arguments about Dutch republicanism harnessing and redirect-ing the passions.[24] 'The Dutch may ascribe their present grandeur to the virtue and frugality of their ancestors as they please,' he wrote in the early eighteenth century. In fact, he retorted with characteristic hyperbole: 'In pictures and marble they are profuse, in their buildings and gardens they are extravagant to folly.' He conceded that there were no great palaces and courts, but '. . . in all of Europe you shall find no private buildings so sumptuously magnificent as a great many of the merchants' and other gentlemen's houses in Amsterdam and in some of the great cities of that small province.'

The papal nuncio to Cologne, Pallavicino, made a more penetrating observa-tion during his visit of 1676. After visiting Amsterdam, where the system of radial canals around the old medieval city was nearing completion, he noted that 'only a nation that does not squander its wealth on clothes or servants could have succeeded in doing all this with so little fuss.' 'All this', of course, was the erection of many thousands of comfortable bourgeois homes, restrained by a 30–40-foot exterior frontage from blatantly advertising the occupants' wealth, but endowed by a 190-foot depth with ample opportunity to achieve a new form of private domestic comfort.

Exotic luxuries from the four corners of the world found their way into these homes. Indeed, in 1697 Peter the Great travelled to Holland, among other reasons, to acquire a fabulous collection of preciosities.[25] The bourgeoisie also possessed costly products of high craftsmanship such as tapestries and furniture. These often came from the southern Netherlands, where craft traditions of long standing were sustained by the patronage of local and Spanish courts.

What the cities of Holland themselves offered were New Luxuries. These products required real craft skills, to be sure, but the objective was not to fabricate something unique. New Luxuries were products capable of multiplication, or capable of being offered in a gradated range of qualities and prices. The canal houses, just as more humble abodes, were decorated with Delft tiles of varying qualities, just as their kitchens and tables made use of the orientally inspired Delft faïence.[26] Similarly, the canal houses were filled with the work of cabinetmakers' wardrobes and linen chests – and much else. Here again, the great pieces were the highest expression of a furniture tradition that came up from below, for even farmers had – albeit more modest – versions of these same items. (See Plate 3.)

Then we come to the paintings. Dutch art, as is well known, was reconstructed after the Reformation from an Old Luxury to a New Luxury as elite patronage gave way to a market economy. By developing both product innovations and process innovations (new themes in the paintings and new techniques of painting), Dutch artists opened new markets, allowing by mid-century some 700–800 masters to be active simultaneously, producing over the course of the century many millions of paintings ranging in price from hundreds of guilders to the *'dozijnwerk'* – work by the dozen – that fetched a guilder or two at the fair. Indeed, if the possession of paintings in Delft can be generalised to all of Holland – the province – then something like three million paintings must have hung on the walls of Holland's houses by the 1660s.[27]

One could go on to discuss clock- and instrument-makers – by 1700 a solid majority of farmers had pendulum clocks hanging on their walls; book publishing – the Republic had 781 printers and sellers in operation by the 1660s, a far higher density than elsewhere in Europe; popular luxuries like tobacco pipes, and decorative and utilitarian silver. In contrast to the exotic extra-European objects, or the most refined material possessions from Brabant or further afield in Europe, the New Luxuries were usually produced in Dutch cities. Some were imitations and adaptations of foreign luxuries, such as Delftware, responding to Chinese porcelain; some were cheaper versions of European luxuries, such as Delft and Gouda's tapestry works, or Amsterdam and Utrecht's silk industry.

Craft production everywhere in Europe depended on specific skills that could be transferred successfully only by the migration of artisans. Thus, the Republic's new crafts and industries inevitably find their origin in diffusion from abroad. Still, in their new home, they developed a particular form, shaped by the nature of Dutch demand – urban, *burgerlijk*, broad-based – and by the prevailing cultural imperatives. These imperatives could be stamped with the label Calvinist, but it might be better to invoke the concept of 'Confessionalisation'.[28] Calvinists, Lutherans, Catholics – every Christian denomination – were concerned in the era of the Dutch Golden Age to consolidate their projects of religious revitalisation, to penetrate to the broad base of society with programmes of education, institutionalisation and greater social control. The cultural dimension of this multi-centred movement left a deep mark on the design of everyday articles, on accessible luxuries, on interior decoration and on clothing. This movement was European rather than specifically Dutch, but it resonated with Holland's social and economic structures more fully and more creatively than elsewhere, which caused the output of Dutch ceramics, paintings, prints, maps, books, furniture, glass, and the dyeing and printing of textiles to be seen as particularly well suited to the temper and purpose of the Confessional era. The integrating rather than differentiating impact of these New Luxuries – their socialising rather than status differentiating function – is revealed in the broader study of material culture. By the late seventeenth century the striking feature of Dutch material culture is its uniformity. The basic forms of expressing status and achieving comfort were remarkably similar between city and country, and between rich and poor. It was the cost and specific quality rather than the types of objects and their general form, that differed.[29]

From the perspective of the outsider, Dutch society seemed to eschew luxury altogether, for the Old Luxury was thin on the ground and hidden from view. But a New Luxury, one we might call modern, or proto-modern, was in fact taking shape – but could not be easily 'read' by the cultural outsider. Nor had Dutch society itself developed a vocabulary or theory to express it adequately.

Its modernity was, however, in some sense premature. By the third quarter of the seventeenth century a new cultural movement spread across Europe, emanating from royal courts, associated with aristocracy, and featuring classical and rococo forms which idealised gallantry and refinement. It affected the Republic too. Its outward manifestations in the Netherlands are often held up as evidence of decadence (the inevitable consequence of a prosperity-fuelled addiction to luxury), but that can be argued only if the Netherlands is studied in complete isolation from the Europe of which it was part. It remains true, however, that the Republic was poorly endowed – whether in social structure, craft skills, mentality or life-style – to offer much that was original to this new cultural project. A European movement that had interacted with Dutch society to create something original and powerfully appealing gave way, after 1670, to another European movement that interacted weakly and derivatively with that same society.

Luxury consumption was not the undoing of the Dutch at the end of the seventeenth century, as is still sometimes claimed by traditional cultural historians. It wasn't even a more than ordinary source of anxiety or embarrassment. Instead, a consumer culture had been established, prematurely perhaps, so that its eighteenth-century development would seem derivative in comparison with its seventeenth-century novelty.

But the Dutch did not fashion its bits and pieces of religious and republican thought into a new discourse to describe and theorise the new reality. Perhaps this was because the new commercial society was too self-evident, and the opponents with whom battle had to be waged were too weak: no political elite to rail against imported luxuries; no Court against which to wrest the power to define fashion; no episcopal hierarchy with the power to add bite to its bark.

It was Adam Smith's achievement, according to Donald Winch, to open up the prospect of a stable way of living in a world in which the wants of the imagination were infinite.[30] He showed that there only appeared to be a conflict between morality and wealth, and that moral choice could sidestep the hitherto inevitable cycles of prosperity and decay. But, in the Dutch Republic they may already have been living this life, harnessing self-love in practice as philosophers later would describe in theory.

Notes

1. The claims for an eighteenth-century consumer revolution are most vigorously made in Neil McKendrick, John Brewer and J.H. Plumb, *The Birth of a Consumer Society: The Commercialization of Eighteenth-Century England* (Bloomington, 1982); Carole Shammas, *The Pre-Industrial Consumer in England and America* (Oxford, 1990). A late-nineteenth century rise of consumerism is charted in John Benson, *The Rise of Consumer Society in Britain, 1880–1980* (New York, 1994); Richard W. Fox and Jackson Lears, eds, *The Culture of Consumption: Critical Essays in American History, 1880–1980* (New York, 1983); Rosalind Williams, *Dream Worlds: Mass Consumption in Late Nineteenth Century France* (Berkeley and Los Angeles, 1982). The emergence of a post-World War II consumer society is analysed in many works. See Gary Cross, *Time and Money. The Making of Consumer Culture* (London, 1993); Christopher Lasch, *The Culture of Narcissism* (New York, 1979); Roland Marchand, *Advertising the American Dream. Making Way for Modernity, 1920–1940* (Berkeley and Los Angeles, 1985).
2. Norbert Elias, *The Process of Civilization* (London, 1981; original German edition, 1939); Harold Perkins, *The Origins of Modern English Society* (London, 1968).
3. Werner Sombart, *Luxury and Capitalism* (Ann Arbor, 1967; original German edition, 1913), pp. 2–5, 60.
4. Sir James Steuart, *Inquiry into the Principles of Political Œconomy*, 2 vols (London, 1767), ch. 22, p. 325; On Montesquieu, see Tjitske Akkerman, *Women's Vices, Public Benefits. Women and Commerce in the French Enlightenment* (Amsterdam, 1992), p. 16.
5. Adam Smith, *Inquiry into the Nature and Causes of the Wealth of Nations* (Chicago, 1976; reprint of Cannan Edition of 1904; originally published, 1776), see esp. Book III, ch. IV, pp. 432–45; Colin Campbell, *The Romantic Ethic and the Spirit of Modern Consumerism* (Oxford, 1987).
6. These are the two cultural purposes of consumption proposed by Mary Douglas and Baron Isherwood, *The World of Goods: Towards an Anthropology of Consumption* (New York, 1979).
7. Sir Dudley North, *Discourses upon Trade* (London, 1691), p. 27.
8. Steuart, *Inquiry*, ch. 21, p. 315.
9. David Hume, 'On Commerce', *Essays: Moral, Political and Literary*, T.H. Green and T.H. Grose, eds., vol. 1 (New York, 1898), p. xx.
10. Bernard Mandeville, *The Fable of the Bees: or, Private Vices, Publick Benefits* (Oxford, 1924, republication of the 1732 edition). Mandeville's poem was first published, as *The Grumbling Hive*, in 1705. In 1714 he republished it, now furnished with explanatory 'remarks'. Successively more elaborate editions appeared in 1723, 1728, and 1732. He died in 1733.
11. John Calvin, *Institutes of the Christian Religion* (Atlanta, 1973; 1536 edition), pp. 109–10, 246.

12. Constantijn Huygens offers a nice illustration of the moral choices before which the Calvinist stands in his satirical poem about the excesses of court life, *The Costly Folly*. Written while Huygens was on a diplomatic mission to the court of King James in England, he reveals his own temptation to use the necessity of dressing for high state office as an excuse to indulge in dandyism. The elaborate and costly dress appropriate to his station was not the problem; rather, it was the unleashing of 'unbridled desire' that the occasion seemed to encourage. Cited in Anne McCants, 'Meeting Needs and Suppressing Desires: Consumer Choice Models and Historical Data', *Journal of Interdisciplinary History* 26 (1995), p. 196.

13. Pieter de la Court, *True Interest and Political Maxims of the Republic of Holland* (London, 1702) [*Het Interest van Holland, ofte Grond van Hollands welvaren* (Amsterdam, 1662)]; Johan and Pieter de la Court, *Politieke Discoursen*, 2 vols (Amsterdam, 1662); Anonymous, but attributed to the de la Courts, *Zinryken fabulen* (Amsterdam, 1685), translated as *Fables Moral and Political, With Large Explications*, 2 vols (London, 1703).

14. On Port Royal philosophy, see Akkerman, *Women's Vices, Public Benefits*; see also William Doyle, *Jansenism* (London, 2000).

15. Mandeville left the Netherlands soon after earning his doctorate at Leiden in 1691. He and his family had been implicated in the 'Costerman Riot' of 1690, an anti-tax riot in Rotterdam. The Mandevilles appear to have authored and distributed a satirical poem directed at Rotterdam's *schout*, or bailiff, whose unpopularity had been intensified by his insistence on applying the death penalty to Cornelis Costerman, a member of the town militia, who stood accused of fatally stabbing a tax collector who had detained a group in possession of a cask of wine on which no excise had been paid. Mandeville's career, even his liberty, were under a cloud, and he decided to leave the country, eventually settling in England. For more on this interesting pre-history of the author of the *Fable of the Bees*, see Rudolf Dekker, ' "Private Vices, Public Virtues" Revisited: The Dutch Background of Bernard Mandeville', *History of European Ideas* 14 (1992), pp. 481–98.

16. Wyger R.E. Velema, 'Ancient and Modern Virtue Compared: De Beaufort and Van Effen on Republican Citizenship', *Eighteenth-Century Studies* 30 (1997), pp. 437–48.

17. Joyce Appleby, 'Ideology and Theory: The Tension between Political and Economic Liberalism in Seventeenth-Century England', *American Historical Review* 81 (1976), pp. 499–515. 'A consumption-oriented model of economic growth threatened major interests of the ruling class that had coalesced in Restoration England. Dangerous leveling tendencies lurked behind the idea of personal improvement through imitative buying' (p. 511).

18. Imports of Indian Cotton Goods (in thousands of pieces per year)

	Dutch East India Co.	*English East India Co.*
1661–70	88	199
1671–80	137	578
1681–90	348	707
1691–1700	278	296

From 1701 to 1740, English cotton goods re-exported to the Netherlands rose from 36 to 51 per cent of the amount brought to England.

19. The possibilities and pitfalls of using visual images as historical sources is discussed in: Jan de Vries, 'Introduction', Jan de Vries and David Freedberg, eds, *Art in History; History in Art. Studies in Seventeenth-Century Dutch Culture* (Santa Monica: Getty Center for the History of Art and the Humanities, 1991), pp. 1–6.

20. Sir William Temple, *Observations upon the United Provinces of the Netherlands*, Sir George Clark, ed. (Oxford, 1972; orig. pub. London, 1673).

21. *Ibid.*, pp. 70, 86, 87, 119.

22. In the view of Bruce Lenman, 'the Dutch had entered an era of consumerism . . . a good generation before the English.' He supports this view by invoking the astonishment of

Samuel Pepys upon being shown round the hold of a captured Dutch East Indiaman in 1665. 'It affected him like a trip to Aladdin's cave,' Lenman relates, for his guides '. . . did show me the greatest wealth lie in confusion that a man can see in the world – pepper scattered through every chink you trod upon it; and in cloves and nutmeg I walked above the knees – whole rooms full – and silk in bales, and boxes of copper-plate, one of which I saw opened.' And then there were the tales of the bags of diamonds and rubies that the English captors had 'taken from the Dutch Vice Admirals neck'. Bruce P. Lenman, 'The English and Dutch East India Companies and the Birth of Consumerism in the Augustan World', *Eighteenth Century Life* 14 (1990), p. 51. Robert Lathan and William Matthews, eds, *The Diary of Samuel Pepys* (London: 1972) 6: 300.

23. For a stimulating discussion of the origins of domesticity, see Witold Rybczynski, *Home: A Short History of an Idea* (New York, 1986), p. 77.

24. Mandeville, *Fable*, the quotations that follow are from Remark Q, pp. 185–9.

25. See: Renée Kistemaker, Natalja Kopaneva and Annemiek Overbeek, eds, *Peter de Grote en Holland. Culturele en wetenschappelijke betrekkingen tussen Rusland en Nederland ten tijde van tsaar Peter de Grote* (Bussum, 1996).

26. In view of the great success of Dutch ceramics, it is instructive to contemplate their failure in developing a porcelain industry. No porcelain industry arose comparable to those of Meissen, Vienna, Copenhagen, Sèvres or Worcester. The technical skills were not missing; rather, the missing element was the court associations essential to design and market what was, in essence, a new 'Old Luxury'.

27. Ad van der Woude, 'The Volume and Value of Paintings in Holland at the Time of the Dutch Republic', in De Vries and Freedberg, eds, *Art in History, History in Art*, pp. 285–330.

28. On this concept, see Heinz Schilling, 'Confessionalization in the Empire', in Heinz Schilling, ed., *Religion, Political Culture, and the Emergence of Early Modern Society* (Leiden, 1992), pp. 205–46; Philip S. Gorski, 'The Protestant Ethic Revisited: Disciplinary Revolution and State Formation in Holland and Prussia', *American Journal of Sociology* 99 (1993), pp. 265–316.

29. Hans van Koolbergen, 'De materiële cultuur van Weesp en Weesperkarspel', in Anton Schuurman, et al., eds, *Aards geluk. De Nederlanders en hun spullen* (Amsterdam, 1997), p. 152; Jan de Vries, 'Peasant demand patterns and economic development: Friesland, 1550–1700', in William N. Parker and Eric L. Jones, eds, *European Peasants and their Markets* (Princeton, 1975), pp. 234–6.

30. Donald Winch, *Riches and Poverty. An Intellectual History of Political Economy in Britain, 1750–1834* (Cambridge, 1996), p. 89.

Plates

1a. Jan Jansz. Van de Velde, 'Still-life with a Pipe-lighter', 1653.
1b. Jan Daridsz. De Heem, 'Still-life of a Banquet Side-table', 1646.
2a. Jacob Backer, 'State Dinner', 1633/34.
2b. Adriaen Backer, 'State Dinner', 1683.
3. Pieter de Hooch, 'Two Women at a Linen Chest with a Child', 1663.

4
Aestheticising the Critique of Luxury: Smollett's *Humphry Clinker*

Michael McKeon

The Expedition of Humphry Clinker (1771) (Plate 4) is the last – and many would say the best – of the novels of Tobias Smollett. As with all great works of litera-ture, its critics have diverged on its interpretation in significant ways; and yet they have tended to agree on one point whose implications for how to read the novel are fundamental. This is the conviction that Smollett's central character, Matthew Bramble, speaks for its author and therefore articulates *Humphry Clinker's* social and ethical norms. As John Sekora puts it, 'the acceptable views expressed in the novel radiate from Bramble'.[1] Sekora's reading is particularly relevant to the con-cerns of this volume because it comes in the context of an authoritative account of western attitudes towards luxury, in which it assigns *Humphry Clinker* a place of special importance: 'By literary standards *Humphry Clinker* is, among other things, the most successful conservative attack upon luxury in any genre during the 1750s and 1760s . . .'[2] In this essay I hope to show the vulnerability of this view, most of all if we read Smollett's novel 'by literary standards'. By this I mean several things. First, I aim to attend to the way Smollett's attitude towards luxury is clarified if we compare it to his use of other controversial categories of the day – enthusiasm, sensibility, pastoral, romance – which have a notably literary reso-nance. Second, and more important, I will suggest how the volatility of these cat-egories infiltrates the formal dimension of *Humphry Clinker*. Formality – the dense network of techniques by which novels, poems and plays implicitly establish their meaning by situating themselves in relation to existing genres, styles and tradi-tions of writing – is the hallmark of literary discourse, not the means by which literary works transcend socio-ethical issues, but the means by which they take a socio-ethical position. To read *Humphry Clinker* within the history of literary forms is to read it most persuasively as a historical artifact.

That *Humphry Clinker* contains a powerful critique of luxury is, of course, not to be doubted. And early on in the narrative, we have good reason to anticipate the sort of novel that Matt Bramble's obsessive preoccupations suggest: namely, an affirmation of the backward-looking values of the paternalistic country gen-tleman, who scours the face of modern Britain lamenting the world we have lost and railing against its replacement. Matt's letters home evince a familial and 'feudal' care for the tenants of Brambleton-hall, evoking an organic community hierarchically stratified by relations of personal dependence. Equally charitable to his tenants and to the poor, Matt shows a notable leniency towards a 'notorious poacher', supposing 'he thought he had some right (especially in my absence) to partake of what nature seems to have intended for common use'.[3] Brambletonhall, thus reflecting the customary view of property as a common use-right, is apparently a 'natural economy' in the sense not only of proper stratification, but also of appropriate land use. And it therefore provides the normative basis for Matt's implacable critique of what luxury has wrought in the rest of Britain, particularly its cities.

In the spa town of Bath, the burgeoning industries of leisure and tourism have aggravated an urban development that is entirely unregulated by principles of necessity or utility. And '[a]ll these absurdities,' says Matt, 'arise from the general tide of luxury, which hath overspread the nation, and swept away all, even the very dregs of the people. Every upstart of fortune . . . presents himself at Bath . . . men of low birth, and no breeding, have found themselves suddenly translated into a state of affluence, unknown to former ages . . . [k]nowing no other criterion of greatness, but the ostentation of wealth, they discharge their affluence without taste or conduct, through every channel of the most absurd extravagance . . .'.[4] 'This portentous frenzy is become so contagious, that the very rabble and refuse of mankind are infected.' And those who have fled Bath 'will be followed by the flood of luxury and extravagance, which will drive them from place to place to the very Land's End . . .'.[5] London is even worse.

> What I left open fields, producing hay and corn, I now find covered with streets, and squares, and palaces, and churches. . . . The tide of luxury has swept all the inhabitants from the open country – The poorest 'squire, as well as the richest peer, must have his house in town, and make a figure with an extraordinary number of domestics. . . . There are many causes that contribute to the daily increase of this enormous mass; but they may be all resolved into the grand sources of luxury and corruption. . . .[6]

Social emulation and the allure of upward mobility have engendered a crisis of conspicuous consumption in which everyone apes their betters. Simplicity gives way to complexity, ordered stability to fluidity and mixture, the natural rule of sufficiency and need to artificial and limitless indulgence of appetite and want. According to Matt, 'the capital is become an overgrown monster; which, like a dropsical head, will in time leave the body and extremities without nourishment and support'.[7] In other words, the Body Politic has become (to adopt one of Matt's favourite figures of speech) 'diseased', 'infected', 'consumed' by a 'contagion' for which only the fast-disappearing natural economy of the countryside, apparently, affords a cure. Or, to adopt another favourite figure – that of tumultuous liquidity – the stable and settled English way of life has been overwhelmed by a 'flood', a 'tide', a 'torrent' of luxury that has 'swept away' the moderation and tradition of the past – even, the relatively recent past of Matt's own youth.

Matt Bramble's lamentations, grounded in the familiarity of pastoral opposition (country versus city, nature versus art, past versus present), thus possess the plausibility of cultural norms. What are the factors that check our impulse to take Matt's lamentations as the norm of Smollett's novel? Most obviously, *Humphry Clinker* is something of an innovation in epistolary form in that it assigns significant narrative roles to five letter-writers, who are sharply distinguished from each other in sex, social status, cultural attitudes, even epistolary style. Read against Samuel Richardson's already canonical precedent, where the letters of the protagonist overshadow all others in both number and authority, Smollett's epistolary novel is an experiment in the multiplicity and relativity of perspective. Matt's letters to Dr Lewis are intermixed with the letters of other family members, whose responses to shared experiences reflect so broad a range of values as to suggest that, in *Humphry Clinker*, the truth of things lies in a composite and mixed view of reality.

Only a little less obviously, Matt's normative status is belied by the ostentatious idiosyncrasy of his judgement. By this I mean not simply his eccentricity, but the fact that the Bramble family travels have been undertaken expressly as a cure for his bodily and mental disorders. Matt is the emergent type of the Man of Feeling, whose ever-present but elusive bodily malady seems to consist most of all in hypochondria – in the fact that his bodily malady cannot be separated from his mental condition. As Matt tells Dr Lewis, he has 'had an hospital these fourteen years within myself, and studied my own case with the most painful attention...'.[8] The problem is that this programme in self-study presumes that separation of mind and body, of subject and object, which Matt's illness precludes: 'I find my spirits and my health affect each other reciprocally...'.[9] In fact, Matt's body provides the perfect analogue for the diseased Body Politic against which he rails.

In accounting for this condition of mixture and reciprocity, Smollett's characters have recourse to the emergent language of sensibility. Thus Matt's nephew Jery muses that his uncle's 'peevishness arises partly from bodily pain, and partly from a natural excess of mental sensibility; for, I suppose, the mind as well as the body, is in some cases endued with a morbid excess of sensation'.[10] Sensibility, if 'excessive', is also 'natural' in its excess, and it plays a role in mixing not only mind and body but also good and ill humour, tenderness and toughness. In Jery's analysis, Matt 'affects misanthropy, in order to conceal the sensibility of a heart, which is tender, even to a degree of weakness...Indeed, I never knew a hypochondriac so apt to be infected with good-humour. He is the most risible misanthrope I ever met with.'[11]

Jery uses the figure of 'infection' here to emphasise a condition of mixture within Matt's body just as Matt uses it in reference to the greater Body Politic; the difference is that the pejorative association of Matt's usage is absent. No doubt this owes to differences in point of view. But what are we to make of the fact that Matt's far-flung travels, prescribed as a treatment for his illness, recapitulate the mixture characteristic of his illness at the macro-level? True, this may be a case of homeopathic medicine, of treating like with like. But at the end of the novel

Matt's reflections on his travels seem to validate them in a more absolute fashion: 'We should sometimes increase the motion of the machine, to *unclog the wheels of life*; and now and then take a plunge amidst the waves of excess, in order to case-harden the constitution. I have even found a change of company as necessary as a change of air, to promote a vigorous circulation of the spirits, which is the essence and criterion of good health.'[12] Here Matt himself positively reconceives the figures of speech that have been so forcefully negative in application to British society and culture at large. Travel helps revalue the condition that had seemed a disease – the condition of mixture, liquidity and excess – as in fact a cure for stagnation.

Mixture is also central to the Bramble family's travelling entourage. Although we might expect this family to reflect the 'feudal' hierarchy and propriety of Brambleton-hall, the Brambles are in fact (as Jery calls them) 'a family of originals' recently and haphazardly conjoined by the death of Matt's sister.[13] Matt and Tabby are not husband and wife but unmarried brother and sister; Jery and Liddy are their orphaned nephew and niece who, having been educated apart, have scarcely met each other as the novel opens; and the party is completed by Tabby's maid, Winifred. As Matt puts it, 'I an't married to Tabby, thank Heaven! nor did I beget the other two: let them choose another guardian: for my part, I an't in a condition to take care of myself; much less to superintend the conduct of giddy-headed boys and girls.'[14] And despite Matt's candour here, throughout the novel there is a strong sense in which these highly extended family members variously act out a scenario of strict familial ties and iron-clad obligations as though to mask the tenuous instability of their family commitments.

This is evident, for example, in the running sub-plot of Mr Wilson, which punctuates the entire narrative from beginning to end, and which, in eliciting diametrically opposed responses from the various family members, also economically demonstrates their utter disparity and mixture. As Liddy is surreptitiously pursued by Mr Wilson, who appears to be a common player, Jery plays, with a passion bordering on the bodily, the antiquated patriarchal role of possessive elder brother enraged at this threat to family honour: 'I must own, my blood boils with indignation when I think of that fellow's presumption . . .'[15] Matt, the putative paterfamilias, is by contrast quite moderate in his response. If we sense in Jery's overemphasis on patriarchal family relations a masquerade that compensates for their insubstantiality, what light does this shed on Matt's patriarchal care for Brambleton-hall?

The tenuousness of Bramble family ties is perhaps most obvious in the fact that we are well into the novel before we even meet its eponymous hero, and are close to the end of it before we discover that he is the missing familial link, Matt's long-lost son. And yet from our first sight of him, Humphry Clinker's identity is self-consciously shrouded in the antiquated trappings of family romance. When the Bramble family first meets him he's 'a shabby country fellow' and a 'beggarly rascal' who none the less has 'a skin as fair as alabaster', a hint of higher origins quickly adumbrated by Matt's charitable donation, by which Humphry 'metamorphosed himself' into Matt's footman 'by relieving from pawn part of his own clothes, with the money he had received from Mr. Bramble'.[16] We may well wonder at the way Matt's charity thus appears to contribute to the social mobility he despises. And Matt himself soon bristles when he finds Humphry holding forth to a crowd in the role of untutored Methodist preacher – a crowd that includes, in Jery's words, 'all the females of our family . . .'.[17] 'What you imagine to be the new light of grace,' says Matt to Humphry,

> 'I take to be a deceitful vapour, glimmering through a crack in your upper story – . . . Heark-ye, Clinker, you are either an hypocritical knave, or a wrong-headed enthusiast; and in either case unfit for my service – if you are really seduced by the reveries of a disturbed imagination, . . . some charitable person might provide you with a dark room and clean straw in Bedlam, where it would not be in your power to infect others with your fanaticism . . .'[18]

Matt's language of 'infection' and 'enthusiast' 'imagination' invites us to see Humphry through his eyes, as a germ of that social disease – the disease of mobility and mixture – which Matt despairs of in the Body Politic. But we cannot help being reminded, as well, of Matt's own diseased body and the mobile spirits unleashed by his sensibility.

By now it is clear that in *Humphry Clinker* Smollett has constructed a dynamic, multi-levelled analogy between the nation, the family and the individual body in which each level serves as a cautionary index to the state of the others. Thus the destabilising excess of upward mobility at the macro-level is replayed by the anomaly of Humphry's elevation into the Bramble family, as well as by the enthusiastic vapour glimmering in his own 'upper story'. However, at any single level of the analogy, the multiplicity of potentially comparable elements challenges us to sustain, or to question, the order of the structure itself. If Humphry's religious enthusiasm is a sign of vapourish excess, what about Matt's sensibility; or the 'family-pride' of his nephew, whom Matt refers to in this state as 'the hot-headed boy'?[19] Although Jery seems to think 'all the females of our family' are susceptible to Humphry's Methodism, sex is complicated here by social status. Liddy temperately remarks that 'as yet I am not sensible of these inward movements, those operations of grace, which are the signs of a regenerated spirit; [however] [s]ome of our family have had very uncommon accessions, particularly my aunt and Mrs. Jenkins . . .'.[20] Later on, Liddy's scepticism about Win has increased: '[A]ll this seems to be downright hypocrisy and deceit – Perhaps, indeed, the poor girl imposes on herself – she is generally in a flutter, and is much more subject to vapours . . .'[21]

In the gendered usage of contemporaries, 'vapours' are to women as the psychosomatic illness of 'hypochondria' is to men. And the vapours that seem truly characteristic of women in particular are those not of religious enthusiasm but of romantic love; as Matt suggests (and as we've already seen in Liddy), 'the passion of love has in some measure abated the fervour of devotion . . . Love, it seems, is resolved to assert his dominion over all the females of our family . . .'[22] Yet Liddy's love reminds us of nothing so much as Matt's hypochondria: according to him 'her colour fades, her appetite fails, and her spirits flag. – She is become moping and melancholy, and is often found in tears.'[23] However, the symptom of spiritual excess that is shared by all the Brambles – the one family trait that truly conjoins this family of originals – is sensibility itself. *Humphry Clinker* is strewn with what its characters refer to generically as 'affecting scenes', moving tableaux of human distress and transfiguration that provide family members a chance to display, with the paradoxical engagement of spectatorial detachment, their sympathetic and charitable responses.[24] The instability of excessive affect – the aesthetic response to life as though it were art and to art as though it were life – is thus paradoxically the stable foundation on which family likeness is grounded, the answer to the question of Bramble family identity.

In time Matt is reconciled to Humphry's Methodism, not because it loses its aura of enthusiastic excess, but because Matt learns to valorise that excess by associating it with the sensible passions he values in a grateful servant. 'If there was any thing like affectation or hypocrisy in this excess of religion, I would not keep him in my service; but so far as I can observe, the fellow's character is downright simplicity, warmed with a kind of enthusiasm, which renders him very susceptible of gratitude and attachment to his benefactors.'[25] Not yet aware of their biological connection, Matt and Humphry are permanently reconciled through a sequence of affecting scenes in which their reciprocal service and care are manifested through figures of liquidity that extend, and positively transform, an image whose negativity is established very early on in the 'tide of luxury' and the filthy waters at Bath. No reader can forget Matt's mounting hysteria at the infectious corruption lurking in these supposedly curative fluids. But if early on liquidity is a disease masquerading as a cure, Matt discovers with Humphry that the process can also be reversed. At first viewing, Matt had mistaken Humphry's preaching for the theatrics of a quack mountebank.[26] Having failed to cure his master through spiritual salvation, at Scarborough, Humphry hears Matt's cry at the coldness of the water and 'took it for granted I was drowning, and rushed into the sea, clothes and all, overturned the guide in his hurry to save his master. . . . [H]e seized me by one ear, and dragged me bellowing with pain upon the dry beach . . . I was so exasperated . . . that, in the first transport, I struck him down . . .'[27]

Three months later, farce recurs as near-tragedy. While attempting to ford a river swollen by rain water, the family carriage is overturned by the 'impetuosity' of the 'flood' and Jery witnesses the 'melancholy spectacle' of Humphry dredging up his apparently lifeless master: 'The faithful Clinker, taking him up in his arms, as if he had been an infant of six months, carried him ashore, howling most piteously all the way, and I followed him in a transport of grief and consternation –' Humphry lets Matt's blood, and 'in a little time the blood began to flow in a continued stream' and Matt is truly saved. The several family members express their fear and relief according to their own peculiar sensibilities. 'As for Clinker, his brain seemed to be affected. – He laughed, and wept, and danced about in . . . a distracted manner . . .'[28]

So Matt, literally saved and reborn by his own son, is chastened and purged by exhibiting, in little, the impetuous liquidity that almost takes his life. As if to recapitulate this contradictory drama on the macro-levels of family and nation, Matt immediately settles on Humphry an annuity that, by rendering him financially independent, provides the social 'circulation' and upward mobility needed to fulfil Humphry's status as a dangerous germ of social disease. Whereupon Smollett, as if to set this act of charity in a more proper light, immediately fulfils his earlier promise of family romance by revealing, with all the self-conscious trappings of romance discovery, that Humphry is really Matt's natural son, born while Matt was still using his mother's name so as to inherit her estate. Or as Matt puts it, Humphry is 'a crab of my own planting in the days of hot blood and unrestrained libertinism', an admission that confirms our sense that Matt and the things he purports to despise are ineluctably mixed.[29] Tabby now affects to see in Humphry's face the signs that he 'hath got our blood in his veins'; however, we know that it is not the genealogical blood of patrilineage, but the 'hot blood' of sensibility, that marks Humphry as a Bramble family member.

Not satisfied with his act of narrative charity, Smollett quickly engineers the other romance discovery we have been waiting for, which elevates Mr Wilson from the lowly status of strolling player to that of a gentleman. Or as Lydia puts it, 'the slighted Mr Wilson is metamorphosed into George Dennison, only son and heir of a gentleman', who also happens to be Matt's old college friend.[30] Win's semi-literate version of this is a characteristically ludicrous transformation of Ovidian metamorphosis itself: 'The player man that came after miss Liddy, and frightened me with a beard at Bristol Well, is now matthewmurphy'd into a fine young gentleman . . .'[31] As is often true, however, Win's malapropism is a disease that bears a cure, a grotesque linguistic mixture that bespeaks the association we ourselves are likely to make between the two discoveries, along with the truth that, in the modern world, proper names are as exchangeable as financial estates.

In the romance tradition, the convention of discovered parentage customarily reconciles outer birth with inner worth, confirming the nobility of character we have already identified in the foundling or bastard by revealing an elevated patriline. Humphry's inner worth is never in doubt; but in Smollett's version we feel not so much the seamless dovetailing characteristic of the traditional family romance as the ragged mixture of authentic upward mobility. Raised in the workhouse and trained as a country blacksmith and ostler, Humphry may be elevated to the status of first-born gentry at the end of the novel, but his actual existence will be as a husbandman on his father's farm, and his demeanour remains the one in which he was socialised by the real world. We might even see this as Smollett's version of realism. Under modern conditions of social fluidity and exchange, it is not improbable that Matt should discover his footman to be his son, and his family to be a micro-version of the burgeoning British nation that has been Matt's spectacle for the past seven months: that is, a heterogeneous collection of individuals.

Smollett parodies the antiquated tropes of 'romance' so as to preserve while suspending them, an experiment whose results are suggested by the way he has his characters use the emergent tropes of the 'romantic'. In the highlands of Scotland, Jery feels 'an enthusiastic pleasure when I survey the brown heath that Ossian was wont to tread', and he finds the banks of Loch Lomond 'agreeably romantic beyond all conception'.[32] Matt agrees: 'Every thing here is romantic beyond imagination.'[33] Romance becomes romantic through the secularisation of spirit, when romance claims to supernatural description can be sublimated into affective response. The sublimity of the Scottish landscape is not a condition of its being but an enthusiastic feeling of its viewer, oxymoronically imagined as that which is ineffably 'beyond' imagination. When both letter-writers note that a 'Mr. Smollett' has his house at Loch Lomond, they remind us that the liminal experience of romantic sublimity – of being poised between subject and object, imagination and reality – is also what we feel in the presence of Smollett's reflexive play with romance endings, suspended between the story and its telling, between what is half-perceived and half-created.

This is also, of course, the mixed state of mind of the aesthetic, which calls for neither belief nor disbelief, but the willing suspension of disbelief. Smollett positively transvalues romance and enthusiasm by aestheticising their critique as error so that it becomes instead an acknowledgement of their pleasing serviceability as fiction. Something similar may be said of his transvaluation of luxury. In *Humphry Clinker*, Smollett holds before us the traditionalistic lamentation of fluidity and excess even as it is replaced by the celebration of Humphry's expedition, his expeditious journey of upward mobility. Matt's ferocious critique of luxury in the Body Politic is never explicitly contradicted – any more than is his dejection at his own bodily disorder. Instead, Smollett suggests that in both cases, the supposedly normative condition of order and stasis is less the cure than the symptom of disease. Midway through his travels, Matt remarks that 'I now begin to feel the good effects of exercise – I eat like a farmer, sleep from mid-night till eight in the morning without interruption, and enjoy a constant tide of spirits, equally distant from inanition and excess . . .'.[34] By the same token, even as Matt continues to condemn the tide of mobility and circulation that engulfs the Body Politic, he shows us that his welfare depends on it. This can be seen if we attend to the way the Bramble family's journey both exemplifies and challenges the traditional tropes of pastoral opposition – of country and city, nature and artifice, need and want.

While still in Bath, Matt writes, 'I have, for the benefit of my health, projected an expedition to the North . . .'.[35] Centuries-long patterns of cultivation in the British Isles had long since made standard the coding of 'south' and 'north' as 'developed' and 'underdeveloped', respectively. But because the Brambles' leisurely and incremental travel northward is experienced and rationalised as a continuous chain of pastoral movements from 'south' to 'north', each link in the chain – for example, crossing the Tweed from England to Scotland – is plausible in itself, yet radically relativised by its placement in a more comprehensive series. Thus the lowlands are to the highlands as England is to Scotland; and epistolary relativity only complicates things further, since where Jery sees industry and prosperity in the farms of Northumberland, Matt finds 'the English side of that river neither so well cultivated nor so populous as the other'.[36] The contradictory Obadiah Lismahago raises the effect to the level of colonialist 'macro-pastoral' when he sets against the barbaric cannibalism of the American Indians their incredulity at the barbarism of a people who 'pretended to create God himself, to swallow, digest, revive, and multiply him *ad infinitum*, by the help of a little flour and water . . .'.[37] The result is that what we are urged at each moment to see as mutually exclusive values and behaviour are repeatedly shown to overlap, mix or lapse into indistinguishability. But this is at least in part because, as Matt's eye for circumstantial detail makes obvious, the modern circulation of commodities renders city and country inseparable, two sides of the same coin.

As we have just seen – and as Matt's cherished natural economy at Brambleton-hall would make us expect – comparisons and contrasts tend to concern matters of agrarian improvement, productivity and consumption. In London Matt is diverted by the contradictory phenomenon of the 'public gardens' at Ranelagh and Vauxhall, and perplexed by the vast urban market of 'Covent-garden', with its 'fresh eggs imported from France and Scotland'; although he also admits it 'affords some good fruit'. Daily life in London mysteriously sustains pastoral antithesis by effacing or inverting it: '[B]y five o'clock I start out of bed, in consequence of the dreadful alarm made by the country carts, and noisy rustics bellowing green pease under my window.'[38] Matt's critique of luxury, undiminished by such scenes, coexists with the accumulation of evidence that Matt himself is quite dependent upon its tidal ebb and flow. In Bath he excoriates the 'mob of impudent plebeians', whose circulation will increase 'till the streams that swell this irresistible torrent of folly and extravagance, shall either be exhausted, or turned into other channels . . .' But in the very next paragraph he remarks to Dr Lewis that '[b]y your advice, I sent to London a few days ago for half a pound of Gengzeng; though I doubt much, whether that which comes from America is equally efficacious with what is brought from the East Indies . . .'.[39] Like his bastard son Humphry Clinker, Matt's ginseng is the sign of his secret role in the modern circulation of things. Is the exotic medicinal herb a 'need' or a 'want'? Already in the habit of capitalising on the international market, Matt is slowly revealed to be fully, and knowingly, submerged in the cultural liquidity from which he stridently attempts to distance himself.

The revelation culminates in the highlands of Scotland, and then in the romance discoveries that bring the novel to its close. North of Inverary, Matt writes home appreciatively about the traditional husbandry of black cattle, and with deep feeling about what he calls the *'patriarchal'* influence the chiefs continue to exert over their clan members. But he also speculates that '[t]he most effectual method I know to weaken, and at length destroy this influence, is to employ the commonalty in such a manner as to give them a taste of property and independence . . .' In Matt's thinking this might be done most effectively by establishing a cod fishery. 'It cannot be expected,' he muses, 'that the gentlemen of this country should execute commercial schemes to render their vassals independent . . . but a company of merchants might . . . Our people have a strange itch to colonize America, when the uncultivated parts of our own island might be settled to greater advantage.'[40]

Matt's modernising ideology of improvement surfaces most decidedly in the final episodes, when his old friend Charles Dennison recounts having used the most advanced methods 'for making experiments in agriculture' to improve his own estate, and Matt himself then helps Baynard toward achieving the same end.[41] We may be surprised to hear Matt apply to these improvements the same idealising pastoralism that he has used to describe the natural economy of Brambleton-hall. Indeed, the process is depicted less as a modernisation than as a restoration: '[T]he pleasure-ground will be restored to its original use of corn-field and pasture,' and Matt orders Baynard's gardener to 'turn the rivulet into its old channel, to refresh the fainting Naiads . . .'[42] Thus Matt employs pastoral idyll to accommodate and familiarise agrarian reality. And as he makes epistolary preparations for the family's return to Brambleton-hall and we find that no modernising improvements are required there, we are confronted by a final discovery – that the traditionality of Brambleton-hall and its paterfamilias has all along been a self-conscious pastoral trope, a late allusion to the country-house poem.[43] The social norm is really social theatre, a performance of pastoral convention that is no less a pleasing fiction than the romance convention of discovered parentage.

A passionate critic of luxury and extravagance, Matt ends by showing his involvement in, and tacit approval of, precisely those socioeconomic developments on which the rise of luxury has depended. On the face of it this sounds, at worst, like sheer hypocrisy, at best like a radical conversion. In fact, it feels more like the disclosure of character traits that have always been there, just below the surface of performative archaism. Something similar can be felt in the romance discoveries that provide formal closure for Smollett's novel, whose old-fashioned incredibility is refashioned as the aesthetic enjoyment of a self-conscious trope made realistic by the fluidity of modern social intercourse. In the end, reading *Humphry Clinker* is a lesson in learning to discern, beneath the broad façade of traditionality, the innovative modernisations which that façade helps facilitate and humanise.

Notes

1. John Sekora, *Luxury: The Concept in Western Thought, Eden to Smollett* (Baltimore, 1977), p. 240.
2. Ibid.
3. Tobias Smollett, *The Expedition of Humphry Clinker*, ed. Lewis M. Knapp and Paul-Gabriel Boucé (New York, 1984), pp. 14–15; see p. 5.
4. Ibid., pp. 36–7.
5. Ibid., p. 57.
6. Ibid., pp. 86–7.
7. Ibid., p. 87.
8. Ibid., p. 23.
9. Ibid., p. 154.
10. Ibid., p. 17.
11. Ibid., pp. 28 and 49.
12. Ibid., p. 339.
13. Ibid., p. 8.
14. Ibid., p. 12.
15. Ibid., p. 224.
16. Ibid., p. 83.

17. Ibid., p. 137.
18. Ibid., p. 138.
19. Ibid., pp. 144 and 145.
20. Ibid., pp. 135–6.
21. Ibid., p. 260.
22. Ibid., p. 208.
23. Ibid., p. 235.
24. Compare ibid., pp. 20–3, 185–6, 263–4.
25. Ibid., p. 154.
26. Ibid., pp. 99–100.
27. Ibid., p. 184.
28. Ibid., pp. 313–14.
29. Ibid., p. 319.
30. Ibid., p. 336.
31. Ibid., p. 337.
32. Ibid., pp. 240 and 238.
33. Ibid., p. 248.
34. Ibid., p. 219.
35. Ibid., p. 66.
36. Ibid., pp. 214 and 207.
37. Ibid., p. 193, p. 196.
38. Ibid., pp. 88–9 and 120–2.
39. Ibid., pp. 37–8.
40. Ibid., pp. 253–6.
41. Ibid., pp. 320–8 and 343–4.
42. Ibid., p. 343.
43. Ibid., pp. 350–1.

Plate

4. 'Matthew Bramble Recognises Some Ancient Friends', from Tobias Smollett, *The Expedition of Humphry Clinker*, 1793.

Part II
Delectable Goods

Luxury was material goods and their acquisition as much as it was discourse. Dena Goodman, in Chapter 5, 'Furnishing Discourses', analyses the characteristics of particular luxury goods such as furniture as a material manifestation of the discourse of luxury. Goodman sets out a debate on luxury from the mid-eighteenth century in France conveyed in terms of Old versus New Luxury. Like the categories set out by de Vries for the Dutch Republic, these counterpoised wealth, status and power with commerce, utility, taste and comfort. Modern commerce displaced barbaric luxury. The French writing desk made for women epitomised the modern luxury consumer good. It conveyed the transformation of luxury into a fashion economy. Furniture-makers produced writing desks in a whole range of types and qualities. They developed new techniques in veneers, varnishes and lacquers, marquetry and spring mechanisms, and made use of exotic woods of the Old and New Worlds. And it shifted the status categories of old luxury to the gender categories of new luxury.

Chapter 6, 'The Circulation of Luxury Goods in Eighteenth-Century Paris' shows how the luxury goods and novelties which flooded Paris over the course of the eighteenth century were circulated and exchanged in a sophisticated business economy of intermediaries. Laurence Fontaine argues that the goods themselves circulated as an alternative currency, goods easily turned to cash through pedlars, pawnbrokers or *revendeuses à la toilette* in order to settle gambling debts or pay for other expenses. Pedlars conducted an international luxury goods trade through an extensive range of shopkeepers. These goods also circulated at all levels of society through a wide range of dealers, secondhand clothing sellers and those who dealt in fabrics, lace and jewellery in visiting their clients at home. Fontaine provides us with a taxonomy of the metropolitan trade in luxury goods, and the distribution and credit networks that diffused from an economy of luxury to one of fashion.

Luxury was not, however, simply a discourse and material world of the wealthy and the middling orders, but was also one of the poor. John Styles, in Chapter 7, 'Custom or Consumption? Plebeian Fashion in Eighteenth-Century England', argues that clothing conveyed respectability, status and fashion. Even amongst the poor, new and relatively luxurious clothing was bought at particular stages of the family life cycle. Young men and women invested their first adult earnings in suits or dresses in the best materials they could afford to reflect recent fashion trends. Styles incorporates the labouring poor into the broader consumer culture, but sets this expenditure within a customary economy where best clothing was worn at occasions shaped by the festive calendar.

5
Furnishing Discourses: Readings of a Writing Desk in Eighteenth-Century France

Dena Goodman

When you stop in front of a little eighteenth-century writing desk in one of the furniture galleries of a museum such as the Louvre, the Victoria and Albert or the Metropolitan Museum of Art today, what do you see? (See Plates 5 and 6.) What world does that piece of furniture disclose to you? I imagine that for most people, the exquisite marquetry, gilt bronze mounts and feminine curves of such a piece call up the opulent, aristocratic world of court and salon in the waning years of the French monarchy – a world in which ridiculously and unfairly wealthy women and men performed their inherited status and privilege in sumptuously decorated surroundings at the expense of the great mass of the people. The feelings called up in this moment of encounter probably contain a mixture of romantic nostalgia for the beauty, elegance and innocent pleasures of such a life and moral condemnation for its corruption, decadence and the guilty oppression of those whose poverty and hard work sustained it.

This moralised vision of a desk and the world it evokes is indebted to both the French Revolutionaries who justified their extra-legal actions as the necessary and moral destruction of such a world, and to the Romantics and Reactionaries who, taking the Revolutionaries at their word, mourned its loss. It has been renewed culturally many times over in the intervening years. In the novels of Balzac, for example, the greed and ugliness of the post-revolutionary bourgeoisie always evoked the beauty and lost innocence of the old regime. More recently, films such as *Ridicule* (1996) have moralised on that beauty by showing the pleasures to be saturated by cynicism; and art exhibitions such as 'The Splendors of Versailles' (1998), which brought furniture, paintings and other artifacts from the royal palace to Jackson, Mississippi, have made sure to moralise even as they glamorised it.[1]

Mary Sheriff suggests that it was the nineteenth-century German cultural historian Jacob Burckhardt 'who generalized the term *rococo* and used it to describe the dissolution he saw in the late phases of all periods and styles. Rococo, in other words, was synonymous with degenerate.'[2] Perhaps this is where Karl Toth, writing in Germany after World War I, got the idea of the rococo as 'the quintessence of French Femininity' and the 'most feminine of Epochs'. For Toth, 'French culture is therefore artificiality, [the] cultivation of luxury.'[3] French culture had a 'secure

71

and unique place in mankind's cultural household', as the luxury of civilisation itself, according to Toth, but it had to be stripped of all power and simply 'carefully cherished'. What he called 'German labour-culture' would regenerate civilisation by assuming the power wrested from feminine France in the name of world peace.[4]

The metaphorical identification of eighteenth-century furniture with a moralised and gendered historical and cultural construction of the old regime is not always so inflammatory, but it remains prevalent. For example, it underlies Leora Auslander's argument in *Taste and Power: Furnishing Modern France*. 'Objects, especially domestic objects, played a distinctive role in the representation of power under absolutism,' she writes; 'the crown displayed its strength both through its possessions and through its control of those who made, sold, and bought them. An absolute monarchy would in principle have only one style in domestic objects, and the state would determine it.'[5] Although Auslander goes on to glorify furniture-makers by asserting that 'actual creativity and innovation could only come from the artisans themselves', the thrust of her argument is that furniture reflects the social and political order, and the old regime was an order shaped by an absolute monarchy concerned only with the display of power.[6] Thus, the historical meaning of an eighteenth-century writing desk lies in the way it reflects royal taste and displays the power of monarchy through the emulation of royal style by the owner of the desk.[7]

Such a historical interpretation of old regime furniture is problematic on two counts. First, its mimetic reading is based on a kind of pathetic fallacy whereby it transfers (although does not ascribe) to inanimate objects a human moral judgement. Second, the simple picture on which it is based of a royal and aristocratic old regime concerned exclusively with the maintenance and display of power can be seen as itself moralistically driven in the light of more than a decade of revisionist scholarship on the old regime and the French Revolution that has revealed a vibrant public sphere (in which the monarchy was one player among many); a breakdown of the traditional social order; and a dynamic, commercialised economy well before 1789.[8] If we want to turn the writing desk into a mirror of the old regime, we could see reflected in it the dynamic processes of commerce and consumption that were tearing apart the traditional world that Auslander evokes. And indeed, in this chapter I will try to remove our writing desk from the romanticised pre-modern world of noble artisans, powerful kings and courtly aristocrats in order to situate it within the framework of the modern world of consumer culture that began to take shape in Paris in the eighteenth century.

This essay is thus presented as a contribution to the understanding of the dynamic of French commerce and consumption in the eighteenth century, the culture and society which they shaped, and the way in which we read furniture historically. But rather than making the writing desk stand for this alternative vision of eighteenth-century French society, I propose that we look for its meaning in the discourses and debates in which members of that society sought to make sense of a changing world. In particular, I propose to dissociate the rococo writing desk from the descriptive marker 'luxury', typically associated with the old regime, and to relocate it in relation to competing discourses of luxury and commerce in the matrix of which attitudes towards material goods were and continue to be articulated. In this way I hope to excavate the desk from the layers of discursive meaning in which it is embedded, while at the same time contributing to a better understanding of a culture constituted by those layers of discourse constructed upon a small but significant piece of furniture.

*

The French writers who engaged in the eighteenth-century debate on luxury marshalled moral, political and economic discourse in an effort, in Daniel Roche's words, 'to understand the power of things'.[9] Roche has laid out the debate well, dividing it into several stages. In traditional society, he argues, there was no serious debate about luxury because luxury supported rather than challenged the social order in its limitation to the few, and because, in the greater scheme of things, the Christian notion of charity was meant to compensate for the inequality luxury defined.[10] The first modern critique of luxury emerged in response to the great political changes wrought by Louis XIV in the last decade of the seventeenth century. An aristocracy humbled by the redistribution of wealth and power to 'new men' at their expense learned to deploy the language of the 'common good' to legitimise a new public role for themselves as representatives of the nation and champions of social order. They attacked luxury (in the wrong hands) as disruptive of that social order and called for moral leadership to arrest its growth. They invoked both Christianity and the ancients in defence of their position.

By 1730, Roche shows, a defence of luxury had been articulated that attacked 'ancient frugality' as a myth and argued that luxury created work and thus engendered rather than squandered wealth. Whereas the attack on luxury was propelled primarily by political change, the defence of luxury was a validation of an expanding economy. By 1740, when the first French translation of Bernard Mandeville's *Fable of the Bees* appeared, the ground was already laid for its reception. Mandeville's radical refusal to moralise economic behaviour, as well as his location of that behaviour in human nature, stimulated a debate on economic matters in salon, academy and print that continued through to 1789. Voltaire, champion of the moderns, weighed in in the 1730s; various encyclopedists and physiocrats dominated the discussion in the 1750s, within and without the pages of the *Encyclopédie*; while at the same time, Rousseau staked out his position against the Enlightenment as an attack on luxury.

By the 1760s, the Rousseauian reaction seemed to have won the day. Sarah Maza has argued recently that in the second half of the eighteenth century, 'luxury' was not so much the key term in a debate as it was the marker for a certain anxiety – 'a convenient code for all of society's perceived problems'. Whereas Voltaire and other early eighteenth-century French anglophiles had defended luxury as a stimulus to the economy, industry and invention, by the 1760s, luxury had lost its defenders. Maza suggests that as France entered a period of social crisis leading up to the French Revolution, luxury came to be associated again with social disorder, with the England that had humiliated France in the Seven Years' War – indeed, with change of all sorts. It was invoked out of concern for, among other things, 'aristocratic profligacy, the effects of commerce and consumerism on society, and the condition of the countryside'.[11] In other words, the aristocratic attack on luxury launched at the end of the seventeenth century had been turned back on the aristocracy by Rousseauian moralists who now attacked luxury throughout society and society through luxury. No longer able to represent themselves as the victims of court-supported luxury, the aristocracy were now the object of their own critique. And modernising commerce, far from reordering society by following Mandevillian human nature, simply destabilised it further. There was no longer an economic justification for, or a proper social location of, luxury; there was no place for it to hide.

Maza's interpretation explains the demise of the defence of luxury in the 1760s, but it does not explain what happened to the arguments in favour of luxury that had been central to the defence of modernity, civilisation and Enlightenment itself right through the 1750s. For the champions of modernity, civilisation and Enlightenment gained momentum just as the chorus of attacks on luxury swelled. The 1760s and 1770s were, by all accounts, the high point of the high Enlightenment. My point here is not to dispute that for many commentators 'luxury' served as a convenient portmanteau in which to toss all the things that they associated with the social anxiety they felt in the face of significant social change. Rather, I would like to suggest that it was possible to use 'luxury' in this way only once a new discourse had come into use to contain the rivers of goods flowing into Paris from around the globe and the even greater number of novelties being produced in the workshops of Parisian artisans and provincial manufacturers for a broadening public of consumers.

In the first half of the eighteenth century, 'luxury' and 'necessity' – categories which had developed in a world of few objects where there was a large gap between the many who made do with the simple objects of necessity and the very few who asserted their power and status by displaying the extravagant objects of luxury – became increasingly inadequate. As the number of objects in circulation increased along with their diffusion through society, the words 'luxury' and 'necessity' lost both meaning and power. At the same time, 'luxury' was hopelessly burdened with a set of moral and political connotations that could not be shaken off.

We can see in the attempts of various men of letters before the 1760s to defend luxury their struggle to comprehend this new world of goods within an old discourse before abandoning it altogether. Voltaire's approach, for example, was simply to declare a new definition of luxury by shifting its associations: 'We have finally arrived at the point where luxury resides only in taste and in comfort,' he wrote in the *Siècle de Louis XIV* (1751). 'We have left vain and exterior pomp to the nations who still know only how to display themselves in public and where the art of living is unknown.'[12] But even Voltaire could not legislate in matters of definition, and his attempt to change the meaning of 'luxury' by associating it with a new culture of taste and comfort only contributed to the proliferation of meanings of it.

'Luxury' had come to mean so much and so little that Saint-Lambert, who tackled the subject for the *Encyclopédie*, was forced to admit that he could not 'claim to assemble here all the good and the bad that has been said of *luxury*'. He would limit himself to the main arguments for and against it, and 'to showing that history contradicts all of them'.[13] In the article 'Encyclopédie', Diderot chose *luxe* as his example of a word in desperate need of definition. 'We say, without any of us being mistaken, of an infinity of objects of all sorts, *that they are luxuries*,' he wrote, 'but what is this *luxury* that we attribute so infallibly to so many objects? Here is the question which will not be answered with any precision except as a result of a discussion which those who demonstrate the most accuracy in the application of the word *luxury* have not had, are not perhaps even in a position to have.'[14]

Diderot's use of *luxe* as an example of a word in need of definition suggests the impasse which the debate on luxury had reached in the 1750s. Arguing that there were different kinds of luxury – an old-style luxury which functioned as a display of power, and a new kind of luxury which stimulated commerce while demonstrating and orchestrating politeness and civility – only confused the issues. What *philosophes* such as Diderot and Saint-Lambert needed was a new discourse in which it would no longer be necessary to devise or defend such distinctions as that between *luxe d'ostentation* which entailed 'unproductive expense' and *luxe de commodité*, which contributed to 'creative labour'; or more simply, between *luxe vicieux* and *luxe utile*.[15] Since attitudes towards the word *luxury* were clearly going to be harder to change than those towards the goods and practices it was being asked to describe, the new world of goods that was making Paris a mecca for shoppers would be situated within a new discourse of commerce in which fashion, taste, utility and comfort, rather than wealth, status or power, were the key determinants of meaning and value. Luxury would remain as a moral category with which to condemn those consumers whose practice of consumption was seen as morally wrong, socially useless and politically harmful.

*

'It is by means of the Merchant that gold circulates, that the agreeable is joined to the useful, that the world is enriched, and that France makes known in all countries its fashions, its nice things, its industry,' declared Louis-Antoine Caraccioli, in *Paris, le modèle des nations étrangeres, ou l'Europe française* (1777). 'Work then, ingenious Lyonnais, elegant Parisians,' he continued; 'everything you do will be exalted as a masterpiece, so much confidence is there in your talents. ... The most minor bagatelle that leaves your hands carries the imprint of delicacy and taste.'[16] Was Caraccioli advocating luxury? 'I will not discuss here the advantages and disadvantages of luxury; that is not my point,' he declared.

I will leave it to some to say that it is the cause of all our misfortunes; to others, that it is the soul and spring of Monarchies; and while they are arguing, I'll go to sleep, rousing myself only to observe that Europe without French elegance remained gothic, and would still be buried under its gold, and that in contracting the happy habit of spending wisely and with taste, it has emerged from its lethargy, and the agreeable is mixed with the useful to render life sweet and comfortable.[17]

Rather than debate the virtue and value of luxury, men of letters such as Caraccioli effectively changed the subject by focusing on questions of productivity, utility, taste, comfort, industry, improvement and innovation. By the 1770s, the abbé Raynal was no longer contrasting bad luxury and good luxury, but luxury and commerce. In the historical introduction to his *Histoire des deux Indes*, a best-selling compendium on European colonialism and global trade, Raynal praised the commercial Arabs of the Middle Ages, who used their wealth to cultivate 'the arts and letters, and were the only conquering nation to have advanced the reason and industry of men'. By contrast, 'barbaric ostentation' characterised the French nobility before the commercial revolution. 'The expense of their table was excessive; and this savage luxury, of which there are still too many vestiges, afforded no encouragement to any of the useful arts,' Raynal declared.[18] Modernising commerce had eventually overthrown the regime of medieval luxury – but it was also responsible for the modern barbarism of slavery. When Raynal contemplated how to bring those whom commerce had enslaved into civilisation after securing their freedom, he recommended not only that they be given European 'laws and manners', but also 'our superfluities. We must give them a country, give them interests to study, productions to cultivate, and articles of consumption agreeable to their respective tastes,' he urged.[19] For Raynal as for Voltaire, the point was not to condemn all that went beyond bare necessity as sinful luxury, but to contrast the unproductive and selfish display of wealth with the productive and socially beneficial use of it. By associating it with commerce, the superfluous could now be embraced as a civilising force in modern society without carrying the taint of barbarous luxury.

If the debate on luxury became one-sided in the second half of the eighteenth century, it was because a new language had been developed in which to appreciate and promote the production and consumption of a rapidly expanding range of goods that could no longer be comprehended within the moral terms of the traditional opposition between luxury and necessity. Even as luxury was condemned, superfluities, comfort, circulation, industry and novelty were loudly celebrated as indications of a healthy commercial economy, polite society and modern civilisation. The universal condemnation of luxury was as much a part of the celebration of commercial society as it was a symptom of a rising anxiety about social change and dynamism. The Rousseauian ancients and Christian moralists who condemned modernity were joined by enlightened moderns who now contrasted a barbaric luxury with modern commerce and the production, consumption and circulation of goods that were central to modern society, civilisation and progress.

The criterion of taste and the concept of fashion were crucial to the development of the discourse of commerce. They allowed men of letters to condemn ostentation as bad taste, while allowing merchants to offer customers of widely diverging means a broad range of goods which all fell within the canons of approved taste and fashion. As Jennifer Jones has shown in the case of clothing, Parisian merchants, with the help of the press, promoted commerce by abandoning luxury and adopting taste as the fundamental criterion of fashion.[20] They made fashion a function of knowledge rather than wealth, and gave power to those who carried the authority of taste.[21]

As Carolyn Sargentson has shown, the Parisian *marchand-merciers* were key to the transformation of the luxury trade into a fashion economy. The *merciers* had been incorporated as a guild in the early fifteenth century to handle the increasing number of goods that were either imported or fell between the provenance of the different guilds that produced finished goods; by the eighteenth century they were taste-setters who specialised in the exotic and in the realm of *'enjolivement'*.[22] This could mean having three Chinese porcelain cups set into gilded bronze holders, mounting them on a Japanese lacquer tray and selling them as an *écritoire* or inkstand. Or it could mean knocking down Japanese lacquer chests into panels and sending them out to *ébénistes* to be veneered onto furniture frames of French design. In these ways, the *merciers* contributed to the stylistic blending of East and West they dubbed *chinoiserie* and created a market for goods defined by fashion and taste.[23]

Taste allowed one to discriminate, but it was also deliberately inclusive. As Jennifer Jones points out, 'the insistence that taste, rather than luxurious fabrics and jewels which only the wealthy could buy, was the most important quality for dressing fashionably served, on the one hand, to distinguish true taste from mere wealth, but it also worked to broaden the potential market for Parisian fashion.'[24] If, for example, a dress could not be praised simply for being made of expensive fabric, nor could it be condemned on these grounds: as independent markers of value, fashion and taste could be had cheaply but also very expensively. In Jones's words, those involved in what we might rather call the fashion trades than the luxury trades, 'organised the economy of taste not around class, but rather around gender and nationality, with French women possessing the most refined taste'.[25] Everyone, from shopgirls to Madame de Pompadour, could participate in and contribute to the profits of the fashion trade and in so doing contribute to French national pride and economic power.[26] Men of letters, from journalists to *philosophes*, would assert their own authority by challenging both the royal court and its aesthetic of ostentatious display by means of the notion of taste. Paris and not Versailles would be promoted as the capital of the modern, civilised world, as 'the centre where all talents, all arts, and all taste come to perfect themselves and flower', as one journalist enthused.[27]

Furniture-making was not the least of these arts. We can see in the evolution of the furniture trade in the eighteenth century a shift from an economy rooted in the discourse of luxury to one that operated within the new discourse of commerce, in which taste and fashion played key roles. Louis XIV made Paris the

European salespoint for luxury goods; in the eighteenth century, the *marchand-merciers*, with the help of men of letters, made it the centre of fashion.

*

The Parisian furniture trade was given a major boost in the seventeenth century by Louis XIV's personal, political and economic interest in luxury. Like the Gobelins tapestry works, the Gobains glassworks and the Lyons silk industry, the work of the *ébénistes* was both to furnish the court and boost the economy. Indeed, from the second half of the seventeenth century to the present, Paris has remained associated with the trade in 'luxury'.[28] Louis XIV and his successors were responsible for bringing to Paris a few notable *ébénistes* to produce furniture directly for the Crown as *artisans privilégiés*. They were followed by many others, mostly from the Low Countries and Central Europe, encouraged by a broadening market. The newcomers settled into the Faubourg Saint-Antoine and other areas of the city where they could work out of the control of the guild of *menuisiers* and hoped eventually to join them. By the end of the seventeenth century, the standard in both technology and design in fine cabinetry was set in Paris rather than in Augsburg, Antwerp or Florence, as it had been in the past.[29]

As Michael Sonenscher has pointed out, luxury goods were soon 'more than an array of ornate objects left to a grateful posterity for careful identification and display: they were one of the most substantial components of the eighteenth-century urban economy'.[30] That is, 'luxury' goods and the 'luxury' trade had expanded far beyond the practice of luxury as display associated with the aristocratic elite of the court, just as discussion of them had burst the bounds of the moral discourse of luxury. The furniture and other expensive, elegant and exotic goods purchased by the traditional elite were now a niche in the roomier space of the fashion economy. Luxury was now located at one end of a continuum of consumption whose unity was defined by fashion.

The novelty and taste which characterised fashion stimulated builders and merchants to invent specialised furniture, such as the *voyeuse* – a chair on which a woman was meant to kneel backwards, resting her elbows on the upholstered top rail for ease of watching others play at cards – as well as multifunctional pieces, such as a table fitted out for letter-writing, needlework and tea-drinking.[31] Innovation was evident in veneers and shapes of furniture, as well as in techniques of making and marketing it. Those who supplied consumer demand developed ways to make existing goods cheaper in order to reduce costs and reach a widening market while devising expensive new designs and products to satisfy their most exclusive clients. The fashion economy also stimulated people of means to trade in old pieces for new ones, thus boosting the stocks of dealers in second-hand goods who sold them to lesser folk at a significant reduction in price.[32] The dual imperative to reduce prices while maintaining an exclusive high-end defined the fashion continuum along which commerce hummed.

Writing desks such as the one that caught our eye in the museum were a mid-eighteenth-century invention. They were, first, a specific market response to rising consumer demand, as letter writing took hold as a fashionable practice (especially among women).[33] They were also a subset of the profusion of small, specialised tables that flooded the market and filled the apartments and *hôtels* of Paris. From the 1740s on, the variety of writing desks on the market went well beyond the stylistic shifts by which furniture historians have associated the shape of a leg with the reign of a king. They were designed and marketed in a remarkable array of shapes, from slant-fronts to roll-tops to elaborately engineered mechanical desks.[34] This multitude of forms and the engineering of the clockwork mechanisms within them are obvious testimony to the inventiveness of *merciers* and *ébénistes*. The veneers of lacquer, wood marquetry or porcelain which covered them, however, are, to our post-industrial eye, more often seen as the epitome of traditional craftsmanship. Yet even veneers demonstrate the modern fashion economy at work.

*

Writing desks first started to be made in Paris around 1745. From the beginning there were very expensive and very modest models available, even at the most fashionable shops. This was not a case of an exclusive item designed for royalty trickling down to less elevated consumers. A *mercier* might display one desk veneered with rare and expensive Japanese lacquer for the most exclusive clientele, while furnishing a desk in the same style and taste, but veneered in the cheaper Chinese lacquer or French *vernis martin*, to a much broader, but equally fashion-conscious market.[35] In fact, the same client might purchase both. In 1752, Madame de Pompadour bought two writing desks veneered in Japanese lacquer for 560 livres apiece. Three years later, she had one veneered in Chinese lacquer for only 48 livres. She bought both from the same *mercier*, Lazare Duvaux, who also sold pieces veneered in the even cheaper French imitation.[36]

French *vernis martin*, which had come to dominate the Parisian market for light furniture by the 1740s, made fashionable *chinoiserie* accessible to a broad market.[37] Meanwhile, in the shops of the *merciers*, where pieces veneered in French, Chinese and Japanese lacquer stood side by side, customers learned to practise the discrimination that would define connoisseurship. Within the world of fashion, the elite and those who catered to them learned to use taste to add value to certain goods.[38] Thus, while the Martin brothers brought down the price of lacquer with their invention of *vernis martin*, the *merciers* taught their elite clients to value Japanese lacquer even more, both because of its rarity and because of its quality – apparent only to the true connoisseur.

A similar dynamic of product innovation and marketing can be seen at work in marquetry veneers. Marquetry veneering had been used since the Renaissance to hide carcasses of common wood (oak or even pine) and not particularly notable construction.[39] The aesthetic of marquetry was based on the mosaic which required inlay pieces of various sharply defined colours; its value was enhanced by the richness and rarity of the inlaid materials: the semi-precious stones of pietra-dura, which came to France from Italy early in the seventeenth century;

and the ebony inlaid with ivory, tortoiseshell, mother-of-pearl and precious metals with which Louis XIV's *ébénistes* made the pieces that furnished his court.

The great innovation of the eighteenth century was to substitute exotic hardwoods newly available from America for the more expensive precious metals, stones, ivory and mother-of-pearl.[40] These *bois des Indes* could be sliced more thinly and worked more intricately than native European woods because of their firmness and close grain; they also came in a breathtaking array of colours, unlike anything coming out of European forests, and in colourful contrast as well to the ebony that had been coming in from Africa, Madagascar and India.[41] America, wrote the author of the *Dictionnaire du citoyen* (1762), 'can be regarded as the wealth of Europeans'. Among the various products it furnished Europe, from gold, silver and diamonds to sugar, coffee, tobacco and cotton, were 'woods for marquetry and construction'.[42] These included the dark Amaranth or purplewood from Dutch Guiana, which contrasted nicely with the golden *bois de Cayenne* or the pale yellow *bois de citron* from Saint Domingue. In the 1740s, pinkish-yellow Tulipwood from Brazil came into use; by 1750 it had become the most popular ground for floral marquetry. By the 1760s, the use of mahogany from Cuba was widespread, and during the years of Louis XVI's reign demand for it increased. The 1780s saw the introduction of pale yellow satinwood from the Antilles, which contrasted well with the dark red mahogany.[43]

Wood marquetry was considerably cheaper to produce than either pietra-dura or the ebony-based *ébénisterie*, which came to be known as 'Boulle marquetry' after Louis XIV's *ébéniste*, André-Charles Boulle (1642–1732).[44] Wood marquetry, however, required different skills and technology – specifically, the ability to slice wood thinly and jigsaw it into curved pieces. As the veneers got thinner, the likelihood of ruining a piece of expensive wood with the jigsaw increased. The cutting of these leaves of exotic woods into small, intricate shapes was the most demanding part of the *ébéniste*'s job.[45] Thin veneers were not simply a *tour de force* of craftsmanship, however, they were the result of technological innovation and a significant means of lowering the cost of materials. In the eighteenth century, materials, not labour, determined the price of finished goods.[46] In 1772, the *Avant Coureur*, a Parisian weekly, published the description of a new spring-driven jigsaw that was less prone to break the piece of wood being sawn.[47] When the *ébénistes* reached the limits of their saws, they cut costs by avoiding imported woods whenever possible. This could be done by dyeing domestic woods such as maple to cover large surfaces that did not require fine cutting.[48] Connoisseurs learned to tell the difference between exotic and dyed woods, as they distinguished among Japanese, Chinese and French lacquer (see Plates 5 and 6).

As innovation brought down the cost of materials, and wood marquetry became fashionable, the demand for skilled woodworkers increased in Paris and London, where demand was high enough and guild restrictions were minimal enough to support specialists in cutting and veneering.[49] Not just the wood, then, but the craftsmen were imported, mostly from the Low Countries and Germany. The names of the most well-known *ébénistes* of the eighteenth century are largely Flemish, Dutch or German: Criard from Brussels, van Risamburgh from

Gröningen, Vandercruse, also Dutch, Molitor from Luxembourg, Latz from Cologne, Oeben from Heinsberg near Aix-la-Chapelle and the Dutch border, Cramer and Weisweiler from the Rhineland, Riesener and Roentgen from Westphalia.[50] The number of *ébénistes* multiplied in the Faubourg Saint-Antoine, where foreigners and labour costs were unencumbered by guild restrictions, direct sales to the public avoided the *mercier's* mark-up, and those without the polish of the elite were perhaps more welcome as customers.

But the privileged artisans and the *merciers* in the rue Saint Honoré were certainly not losing business. The *merciers* started ordering expensive porcelain plaques from the royal factory at Sèvres and having *ébénistes* mount these on desk frames; the privileged artisans started to produce signature designs in expensive materials, like the cube marquetry and mechanical tables of Oeben, or the gilt-bronze mounts in classical motifs of Weisweiler, that would make their work recognisable and expensive, and would carry prestige without violating the canons of taste which made it fashionable. In the 1770s and 1780s, the most expensive writing desks made for the most exclusive clientele (the international court elite) were veneered in Japanese lacquer, Sèvres porcelain and Cuban mahogany, yet they were part of the same fashion system and represent the same taste as the more modest desks veneered in wood marquetry.[51] As in the case of lacquer, developments in marquetry materials and techniques both responded to demand for fashionable writing desks among an expanding letter-writing public, and stimulated design innovations that kept the top segment of the market securely exclusive.

Merciers and *ébénistes* together expanded the market for fine furniture by maintaining fashionability, while assiduously catering to the high end with new and rare veneers whose appreciation demanded a cultivated and refined taste – as well as a hefty outlay of money, of course. Even the most fashionable shops on the rue Saint Honoré catered to both ends of the market by selling goods in a broad price range. The most modest writing desk sold by Lazare Duvaux to one of his female clients cost a mere 30 livres. He described it as 'a small table, with a writing slide and a drawer, veneered in satinwood.' Six months earlier, Madame de Pompadour had bought a similarly described desk, but veneered in lacquer and equipped with silver fittings ('a lacquer table, with a drawer and a writing slide, the jars in silver'), for 534 livres.[52] Beyond the veneer, silver fittings and, more frequently, gilt bronze mounts, made a fashionable desk into a luxury item. The cost of materials more than the workmanship jacked up the price. Yet even here, the rich and powerful could not simply heap on the gold and silver. Luxury had to be in good taste and within the parameters of fashion if its owner were to be admired. As Caraccioli told his readers:

If one means by luxury that massive sumptuosity that knows only how to gild and tinge with blue and spend profusely, the Europeans do not owe to the French the glory of having succeeded in this regard; if, on the contrary, it is a question of charm, of graciousness, of comforts, and even of magnificence, they are indebted both to the Parisians and to the Lyonnais. They commission them to furnish [their homes] and to clothe them, and never was a commission better executed.[53]

Trusting to the good offices of a respected merchant like Lazare Duvaux and the name of a well-known *ébéniste* assured the client that her purchase would testify to her refinement and good taste. By the last decades of the century she could turn to the fashion press for guidance as well. In the 1780s, the *Cabinet des Modes* declared itself a 'work that gives an exact and prompt knowledge, as much concerning new Clothes and Hairstyles for both sexes, as of new Furniture of all sorts, ... & generally of all that Fashion offers that is singular, agreeable, or interesting in all genres'.[54]

*

The writing desk known as the *bonheur-du-jour* epitomised the fashion trade in furniture. This joint creation of enterprising *ébénistes* and *merciers* came in the full range of shapes, styles and veneers, from whimsical, but not particularly expensive wood marquetry to the most expensive porcelain (see Plates 7 and 8). At the same time, it was eminently practical for serving the letter writer's needs: its writing surface was supplemented by one drawer fitted with an *écritoire*, and an additional set of locked drawers and pigeonholes for letters received, blank paper and other epistolary needs. It is generally thought to have been aimed specifically at the new female market associated with fashion consumption and the fashionable practice of letter-writing. An *ébéniste* may have invented the design, but Pierre Verlet assures us that the *merciers* were responsible for popularising it with the catchy name that evoked novelty, fashion and a comfortable happiness.[55] Art historian Geneviève Souchal calls the *bonheur-du-jour* 'one of the most graceful inventions of a century abounding in such inventions'.[56]

Our little desk, the one that first caught our eye in the museum, is a *bonheur-du-jour*. Is it a 'luxury' good? Or is it, rather, a commodity, a consumer good? Was its purpose to display the good taste of its owner, or to be useful in her daily practice of letter-writing? Was the woman who sat at this desk to write a letter – to a friend, a daughter, a sister, a husband or a son – a modern consumer whose friends and family were dispersed by commerce, state expansion, and an infrastructure of roads, coaches, packet boats and sailing ships? Or was she a decadent aristocrat, scribbling a note to her young lover while her husband was off, minding his own affairs or the king's? Her silk dress is cut and beribboned in the latest fashion; the walls of the room in which she sits are papered, also in the latest fashion, and hung with mirrors and genre paintings by fashionable modern painters; in the comfortable chair near the fire lies a novel, half-read, that was recently favourably reviewed in the *Avant Coureur*; children can be heard reciting their lessons in another room; servants, including the letter-writer's personal maid, are at their work throughout the house. But none of these things tells us if she is an aristocrat concerned with the display of social power, or a courtesan in good times, or the wife of a successful merchant – only that she is wealthy. Nor do they tell us if she is corrupt or virtuous – only that she is fashionable. This scene cannot reassure us, any more than the desk can, that she and her world were decadent and deserved their imminent destruction, or that, to the contrary, they were vibrant and dynamic and poised to triumph.

What is perhaps most interesting is the possibility that whether this woman and this desk are viewed in terms of luxury and display, or as representing fashion and modern practices of consumption, she, in her association with it, will be equally susceptible to charges of feminine vanity and frivolity, wastefulness and moral laxity. For although Maxine Berg and Helen Clifford are right in saying that the champions of the modern commercial economy made every effort to shift the debate about things from a moral to an economic discourse,[57] it is nevertheless true that by shifting the marker of *consumption* from the status category of aristocracy to the gender category of women, consumption was remoralised, even as commerce and the commercial economy retained their masculine associations.[58] By the nineteenth century, the gendering of consumption as feminine was secured by the masculinising of its binary opposite, production. This has resulted not only in the gendering of the working class as male producers, as Joan Scott has shown, but the writing of economic history from the perspective of supply rather than demand.[59] Even the new interest in the 'Consumer Revolution', as Amanda Vickery points out, has shifted attention to the male entrepreneurs and middlemen who created or met demand, rather than to consumers themselves, still considered irrational, manipulable, fickle, in a word – feminine.[60]

Like any other object, the *bonheur-du-jour* is neither feminine nor masculine. In itself it represents neither the decadence of the Old Regime, nor its craftsmanship, civilisation, or commercial dynamism. It exists as the subject of various discourses, past and present, each of which gives it meaning while using it to lay out a certain vision of the culture and history in which it is seen to figure. The *bonheur-du-jour* helps to reveal these multiple discourses and the concerns of those who deployed them. Unlike an object of nature (a tree, a mountain, a seashore), however, the *bonheur-du-jour* is not already there, simply to be played upon by competing discourses. Its very existence is a function of a set of practices of production, distribution and consumption that are historically defined and discursively situated. For this reason, a desk produced, marketed, purchased and used within a discourse of luxury in which power is displayed through ostentatious wealth must differ in some way from one produced, marketed, purchased and used within a discourse of commerce in which value is ascribed in terms of notions of taste and fashion, and where utility and novelty are legitimising factors. Perhaps the best way to understand the *bonheur-du-jour* and its world is at the intersection of these two discourses and the practices they shaped. In so doing, we can perhaps break down both the Enlightenment opposition between barbaric aristocratic luxury and modern consumption and the nineteenth-century opposition between feminine consumption and masculine production. We can thus perhaps break free of the moralising they entail to come to a more complex understanding and appreciation of a writing desk and, by extension, of the woman who used it.

Notes

1. 'Styles of furniture reflected the personalities of the three monarchs. Louis XIV had furniture built for show, rather than for comfort. He was not concerned about whether people had a place to sit while waiting for his royal appearance.' 'Teachers' Guide' to 'Splendors of Versailles', Http://www.splendors-versailles.org/index2.html.
2. Mary D. Sheriff, *Fragonard: Art and Eroticism* (Chicago, 1990), p. 27.
3. Karl Toth, *Women and Rococo in France*, trans. Roger Abingdon (Philadelphia, 1931), p. 341.
4. *Ibid.*, p. 371.
5. Leora Auslander, *Taste and Power: Furnishing Modern France* (Berkeley, 1996), p. 29.
6. *Ibid.*, p. 110.
7. *Ibid.*, esp. pp. 35–40, 58. It should be pointed out that Auslander is following rather than establishing a model interpretation here. As Carolyn Sargentson notes, citing classic sociologists Norbert Elias, Werner Sombart and Thorstein Veblen, 'France has been held up as a paradigm of court culture, a society whose consumption is driven by the observance of the behaviour of the court and the emulation of it by city consumers.' Sargentson, *Merchants and Luxury Markets: The Marchands Merciers of Eighteenth-Century Paris* (London and Malibu, 1996), p. 5 and n. 19.
8. The 'revisionism' that now undergirds scholarship on the old regime and the French Revolution came into its own in the late 1980s. Useful review essays include Sarah Maza, 'Politics, Culture, and the Origins of the French Revolution', *Journal of Modern History* 61 (1989), pp. 704–23; Jack R. Censer, 'Commencing the Third Century of Debate', *American Historical Review* 94 (1989), pp. 1309–25; Lynn Hunt, 'Forgetting and Remembering: The French Revolution Then and Now', *American Historical Review* 100 (1995), pp. 1119–35; Suzanne Desan, 'What's after Political Culture? Recent French Revolutionary Historiography', *French Historical Studies* 23 (2000), pp. 163–96. On the economic dynamism and consumer culture of the old regime, see Daniel Roche, *The People of Paris: An Essay in Popular Culture in the Eighteenth Century*, trans. Gwynne Lewis (Berkeley, 1987); *A History of Everyday Things: The Birth of Consumption in France, 1600–1800*, trans. Brian Pearce (Cambridge, 2000); Colin Jones, 'Bourgeois Revolution Revivified: 1789 and Social Change', in Colin Lucas, ed., *Rewriting the French Revolution: The Andrew Browning Lectures 1989* (Oxford, 1991), pp. 69–118; and 'The Great Chain of Buying: Medical Advertisement, the Bourgeois Public Sphere, and the Origins of the French Revolution', *American Historical Review* 101 (February 1996), pp. 13–40; Cissie Fairchilds, 'The Production and Marketing of Populuxe Goods in Eighteenth-Century Paris', in John Brewer and Roy Porter, eds, *Consumption and the World of Goods* (New York, 1993), pp. 228–48; Robert Fox and Anthony Turner, eds, *Luxury Trades and Consumerism in Ancien Régime Paris: Studies in the History of the Skilled Workforce* (Aldershot, Hampshire and Brookfield, Vt., 1998), esp. the articles by Michael Sonenscher and Gillian Lewis; Colin Jones and Rebecca Spang, '*Sans-culottes, Sans Café, Sans Tabac*: Shifting Realms of Necessity and Luxury in Eighteenth-Century France', in Maxine Berg and Helen Clifford, eds, *Consumers and Luxury: Consumer Culture in Europe 1650–1850* (Manchester: Manchester University Press, 1999), pp. 37–62.
9. Daniel Roche, *France in the Enlightenment*, trans. Arthur Goldhammer (Cambridge, Mass., 1998), p. 562. The following discussion is based on Roche's analysis of the luxury debate, pp. 561–74.
10. On the seventeenth-century defence of luxury as a means of reinforcing the social order when limited to the traditional elite, see Carolyn C. Lougee, '*Le Paradis des Femmes*': *Women, Salons, and Social Stratification in Seventeenth-Century France* (Princeton, 1976), pp. 94–7.
11. Sarah Maza, 'Luxury, Morality, and Social Change: Why There Was No Middle-Class Consciousness in Prerevolutionary France', *Journal of Modern History* 69 (June 1997), p. 217.

12. Voltaire quoted in Philippe Perrot, 'De l'apparat au bien-être: Les avatars d'un superflu nécessaire'; in J.-P. Goubert, ed., *Du Luxe au confort* (Paris, 1988), p. 42. Perhaps Jean-François de Saint-Lambert was thinking of luxury as comfort, too, when he wrote in the article, 'Luxe': 'Thus there is a *luxury* in all estates, in all societies: the savage has his hammock, which he buys with animal skins, the European has his couch, his bed.' Denis Diderot and Jean Le Rond d'Alembert, eds, *Encyclopédie, ou Dictionnaire raisonné des sciences, des arts, et des métiers* (Paris, 1751–65), 9:763. On the eighteenth-century distinction between furniture of display and furniture of comfort, see Pierre Verlet, *La Maison du XVIIIe siècle en France: Société, décoration, mobilier* (Paris, 1966), p. 11; on the new meaning of comfort in eighteenth-century Anglo-American society and its role in reshaping consumption, see John E. Crowley, 'The Sensibility of Comfort', *American Historical Review* 104 (June 1999), pp. 749–82.

13. Saint-Lambert, 'Luxe', *Encyclopédie*, 9:764.

14. Diderot, 'Encyclopédie', *Encyclopédie*, 5:635A. Keith Baker reads Diderot's spotlighting of luxury here as a marker of 'the more profound problem of a society in structural disarray'. *Condorcet: From Natural Philosophy to Social Mathematics* (Chicago, 1975), p. 19. See also Pierre Rétat, 'Luxe', *Dix-Huitième Siècle*, no. 26 (1994), pp. 79–88.

15. Perrot, 'De l'apparat au bien-être', p. 42; Saint-Lambert, 'Luxe', 9:766.

16. Louis-Antoine Caraccioli, *Paris, le modèle des nations étrangeres, ou l'Europe françoise* (Venice/Paris, 1777), pp. 55–7.

17. Caraccioli, *Paris, le modèle des nations étrangeres*, p. 120.

18. Guillaume Thomas François Raynal, *Histoire philosophique et politique des établissemens et du commerce des Européens dans les deux Indes* (Geneva, 1782), 1:12, pp. 20–1.

19. Raynal, *Histoire philosophique*, 5:137.

20. Jennifer M. Jones, 'Repackaging Rousseau: Femininity and Fashion in Old Regime France', *French Historical Studies* 18 (Fall 1994), p. 947.

21. The *marchande de modes* and the *marchand mercier* were in this sense like the *salonnière*, whose taste was expressed in her selection of guests based on individual merit and her ability to elicit from them both brilliance and harmony. These essentially aesthetic criteria contested the rank-based society of display that was the social counterpart of ostentatious luxury associated with the royal court. See Dena Goodman, *The Republic of Letters: A Cultural History of the French Enlightenment* (Ithaca, 1994), ch. 3.

    It should be noted that in matters of taste, authority is always unstable and subject to contestation, as Reed Benhamou emphasises in her discussion of the change from a baroque style based on symmetry, formal rules, and repeated motifs to a rococo style based on novelty and imagination. Benhamou, 'Furniture Production in 18th-Century France: An Interactive Process', *European Studies Journal* 1 (1984), p. 49.

22. Sargentson, *Merchants and Luxury Markets*. See also the pathbreaking article of Pierre Verlet, 'Le Commerce des objets d'art et les marchands merciers à Paris au XVIIIe siècle', *Annales E.S.C.* 13 (January–March 1958), pp. 10–29; and Cissie Fairchilds, 'The Production and Marketing of Populuxe Goods in Eighteenth-Century Paris', in Brewer and Porter, *Consumption and the World of Goods*, pp. 228–48.

23. Sargentson, *Merchants and Luxury Markets*, ch. 4.

24. Jones, 'Repackaging Rousseau', p. 959.

25. *Ibid.*, p. 960.

26. By 1793, a character in one of Isabelle de Charrière's novels (a French duchess who has emigrated to London), could say obnoxiously to the English Lady Caroline Dupont: 'You could really be taken for a Frenchwoman . . . you have the taste of one, you have the figure: Wasn't your mother in Paris a few months before your birth?' *Lettres trouvées dans des portefeuilles d'émigrés* (Paris, 1993), p. 45.

27. *Magasin des modes nouvelles* [new volume], pp. 1–2; quoted in Jones, 'Repackaging Rousseau', p. 962.

28. See Steven L. Kaplan, 'The Luxury Guilds in Paris in the Eighteenth Century', *Francia* 9

(1981), pp. 257–98; Sargentson, *Merchants and Luxury Markets*; and the recent volume edited by Fox and Turner, *Luxury Trades and Consumerism in Ancien Régime Paris*.

29. Louis XIV was the first French king to make furniture a significant royal expenditure; his predecessors had invested mainly in jewellery and tapestries. See Alexandre Pradère, *French Furniture Makers: The Art of the Ébéniste from Louis XIV to the Revolution*, trans. Perran Wood (Malibu, Ca., 1989), pp. 9–11; Michael Stürmer, 'An Economy of Delight: Court Artisans of the Eighteenth Century', *Business History Review* 53 (Winter 1979), pp. 496–528; Verlet, *La Maison du XVIIIe siècle*, pp. 17–18.

30. Michael Sonenscher, *Work and Wages: Natural Law, Politics and the Eighteenth-Century French Trades* (Cambridge, 1989), p. 211.

31. Mimi Hellman discusses these objects and many others that 'structured and delimited the behavior and appearance of individuals according to culturally specific codes of social conduct', in 'Furniture, Sociability, and the Work of Leisure in Eighteenth-Century France', *Eighteenth-Century Studies* 32 (Summer 1999), pp. 415–45. See also Pierre Devinoy, *Le Meuble léger en France* (Paris, 1952), p. 19.

32. Pradère, *French Furniture Makers*, pp. 24–5. Here are three ways we can see the circulation of second-hand furniture: (1) The Parisian *marchand-mercier* Lazare Duvaux notes in his daybook that on 9 December 1748, he sold a writing table to the Marquise de Coëtlogon for 240 livres, and then bought it back from her in 1749 for 192 livres [*Livre-journal de Lazare Duvaux, Marchand-bijoutier ordinaire du Roy, 1748–1758*, ed. Louis Courajod (Paris, 1965), vol. 2, transaction #64]; (2) Madame de Genlis relates in her memoirs that it was the purchaser of her late father-in-law's desk, which she was in the process of selling, who discovered his will upon springing open a secret drawer [*Mémoires inédits de Madame la Comtesse de Genlis, sur le dix-huitième siècle et la révolution françoise, depuis 1756 jusqu'à nos jours* (Paris, 1825), 3:331]; (3) under the rubric *Effets et Marchandises à Vendre*, the French commercial press known collectively as the *Affiches* gave the public notice of auctions of seized goods, including household furniture and the inventory of bankrupt businesses dealing in furniture (see, e.g., *Annonces, Affiches et Avis Divers de Picardie, Artois, Soissonnois et Pays-Bas François*, 13 August 1774, no. 33).

33. Elizabeth C. Goldsmith, 'Authority, Authenticity, and the Publication of Letters by Women', in Goldsmith, ed., *Writing the Female Voice: Essays on Epistolary Literature* (Boston, 1989), pp. 46–59; Katherine A. Jensen, 'Male Models of Female Epistolarity; or, How to Write Like a Woman in Seventeenth-Century France', in Goldsmith, ed., *Writing the Female Voice*, pp. 25–45. See also Jensen, *Writing Love: Letters, Women, and the Novel in France, 1605–1776* (Carbondale, IL, 1995); Susan Lanser, *Fictions of Authority: Women Writers and Narrative Voice* (Ithaca, 1992).

34. Devinoy, *Meuble léger en France*, pp. 18–19; Verlet, *La Maison du XVIIIe siècle*, pp. 162–4, pp. 193–4.

35. The first writing desks documented by Pradère are two *secrétaires en pente*, one carrying the stamp of the ébéniste Jacques Dubois, and the other B.V.R.B. One is veneered in Japanese lacquer and the other in *vernis martin*. Pradère dates both to 1745–49. Pradère, *French Furniture Makers*, pp. 170 and 192. Guillaume Janneau dates both the *toilette* and the 'bureau de dame' after 1735, and notes that they appear at the same time. Janneau, *Le Mobilier français: Le Meuble d'ébenesterie* (Paris, 1993), p. 68. He notes that the *secrétaire à dessus brisé* (i.e., *secrétaire en pente*) appeared in Wallonie in the 1730s and in Paris a decade later (p. 80). See also Pierre Verlet, 'Le Commerce des objets d'art et les marchands merciers à Paris au XVIIIe siècle', p. 17.

36. Louis Courajod, ed., *Livre-journal de Lazare Duvaux, Marchand-bijoutier ordinaire du Roy*, vol. 2: transaction #1138 (3 June 1752); transaction #2189 (3 July 1755).

37. Sonenscher, *Work and Wages*.

38. Sargentson, *Merchants and Luxury Markets*, p. 74.

39. John Whitehead, *The French Interior in the Eighteenth Century* (New York, 1993), p. 127.

40. Whitehead gives the credit for this innovation entirely to the competitive practices of

the *marchand-merciers* who, as he notes, specialised in exotic goods and materials. *French Interior in the Eighteenth Century*, p. 130.

41. *Encyclopédie méthodique, ou par ordre de matières*, par une Société de Gens de Lettres, de Savans et d'Artistes.: *Arts et métiers mécaniques* [by Jacques Lacombe] (Paris and Liège, 1782–91), 27: pp. 301–2; Michael Stürmer, '"Bois des Indes" and the Economics of Luxury Furniture in the Time of David Roentgen', *The Burlington Magazine* 120 (December 1978), pp. 800–1.

42. *Dictionnaire du citoyen, ou abregé historique, theorique et pratique du commerce* (Amsterdam, 1762), 1:viii.

43. Pradère, *French Furniture Makers*, p. 431. Michael Stürmer writes that the price of mahogany only came down low enough to bring it into general use in 1770. Stürmer, '"Bois des Indes"', p. 800.

44. In the second half of the eighteenth century, authentic Boulle pieces veneered in old lacquer were the only furniture to have value as antiques rather than as novelties. They were the first type of furniture to be collected. Their value rose with time, while other furniture was simply considered old or used and thus was cheaper than new pieces which reflected the latest fashion and the most modern taste. See Pradère, *French Furniture Makers*, p. 24. It should also be noted that Boulle pieces were used for the old-fashioned purpose of decorating *appartements de parade*, which were themselves going out of fashion. Imitation Boulle of 'ebonised wood' was used for large *bureaus plats* meant to impress, but never for the small letter desks discussed here. Whereas a *bureau plat* of real Boulle marquetry could run to 1,000 livres, one of ebonised wood was sold for a mere 96. See Sargentson, *Merchants and Luxury Markets*, p. 25; Whitehead, *French Interior*, p. 130.

45. Abbé [Pierre] Jaubert, *Dictionnaire raisonné universel des arts et metiers* (Paris, 1773), 3: p. 112. 'The veneers were hand-cut to a thickness of about $\frac{1}{12}$ of an inch by craftsmen "who do only this work. . . . These sawyers are paid by the pound, that is, on the basis of the piece of wood brought to them . . ."' Roubo, quoted in Benhamou, 'Furniture Production', p. 46.

46. Pradère, *French Furniture Makers*, pp. 24–5.

47. *Avant Coureur*, no. 28, 13 July 1772.

48. Stürmer, '"Bois des Indes"', p. 802; Jaubert, *Dictionnaire raisonné*, 2: pp. 88–9, 3: pp. 112; Benhamou cites Guillaume Janneau, *L'Epoque Louis XV* (Paris, 1967), 81–2 for her detailing of the available dyes as follows: 'One silver-gray, three greens, four blacks, 17 whites, 21 yellows, and 33 reds' ('Furniture Production', p. 46). On colour innovation in eighteenth-century France see Sarah Lowengard, 'Colours and Colour Making in the Eighteenth Century', in Berg and Clifford, *Consumers and Luxury*, pp. 103–17.

49. Stürmer, '"Bois des Indes"', pp. 800–1.

50. Lesser-known *ébénistes* include Schneider from Augsburg, Baumhauer, Benneman, Schwerdfeber, and Stockel also from Germany. See Pradère, *French Furniture Makers*, for sketches of all the major ébénistes.

51. Of the many books on eighteenth-century French furniture, Pradère, *French Furniture Makers* is the most exhaustive and the most lavishly illustrated. The reader will find in it excellent examples, often illustrated in full colour, of every sort of writing desk in every possible veneer.

52. *Livre-Journal de Lazare Duvaux*, transactions #804 (8 May 1751) and #650 (22 November 1750).

53. Caraccioli, *Paris, le modèle des nations étrangeres*, p. 119.

54. *Cabinet des Modes/Magasin des modes nouvelles, françaises et anglaises* (Paris, 1785–90). See also the francophone *Journal [des Luxus und] der Moden*, edited by F.J. Bertuch and G.M. Kraus (Weimar, 1786–99), which featured many plates of fashionable furniture, including a *sécretaire en pente* and a rolltop desk in 1787.

55. Pierre Verlet, *La Maison du XVIIIe siècle en France*, pp. 204–5. See also Henri Havard, *Dictionnaire de l'ameublement, et de la décoration depuis le XVIIe siècle jusqu'à nos jours* (Paris, 1887–90), 1: pp. 352–3. Pradère credits the *marchand merciers* with the invention of the *bonheur-du-jour* (*French Furniture Makers*, pp. 39–40), while Whitehead more diplomatically claims only that they *provided* customers with the variety of small tables for letter-writing which they demanded, including the *bonheur-du-jour* (*The French Interior in the Eighteenth Century*, p. 135).
56. Geneviève Souchal, *French Eighteenth-Century Furniture*, trans. Simon Watson-Taylor (New York, 1961), p. 67.
57. Maxine Berg and Helen Clifford, 'Introduction', to *Consumers and Luxury*, 3.
58. See especially Jennifer Jones, 'Repackaging Rousseau', p. 960. Both Jones and Daniel Roche show how women came to be the target market for consumer goods as luxury gave way to fashion. See Roche, *France in the Enlightenment*, pp. 554–5, and *The Culture of Clothing: Dress and Fashion in the Ancien Regime*, trans. Jean Birrell (Cambridge, 1994).
59. Joan Wallach Scott, 'Women in the Making of the English Working Class', in *Gender and the Politics of History* (New York, 1988); Neil McKendrick, 'Introduction: The Birth of a Consumer Society: The Commercialization of Eighteenth-Century England', and 'The Consumer Revolution of Eighteenth-Century England', in Neil McKendrick, John Brewer, and J.H. Plumb, *The Birth of a Consumer Society: The Commercialization of Eighteenth-Century England* (Bloomington, In., 1982), pp. 1–33.
60. Vickery, 'Women and the World of Goods: A Lancashire Consumer and Her Possessions, 1751–81', in Brewer and Porter, *Consumption and the World of Goods*, p. 274.

Plates

5. *Bonheur-du-jour*, open, attributed to Topino, Louis XV period.
6. The same *bonheur-du-jour* closed.
7. One of a pair of oval *bonheur-du-jours*, stamped Topino, *c*. 1775.
8. Lady's *bonheur-du-jour* writing table, 1765.

6

The Circulation of Luxury Goods in Eighteenth-Century Paris: Social Redistribution and an Alternative Currency

Laurence Fontaine
Trans. *Vicky Wittaker*

Until recently research has laid emphasis more on how luxury goods were pro-duced and consumed than on the actual business activity surrounding them, even though light is beginning to be shed in certain areas. An analysis of the whole spectrum of activities involved in distributing luxury and fashion goods is out of the question here: the task is too great. I am not attempting to determine all merchant circuits in which luxury and fashion goods played a part; in particular I shall not discuss those merchants involved with the court, the aristocracy and tourism, to which Carolyn Sargentson has recently devoted an excellent study, just as I will not be tackling the role of fairs – such as those held in Saint-Germain and Saint-Laurent – where whole sectors specialised in these types of goods.[1] I shall concentrate on more ordinary and lesser-known distribution circuits, and on those distribution circuits which lay at the heart of the ways in which luxury and fashion goods were introduced and circulated in the city.

I must first stress how difficult it is to circumscribe and accurately define what constituted a 'luxury' item or a taste for luxury because 'luxury' is a changing social and cultural category. Cultural and political models which are diverse and change over time shape forms of consumption. These forms and the things them-selves are metamorphosed into objects of luxury, desire or fashion. In doing so, they bear witness also to the power of those who classify them into something to be coveted. It is not therefore surprising that the dictionary of commerce written by Savary des Bruslons has no entry for luxury, although it does have one for fashion. In its own way it explains that 'luxury' is a cultural category and a notion expressing social relations.

The goods considered as luxury items in eighteenth-century Paris varied widely over time and between social groups. For some people luxury was represented by a pair of stockings or a cheap watch; for others it meant diamonds, curios or even an abundance of those same objects which were held in esteem by the poor. Louis Sébastien Mercier was scandalised by the spread of luxury in the capital: 'The

Parisian who does not have an income of ten thousand livres ordinarily has neither bedsheets, nor towels nor undershirts; but he has a repeater watch, mirrors, silk stockings, lace . . .'[2] In Diderot's *L'Encyclopédie*, Saint-Lambert eloquently expresses under the heading 'luxe' how society in its entirety was concerned with luxury: 'without an abundance of luxuries, men of all ranks believe themselves to be poor'.[3]

Caught between pleasure and social competitiveness, luxury goods created new business opportunities and new low-level jobs at all levels of society, and it is this which interests me here. Though it is a necessary area of study, I shall not reflect upon the changing goods which came upon the market, nor on the way in which these goods changed character as they changed hands. My main concern, then, will be to examine how such goods circulated away from the established shops, what the informal practices of sale and resale were, and how luxury goods became part of the city's financial economy. I shall first examine the relationships between shops and pedlars, then I shall highlight how luxury goods were also part of two other economic circuits. The first circuit is linked to the resale market: one of the intrinsic mechanisms of the economy of luxury goods and of the ways in which goods were acquired and circulated within society. The second circuit, although affected by the economic cycle of fashion, was primarily the result of other influences: it was a reflection of the precariousness of the economy throughout the ancien régime, poorly developed monetarisation, the 'flexibility' of the job market and the lack of financial institutions. Luxury goods circulated not just as themselves but as an alternative currency – not just for legal (or illegal) traders in difficulty, but for the majority of private individuals. As a result, this second circuit played a significant role in the economy of luxury goods and of the city itself, to which it lent an indispensable flexibility.

It is not an easy task to bring these circuits out of their obscurity and study them more closely because there is a lack of material: we are often dealing with an informal economy which, unless its activities became criminal, almost entirely escaped being recorded. Hence I shall take as my guide the commentators of the time, in particular Louis Sébastien Mercier, who will be my first point of entry into this urban economy. His pen may be readily moralising, determined to castigate licentiousness and the decline in morals, or lecturing when an opportunity for praising family values arose, but his eye is extremely sharp. His ability to apprehend, whenever they existed, economic micro-circuits, the social and cultural practices attached to them and the menial jobs they created is always corroborated by other sources.

Luxury goods and trade circuits

Shopkeepers and pedlars

When considering the circulation of luxury goods it is traditional to focus upon two markets: the market supplied by the elegant boutiques whose customers were the aristocracy and the rich bourgeoisie, and that supplied by pedlars who catered for the ordinary people, with goods moving from the first market to the second market when objects became too common for the rich to consider them worth having any more.[4] I want to show here that the ways in which luxury goods were circulated were more complex than this and that the boutique and peddling worlds interpenetrated at all levels.

The boom in trade that took place in the eighteenth century was characterised by an increase in the number of shops, and although Mercier expressed concern about the rush by 'people with nothing to sell' to set up shop, given how rapidly they came unstuck, he was pleased that this meant that salesmen no longer paced 'the landings of firms, ready to catch the regular customers' but became upholsterers and decorators busy looking after their window displays.[5] In contrast to the sedentary businesses, the itinerant merchants criss-crossed the markets and streets, climbed up and down stairwells, and went into the inns – which then looked just as much like bars as multiform markets where deals were struck (or settled), and where the pedlar would spread out his new wares and his smuggled goods.[6]

In the city sedentary businesses and travelling merchants were still largely intermingled – even though the boutiques selling luxury goods had begun to dominate certain streets – but drawing the line between them is made no easier by comparing social origins and business practices.[7] Many of the shopkeepers were actually from the ranks of itinerant merchants, even if the city archives conceal this fact, just as the shopkeepers themselves, once successfully established, were very reluctant to reveal their social trajectory. The peddling profession was also one in which success meant setting up shop and the first setback a return to the road. At the end of the day, over and above the competition between them, shopkeepers and pedlars made use of one another and relied on one another to sell their goods.

In France, until the eighteenth century, the majority of pedlars operating in the city belonged to extensive networks made up of family and countrymen. These peddling networks relied on emigrants who had succeeded in opening up a shop in the city. Their business structure operated on two levels: the first was constituted by immediate family and other relatives who supported a family banking system and, by opening warehouses and city shops, extended over a huge geographical area. The second level was a distribution system which was tied to migration. This was a tightly circumscribed structure with a clear hierarchy, built on temporary migration and the manpower of men from the home village.[8]

The role played by peddling in the distribution of objects of modernity has already been shown: travelling merchants have always added small luxury and fashion items to their basic stock. In the eighteenth century watches and printed matter were among the goods popular with packmen. All account books, no matter how modest, bear this out, and many examples can be found by going through the business ledgers held in the Paris archives.[9] As was the case with printed matter, and at the same time as watches started to appear in pedlars' stock, certain families began to specialise in clocks and watches, and jewellery. In France these families were from the Savoie.[10] Analyses of these pedlars' circuits and of their business practices demonstrate the central role which they played in the sale of luxury goods, distributing as many upmarket goods as inexpensive items, and supplying the aristocracy and a number of other merchants (both sedentary and itinerant) as well as a more humble clientele.

Let us briefly consider Pierre Rullier, a Savoyard pedlar who covered the north and east of France, using Paris as a base. He rented a room for the year in Paris at Mme Lanoe's where he kept his business ledgers and a certain amount of merchandise. His landlady also forwarded his mail if he had to change his itinerary. Pierre's circuit had two geographies: one physical, the other epistolary. In the first he met customers in the towns and at fairs, in the second – and this is what fills the pages of his ledger – he undertook to supply them with goods at their request. To do this he used the postal service, stagecoaches and his nephews; and maintained a network of postboxes which enabled him to receive goods and have them forwarded to wherever his clients asked. His intermediaries were innkeepers, relatives and faithful customers, all of whom were merchants, and, lastly, the firms who acted as intermediaries with his own foreign suppliers. Some examples: on 28 November 1771 he was in Boulogne and had goods sent to Paris for one of his customers; on 28 December he was in Saint-Quentin and was paid for a watch which he had had sent from Paris to his customer on 27 June; on 11 June 1772 he was in Arras putting 'a package of goods in the coach for Paris', etc.

The Rullier brothers – because Pierre's brother was also a pedlar but in a more northern territory, since he covered northern France and southern Belgium – sold watches and gold and silver jewellery: snuff-boxes, earrings, crosses, rings, chains, buttons, tumblers and goblets. They also sold these precious metals as ingots or bullets to jewellers and supplied goldsmiths with watchmaker's tools and with watch-glasses. The only objects they sold which fell outside this specialisation were Langres knives. Their suppliers came from the great centres of European watchmaking: Switzerland and England via a great variety of channels.[11]

Establishing the value of the goods Pierre Rullier sold has proved extremely difficult because he rarely recorded the details of his transactions: at most he indicated the total value of the parcel of goods he had received. Moreover for transactions concerning a single item, particularly watches, he preferred to note the code of four to six letters for which he knew the corresponding financial value, and only rarely specified (as in the following two examples) that the watch coded 'aadp' was worth 475 livres and the one coded 'aabp' was worth 1,230 livres. However the originality of his methods of bookkeeping means that some ranges of prices can be established.

What do the prices which the pedlar charged tell us? Rullier sold silver snuff boxes for between 27 and 49 livres and bought them in Geneva for between 23 and 33 livres. Crosses were available in five different styles, ranging from 12 to 25 livres for the biggest. But he also sold a diamond cross for 84 livres. Watches, which were the articles that sold the most for this type of business, were available in an even wider price range: between 4 livres and 1,230 livres.[12] If we consider low prices charged for watches, then we can understand why they spread so quickly: for most people the price only represented a few days' work.

The novel aspect of Rullier's account book lies in the fact that the vast majority of his clients were shopkeepers. This adds a previously unsuspected dimension to peddling and, where these particular goods were concerned, gives the pedlar the advantage in the question of market share between sedentary businesses and travelling merchants. Rullier in fact supplied shopkeepers along the way, but also by mail. The time he spent writing letters and sending goods to his customers, or having goods sent, demonstrates the importance of this aspect of his business. Individual customers, on the other hand, were rare. Admittedly, he might have sold small items for cash, which he didn't bother to write down as his account book was more of an aide-mémoire as far as his correspondence was concerned than a usable accounting document. The few individual customers who do appear in it had purchased expensive items – a gold repeater watch for the innkeeper from Maubeuge, or a cross inlaid with diamonds, perhaps even silver watches of lesser value.

Another original aspect of Rullier's business was how he sold items to individuals via his customers' shops, leaving watches and items of jewellery for the shopkeeper to sell, fixing usually a minimum price and specifying that if the shopkeeper managed to get a better price for it they would split the profit. He would collect the unsold item when he would next return. Rullier also undertook repairs, but it is difficult to see how this worked except that he would easily give the customer another watch while the first was being repaired.

Lastly, Pierre lent large sums of money to some of the merchants who had stalls at the fairs (789 livres, for example, to a merchant from Reims; 531 livres and then another 203 livres to another 'ordinarily resident at Abbeville, travelling with the fairs'). This was a classic example of a supply chain, following the same patterns as the peddling hierarchy.

The Rulliers illustrate that pedlars were not just occasional and archaic vehicles in a rapidly changing business world, nor makeshift solutions to the slow development of the shopkeeping network, nor those left behind by the commercial boom. Many of them were able to take advantage of the possibilities created by rapidly expanding markets – in particular the markets for luxury goods and new products – and became intermediaries between the manufacturers and the shopkeeper, while continuing to look for sales to individuals, either directly or by using the shops as intermediaries.

Chambrelans and *revendeuses*[13]

Let us also mention the better-known figure of the *chambrelan* who sold goods illegally, that is without licence or in breach of commercial regulations, or used the pedlar to sell his products for him.[14] The wives of craftsmen would often sell their husbands' products illegally, ignoring the statutes of craft corporations or retailing regulations. Women selling fans would position themselves on bridges or at church doors where they could reach a large female clientele. Fraud and illegal sales, which took place at all stages of a product's life, were so common that the police ignored them unless a particular complaint was made by one of the guilds.[15]

In fact the police tolerated and made use of the *revendeuses* (women selling secondhand clothes). Some of them worked as a group and were in touch with the police informers; others managed to combine the two roles and were informers and sold stolen clothes at the same time.[16] The *revendeurs* and *revendeuses* had much in common with the pedlars. Like them they ranged in status from rich merchant to occasional dealer who was practically a beggar; again like the pedlars they not only sold to individuals but also acted as the link between different merchants, and their practices were often similar since they too used the shops to sell certain items which their street clientele was not in the habit of buying. Secondhand clothes were at the heart of this business which was controlled by the secondhand clothes dealers and the *revendeurs* of both sexes.[17]

Public sales

These took place on three types of occasion: when an inheritance was being settled, when a business had failed and when objects were being disposed of which had been pawned, but not recovered. Louis Sébastien Mercier denounced in general terms the way in which the shopkeepers dominated these sales, doing everything in their power to prevent access to private individuals. These sales, he declared, were in the control of the *grafinade*:

> These are a group of merchants who do not outbid each other at sales because all those who are there when an object is purchased have a share in it; however when they see that an individual desires a particular object they force up the price of it and bear the loss which, although significant for a person acting alone, becomes slight when divided between all the members of the league. These leagues exist for jewellery, diamonds, clocks and watches: they prevent the public from taking advantage of inexpensive goods . . .

The women selling old hats and the *revendeuses*, adds Mercier, act similarly and documents belonging to the most successful merchants on the rue du faubourg Saint-Honoré confirm that they were in the habit of getting part of their stock from the public sales.[18]

According to Mercier the merchants' success in controlling these sales meant that *Les petites affiches*, one of the first French newspapers to announce the auctions which took place after a death, 'are only of service to upholsterers, jewellers, merchants in the fashion business, and the young men who trade in horses, pictures and diamonds', whereas by making the information about these sales easily accessible the paper should have been helping individuals to break into this type of business.[19]

The '*curieux*'

The upper classes, with their cabinets full of curios, took part in this business too:

> Our great lords call themselves 'curieux' [collectors of curios], yet are more often than not glorified *brocanteurs* [secondhand dealers] who buy not from

need or passion, but so that they may have jewellery, horses, pictures, antique prints and so forth cheaply. They set up stud farms or cabinets which rapidly become shops: we believe them to be fervent enthusiasts of the fine arts; in actual fact they love money. The vases, bronzes and masterpieces to which they seem so attached and appear to idolise are available to anyone who'll relieve them of them for gold.[20]

The entries for '*curieux*' and '*brocanteur*' in *l'Encyclopédie* back up Mercier on this.[21] Moreover, paying for new objects by getting rid of older ones was common practice between the aristocrats and their suppliers.[22]

Luxury goods and financial circuits

I do not intend to analyse here the financial sectors, nor go into the complexities of credit, but to understand the role of luxury goods in financial circuits certain characteristics of eighteenth-century financial practices should be highlighted. Credit was still largely a matter between individuals and the ways in which it operated were very specific depending on who was borrowing and who was lending. Everything hung on the time allowed (or refused) to repay the loan, and not everyone had equal access to time. It depended on social status: the higher you were in society, the more time played in your favour and against your creditor. As a result those without social status – the majority – all those who had no property on which to secure their loans, would have access to credit (excepting credit within a community) only by pawning their possessions – effectively a deferred sale.

However, there was one type of debt which fell outside of the equation linking time and social status: gambling debts, which had to be paid without delay. Indeed, gambling debts fall outside the ordinary culture of credit since, by its very nature, to gamble is to consume money. It is therefore out of the question, since it risks distorting the very act of gambling, to include these debts within an economy of credit which was oriented towards the future when they were really part of a consumer economy rooted in the present. Gambling was extremely common both at the court and in the town.[23]

Revendeuses à la toilette and courtiers

The absence of financial institutions combined with the poor circulation of money and the numerous occasions on which people needed cash created openings for intermediaries, positions which required discretion and the ability to enter into every type of home. Moreover, the aristocracy could not openly engage in business. Some of these professions, such as *revendeuse à la toilette*, were the province of women; others, like *courtiers* (brokers), were exercised by both sexes.

The *revendeuse à la toilette* is welcome anywhere. She brings you fabrics, lace and jewellery which belonged to someone who needed cash to pay gambling debts. She is in the confidence of the finest ladies, who ask her opinions and arrange several matters on the basis of her advice. She is entrusted with curious secrets, and generally keeps them fairly faithfully.

It has been said that a *revendeuse à la toilette* must prattle endlessly but none the less maintain unfailing discretion, must possess boundless agility, a memory for objects, unflagging patience and a strong constitution.

Women such as this only exist in Paris. They make their fortune in a very short time.[24]

Trevoux's dictionary also mentions their existence: 'In Paris those women who go to private houses with old clothes or jewels which others wish to be rid of are called *revendeuses à la toilette.*'[25] Savary too stresses that this profession existed only in Paris, but he also highlights the role they played in the circulation of contraband. 'In Paris those women who go to people's houses to sell second-hand clothes and jewellery which others wish to get rid of are called *revendeuses à la toilette.* They are also often involved in the clandestine sale of smuggled or illegally imported goods, such as fabrics from the Indies, Indies painted canvases, Flanders lace, and so forth . . . either on their own account or acting on behalf of someone else.'[26] (See Plate 9.)

Mme Leonard, '*courtière* and *revendeuse à la toilette*', owed five creditors nearly 30,000 livres for 'merchandise entrusted to her', amongst whom were two haberdashers, and she dealt in all kinds of goods: Persian rugs, fabrics from the Indies, satins, dresses, jewellery, watches.[27] Marie-Anne Riffant was another *revendeuse à la toilette* who specialised in cloth and muslins, competing illegally with the women who sold household linen. She also lent money to other (female) usurers.[28]

Let us turn once again to Mercier as he describes the activities of the *courtiers*:

The man who offers you money looks gaunt and half-starved; he wears old clothes. He is always tired; he sits down when he comes in, for in a day he covers all parts of the city in order to match sales and purchases and to link the frequent exchanges of various goods.

First, you place in his hands your bills of exchange. He leaves: within the hour they will have been scrutinised by the entire clique of courtiers. Then he comes back to offer you cheap stockings, hats, braid, cloth, raw silk, books – he'll even offer you horses. It's up to you to turn these objects into money. Suddenly you're a hatter, a hosier, a bookseller or a horse dealer.

Your bill of exchange has been paid in merchandise; sometimes you'll get a quarter of it as cash. And the same courtier, whom you're obliged to turn to again, is also the man to take this merchandise off your hands: a new piece of sharp practice which soon reduces your bill of exchange to a third of its original value.[29]

The lack of ready cash was therefore sometimes a reason for and sometimes a pretext for the parallel circulation of goods.

'Affaires'

Selling secondhand clothes was an important activity between individuals, as well as for the dealers who were behind some of the collectors. This activity was simply called '*affaires*'.

> This is the generic term to describe any form of trading in secondhand goods. Rings, cases, jewellery and watches circulated in place of money. If someone needs money, he starts out with the contents of a shop. He will lose, it is true, more than half his investment when he wants to turn it into cash; but this is what is called '*affaires*'.
>
> Young people are often involved in this type of business. Dresses, skirts, negligees, cloth, lace, hats, silk stockings are all traded. They know that they will be tricked, yet need pushes them onwards and they take on all sorts of merchandise. A mass of men are engaged in this destructive industry, and the upper classes are among the most skilful among them.[30]

Further on Mercier returns to this activity: 'There is an enormous trade in jewellery: among rich men items of jewellery are constantly being resold. Certain individuals have in their homes stocks of jewellery to rival the shops of the jewellers themselves: they're jealous and proud of this honourable reputation.'[31] Mercier sees the origins of this circulation of luxury goods between individuals lying in the rapid tempo of changing fashions and in the need to possess several versions of certain objects like snuff-boxes and items of jewellery.[32] In this he agrees with Georg Simmel's analyses which have recently been supported by Carlo Poni's work on the strategies employed by silk merchants in Lyons.[33]

This circulation is generated both by fashion's need to renew itself and by a basic need for money, whether it be to help to acquire the latest stylish objects or for other reasons entirely. The fact remains that jewellery and fashion items circulated as though they were paper money, except that their drop in value was significant and rapid. Those working in the clothing industry were all caught up in this financial circulation, which was essentially usurious given the huge drop in value once an item had been sold on once. The importance of this market can be seen in the numeric division between occupations in the clothing industry: those involved in the production of new clothes around 1725 totalled 3,500 tailors and dressmakers compared with 700 secondhand clothes dealers, as many linen sellers, and between 6,000 and 7,000 *revendeuses*.[34]

Pawning goods

In working-class urban milieux, people pawned objects incessantly when there was no work. This practice is particular to social groups and economies which are too poor to support an economy in which risk can be measured over time; the fragility of their existence forces them to live an unpredictable economy where only the present matters. Pawning which is a sale disguised in a loan is therefore one of the most important financial tools in these economies.

Because this private sector of the economy was extremely active and powerful and more often than not was controlled by the biggest merchants and financiers, it was very difficult for official pawnshops to become established in France. All attempts to set up pawnshops in France – despite the fact that people such as Colbert were in favour of them – failed until the end of the 1770s.[35] At this point the increase in pauperism and the pressure from a group of bankers and politicians who, like Necker, believed in the need for cheap credit and felt that this way of helping the poor was more effective than charity, enabled the creation on 9 December 1777 of the Paris pawnshop.[36] Its success was immediate. Three months later the crowds were such that it was necessary to increase the size of the shops and create several divisions.[37] In fact, the pawnshop was the only institution that enabled the poor to resist the financial practices of private intermediaries who played on lack and necessity.

Let us turn once again to Louis Sébastien Mercier who was present at the opening of this pawnshop:

Nothing better demonstrates how much the capital needed this lombard than the never-ending crowds of applicants. Such peculiar and incredible tales are told that I dare not set them down here without first having sought more precise information which will allow me to guarantee their veracity. There is talk of *forty barrels filled with gold watches*, doubtless to express the prodigious quantities which have been deposited. What I know for sure is that I have seen between 60 and 80 people waiting their turn there, each one come to borrow not more than *six livres*. One was carrying his shirts, another a piece of furniture, another what remained of a wardrobe, and another his shoe buckles, an old picture, some poor clothes, and so forth. They say that there is a new crowd there almost every day, and this gives a very clear idea of the extreme shortage of money from which most of the city is suffering . . .

Rich people borrow as well as the poor. One woman gets out of her carriage, wrapped up in her coat, and deposits 25,000 francs worth of diamonds so that she can go gambling in the evening. Another takes off her petticoat and asks for the price of a loaf of bread . . .

We are assured that a third of the effects are not collected: a further proof of the strange shortage of cash. The sales which take place offer many luxury goods at low prices, which may harm the smaller merchants somewhat. But besides this it is no bad thing that these goods, which were excessively highly priced, should now experience a drop in their phenomenal rates.

It is said that the system is already being abused. The poor are bullied, and the objects offered by the destitute are estimated at too low a price, which means that they are being offered virtually no help. Charity should be the driving force and should be more important than other superficial and vain considerations. It would not be hard to turn this establishment into a *temple of mercy*, generous, active and compassionate. The good work has begun: why should it not be completed in a way which will satisfy the poorest people most?[38]

The letters patent of 9 December 1777 set the loans at four-fifths of the value, measured by weight, of gold and silver; and two-thirds of the estimated value for other objects. The right of the state to retain 2 deniers per livre per month for administrative expenses implicitly capped the interest rates on the loans at 10 per cent. Three livres was the minimum amount which could be borrowed.[39] The Parisian pawnshop appears to have acted as a bank for the Parisian artisanal classes, as the nature of the objects pawned and the smallness of the loans attests. Of the 600,000 loans made in a year, 550,000, ranging from 3 to 24 livres, incurred expenses which were higher than the value of the object.[40] Four divisions of the establishment, each accepting nearly 80,000 articles worth around a million livres, were set aside for clothes, linen, cloth, and fabric remnants. More valuable objects were pawned in three further divisions. Diamonds, jewellery, lace and brand new items were covered by the first of these. In 1789 the total value of the loans for the 52,221 objects of this type pawned was 7,630,667 livres. Figures such as these justify Mercier's claims that the wealthy borrowed just as much as the poor did. Silverware, watches, bronzes, buckles, swords and pictures were pawned in the second division, which was very popular, recording 89,641 articles worth 5,420,145 livres. On 26 August 1783 alone 139 gold watches were deposited. Of the 1,500,000 livres in sales in 1788, 600,000 was made from the clothes of the poor, 300,000 from silverware, 200,000 from watches, 200,000 from jewellery and only 200,000 from merchandise.[41]

In January 1789 in his 'Mémoire sur les calamités de l'hiver 1788–1789', Desbois de Rochefort attributed the unemployment in the watchmaking industry in part to the pawnshop sales; and in the complaint books the merchants who sold feathered fashion accessories also bemoaned the competition posed by the pawnshops. Observations made by employees of the pawnshop enable us to qualify these accusations as they show that it was often the merchants themselves who pawned items, and this claim is backed up by remarks made by the pawn-shop evaluators in their 'Observations sur le Mont-de-Piété' published in 1790. Once again Mercier is right when he says that the establishment of the Parisian pawnshop caused the price of diamonds and luxury goods to fall, which delights him even if 'the smaller merchants suffered a little because of it'.[42]

The activity of the Parisian pawnshop also provokes questions about the enthusiasm of the ordinary people for the gold watches and jewellery which appear in inventories drawn up after a death: their presence may not be explained solely in terms of their usefulness or a desire to imitate the upper classes – they were also valuable objects which were easily turned into cash.[43] On the same morning in 1788, two midwives, a wine merchant and a tailor, amongst others, passed before the estimators at the pawnshop and had their gold watch valued at 84 livres; then a cobbler with silver buckles for which he got 32 livres; a jeweller with a clock for 252 livres; and a middle-class woman from the rue d'Argenteuil who deposited 150 livres worth of silverware. A carpenter brought a seven-volume set of Voltaire's works; a dancer from the Délassements-Comiques pawned his theatre costumes; someone else deposited four pictures estimated at 260 livres, and so forth.[44]

The operation of the pawnshop – and of the numerous organisations offering similar loans – demonstrates how important it is to locate the act of buying and selling objects not only in a symbolic economy but also within the real workings and the constraints of the day-to-day economy: in the eighteenth century money was scarce, work and life precarious and financial institutions were heavily involved with merchandise.

Notes

1. Carolyn Sargentson, *Merchants and Luxury Markets. The Marchands Merciers of Eighteenth-Century Paris* (London, 1996), p. 66. Robert M. Isherwood, *Farce and Fantasy: Popular Entertainment in Eighteenth-century Paris* (Oxford, 1986). Mickael Szanto, 'Liberatus artibus restituta. La foire Saint-Germain et le commerce des tableaux. De l'échoppe Goetkindt aux loges Valdor (1600–1660)', *Economia e Arte Secc. XIII-XVIII, Istituto Internazionale Di Storia Economica 'F. Datini'*. Prato, 33, 2002, pp. 149–86.
2. Louis Sébastien Mercier, *Tableau de Paris*, text edited by Jean-Claude Bonnet, 2 vols (Paris, 1994), p. 1088.
3. Saint-Lambert, 'Luxe', in Denis Diderot and Jean Le Rond d'Alembert, eds, *Encyclopédie, ou Dictionnaire raisonné des sciences, des arts, et des métiers* (Paris, 1751–65), 9, 764.
4. Cissie Fairchild, 'The Production and Marketing of Populuxe Goods in Eighteenth-century Paris,' in *Consumption and the World of Goods*, John Brewer and Roy Porter eds. (London, 1993), pp. 228–48, p. 242.
5. Louis Sébastien Mercier, *Le Nouveau Paris*, Etalages, pp. 1212–14. Surveys around 1680–1700 recorded the population of Paris as between 400,000 and 500,000 people; around 1750 this would have been close to 600,000, and it exceeded the 700,000 mark just before the Revolution. Daniel Roche, *La Culture des apparences* (Paris, 1989), p. 71 and *Le Peuple de Paris* (Paris, 1981), pp. 254–6.
6. Pierre Verlet, 'Le commerce des objets d'art et les marchands merciers à Paris au XVIIIe siècle', *Annales ESC*, (1958), XII, pp. 10–29, pp. 15–17; Jean Hillairet, *Dictionnaire Historique des rues de Paris*, 2 vols (Paris, 1963). Carolyn Sargentson, *Merchants and Luxury Markets*; Claire Walsh, 'Shopping in Early-Modern London c. 1660–1800,' PhD thesis European University Institute, 2001.
7. Sargentson, *Merchants and Luxury Markets*, pp. 18–20.
8. Laurence Fontaine, *History of Pedlars in Europe* (Cambridge, 1996).
9. Archives de la Seine, D5 B6 889. As well as the fabrics which constituted his core business, in the 1780s, Jean Baptiste Duport the elder sold a number of gold watches for around 175 or 200 livres – 60 livres for silver ones – and some cardboard snuffboxes. Similarly Cahen – who left a 15-page notebook detailing his purchases, sales and expenses in 1770, a year in which he planned to travel as far as Poland – bought and sold calico handkerchieves, watches, gloves and small items of jewellery. Bookselling pedlars also always added watches to their wares. Archives de la Seine D5 B6 592, account book belonging to Gilles Noël, a bookselling pedlar, who also sold gold watches from Geneva for 300 and 280 livres, and repeater watches with gold cases from Paris for 312 livres.
10. Fontaine, *History of Pedlars*. Hélène Viallet, *Les Alpages et la vie d'une communauté montagnarde: Beaufort du moyen âge au XVIIIe siècle*, Mémoires et Documents publiés par l'Académie Salésienne vol. 99, Documents d'ethnologie régionale, n° 15, 1993.
11. For more details see Laurence Fontaine, 'Pierre Rullier colporteur horloger-bijoutier savoyard au XVIIIe siècle', in *Quand la Montagne aussi a une Histoire. Mélanges offerts à Jean-François Bergier*, Martin Körner and François Walter, eds. (Berne, 1996), pp. 167–75.
12. This is the range of prices and quality which we have been able to ascertain. Rullier sold a gold repeater watch with an enamel portrait of a figure, a diamond hoop and a

diamond push button for 1,230 livres; a gold repeater watch for 475 livres; engraved gold watches for between 160 and 200 livres; gold watches for between 182 and 123 livres; silver watches for between 90 and 60 livres; a gold chain for 200 livres; and other silver ones for which he hoped to get 120 livres. Alongside these jewellery watches he also had six watches with spring mechanisms from Paris which he'd bought for 12 livres, and 45 'non-gold' watches which he'd acquired for 406 livres 10 sols, which puts watches at scarcely more than 9 livres each. Finally there is an enigmatic reference to two watches for 4 livres. For more information on repeater watches, see David S. Landes, *Revolution in Time. Clocks and the Making of the Modern World* (Cambridge, 1983).

13. There are many terms in French for 'secondhand dealers' – *brocanteur, revendeur*, etc. – and not enough English equivalents, so I have chosen to keep their terms in the original French, since they are later defined. ('Seller on', or even 'seller', would not be appropriate in English.) Note of the translator.

14. Fairchild, p. 237. Steven L. Kaplan, 'Les corporations, les "faux-ouvriers", et "le faubourg St Antoine au XVIIIe siècle"', *Annales ESC* (1988), pp. 353–78, and 'Les "faux ouvriers" de Paris au XVIIIe siècle', in *La France d'ancien régime: Etudes réunies en l'honneur de Pierre Goubert*, vol. 1 (Toulouse, 1984), pp. 325–31. Michael Sonenscher, *Work and Wages: Natural Law, Politics and the Eighteenth-century French Trades* (Cambridge, 1989). Raymonde Monnier, *Le faubourg Saint Antoine (1789–1817)* (Paris, 1981), pp. 49–81.

15. Fairchild, pp. 240–1.

16. Roche, *La Culture des apparences*, pp. 318–19.

17. *Ibid.*, pp. 313–45. For more information on secondhand clothes dealers who specialised in clothes from the court, see Sargentson, *Merchants and Luxury Markets*, pp. 106–7.

18. Mercier, *Tableau de Paris*, vol. 2, pp. 109–11; Sargentson, *Merchants and Luxury Markets*, p. 32.

19. Mercier, *Tableau de Paris*, vol. 2, p. 312.

20. Mercier, *Tableau de Paris*, vol. 1, pp. 808–9.

21. See also Annie Becq, 'Artistes et marché', in *La Carmagnole des Muses. L'homme de lettres et l'artiste dans la Révolution*, Jean-Claude Bonnet ed. (Paris, 1988), pp. 81–95.

22. Carolyn Sargentson, *Merchants and Luxury Markets*, pp. 32–3.

23. Francis Freundlich, *Le Monde du jeu a Paris (1715–1800)* (Paris, 1995).

24. Mercier, *Tableau de Paris*, vol. 1, p. 392.

25. *Idem*, p. 392, note 1.

26. Jacques Savary des Bruslons, *Dictionnaire universel de commerce, d'histoire naturelle et des Arts et Métiers*, 5 vols. Copenhagen, 1759. Art. *revendeur, revendeuse*.

27. Roche, *La Culture des apparences*, p. 336.

28. *Ibid.*, pp. 336–7.

29. Louis Sébastien Mercier, *Tableau de Paris*, vol. 1, ch. DLIII, Courtiers, vol. 2, pp. 57–60.

30. Mercier, *Tableau de Paris*, vol. 1, pp. 365–6.

31. *Ibid.*, p. 415.

32. 'Such as different snuff boxes for summer and winter; the former light, the latter heavy, and which have to be changed every day. This is how one knows [recognises] a man of taste. One is excused from having a library, a natural history collection and pictures if one has 300 boxes and as many rings'. *Ibid.*

33. Georg Simmel, 'Fashion', originally published in *International Quarterly*, 10, 1904 – Georg Simmel, *On Individuality and Social Forms. Selected Writings*, edited with an introduction by D.N. Levine (Chicago, 1971) pp. 294–323; Charles F. Sabel and Jonathan Zeitlin, 'Historical Alternatives to Mass Production: Politics, Markets and Technology in Nineteenth-Century Industrialisation', *Past and Present* 108 (1985) pp. 133–76; Carlo Poni demonstrates how silk merchants exploited this inherent characteristic of fashion: 'Fashion as flexible production: the strategies of the Lyon silk merchants in the eighteenth century', in *Worlds of Production: Flexibility and Mass Production in Western Industrialisation*, Charles F. Sabel and Jonathan Zeitlin eds. (Cambridge, 1997) pp. 37–74. See also Sargentson, *Merchants and Luxury Markets*, ch. 5, p. 97f.

34. Roche, *La Culture des apparences*, pp. 328 and 344.
35. Yannick Marek, 'Au carrefour de l'économique et du social: l'histoire du mont-de-piété de Rouen (1778–1923)', *Le Mouvement social*, n° 116, 1981, pp. 70–1 et *Le 'clou' rouennais des origines à nos jours (1778–1982) du Mont de piété au Crédit municipal. Contribution à l'histoire de la pauvreté en province* (Rouen, 1983). Jean-Pierre Gutton, 'Lyon et le crédit populaire sous l'ancien régime : les projets de monts-de-piété', in *Studi in memoria di Federigo Melis*, vol. IV, Giannini Editore (1978), pp. 147–54.
36. Marek, p. 70.
37. In 1783, there were 406,428 articles worth 16.5 million livres (16,659,733); in 1787, there were a further 70,000 (477,666) worth 18 million (18,212,019). In 1780, there were 50 employees; in 1782, 60; in 1787, 84. In 1789 the great upheaval of the two previous winters required 7 warehouse men, 82 pawnbrokers, and 88 clerks which, added to those managing it, made a total of 194 officials. Robert Bigo, 'Aux origines du Mont de Piété parisien', *Annales d'histoire économique et sociale* (1932), pp. 113–26, p. 118.
38. Mercier, *Tableau de Paris*, vol. 1, pp. 662–4.
39. Bigo, p. 121.
40. *Ibid*.
41. Bigo, pp. 121–5.
42. Mercier, *Tableau de Paris*, pp. 662–3.
43. In Paris in 1700 13 per cent of servants and 5 per cent of wage-earners owned a watch. Watches spread rapidly throughout the eighteenth century and, in the 1780s, 70 per cent of inventories relating to servants mention them, as do 32 per cent relating to wage-earners. Roche, *Le Peuple de Paris*, p. 226. Initially it was cheap watches which people bought (27.1 per cent in 1725 and 17.2 per cent in 1785), but the major phenomenon was the lightning increase in ownership of gold watches (7.1 per cent in 1725 compared with 54.7 per cent in 1785). The same trend can be observed for jewellery, and the number of inventories in which they figured rose from 49.2 per cent in 1725 to 78.1 per cent in 1785. Fairchilds, p. 230. The fall in the number of cheap watches should be approached carefully: it might simply mean that they were no longer considered by many as being worthy of recording in an inventory. Fairchild, *ibid*.
44. Bigo, p. 124.

Plate

9. 'The Modiste'. Ascribed to François Boucher.

7

Custom or Consumption? Plebeian Fashion in Eighteenth-Century England

John Styles

Bread, cheese, butter, meat and potatoes: the '5 principel Things that poor Peple want to bye,' asserted an anonymous threatening letter received at Lewes in Sussex during the famine year of 1800.[1] Although the precise composition of the plebeian diet varied from region to region, there is little doubt that in good years, as in bad, basic foodstuffs represented the largest single item in the budgets of plebeian families in eighteenth-century England. But should we assume that because basic foodstuffs were the principal things that plebeian men and women wanted to buy, they were the only things that they wanted, or, for that matter, were able to buy? Did they aspire to purchase, or succeed in purchasing, commodities that we might usefully describe as luxuries?

There is currently a tendency among historians whose sympathies lie with 'those whom the consumer society consumed' to deny that labouring people were much affected by those changes in consumption that have been identified as comprising an eighteenth-century consumer revolution, and then mainly to their disadvantage.[2] For Edward Thompson, throughout the eighteenth century 'capitalist process and non-economic customary behaviour are in active and conscious conflict, as in resistance to new patterns of consumption'. It was only in the aftermath of the Industrial Revolution and its accompanying demographic revolution, well into the nineteenth century, that, according to Thompson, the 'needs' of working people were remodelled, the threshold of their material expectations raised, traditional cultural satisfactions devalued and the authority of customary expectations destroyed.[3] For Robert Malcolmson, the 'expanding culture of consumerism . . . was almost entirely inaccessible to the great majority of the nation's population'.[4] In a more technical vein, Adrian Randall and Andrew Charlesworth worry that 'the boundary line between the consuming classes and the poor may have been set rather higher than some of the more optimistic accounts of market penetration might presume'.[5]

Like almost all the opinions expressed by historians on the subject of plebeian consumption in the eighteenth century, these views are not grounded in substantial empirical work. Rather, their proponents assert a number of powerful objections to those meliorist interpretations of eighteenth-century England that have presented it as a socially inclusive 'consumer society', in which the labouring poor enjoyed increased access to what are defined as luxuries or conveniencies, as opposed to necessities. They offer three main objections. First, a straightforward denial of Neil McKendrick's influential claim (itself based purely on the views of polite commentators) that his eighteenth-century consumer society extended to many among the labouring poor; that 'the expansion of the market [for fashionable clothing], revealed in the literary evidence, occurred first among the domestic-servant class, then among the industrial workers, and finally among the agricultural workers'.[6] Second, a reassertion of the pessimistic view of the effects of early factory industrialisation on working-class living standards. Third, an insistence that any increase in the threshold of material expectations among plebeian men and women was incompatible with the continuation of their traditional customary satisfactions and defences.

This chapter intervenes in the argument between pessimists and optimists by considering the ways plebeian women and men spent on clothes in eighteenth-century England. Clothing is crucial to this argument because it was the element of plebeian expenditure most likely to embrace fashionable display. The capacity of fashionable display to provoke emulation has been a central element in efforts to define and explain plebeian luxury, whether by eighteenth-century commentators, or by modern historians. The chapter argues that McKendrick and other optimists have been right to insist on the capacity of large numbers of young adult plebeians to indulge in the pleasures of stylish clothing, although the evidence they use is of questionable value. The chapter goes on to argue, however, that such behaviour did not necessarily require these young plebeian consumers to give up the commitment to custom that Edward Thompson saw as the principal defence of working people against the rigours of the free market.

*

Custom and consumption were often allies, not enemies. Plebeian custom embraced the market as often as it resisted it. The customary assumptions and practices that ordered many aspects of plebeian life in early modern England were symbiotically entwined with the development of the early modern market economy. Often they flourished precisely because they provided opportunities and legitimising excuses to participate in attractive forms of commercialised consumption. As Hans Medick has argued, '[Edward] Thompson's work lacks an analysis of those quieter, but equally "communal" characteristic manifestations of the everyday life of the plebeian lower orders, which developed – to a considerable extent in harmony with the growth of capitalistic markets – in consumption, fashions and especially in drinking culture.'[7]

Even Medick, however, puts too much stress on the elements of resistance and picaresque 'irrationality' in everyday plebeian consumption, so concerned is he to distinguish plebeian life from the stereotype of an emerging, rational 'bourgeois' culture. Such cultural stereotypes, too often derived uncritically from eighteenth- and nineteenth-century models, can be profoundly misleading in the study of eighteenth-century consumption. This is true at every social level.

Thus the stereotype of the ultra-fashionable, gambling, spendthrift aristocrat, itself assiduously cultivated and disseminated in the late eighteenth century by the circle around Georgiana, Duchess of Devonshire and the Prince of Wales, entirely ignores those prudent and pious nobles whose sympathies lay with George III. Equally, the stereotype of the rational, calculating, self-denying bourgeois fails to comprehend the often ruinous expenditure on personal and commercial display incurred by many eighteenth-century businessmen.[8] In the same way, the stereotypical view of eighteenth-century plebeian culture, which presents it as collectivist, anti-individualistic, immune to economically rational calculation and overwhelmingly short-term in its time horizons, ignores the obvious variations of plebeian experience which grew out of differences of gender, age, location, and employment. Even among single adult working men, who were perhaps the group in the plebeian population most likely to fall into unpredictable, picaresque lives, patterns of consumption varied considerably.

At one extreme was Johnny Chapman, the pitman employed by the father of the wood engraver, Thomas Bewick, on the banks of the Tyne in the 1750s and 1760s. Bewick describes him, not unsympathetically, in the *Memoir* he wrote towards the end of his life as dressing in rags, living on the most meagre of diets and spending all his spare cash on periodic drinking binges in Newcastle.[9] At the other extreme were working men like the teenage William Hutton, in 1739 an impoverished apprentice stocking weaver at Nottingham, who spent two long years 'with a little over work and a little credit, to raise a genteel suit of clothes' and who goes on in his autobiography to plot the failures and successes of his late teens and early twenties in terms of his ability to accumulate clothes that were stylish by the standards of his peers.[10]

Not that we should conceptualise patterns of consumption among single plebeian men as a single spectrum bounded by these two extremes. There were working men hungry to acquire petty, fashionable luxuries like watches or laced hats, who subsequently discarded them with little concern for accumulation – many deep-sea sailors appear to have behaved in this way while on shore. There were also working communities which enforced limits on sartorial display. The buckle-maker James Gee, who arrived in Walsall from Dublin looking for work in the 1760s wearing a cocked hat that was smart by Dublin standards, was reluctantly obliged to conform to what he called 'the custom of the place' and wear a round hat with a brim that flapped down over the face.[11] Nor were these variations simple reflections of occupational or residential stability. It was the improvident pitman Johnny Chapman who enjoyed settled residence and employment, and the calculating, accumulating apprentice William Hutton who took to the road in search of material self-advancement.

What follows is an exploration of the clothing practices of some important sections of the young adult population between the 1740s and the 1790s. It indicates that the material aspirations of plebeian English women, in particular, were higher and more dynamic than the pessimists contend.[12] It also suggests how, at some stages in their lives, they might have enjoyed the means to fulfil those aspirations. But let me begin in the harsh final decade of the eighteenth century, with some of the most impoverished groups in English society – the labouring families whose budgets were recorded and analysed by the Reverend David Davies in his *Case of the Labourers in Husbandry* of 1795 and by Frederick Morton Eden in his *State of the Poor* of 1797. Both these men collected detailed information on income and expenditure for large numbers of labouring families spread across Britain, including information on clothing. The picture that emerges is a dreary one of shabby clothes made from coarse materials that were worn for too long. Things do not appear to have been so bad that adults were obliged to wear all the clothes they owned at once; most of the budgets allow for a change of undergarments, stockings and, in some of the more fortunate cases, outer garments and even footwear. Usually adults (although sometimes not their children) appear to have possessed all the basic elements that constituted a decent eighteenth-century English wardrobe, in contrast to some of their Scottish equivalents. But for a number of the families it was only with extraordinary difficulty that these minimal standards were sustained.

This bleak picture of the clothing of the labouring poor is in marked contrast to the generally positive impression of their dress offered by foreign commentators such as the Swede Kalm, the Frenchman Grosley and the German Moritz between the 1740s and the 1780s.[13] The immediately obvious reason for these inconsistencies is chronological. The researches of both Davies and Eden were prompted by concerns about deterioration in the economic position of the labouring poor in the 1780s and 1790s, as registered in the rising cost of poor relief. There is little doubt that the progressive rise in the cost of basic foodstuffs in the second half of the eighteenth century, which does not seem to have been matched by a corresponding improvement in wages in the south at least, meant that Davies's southern agricultural labourers were under considerable financial pressure when their budgets were drawn up at the end of the 1780s. Eden's budgets for labouring families were compiled in the war years between 1794 and 1796, the majority of them in the immediate aftermath of the devastatingly bad harvest of 1795. Many of his families faced a ruinous combination of unprecedentedly high food prices, falling industrial wages and reduced opportunities for industrial work.

There remains, however, another crucial consideration – the family life-cycle. Almost all of Davies's and Eden's budgets are for families, mainly families with large numbers of young dependent children. This was the first of the two stages in the life-cycle of the family when the balance between income and expenditure was at its most precarious (the second being old age).[14] As Davies pointed out, mothers with very young children were restricted in the amount of paid work they could undertake, even if it was available. Although children might secure some money income from the age of five or six, their earnings at that early age were very small. This, however, was a limited stage in the life of most parents. Between leaving home and marriage, the majority of labouring people spent a long period during which many of them earned and, at least as far as clothing is concerned, consumed independently. Usually this involved one of the various forms of live-in service or apprenticeship, with adult wages sometimes achieved for men by the age of nineteen.[15] Typically the majority of late eighteenth-century labouring children left home in their mid-teens, but the average age of first marriage was nearly 26 for men and over 24 for women.[16] Earlier in the century, the period between leaving home and marriage was longer still, because both sexes tended to marry later.

Savings and stocks of clothing accumulated in the financially independent years before marriage might see a couple through the first few years of child-bearing, but the need to support several infant children and a nursing mother who could earn little must have progressively impoverished many labouring families. Nevertheless, the heavy initial financial burden of young children began to reduce (assuming both parents remained alive) by the time the parents turned 40, as childbearing ended and children grew older. At this stage, older children and wives who did not have to look after infants could provide an increasing contribution to family income (assuming paid work was available for them). At the same time, some of the older children began to leave home (at least semi-permanently), reducing claims on family resources. It is the fact that most of the families in the Eden-Davies budgets were at or near the first trough in the family poverty cycle that accounts for some of the worst deficiencies in their clothing.

The pressure that infant children placed on family resources was not, of course, just a problem for labouring families. Detailed, long-term family accounts do not survive for eighteenth-century labouring families. It is possible, however, to observe the effects of the family life-cycle on clothing expenditure in the accounts of at least one plebeian family, the Lathams of Scarisbrick in west Lancashire between the 1720s and the 1760s.[17] The Lathams are the poorest family for whom long-term, detailed financial records survive from the period. Nevertheless, they enjoyed many economic advantages not available to the Eden-Davies families. They farmed a smallholding of approximately 20 acres on fertile land suitable for mixed agriculture in an economically expanding region; they had access to grazing and turbary rights on newly reclaimed common land; they lived in an area where industrial outwork for women was increasingly plentiful.

Families like the Lathams are usually identified by historians as part of that extensive middling sort that was such an important feature of the eighteenth-century English social hierarchy. There is good reason to admit them to that category's broad and ill-defined embrace, but we should not forget that the Lathams were far removed from its upper echelons and were in no sense wealthy in the contemporary sense of the word. Unlike most yeoman farmers, they did not employ permanent domestic or farm servants. Indeed, it could accurately have been said of them, just as it was of petty landholders in nearby Cumberland in the 1760s, that 'they work like slaves; they cannot afford to keep a man servant, but husband, wife, sons and daughters all turn out to work in the fields'.[18]

As landholders, the Lathams had a significant economic advantage over the Eden-Davies labourers, but they did not inhabit an alien world of goods. They bought only a very narrow selection of the small domestic luxuries that spread among the middling sort during the first half of the eighteenth century and seem to have become increasingly common among the labouring poor during the second half of the century. Their purchases included books, newspapers, tobacco pipes, and knives and forks, but excluded crockery and tea wares. In terms of access to material possessions, therefore, the Lathams lived a life which was probably no better than, and in some respects may have been inferior to, that of the hard-pressed agricultural labourers at the end of the eighteenth century.[19] Nevertheless, the Lathams were not a typical plebeian family. Their children were disproportionately female and most of them continued to live at home until they were relatively old. Between their marriage in 1723 and the birth of their youngest child in 1741 Richard and Nany Latham produced seven children who survived at least into young adulthood, of whom six were daughters.

The Latham account book covers the 43 years of their married life from 1724 until Richard Latham's death in 1767, including a period after the children had left home. Neither the amount nor the proportion of expenditure devoted to clothes remained constant. Richard and Nany Latham's married life, and their spending on clothes, fell into three distinct periods. During the first 18 years between 1724 and 1741, when their children were young and increasingly numerous, clothes expenditure was limited. The second period between 1742 and 1754, when the children were older and earning more, but still largely resident at home, saw spending on clothes rise dramatically, both in absolute terms and as a proportion of total expenditure. In the third period, after the children left home in the mid-1750s, clothes spending fell back. The focus of this chapter is on the first and second periods.

The experience of the Lathams in the first 18 years of married life was one of intense pressure on the family's budget that bore many similarities to the Eden-Davies labouring families. The early years of marriage and childbearing imposed heavy financial demands and placed considerable restrictions on family earnings. If a money value is ascribed to the cloth the Lathams made at home and is added to the rest of their clothes spending, their average annual expenditure on clothing in these years, at just over 50 shillings, was not very different from Davies's most pessimistic calculation for his Berkshire labouring families. Like several of the Davies labourers, Richard Latham appears to have owned at least two sets of outer garments during this period, but he can have renewed them only very intermittently. Nany Latham appears more abstemious than the labourers' wives in doing without new gowns, but like the adults in the labouring families, both the adult Lathams appear to have been able to acquire footwear and undergarments annually. If anything, Richard and Nany Latham spent less on themselves and more on their children than Davies's labourers. The cost of most of what the adult Lathams bought was low and they purchased virtually no petty clothing luxuries like lace, silk hats, patterned gown fabrics or fine linen aprons.

The second period, the 13 years from 1742 to 1754, witnessed a transformation in the family's spending on clothes. Their annual expenditure on clothing was on average three times higher than in the first period, a leap in expenditure that was funded principally by the Latham daughters' earnings as outwork spinners for the Lancashire cotton industry. The principal beneficiaries were those who made it possible – the older children. We can observe the change in the family's circumstances by examining purchases of two different types of clothing – gowns and accessories.

Before 1742, no adult gown lengths of cloth were purchased for Nany Latham or any of her daughters. Thereafter, as each of the daughters reached her mid-teens, gowns began to be bought. Between 1742, when Betty, the eldest daughter, was 16, and 1749, when she was 23 and had already been in service, she acquired four gowns on the family account. Two of these were relatively cheap, with fabric costing 7s 6d and 12s 4d respectively. They were probably working gowns made from a plain worsted cloth such as camblet at less than $16\frac{1}{2}$d a yard. The other two gowns were much more stylish and expensive, made from patterned cloths. Although the word is not used in the accounts, these were almost certainly her 'best' gowns. When she was 16 Betty acquired $11\frac{1}{2}$ yards of blue flowered damask, costing over 20 shillings, which at $20\frac{1}{2}$d a yard was probably a mixed worsted-silk fabric. Her plain, workaday gowns used only 9 yards of fabric or less, but a gown made from a flowered fabric required a longer (and more costly) length to allow the pattern to repeat harmoniously across the surface of the garment when cut out and assembled. Later, when she was 23, she acquired a printed gown costing 20 shillings, the fabric for which was probably either linen or cotton.[20] A similar pattern emerges for the next daughter, Sara, who acquired four cheap, workaday gowns, costing well under 14 shillings, and two expensive, stylish gowns, one of flowered damask and the other of a printed cotton or linen fabric. Gowns were likewise bought for the four younger sisters once they reached their mid-teens.

The change in the Lathams' clothes purchases after 1742 can also be observed in accessories and footwear. The increase in the number of accessories bought is easily illustrated by hats and handkerchiefs, which between 1742 and 1754 were bought much more frequently than before. In these 13 years, handkerchiefs were purchased in sufficient numbers to provide approximately one every 18 months for each member of the family, compared with approximately one every two years previously.[21] With hats, the contrast is even more marked. The family bought 30 during these 13 years, whereas only eight had been acquired in the previous 18. But it is the increase in the range and the quality of the accessories purchased that is most striking. Neither Nany Latham nor any of her daughters acquired any petty clothing luxuries before 1742. But thereafter, just as with gowns, when the daughters reached their mid-teens, they each began to acquire relatively costly and decorative accessories, such as shag hats, probably made from silk and costing between five and eight shillings, silk handkerchiefs and expensive white aprons made from fine fabrics like cambrick. It is only in this period, moreover, that there are entries in the account book for borders for caps and aprons, and for costly bone lace.

For the Lathams, clothing was a luxury in the technical sense used by economists. As the family's income grew as a consequence of the daughters' industriousness, so did both the amount and the proportion of family spending devoted to clothes. Appropriately, this new spending was led by the unmarried daughters themselves, whose purchases also embraced luxury in a sense more familiar to

eighteenth-century social commentators, in that they purchased stylish accessories and garments in addition to practical, workaday items of clothing. Yet it is
important to stress that the increase in family spending required to make all these
new luxury purchases was small, no more than an extra 1s 8d a week, considerably less than the estimated weekly earnings of just one regularly employed
outwork cotton spinner in the period. Relatively small shifts in family income
could produce dramatic transformations in material culture.

The Latham daughters were unusual in that they stayed at home into their late
teens and early twenties. Was theirs a typical pattern of expenditure and acquisition among young plebeian women? The evidence of female domestic servants'
expenditure on clothing suggests that it was. Service of one kind or another was
the experience of vast numbers, perhaps a majority, of adolescents and young
adults in early modern England. A status as much as an occupation, service could
involve a variety of different kinds of work, but for women domestic service pre-
dominated. Vast numbers of young women entered domestic service. Patrick
Colquhoun's 1806 estimate of 910,000 domestic servants in England and Wales,
of whom 800,000 were women, in a total population of approximately nine
million, may have been exaggerated, but it is suggestive both of the enormous
numbers involved and the sex ratio.[22] A large majority of these women were drawn
from the plebeian classes and were under 25 years of age; in general female domestic servants were expected to be young and unmarried.

Female servants (unlike their male equivalents) were not usually provided with
clothing under the terms of their contract of employment. They received payment
in kind in the form of accommodation, food, heat, light and washing, and in
addition a small money wage. How did they spend it? The records of Robert
Heaton throw some light on this matter.[23] He was a medium-sized manufacturer
of worsted cloth and small landowner who lived high in the Yorkshire Pennines
at Ponden near Howarth in the second half of the eighteenth century. For most
of the period from 1768 to 1793 he had two female servants. Turnover was high:
only three of them stayed with him for more than three years. This was normal.
Where Heaton was unusual was in keeping detailed accounts of how his servants
spent their meagre wages, probably so that he could settle with them for
purchases made on his credit from local retailers. With only one exception, all
Heaton's female servants devoted the bulk of what they spent out of their wages
to the purchase of clothing. Moreover, a majority spent more than they earned
and they did so by borrowing from Heaton.

Like the Latham daughters, their purchases represented a combination of the
stylish and the mundane. The most extreme was Alice Hutchinson, hired by
Heaton in 1781 at an annual wage of 78 shillings. In her first year of service she
actually laid out almost 102 shillings – a 31 per cent overspend. All but 10 shillings
of this went on clothes. She made 28 separate clothing purchases in that year,
including expensive, indeed fashionable, items like a muslin neckcloth for 3s 6d,
a silk hat for 6s 10½d with a paper hat box worth 2 shillings, and a new linen
gown for 20s 6d, as well as shoes, clogs, pattens, other handkerchiefs, a petticoat,
a shift, yarn for stockings and various kinds of cloth, including a length of calli-

manco for 7 shillings, which was probably used to make her a gown for everyday use. She went on to serve for another two years, continuing in debt to Heaton but none the less making yet more expensive clothes purchases, including another gown for 21 shillings, lace worth 12 shillings, a cloak, neckcloths in silk and muslin, and another hat and hatbox. Alice Hutchinson may have been extreme in the number of clothing items she bought, but the items she bought were not uncharacteristic, either of her fellow servants in the Heaton household, or of servants elsewhere whose purchases are recorded in the servants' books kept by drapers and other shopkeepers.[24]

Female servants' money wages may have been small, but like the industrial earnings of the Latham daughters, they were sufficient to provide a range of petty clothing luxuries. Like the Lathams, most of what they bought was new; they appear to have made hardly any purchases on the secondhand market. Of course, their little luxuries did not match either for price or quality the more expensive purchases of the daughters of the local gentry and a great gulf separated them from the clothes bought by those among the nobility who aspired to lead metropolitan high fashion. Nevertheless, the prices these young plebeian women paid for their more expensive gowns, for example, overlapped with the lower end of the range of prices paid for gowns by provincial women from lesser gentry, professional and mercantile families. In so far as the stilted descriptions of the account books allow us to establish, the young plebeian women's more expensive purchases reflected, albeit in a muted, limited manner, the broad trends of high fashion. (see Plates 10 and 11.)

It is not easy from the terse descriptions and figures of an account book to reconstruct the terms in which Robert Heaton's servants or the daughters of the Latham family understood their activities as consumers of clothing, particularly as purchasers of their more expensive and stylish items, those clothes which are repeatedly identified in plebeian and elite sources alike by the adjective 'best'. Yet both daughters and servants probably shared many of the concerns of the 16-year-old William Hutton while apprenticed to a stocking weaver at Nottingham in 1739.

> I was arriving at that age when the two sexes begin to look at each other, consequently wish to please; and a powerful mode to win is that of dress. This is a passport to the heart, a key to unlock the passions, and guide them in our favour. My resources were cut off; my sun was eclipsed. Youth is the time to dress; the time in which it is not only excusable, but laudable. I envied every new coat; I had the wish to earn one, but not the power.[25]

It took Hutton two years, but he did manage to acquire a best suit, and also a best wig and a best hat. 'The girls eyed me with some attention; nay, I eyed myself as much as any of them.'[26] For young adult plebeians, then, stylish or 'genteel' clothes could be a sign of sexual maturity, an emblem of material self-advancement, a means of sexual attraction, a currency in sexual competition and a source of self-regarding pleasure. There were also economic considerations. The romantic success that Hutton believed to flow from stylish clothes could eventually lead to marriage, without which plebeian women especially found it very hard to survive economically. A stock of clothes built up while single could see the owner through the impoverished early years of married life. Being well dressed was one of the criteria that might secure a privileged service in a more wealthy household.[27]

It was not just in sexual encounters or when seeking employment that clothing aroused feelings of respect and shame. Plebeian men and women felt a profound obligation to maintain a decent, respectable appearance before their peers in a variety of settings. Cheshire clergy in the 1778 visitation returns attributed low church attendance among the lower rank to their false shame or pride in not having decent clothes.[28] Significantly, parish vestries hardly ever provided paupers with clothing in the materials or at the prices that distinguished the 'best' clothes bought by the Latham daughters, Robert Heaton's servants, or the young William Hutton, although they might require paupers to wear 'decent' clothing on Sundays, sometimes of a slightly better quality than that to be worn on 'common days'.[29] The significance of these distinctions is confirmed by the fact that the 'best' clothes acquired by the young plebeian adults discussed here, particularly the accessories, were precisely those that bore the brunt of internal discipline among Quakers, who were required to avoid 'the world's customs and fashions in apparrel'.[30]

Yet to locate plebeian consumption of clothing in relation to the historical debates outlined at the start of this chapter, we need to look beyond the personal satisfactions and rewards stylish clothing might afford to those who could acquire it. We need to consider the circumstances in which those satisfactions and rewards were typically enjoyed. The visual distinctions between 'best' clothes and 'work' clothes were rooted in a fashion system that was an integral component of eighteenth-century commercial expansion. Nevertheless, the occasions when 'best' clothes were worn were shaped by a festive calendar that found its legitimacy in emphatically customary usage and sometimes had to be defended against attack by local elites.[31] It was above all on special days like Sundays, Christmas, Easter and Whitsuntide, at fairs and at hirings, at parish feasts and at harvest home that plebeian men and women, especially young men and women, were able to observe and be observed in their finery.

Towards the beginning of the century, Henry Bourne noted in his *Antiquitates Vulgares* (1725) that it was at wakes that the people 'deck themselves in their gaudiest clothes, and have open doors and splendid entertainments, for the reception and treating of their relations and friends, who visit them on that occasion, from each neighbouring town'. Sixty years later, young women continued to come to fairs like the one at Turton in Lancashire 'deck'd in the gayest fashion of the year'.[32] Indeed, wakes and fairs were occasions for the exhibition of plebeian consumer luxuries of all kinds. The radical weaver Samuel Bamford recalled that at Middleton wake in Lancashire in the late eighteenth century, it was the custom for the women of each household to make a display of their 'silver watches, trays, spoons, sugar-tongs, tea-pots, snuffers, or other fitting articles of ornament and value . . . and in proportion as it was happily designed and fitly put together or otherwise, was their praise or disparagement meted out by the public'.[33]

Fairs, moreover, were not simply events where best clothes were worn, but also places where they could be acquired. Retailers of cloth and clothing of every kind set up their stalls in large numbers at fairs, taking advantage of the crowds and providing them with an unusually wide choice of merchandise. Clothing also featured prominently among the prizes offered to the winners of the sporting contests that proliferated at fairs and other recreations. At Boughton Green fair in Northamptonshire in 1721, prizes included two hats worth a guinea each and six pairs of buckskin gloves, each worth 5 shillings.[34] The significance these customary festivities held for plebeian consumers of clothing can, once again, be registered in the attitude of the Quakers, who discouraged attachment to worldly show and were consistently hostile to attendance at fairs. Dorothy Garbutt was disciplined by the Thirsk Monthly Meeting in the North Riding of Yorkshire in 1797 for having two sorts of dress, one to attend meetings, the other for fairs and markets.[35]

*

The unfortunate Dorothy Garbutt was one of a large number of young plebeian men and women who, as this chapter has argued, enjoyed disposable incomes sufficient to acquire petty luxuries, especially clothes. Their choices as consumers of clothing suggest a set of material expectations profoundly influenced by the operation of the fashion system in the commercial marketplace. Yet these material expectations found fulfilment in modes of self-representation rooted in the customary calendar which ordered so many of the key life decisions – courtship, marriage, employment – of young plebeian adults. In the sphere of clothing at least, custom and consumption were not incompatible.

Notes

1. R. Wells, *Wretched Faces. Famine in Wartime England, 1793–1801* (Gloucester, 1988), p. 13.
2. E.P. Thompson, quoted on the dust jacket of P. Linebaugh, *The London Hanged* (London, 1993).
3. E.P. Thompson, *Customs in Common* (London, 1991), pp. 12 and 14.
4. R.W. Malcolmson, *Life and Labour in England, 1700–1780* (London, 1981), p. 149.
5. A. Randall and A. Charlesworth, eds, *Markets, Market Culture and Popular Protest in Eighteenth-Century Britain and Ireland* (Liverpool, 1996), p. 8.
6. N. McKendrick, 'The Commercialisation of Fashion', in N. McKendrick, J. Brewer and J.H. Plumb, *The Birth of a Consumer Society* (London, 1982), p. 60.
7. Hans Medick, 'Plebian Culture in the Transition to Capitalism', in R. Samuel and G. Stedman Jones (eds.), *Culture, Ideology and Politics* (Routledge, London, 1982), p. 89.
8. Julian Hoppit, *Risk and Failure in English Business* (Cambridge, 1987), pp. 71–2 and 168–9; also Daniel Defoe, *The Complete English Tradesman*, vol. 1 (London, 1745), chapters 10 and 22.
9. Iain Bain, ed., *A Memoir of Thomas Bewick Written by Himself* (Oxford, 1979), pp. 28–9.

10. William Hutton, *The Life of Willam Hutton* (London, 1817), passim. A similar use of clothing as a measure of personal advancement can be found in the autobiography of Francis Place; see Mary Thrale (ed.), *The Autobiography of Francis Place* (Cambridge, 1972), passim.

11. Walsall Local History Centre, 'The Life and Times of James Gee of Walsall, 1746–1827', unpaginated typescript, chapter 4.

12. The most comprehensive statement of the pessimist position with regard to clothing is to be found in John Rule, *The Labouring Classes in Early Industrial England, 1750–1850* (London, 1986), pp. 66–71, which covers a slightly later period than that addressed here. Based mainly on the evidence of contemporary commentators, it notes that little is known about actual plebeian consumption patterns.

13. P. Kalm, *Account of his Visit to England ... in 1748* (London, 1892); M. Grosley, *A Tour to London* (London, 1772); K.P. Moritz, *Travels chiefly on foot, through several parts of England in 1782* (London, 1795).

14. See Keith Snell, *Annals of the Labouring Poor: Social Change and Agrarian England, 1660–1900* (Cambridge, 1985), pp. 358–9.

15. Snell, *Annals of the Labouring Poor*, p. 333.

16. E.A. Wrigley and R.S. Schofield, *The Population History of England, 1541–1871* (Cambridge, 1981), p. 424.

17. The following discussion is, unless otherwise indicated, based on L. Weatherill, *The Account Book of Richard Latham* (London, 1990), a transcription which does contain inaccuracies; see the review by S. Harrop and P. Perrins in *Transactions of the Historic Society of Lancashire and Cheshire*, 141 (1991), pp. 234–6. In using the accounts for this chapter, inconsistencies within the printed text have been corrected, but it has not been possible to check the whole of the printed text against the original manuscript. As most of the inaccuracies are minor, it is unlikely that they have a substantial effect on the conclusions. I would like to thank Andy Gritt of the University of Central Lancashire for additional information on the Latham family.

18. *Gentleman's Magazine* (1766), p. 582.

19. For a pessimistic assessment of the material circumstances of agricultural labourers at the end of the eighteenth century, see I. Dyck, *William Cobbett and Rural Popular Culture* (Cambridge, 1992), chapter 5, and J.M. Neeson, 'An Eighteenth-Century Peasantry', in J. Rule and R. Malcolmson, eds, *Protest and Survival* (London, 1993), pp. 51–8. For a more optimistic assessment of their access to material possessions, see P. King, 'Pauper Inventories and the Material Lives of the Poor in the Eighteenth and Early Nineteenth Centuries', in Tim Hitchcock, Peter King and Pamela Sharpe (eds), *Chronicling Poverty. The Voices and Strategies of the English Poor, 1640–1840* (London, 1997).

20. Shopkeepers' inventories for the period 1720 to 1750 often include cloth described as printed linen and printed cotton. Occasionally printed flannel and printed linsey woolsey also occur.

21. Based on the average cost of the Lathams' purchases of handkerchiefs where prices are itemised between 1742 and 1754, the total sum spent on handkerchiefs, and the number of family members alive and resident in each year.

22. P. Colquhoun, *A Treatise on Indigence* (London, 1806), p. 253.

23. West Yorkshire County Record Office (Bradford), B149, Heaton of Ponden Mss., account book of Robert Heaton, 1764–92. For an extended analysis of this source, see John Styles, 'Involuntary Consumers? Servants and their Clothes in Eighteenth-Century England', *Textile History*, 33 (2002), pp. 9–21.

24. Hampshire. R.O., 96M82 PZ25, Account book of Mary Medhurst and Thomas North, drapers, 1762–81; University of London Library, Mss. 625/3, R. Flowers, grocer and draper at Westoning, Bedfordshire, Servants Book. It is not possible to reconstruct individual servant's clothes purchases as a whole from these books, because they must almost always have bought clothing from more than one supplier.

25. Hutton, *The Life of Willam Hutton*, pp. 96–7.

26. Hutton, *Life of Willam Hutton*, p. 101.

27. Greater London Record Office, MJ/SP, Middlesex Sessions Papers, 1699 Jan/46–7. Margaret Edwards, confessing to the theft of table linen, a spoon and two silver buckles, said she 'intended to dispose of the same to buy herself clothes to put herself into a service'.

28. J. Howard Hudson, *Cheshire, 1660–1780: Restoration to Industrial Revolution* (Chester, 1978), p. 47.

29. Essex R.O., D/P 30/18: Witham overseers miscellanea, /1: Agreement between the Parish of Witham and John Darby for running the workhouse, 1790, and /7: Orders for regulating the workhouse, 1726.

30. Brotherton Library, University of Leeds, Special Collections, Quaker Records, SE 2: Minutes of Settle women's monthly meeting, 1701–38, meeting of 7/3/1735.

31. For attempts to suppress fairs, see R.W. Malcolmson, *Popular Recreations in English Society, 1700–1850* (Cambridge, 1973), passim.

32. Malcolmson, *Popular Recreations*, pp. 53 and 86.

33. Samuel Bamford, *The Autobiography of Samuel Bamford*, vol. 1, Early Days (London, 1967), pp. 149–50.

34. Malcolmson, *Popular Recreations*, p. 57.

35. Jean E. Mortimer, *Quakers in Gildersome* (Leeds, 1990), p. 16.

Plates

1a Jan Jansz. Van de Velde, 'Still-Life with a Pipe-Lighter', 1653 (Ashmolean Museum). [Chapter 3]

1b Jan Davidsz. De Heem, 'Still-Life of a Banquet Side-table' ('*Pronk stilleven met ham*'), 1646 (Toledo (Ohio) Museum of Art. [Chapter 3]

2a Jacob Backer, 'State Dinner' ('*Regentessen van het Burgerweeshuis*'), 1633/34 (Amsterdam Historisch Museum). [Chapter 3]

2b Adriaen Backer, 'State Dinner' ('*Regentessen van het Burgerweeshuis*'), 1683 (Amsterdam Historisch Museum). [Chapter 3]

3 Pieter de Hooch, 'Two Women at a Linen Chest with a Child', 1663 (Rijksmuseum, Amsterdam). [Chapter 3]

4 'Matthew Bramble Recognises Some Ancient Friends', from Tobias Smollett, *The Expedition of Humphry Clinker*, 1793 (Bodleian Library). [Chapter 4]

5 *Bonheur-du-jour*, open, with marquetry of still life, attributed to Topino, Louis XV period (Musée Cognacq-Jay). [Chapter 5]

6 The same *bonheur-du-jour*, closed, with marquetry showing writing instruments (Musée Cognacq-Jay). [Chapter 5]

7 One of a pair of oval *bonheur-du-jours*, with marquetry of teapots and ware in the Chinese style, stamped Topino, c. 1775 (Sotheby's). [Chapter 5]

8 Lady's *bonheur-du-jour* writing table, 1765, tulipwood veneer on oak, mounted with Sèvres porcelain plaques and gilt bronze, by Martin Carlin, c. 1739–85 (The Bowes Museum, Barnard Castle, County Durham/Bridgeman Art Library). [Chapter 5]

9 'The Modiste' ('*La Marchande de Modes: Le Matin*'), ascribed to Francis Boucher (Wallace Collection, London). [Chapter 6]

10 George Stubbs, 'The Haymakers', 1785. All the women wear black silk hats of the style fashionable in the 1780s (© Tate Gallery). [Chapter 7]

11 H. Walton, 'Woman Plucking a Turkey', 1770s. Though at work, this young woman wears a printed cotton or linen bedgown and a cap in the fashionable shape of the 1770s, decorated with a silk ribbon.

12 'The Third State', plate 1 of William Hogarth, *The Analysis of Beauty*, March 1753 (© British Museum). [Chapter 8]

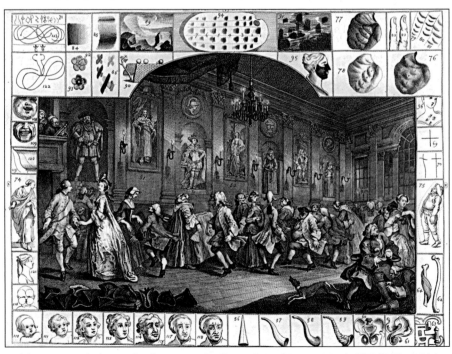

13 'The First State', plate 2 of William Hogarth, *The Analysis of Beauty*, March 1753 (© The British Museum). [Chapter 8]

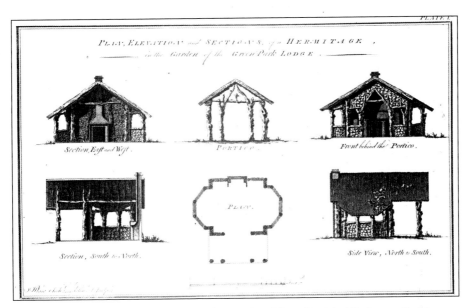

14 John Plaw, 'Plan, Elevation and Sections of a Hermitage', from *Rural Architecture; or Designs, from the Simple Cottage to the Decorated Villa . . .*, London, 1796 (The Winterthur Library). [Chapter 9]

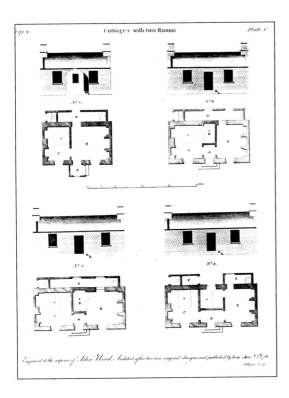

15 John Wood, 'Cottages with two Rooms', from *A Series of Plans for Cottages of Habitations of the Labourer . . .*, London, 1806 (The Winterthur Library). [Chapter 9]

16 James Malton, 'Design 7', from *An Essay on British Cottage Architecture*, London, 1798 (The Winterthur Library). [Chapter 9]

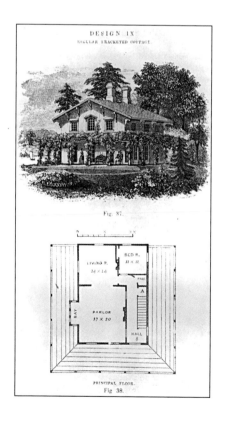

17 Andrew Jackson Downing, 'Design IX: Regular Bracketed Cottage', from *Architecture of Country Houses*, New York, 1852 (The Winterthur Library). [Chapter 9]

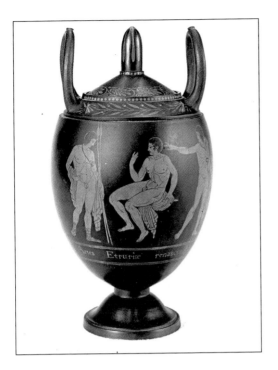

18a Wedgwood, 'First Day Vase', 1769,
the front showing figures (The
Wedgwood Museum Trust Limited,
Barlaston, Staffordshire). [Chapter 10]

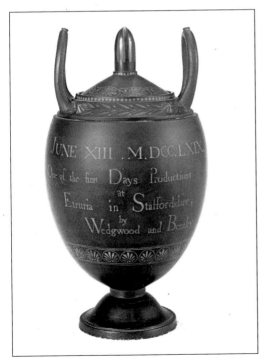

18b Wedgwood, 'First Day Vase', 1769,
the reverse showing the inscription
(The Wedgwood Museum Trust
Limited, Barlaston, Staffordshire).
[Chapter 10]

19 Boulton and Fothergill, *Pattern Book 1*,
p. 129, 'Designs for Tea Urns'
(Birmingham Museum). [Chapter 10]

20 Boulton and Fothergill, 'Pair of
ewers', ormolu and Blue-John,
c. 1772 (Birmingham Museum).
[Chapter 10]

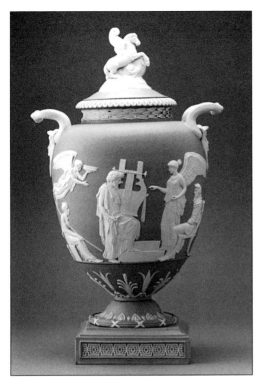

21 Wedgwood, Vase with relief of 'The Apotheosis of Homer', designed by John Flaxman, blue jasper, 1786, front (© The British Museum). [Chapter 10]

22 Benjamin West, preparatory design for a ceiling painting, known as 'British Manufactory Giving Support to Industry', 1791 (Cleveland Museum of Art). [Chapter 10]

23 'The Famous Roxana', frontispiece from Daniel Defoe, *Roxana: or, The Fortunate Mistress*, 1742 edition (Bodleian Library). [Chapter 11]

ROXOLANA, Solyman his beſt beloued wife. 7;9

Frontis nulla fides, nulla eſt fiducia formæ:
Pectore dum ſæuo dira venena latent.
Philtra viro miſcet fallax, miſerumq́ coegit
Sanguine natorum commaculare manus.

Rich. Knollevs.

To faireſt lookes truſt not too farre, nor yet to beautie braue:
For hatefull thoughts ſo finely maskt, their deadly poiſons haue.
Loues charmed cups, the ſubtile dame doth to her husband fill:
And cauſeth him with cruell hand, his childrens bloud to ſpill.

This woman of late a ſlaue, but now become the greateſt empreſſe of the Eaſt, flowing in all worldly felicitie, attended vpon with all the pleaſures her heart could deſire, wanted nothing ſhe could wiſh, but how to find means that the Turkiſh empire might after the death of *Solyman*, be brought to ſome one of her owne ſons. This was it that had (as we haue before ſaid) long troubled her aſpiring mind; and in the middeſt of all her bliſſe, ſuffered her yet to take no reſt. Noble *Muſtapha*, *Solymans* eldeſt ſonne, and heire apparant of the empire, although farre abſent, was yet ſtill before her cies preſent; his credit, his valour, his vertues, his perfections were all bars to her deſires: he was the onely cloud that kept the ſunne from ſhining on her; if he by *Roxolane plotteth the confuſion of Muſtapha.*

Ttt ij any

24 'Roxolana', from Richard Knolles, *Generall Historie of the Turkes*, 1603 (Bodleian Library). [Chapter 11]

25 Portrait of Lady Mary Wortley
Montagu in Turkish dress, attributed to
Jean Baptiste Vanmour (National
Portrait Gallery). [Chapter 11]

26 'An Evening View on Ludgate Hill', satirical print, 1749 (Guildhall Library). [Chapter 12]

27 'Exterior of Montagu House', watercolour (Guildhall Library).
[Chapter 13]

28 Joseph Bonomi, 'Mrs Montagu's Great Room, Montagu House' (RIBA Library). [Chapter 13]

29 Joseph Bonomi, 'Design for the Great Drawing Room, Montagu House, for Mrs Montagu' (RIBA Library). [Chapter 13]

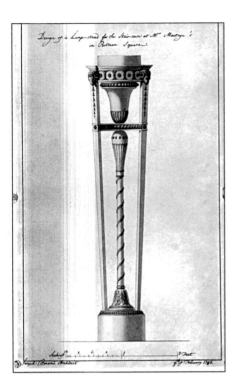

30 Joseph Bonomi, 'Design for a
Lampstand for the Staircase, Montagu
House' (RIBA Library). [Chapter 13]

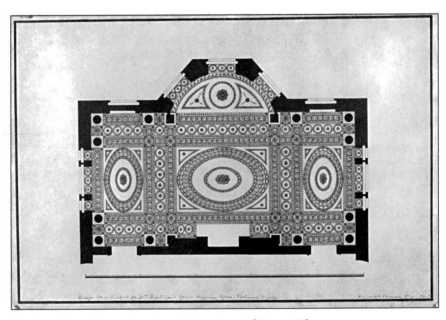

31 Joseph Bonomi, 'Design for a Carpet' (RIBA Library). [Chapter 13]

32 Ewer with the arms of peers,
porcelain with overglaze
enamel decoration and gilding.
China, c. 1730, height 20.5 cm
(Ashmolean Museum). [Chapter 14]

33 Porcelain dish with underglaze blue and
overglaze enamel decoration, depicting
characters from the novel *Shuihu
zhuan* (*The Water Margin*). China,
c. 1700, diameter 20 cm (Ashmolean
Museum). [Chapter 14]

34 Chair cover (*left*), silk and gold thread *kesi* tapestry weave. China, eighteenth century, 171.5 by 52 cm (Ashmolean Museum). [Chapter 14]

35 Silk panel (*right*), probably from a screen, depicting peach, bamboo, narcissus and fungus, embroidered in satin stich. China, eighteenth century, 126 by 46 cm (Ashmolean Museum). [Chapter 14]

36 Cope made up from sections of Chinese embroidered silk satin, late eighteenth-early
nineteenth century. L. 149.5 cm, w. 304 cm. By kind permission of the Deans and Canons
of Christ Church Cathedral, Oxford.

37 This Ecuadorian lady's dress consists almost entirely of lace and brocade. She wears many necklaces, pearl bracelets and elaborate earrings, while her shoes sport golden buckles. The black slave, who hands her mistress a slice of papaya, wears clothing of almost equal fineness. Her gold necklace shines prominently at her throat. Vicente Albán, 'Distinguished Lady with her Black Slave', Quito School, 1783 (Museo de América, Madrid). [Chapter 15]

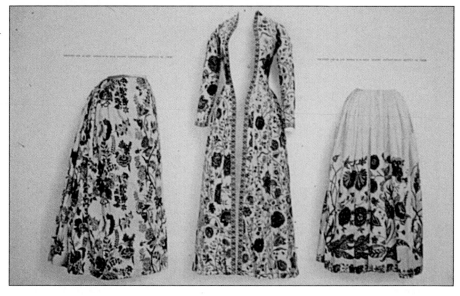

38 Skirt and frock of cotton, hand painted in India, made up in Europe (Bodleian Library/Arnold Publishers). [Chapter 16]

Col. Pl. 6. Cat. No. 112.

39 Chintz overdress, painted and dyed cotton (Bodleian Library/Royal Ontario Museum). [Chapter 16]

40 Chinese octagonal plate, *c.* 1736, with European Delft tile, used as a pattern, *c.* 1745, diameter of plate 22.8 cm (Sotheby's). [Chapter 16]

41 Saucer and cup with handle ('*Handle Chocolatettes*'), *c.* 1720, diameter of saucer 14.6 cm (Sotheby's) copied from European shapes. [Chapter 16]

Part III
Beauty, Taste and Sensibility

The essays in this part explore the relationship between luxury and aesthetics through the mediating concept of taste in its real and metaphorical senses. Here the contributors reveal the close relation between a history of material improvement and broader histories of education, taste and desire, tracing the profound relationship between visual and literary culture in the development of an aesthetic of luxury. In Chapter 8, 'From the Moral Mound to the Material Maze: Hogarth's *Analysis of Beauty*', Annie Richardson provides a groundbreaking new reading of Hogarth's polemical incursion into the field of aesthetic theory in the *Analysis of Beauty* (1753). The chapter focuses on Hogarth's definition of beauty as the visual pleasure produced by serpentine lines and curves, based on the material human body. Richardson observes that the *Analysis* naturalises, rationalises and validates contemporary, fashionable tastes and the practices of everyday life. This is particularly the case with the contemporary rococo style of asymmetrical curved ornamentation in interiors, furniture and dress. Richardson's lively readings of the conduct and dance manuals contemporary with Hogarth's *Analysis*, demonstrate that polite science is put in the service of the explanation and practice of taste in a way that allows the human body to meet a version of itself wherever it looks. A key function of Hogarth's book, argues Richardson, is to enable the culturally enfranchised reader to be 'at home' in the various worlds of discourse and practice he or she is called upon to inhabit.

In Chapter 9, 'From Luxury to Comfort and Back Again: Landscape Architecture and the Cottage in Britain and America', John Crowley explores the nature of domestic comfort more directly. He argues that physical comfort was an innovative aspect of eighteenth-century Anglo-American culture, arising from the discussion of the differences between luxury and necessity at the beginning of the century. Adam Smith's paean to the 'universal opulence which extends itself to the lowest ranks of the people' in the first chapter of *The Wealth of Nations* provides the starting point for a discussion of the history and uses of comfortable cottages, in which Crowley traces the links between sensibility and technology in the social application of luxury.

Finally, Jenny Uglow's essay explores the cultural history and significance of Britain's 'vase mania' of the 1760s and early 1770s. At a time of great political and social unrest the polite world became obsessed with classical vases. Uglow traces the classical vases' changing status, from fashionable craze to symbol of British craftsmanship as a whole. The British were proud of the manufacturers Josiah Wedgwood and Matthew Boulton, clear examples that modern industry could rival the greatest achievements of the ancient world. Uglow argues that the mass production of fine objects raised new questions about the nature of art, craft and originality. From the perspective of production or consumption, a simple vase could carry complex meanings. Affordable luxury lay at the heart of a new sense of national identity.

8

From the Moral Mound to the Material Maze: Hogarth's *Analysis of Beauty*

Annie Richardson

This essay investigates the luxury debates as context for one of the most challenging treatments of aesthetics in eighteenth-century Britain: the artist William Hogarth's *Analysis of Beauty* (1753).[1] Our understanding of the *Analysis* benefits from contextualisation, since it is significantly different from other texts in the field of philosophical aesthetics in eighteenth-century Britain.[2] It engages with its central concerns, but declares its opposition and superiority to the field, and reshapes its framework. The aim here is to elaborate on the nature of this opposition and difference in which the aesthetic values associated with beauty are grounded in the substances of the human body, and in a psychology which allows appetite a key role, as a version of materialism which makes particular sense in the context of the luxury debates.

To present-day readers of the *Analysis*, it will seem unremarkable that aesthetic values associated with beauty should be grounded in the body and its appetites. Yet the dominant paradigm for philosophical aesthetics in early eighteenth-century Britain grounds its aesthetic values in the divinely ordained response to the abstract qualities of orderliness in the universe, and to moral character in human beings. Puzzling to the present-day reader is why Hogarth has little to say about what a beautiful human body is like in terms of specific features, and yet has a lot to say about how a beautiful body stands, sits, gestures, moves and dances. In this too the *Analysis's* departure from the parameters of aesthetic writings can be understood more clearly in relation to the luxury debates.

The contention here is that aspects of Hogarth's position are shared with the modernisers in the luxury debates. In this context, the *Analysis's* materialism and apparent 'amorality', in comparison with the moralising project of philosophical aesthetics, can be seen as in line with those modernisers who sought to demoralise, that is undermine the purchase of moralism, in the analysis of social and economic change. Hogarth also shares attitudes compatible with modernising materialism with the writers of dance manuals: the celebration of the physical and psychological basis of the human love of variety and change, and pragmatic support for the human need for social distinction through the confident exercise of self-presentation.

Hogarth's position is not viewed here as a personal politics. The idea is rather to relate the *Analysis* to those broader positions on modernity with which philosophical aesthetics engaged, and which give the *Analysis* its underlying consistency. In privileging the perception of variety as the most significant constituent of beauty, Hogarth was identifying with particular notions of the modern, and consciously reversing the definition of beauty as the perception of uniformity amidst variety given by his implicit target Francis Hutcheson, in the latter's *An Inquiry into the Origin of our Ideas of Beauty and Virtue*, 1726.[3] Viewed in the most general terms, the employment of variety and uniformity in aesthetics drew on classical values, particularly immaterial ideal beauty, and engaged with the modern in other fields, particularly in moral and economic philosophy and the sciences. Debates in aesthetics on the relative value of variety can therefore be seen as contributions to wider debates about human nature in the context of modernity. The concept of variety had an important role in several influential fields of knowledge associated with modern thinking: in Newtonian theories of matter, in materialist psychology and the notion of humans as driven by appetites, a notion deployed by modernisers in luxury discourse, and in John Locke's concept of the mind and the imagination as containing 'endless variety' because it learns through observation and experience rather than through innate ideas.[4]

Several Hogarth scholars have already insightfully linked Hogarth's serpentine aesthetics to a sympathy with modernity as *mentalité*, based on engagement with empirical philosophy and with pluralistic, horizontal models of society.[5] Exploring the embeddedness of the *Analysis* in the luxury debates enables us to gain additional purchase on why and how variety, intricacy and serpentine curvature, the core constituents of Hogarth's definition of beauty, were chosen as the key values for an aesthetic of modernity.

Viewing the *Analysis*, the *Inquiry*, and other comparator texts in their discursive context and as vehicles for agendas connected to the representation of modernity, begins by recognising that philosophical aesthetics can be grouped, along with rational and natural theology, moral and economic philosophy and psychology, under the umbrella of the luxury debates. They register ambivalence about the effects of economic modernisation through debates about the legitimacy of hedonism and types of leisure and consumption traditionally associated with luxury. They are unified, not by their positions, but by their deployment of Lockeian sense-based psychology and a cogent new scientific model of man 'as a self-contained machine or physical organism, governed by a tendency to pursue pleasure and avoid pain'.[6]

This pleasure–pain model was supported by the authority of science to provide arguments about the pursuit of pleasure as natural, and therefore legitimate. When writers claimed that certain pleasures were basic to human nature, operating at a relatively primary, sensory level, entailing immediate responses to the qualities of objects, they could also claim the legitimacy and value of the pleasure and its objects. Representing beauty in terms of a mental match to aesthetic qualities in objects, that is, in terms of objective correlatives, tended to homogenise objects in the spheres of nature, culture and fashion, and to naturalise the pleasures in them.[7] These are the typical discursive moves in the legitimisation of leisure and consumption that we find in philosophical aesthetics.

A dominant moral-sense paradigm arose in British aesthetics through its engagement with luxury discourse and discomfort with the idea that self-interest was the basic human motivation. One of the acknowledged 'founding fathers' of aesthetics, Anthony Ashley Cooper, the third Earl of Shaftesbury, wrote on aesthetics only incidentally as part of his project to combat what he saw as Hobbes' and Locke's representation of morality as arbitrarily imposed by religion and culture. Concerned to set man's ethical behaviour on the sound foundations of natural behaviour at the level of the senses, he likened the moral sense to the sense of beauty and conflated ethical and aesthetic judgement.[8] It was Hutcheson's *Inquiry*, however, which developed the moral-sense paradigm for philosophical aesthetics as such. It was written to marshal Shaftesbury's moral sense against Bernard Mandeville's *Fable of the Bees* (1705, 1714, 1723), a notorious catalyst in the luxury debates.[9] Mandeville's provocation consisted not in rejecting the traditional idea that luxury was a vice, but in arguing that it was the inevitable concomitant and generator of general prosperity in a modern, commercial society. Far from being against human nature, luxury was rooted in human nature, conceived along the lines of morally pessimistic theology and materialist psychology: 'real pleasures', what really motivated people, was the gratification of material and social appetites with the pleasures of prosperity, power, self-interest and self-improvement.[10]

To replace this pessimistic view of human nature, and the representation of luxury as a necessary vice, the *Inquiry* separates rationality from self-interest by reconstructing rational man at the level of the senses. When man responds with sensory pleasure to uniformity, he is confirming his rational agency in a divinely authored universe which he has been constituted to preserve. Sensory pleasure, in the cause of knowing and preserving the universe, operates 'antecedent to prospect of advantage', 'antecedent to custom or interest', and the sense of beauty is very different from the desire for objects.[11] Consumption and the consumer of luxuries are rehabilitated: wealth and power are not ends in themselves, their end or purpose is the innocent gratification of a sense of taste for which property is 'of little consequence'.[12] Hutcheson's view of the appreciation of beauty in the body as reducible to the appreciation of moral qualities, reiterates Shaftesbury's immaterial, body-repressing ideal beauty, and rejects Mandeville's scepticism about politeness and the polite body as the means to disguise appetite. It is hard to overestimate the impact of Mandeville's views on self-interest, appetite, consumption and politeness on aesthetics. To represent morality in the context of modernity in a secular idiom which could claim to represent how people really were, aesthetics resorted to the same, increasingly prestigious, sense-based psychology which was being deployed to naturalise pleasure and consumption in luxury discourse.

The agenda of the moral-sense paradigm – to represent the gratification of a sense rather than wealth as an end of human behaviour – guides the argument of Alexander Gerard's *Essay on Taste* (1759).[13] This makes a further useful comparison for the *Analysis* since it acknowledges the *Analysis* and indicates the continued functional importance of rehabilitating luxury. While admitting that the connection between taste and morals cannot be proved, Gerard nevertheless acknowledges Hutcheson as the founder of the concept of taste as a 'reflex' sense, that is somewhat above the most basic level, and restates his arguments in attenuated form. 'Taste stamps a value upon riches, as the procuring its gratifications is the great end for which they are desired and the worthiest use to which they can be applied, the execution of benevolent and virtuous designs alone excepted.'[14] Through taste's 'innocent' pleasures, the mind is predisposed to moral goodness, and enabled 'to disregard the calls of appetite'. It can therefore only be perversions of taste which give rise to luxury.[15]

The *Analysis* does not represent the sense of beauty as antecedent to wealth, nor as part of a divine plan, of which there is only the most equivocal hint, where Hogarth writes of the response to beauty as 'implanted in our natures . . . for necessary and useful purposes.'[16] While operating with sense-based psychology and the pleasure–pain model, Hogarth's understanding of the sensory response to beauty is very different from the moral-sense response.

In the moral-sense paradigm, the perception of uniformity provides man with an ideal state of happiness described in terms of equilibrium and quietude. Arguing explicitly against the excessive weight Hogarth had placed on variety, Gerard writes that without uniformity boundless mental energy would produce 'fatigue, pain, no end to labour, bafflement and toil'. With uniformity, humans experience an ideal equilibrium between mutually mellowing 'facility and exertion'.[17] The psychological pleasure–pain equilibrium is thus also framed in terms which suggest class and occupation. By comparison, Hogarth's description of the pleasures of intricacy, a species of variety, is of an active condition of mental stimulation. 'The active mind is ever bent to be employ'd. Pursuing is the business of our lives; and even abstracted from any other view gives pleasure. Every arising difficulty, that for a while attends and interrupts the pursuit, gives a sort of spring to the mind, enhances the pleasure, and makes what would else be toil and labour, become sport and recreation.'[18] The hunting metaphor is likely to have come from Locke's own use of a hunting metaphor for the mind's pursuit after truth.[19] This pleasure in the process of inductive thinking contrasts with Hutcheson's rational agent at the final stage of deductive thinking, confirming scientific laws.[20]

Hogarth's concept of the pleasures of pursuit includes physical as well as mental stimulus, as is clear in his exemplification of the pleasures of intricacy, defined as a response to serpentine lines which lead the eye 'a wanton kind of chace' whether the object observed is moving or at rest.[21] The cause of the pleasure is identified with the movement of the eye, but, when Hogarth's examples move in rapid succession from a winding jack, to a stick and ribbon carved ornament, to the sight of a female dancer, the pleasure is heightened by more than eye movement. The bewitching woman is a stimulus-object in the sense in which the concept was elaborated in physics and psychophysics a century later, both a physical object emitting energy, and a social-emotional-libidinal event.[22] 'But the pleasure it gives the eye is still more lively when *in motion*. I never can forget my frequent strong attention to it, when I was very young, and that its beguiling movement gave me the same kind of sensation then, which I have since felt at seeing a country-dance; though perhaps the latter might be somewhat more engaging; particularly when my eye eagerly pursued a favourite dancer, through all the windings of the figure, who then was bewitching to the sight, as the imaginary ray, we were speaking of, was dancing with her all the time.'[23] For Hogarth, making beauty a sensory response did not mean it was different from desire.

Hogarth's dynamic mental and physical response to dancing bodies compares with the way the dancing master John Weaver writes about the psychological and bio-mechanical foundations of dance movement and its pleasures in his *Anatomical and Mechanical Lectures upon Dancing* (1721).[24] The bio-mechanics of 'easy' movement, that is, alternating tension and rest in the muscles, movement in alternating limbs, and relatively moderate flexion of joints, and the psychology of variety, 'the desire and love of change' make dancing as a heightened, extended and varied form of easy walking, both pleasurable and graceful.[25] Although variety is not an explicit aesthetic value for Weaver's concept of grace, it is implicit in his view of human psychology and the matching bio-mechanical body with its movements necessarily alternating, according to the laws of mechanism and motion.

Movement, sexual attraction and variety all appear in Addison's 'Pleasures of the Imagination'.[26] For Addison too eye-response is important. The eye responds to variety since this allows the travelling eye to lose itself. Addison's and Hogarth's journeying eyes are directly opposed to the moral-sense eye of Shaftesbury and Hutcheson which should not be 'distracted', and sees through matter, rather than being pulled across its surfaces. Although Addison used landscape examples rather than the body in writing about the visual pleasures of variety and novelty, movement was fundamental to the experience. His psychology of pleasure includes physiological processes of movement in the body: the healthy flow of 'animal spirits' affects mind and body, and such pleasure is heightened further when the object is moving, such as prospects with waterfalls or rivers. Hogarth mentions serpentine walks but has comparatively few landscape examples while most of Addison's are of landscape or literature. Hogarth's concept of intricacy comes close to Addison's description of variety and novelty. Beauty is associated by Addison with the physical body since he assumed that its purpose was to tempt humans to multiply. Unlike the moral-sense paradigm thus far, what Addison shared with it was insistence on the divine framework which made the human responses useful, and the multiplication of categories beyond beauty (novelty and the grand or sublime).[27]

Addison has a limited concept of beauty as such, as the physical response to the physical qualities of objects, particularly symmetry and proportion, and associates the novel and the grand with more powerful responses. Hogarth appears to have incorporated Addison's novel with its quality of variety and the active physiological processes associated with its pleasures, into his concept of ornamental beauty, and particularly to the body.[28] Gerard restated the category of the novel, perhaps partly in response to Hogarth's emphasis on variety, which Gerard acknowledged as correct but going 'too far'. Gerard's novel accommodated 'moderate difficulty', variety, intricacy and Chinese and gothic ornament.[29] Hogarth refers to Chinese and gothic as part of a call for greater 'latitude' in the ornamentation of buildings since the natural eye regulates the necessary amount of variety in any style. Thus *any* style can be beautiful.[30] It was clearly important to Hogarth not to multiply categories of aesthetic response, and certainly not to marginalise contemporary fashions and styles into the category of the novel associated with consumer behaviour in the luxury debates.[31] Hogarth wanted his theory to centre on beauty alone, perhaps so that its endorsement of fashions and the proliferation of styles beyond the Palladian would be all the more prominent, and the common meanings beauty has in discourses other than aesthetics, would be retained. In fictional and satirical literature the term beauty frequently referred to physically desirable women.

Hogarth's pleasures of intricacy and his dancing woman probably connected the reader to a very different world of discourse around beauty to that of philosophical aesthetics. He compared the response to intricacy to the stimulus of plots, riddles and the threads of plays, as well as to social dance.[32] In seventeenth- and eighteenth-century comic dramas, the country dance, a fashionable urban pastime which belied its name, featured commonly as spectacle and symbol. It frequently accompanied the announcement of a marriage and was used as a metaphor for marriage, courtship and sex. The complex floor patterns of country dances, seen to best advantage in the theatre from above, as Hogarth mentions, also symbolised the skilfully choreographed complexities and resolutions of multilayered plots, driven by a variety of modern, competitive, aspirational types and their sexual, love and financial intrigues. Beauty in these plays referred explicitly to women, desirable for their physical beauty and their witty verbal dexterity and cunning, attractive to their rakish pursuers since it mirrored their own, and the playwrights', most prized qualities. Their beauty was often referred to through a display of their dancing with the idea of their footwork and wit being equally 'nimble'.[33]

Philosophical aesthetics required objective correlatives. In the *Analysis* these are the waving line of beauty and the three-dimensional serpentine line of grace, more specific than qualities such as variety alone. None of the comparator texts refers to lines. Hogarth's insists on lines as the foundation of his definition of beauty. It is lines 'which serve to raise in the mind the ideas of all the variety of forms imaginable'. Hogarth's serpentine lines are 'principally concern'd' with the human body.[34] They match mind and body, object and response, and are associated with infinity and plenitude. Projected lines constitute models for the eye to traverse the interior as well as exterior contours of objects and envisage them in totality. Lines are basic, classifiable units, which make up the complex surfaces of all objects and are infinitely combinable into new ones. Represented lines are imagined as present, but are also literally present in the body, in the forms and substances of bones, muscles and veins. They occupy an interesting intermediary territory being both immaterial, as the product of thought, and material, as appropriate to an objective correlative. Where Hogarth suggests his easy method to produce a graceful serpentine gesture by chalking a serpentine line on an ogee moulding, we see how closely he wants us to see beautiful objects as having an affinity with human form.[35] This insistence on concrete objective correlatives in lines, and the body as an underlying, formative presence, is completely lacking in the moral-sense paradigm.

Discussions of the 'end' of taste in the divine plan are the *sine qua non* of the moral-sense paradigm, placed by both Hutcheson and Gerard at the end of their texts. There is no evidence in the *Analysis* of Hogarth having a teleological concept of an end for beauty. If we ask what more mundane sense of purpose for taste we find in the *Analysis*, it is self-presentation, and the legibility of the expressive body, which is the real subject of his final chapters. Did Hogarth view human mechanisms as ends in themselves? I offer the suggestion that as a materialist, Hogarth could well have considered body and motion as sufficient explanation, and thought, like Hobbes, that body and motion were primary terms which could be developed through geometry, physics and psychology, to construct the best if not the ultimate knowledge.[36]

Newtonian laws of gravity and motion were amongst Hutcheson's examples of beauty as uniformity. While rejecting the moral-sense paradigm, Hogarth does not reject the framework of using modern psychology and modern science to situate beauty in the modern world. In a rejected passage Hogarth made clear why he thought he needed to reshape the existing paradigm. His concept of beauty was not the natural philosophers' 'universal beauty, as to the harmony and order of things' but 'Natures more superficial beautys, of sportiveness, and Fancy'.[37] Although there is no scope here to correlate Hogarth's arguments with contemporary science in detail, it is likely that Hogarth's views were as informed by science as Hutcheson's.[38] Where Hogarth wrote about the wrong-headedness of the natural philosophers, he uses a labyrinth metaphor in a way which suggests that his preference for variety is based on an understanding of contemporary concepts of matter and that his superficial beauty refers to material beauty. He accuses the natural philosophers of getting bewildered in the 'labyrinth of variety' and ascending the 'mound of moral Beauty, contiguous with the open field of Divinity'.[39] What were the relevant phenomena in the labyrinth that they left behind? Hutcheson and Addison also referred to labyrinths. Hutcheson had written of a labyrinth of confusion and dissimilitude which would result from the perversity of finding irregular objects beautiful, which would work against the divine plan.[40] Addison had used a labyrinth metaphor to refer to the new worlds opened up by science: the infinite scope of planetary and microscopic worlds and the 'inexhausted fund of matter'.[41] Hogarth's labyrinth of variety refers, I think, to a modern, materialist reduction of the scope of scientific enquiry, to materialist concepts of matter, to the human body, in all its labyrinthine structures, and to its sensing and thinking processes.

Two powerful Newtonian concepts of matter, first forces of attraction and repulsion operating on indivisible particles and, increasingly after 1740, fiery or fluid aether substances, were being used in physics, chemistry and physiology to explain basic processes.[42] For some scientists, the same matter-in-motion processes appeared to be the basis of all organic operations, such as blood circulation and muscular motion, and even of sensation itself, as well as being involved in heat, fire or electricity. Since the few art theories Hogarth finds correct in defining grace are those which refer to flame and serpent forms, it is worth recognising how matter-in-motion was being represented in all-embracing theories of life processes which modelled them on the elasticity or fluidity of fire and electricity.[43] Body-matter was represented as animated at the microscopic level by dynamic recipro-cal motions conceived as similar to those in electricity and fire. It would not be an improbably huge leap from this representation of organic processes as flame-like, for Hogarth to be prompted to synthesise the serpent as symbol of desire, the flame form of grace from art theory, serpentine forms of human structures, and physiological processes also conceived as like fire in their motion.

Hogarth would have found the inspired neuropsychology of David Hartley's *Observations on Man* (1749) even more suggestive since he synthesised Newtonian wave-form aether vibrations with Locke's concept of the mind's associative powers to theorise the brain structure itself as modified over time into the wave forms that vibrated on it from the nerves.[44] Such mind–body homology would have been suggestive to Hogarth whose materialism also requires what happens in the mind to be closely correlated to the forms and processes of the body.

Hutcheson's and Hogarth's ambitions for aesthetics included producing a definition of pleasure that was a pleasure in a sense of self as ideally defined, and with reference to modern science. Hogarth's equivalent to Hutcheson's Newtonian rational agent is a holistically viewed, active, desiring, sensing and thinking agent, which took its cue from prestigious explanatory concepts of basic life-processes which appeared to apply to both mind and body. Given the excite-ment at mid-century in aether theory, and its identification with electricity in order to explain 'all varieties of phenomena', a wave-form might have seemed to Hogarth a way of representing sensation and thought diagrammatically with a form that inhered in the substances and processes of the body.[45] Criticism of Hogarth's serpentine line for being as formulaic as the mystical *je ne sçais quoi* concept of grace he aimed to replace, should at least recognise the potentially comprehensive explanatory power of wave vibrations.

Compared with the moral-sense paradigm, the final section of the *Analysis* im-plied that the 'end' of taste is self-advancement through impression-management. This is aimed at Hogarth's socially inclusive readership, for whom he takes for granted that it will be useful to acquire the ornamental body-language of the genteel, and to gain that other vital ingredient for controlling how others see you: self-confidence. The body is also legible in the moral-sense paradigm. The differ-ence is that in Hutcheson and Gerard its legibility depends on the judgement of the viewer and is assumed to be a relatively reliable procedure, whereas in Hogarth it also depends on the skills of its inhabitants, who are told to marshal every expressive resource at their disposal to appear good and genteel. The body is a theatrical body, a cultural artefact which needs to be fashioned into semiotic plenitude with the aid of facial expressions, deportment, words and actions. The power of the semiotically fashioned body simply defeats the artist and reader since the hypocrite can 'manage his muscles'.[46] While Shaftesbury himself, who found the theatrical body of the hyper-sociable personality abhorrent, acknowledged that the body had to be fashioned into a behavioural ideal of sociability balanced against reserve and self-control, Hogarth appears to encourage an unashamedly theatrical approach, with corporeal codes operating on a quantitative rather than qualitative scale of 'more or less noble'.[47] Hogarth's rationale for his polite body is the same rationale of self-advancement and the same concept of picturesque self-presentation found in the dance manuals.[48] Hogarth's concepts of the theatrically polite body come close to that in dance manuals: the ideal golden mean for postures which signify a golden mean of character, summed up in the term complaisance; a semiotically rich bending and twisting polite body neatly but paradoxically mapped onto the bio-mechanical body conceived as naturally 'a little bent' in the joints, for counter-weighted alternating motion.[49]

If the *Analysis*'s material and theatrical bodies oppose the moral-sense paradigm, so too does his functionally beautiful body to which concepts of interest, advantage and custom (Hutcheson's bugbears) apply. Hutcheson had argued that judgements of strength and proportion could not count as absolute beauty since they were mixed with notions of interest.[50] Hogarth directs himself pointedly at Hutcheson then, at the same time as addressing his inclusive readership, when he notes that everyone can draw on extensive experience, cultural knowledge and 'interest' in judging bodies as fit for tasks, as when even a butcher, familiar with boxing, who has an 'interest' in the outcome, could judge which of two bodies would win a match.[51]

The dancing body, which the *Analysis* presents as the ultimate in beauty, is thus logically ideal in Hogarth's framework, since it is ideal in terms of all three of Hogarth's categories of body: it displays the human machine in its most exquisite functional capacities, offers a symbolic and ornamental spectacle of visual and social intricacies, and is also the ideal vehicle for the display of the social self. In the *Analysis* the sense of the wealth of real, competitive, social contexts in which the body is judged, is powerfully present.

The dynamic nature of the experience of beauty, the homology or affinity of mind and body around serpentine form, concrete objective correlatives, the lack of embarrassment in the role of interest in judging and presenting the body, and of course the return of the repressed material and theatrical body are all ways in which Hogarth reshaped the moral-sense paradigm in favour of a materialist perspective. These key differences can all be given further meaning in terms of the luxury debates.

The de-moralising supporters of luxury drew on contemporary philosophy. They operated with a materialist perspective which saw wants of the body applying equally to 'wants of the mind', as Nicolas Barbon phrased it, so that senses demand rarities for their gratification. The senses hunger for luxury.[52] Mandeville expresses the idea of man as materially driven very starkly: 'man is skin, flesh bones, etc.', and 'a compound of various passions that . . . govern him by turns, whether he will or no'.[53] His passions – self-love, avarice, pride and shame – explain all of human behaviour. 'Getting real' in analysing human behaviour means including the needs of the body and making a parallel between mind and body, recognising appetite, desire, and vice, the real 'springs more immediately required to continue the Motion of our Machine', which compare with the 'trifling Films and little Pipes' responsible for the life of the body.[54] Echoing Barbon, Mandeville notes that the wants of man are innumerable so that excesses of luxury are required, no longer to be meaningfully distinguished from necessities. But these are not to be condemned as harming the constitution, like overindulging the body, since they merely meet the inevitable and natural appetites for 'refin'd pleasures' and reputation from the administrative, officer, and other quality sections of society.[55] Set Hogarth's variety within the discourse of luxury, and you are referred to the de-moralised, materialist view of man's infinite wants. 'The rich have a variety of dishes, several suits', hence all the employment they give to infinite trades, and the stimulus to emulation, says Barbon.[56] The representation of wants as infinite and self-generating makes luxury consumption, indeed, all consumption, a matter of variety in commodities.

Hogarth too operates from this materialist perspective on the motions of the human machine. His sense of beauty is not to be diluted with reflection, compounded with morality, or subordinated to the sublime. It is simply a sense, with no need for a qualitative or epistemological distinction between a sense delighting in the visual pleasure of ornament, in the female body, and in confident self-display. His sense is a comprehensive appetite for visual and sensory richness, and social status, like the concept of appetite held by Mandeville. Social appetites are natural appetites in Mandeville's and Hogarth's view. The moral-sense school allowed esteem to follow from concern with art. Hogarth, however, presents appetite for esteem as part of the desire for beauty. Unless we understand the conflation of social aspiration with visual and sensory appetites in Hogarth's perspective, the sections on controlling bodily self-presentation at the end of the book appear eccentric. One finds oneself wondering whether this is some sort of appendix for the socially inexperienced reader, and with what distant perspective from a past era beauty could be largely a matter of deportment. When we see how the power of all-encompassing appetite is used by luxury's supporters to de-moralise desire for ease, refined objects, self-esteem and self-display, and the link between appetite and self-interest, we understand how Hogarth's various 'bodies', the theatrically polite, the functional and the ornamental, can all be understood as beautiful objects of desire. For Mandeville appetite is largely male appetite, 'more violent and ungovernable' than that of women.[57] Courtship rituals therefore offer a particular instance of the intricacies of social behaviour in which passions are hidden, crafted into form, and the goal of multiple gratification is gained. (You get the woman *and* the self-esteem accompanying self-management.) If the *Fable of the Bees* itself were read for an aesthetic, then the intricate rules of social behaviour that both hide but gain gratification of the appetites would provide it, and Hogarth's male-centred image of intricate dancing would seem a highly appropriate example.

The materialist perspective attributed the concept of motion with great explanatory power, and not only in the natural sciences, since it appeared to correspond with the very evident mutability associated with fashion and social emulation in the modern world. Man was the creature of desire in the self-consciously modern view put forward by Hobbes in *Leviathan*. For Hobbes motion or uneasiness was 'the way the world (including mankind) is'.[58] Hence perhaps the dynamic flow of 'animal spirits' around the body in Addison's account, and his argument that moving objects give heightened pleasure. Hogarth's dynamic account of the pleasure of intricacy is also based on a materialist concept of desire as 'pursuit'. Materialist dynamism makes the country-dancing woman, and the spectacle of dance on the stage, a logical, over-determined choice for the exemplification of beauty in this perspective. The body is a machine in motion, the appetites of the viewer are reciprocally stimulated, and on stage the dances symbolised complex actions resulting from the freedom of modern appetites. Like luxury, dance was defended with a long-standing rhetoric of apology, which argued that it was damaging only if accompanied by excessive behaviour. Appetite and imagination, conceived in terms of the springs of motion in materialist mind–body homology, linked modern concepts of trade, money and fashion to an 'ineradicable fluidity' in Berry's memorably apt phrasing.[59] Materialist perspectives in science and economic philosophy found this a suggestive concept.

In luxury discourse the dynamic nature of pleasure was part of a modernising agenda. We have noted the contrast between Gerard's and Hutcheson's ideal states of equilibrium in which leisure appears to be contrasted with work, and Hogarth's and Addison's more active states. Mandeville's arguments for the legitimacy of varied types of pleasure equated the pleasure in ceaseless money-making of the capitalist 'Laborio', and the hard-working but profligate type 'Urbano', since getting and spending were part of the same capitalist continuum, whose *mentalité* needed to be established and defended. Mandeville rejected the way of life of the gentleman landowner, whose incomprehension at Laborio's pleasure is expressed through a hunting metaphor: 'but he that neglecting the Aim which can only justify his Labours, in the Pursuit of Happiness falls in Love with the Chase'.[60] Hogarth's 'wanton chace' also refers to the pleasures of pursuit generalised to cover work, the 'business of life', which 'even abstracted from any other view, gives pleasure'.[61] It is hard not to equate Hogarth's presumed reader with a Laborio who, unlike Mandeville's, could identify with the spirit of hunting even though he was unlikely to do it himself. For him, dancing was a more likely leisure pursuit. Concepts of pleasure as activity versus ease or indolence were used not only to express the legitimacy of certain types of pleasure, but also pleasure in the image of particular groups. Defoe celebrated the achievements of tradesmen and manufacturers, who lived from their own industry, promoted trade and were irrelevantly accused of luxury, with the phrase 'Employment is life, Sloth and Indolence is Death'.[62] Hume, in his argument for the moral neutrality of luxury, and for the claim that the ages of refinement are the happiest and most virtuous, defined happiness as having three ingredients: action, pleasure and indolence. He quickly dismissed indolence as 'only agreeable for a moment'. The mind is naturally full of spirits and vigour, with 'natural appetites'. When industry and the arts flourish, men are kept in 'perpetual occupation, and enjoy as their reward, the occupation itself, as well as those pleasures which are the fruits of their labour.

The mind acquires new vigour; enlarges its powers and faculties; and, by an assiduity in honest industry both satisfies its natural appetites, and prevents the growth of unnatural ones . . .' Both art and industry provide the pleasures of action. Hume believed the spirit of such an age put the mind into 'fermentation'. [63] Thus refined arts and industries inevitably accompany one another. As for Hogarth, the notion of the active mind underwrites the pleasure in action, the legitimacy of the pleasures of appetite, and the close relation between arts and industry, leisure and work.

Modernisers in the luxury debates attempted to defeat classical notions of fixed ends and limits. Equilibrium and the golden mean were attached to concepts of limits, and seen as incompatible with infinite wants. Hogarth refers to the concept of the golden mean as attaching to the 'precise serpentine line'. On the other hand, his description of the active mind's pleasure in the stimulus of the waving line, and his initial description of the three-dimensional serpentine line, suggest something more like a continuum. The serpentine line is represented as a part of a larger curved grid, which really exists for the imagination. As a fundamental constituent of the body's surfaces, and interior, it suggests endlessness or the plenitude of thought and the life processes. Human bones and muscles are 'a continued waving of winding forms' as in figure 64, plate 2 and figure 65 plate 1 (reproduced here as Plate 12).[64] To apprehend fully the human body, according to Hogarth, the mind's eye has to imagine a wire in an uninterrupted flow across the body's surfaces. It can be no coincidence, surely, that before demonstrating the presence of the serpentine line in the body, he refers to a horn and provides an increasingly rich series of imaginary lines going round a twisted and bent horn. He refers to this as a cornucopia. Horns were also symbols of the cuckold whom Hogarth illustrates on the right hand side of the main illustration in Plate 2 (reproduced here as Plate 13).

The serpentine line then is largely thought of as a part of a series, part of an experience of projection or gratification. The ash-tree ornament near figure 67 in Plate 1 is given as an illustration of ornamental beauty, designed to entertain the eye. Its placement next to the anatomical drawings reinforces Hogarth's point that the body itself is ornamental, inside and out. The line is both a symbol of the idea of gratification, and a fragmentary, diagrammatic representation of the chasing pleasure of the eye. The time-dimension is significant. Frédéric Ogée has suggested this relates to the effects of empiricism on the development of an aesthetics of modernity.[65] In the context of the luxury debates, the prolonged and subjective nature of serpentine pleasure, controlled by the projections of the eye but also invited by the richness and complexity of linear networks evoking the human body, relates to the power of unleashed desire, envisaged as a bodily appetite. Hogarth's frontispiece makes his line into a serpent with a serpent's head and places over it an epigraph referring to Satan's luring of Eve with a wanton wreath in Milton's *Paradise Lost*.[66] The temptation of Eve was certainly connected to Christian concepts of luxury as a cardinal sin combining carnality and desire for worldly power which, as Sekora shows, was almost always symbolised visually by female figures including Eve.[67]

The concept of natural limits was connected in traditionalist luxury thinking to the 'natural legislators' whose birth and wealth gave them the independence to judge the norms of taste. The presence of moneyed men in government suggested that the natural legislators were not those in actual power and that luxury was a contemporary threat to the nation.[68] Hogarth's vituperative attacks on the bigotry of 'connoisseurs', with their dogmatic mystificatory theory of grace as the *je ne sçais quoi*, false beliefs in straight lines, the canon as the norm of beauty, and art whose prices they want to control, would appear to voice from below a call for circuiting the natural guardians. Hogarth's address to the reader is a warm embrace from a practitioner, rather than the intellectual, to those open-minded consumers of his art who already practise serpentine aesthetics when they decorate their houses, accessorise asymmetrically, or incline the head, without thinking of these practices as principles. Hogarth presents the existing practices of the fashionable consumer, the non-connoisseurial everyman and his and her quotidian aesthetics as the basis and confirmation of his theory.

As we have seen, Hogarth differs radically from the moral-sense paradigm on the closely connected issue of being and appearance. Appearance should not belie rank and the appearance of those above should not be aped by those below. A typical if late statement of the anti-luxury, natural-legislator position on being and appearance runs: 'appearance in the vulgar eye passes for the only criterion of true worth; everyone is ready to assume the marks of a superior condition; in order to be esteem'd more than what he really is'.[69] In modernising luxury discourse self-improvement was a natural appetite, based on the love of approbation and esteem.[70] Hogarth's assumption is that his reader has invested in acquiring the means to genteel appearance. Interestingly, while Hogarth continually claims it is easy to judge art since a 'real connoisseur' need only be capable of envisaging objects in terms of his curved grid, he makes no such claim for deportment. His book can provide the 'confidence' of knowledge equivalent to the confidence of those with rank or fortune, but there is no short cut to genteel body language. Hogarth's ready equivalence between grace and gentility evokes the concept of skills as opposed to inherent qualities. As Sekora says of the opposition's abhorrence for Walpole and the moneyed men's statecraft as mere administrative skill: 'A skill might be learned by anybody, when to be anybody was to be nobody.'[71] The idea of managerial skills was used by Mandeville to describe the way most individuals control and manage appetites through the rules of polite behaviour, and control by government. Mandeville connects the two since the rules of politeness enable the controlled society, which politicians need, as well as the satisfaction of the individual's passions of pride and shame. Thus control of appetite in politeness itself stems from appetite. There is no alternative 'natural' behaviour, other than brutishness, for most people since pride and shame are such strong passions. 'The Rules I speak of consist in a dextrous Management of our selves, a stifling of our Appetites, and hiding the real Sentiments of our Hearts before others.'[72] Gratification of appetites is about hiding appetites and passions, rather than subduing them. Such pragmatism at the management of the polite body was shared by Hogarth and is represented vividly in plate 2 where the only thing the reader can say with certainty about the leading couple is that they are graceful and *appear* genteel. This representation of social dance, commensurate with its use in comic drama to point up the frailty and transience of the moral super-structure, also appears to endorse Mandeville's view of civilisation as a managed superstructure, beautifully coherent in spite of and because of the drive-directed behaviour of his egoists, but constantly subject to change and improvement along the lines dictated by the quality.

Notes

1. William Hogarth, *The Analysis of Beauty*, 1753, edited with an introduction and notes by Ronald Paulson (New Haven and London, 1997).
2. Philosophical aesthetics is recognised as a distinctive field of discourse which emerged in eighteenth-century Britain though it was referred to only subsequently as aesthetics. Its distinctiveness rests on its concern to define taste in terms of mental operations as represented through empirical sense-based psychology, on its production by intellectuals rather than by artists, in which of course Hogarth is an exception, and its agendas of secularising ethics and legitimising, separating, or sanitising relations between art, money and fashion. See Andrew Hemingway, *Landscape Imagery and Urban Culture in Early Nineteenth-century Britain* (Cambridge, 1992), Paul Mattick, Jnr., ed., *Eighteenth-century Aesthetics and the Reconstruction of Art* (New York, 1993), Walter John Hipple, *The Beautiful, the Sublime and the Picturesque in Eighteenth-century British Aesthetic Theory* (Carbondale, 1957), Preben Mortensen, *Art in the Social Order: the Making of the Modern Conception of Art* (Albany, New York, 1997), and Michael McKeon, 'Politics of Discourse and the Rise of the Aesthetic in Seventeenth-century England', in Kevin Sharpe and Steven N. Zwicker, eds, *Politics of Discourse: the Literature and History of Seventeenth-century England* (Berkeley, 1987).
3. Francis Hutcheson, *Inquiry into the Origin of our Ideas of Beauty and Virtue*, 1726, fourth edition (London, 1738).
4. John Locke, *Essay Concerning Human Understanding*, 1689, Peter H. Nidditch, ed. (Oxford, 1975), II.i.2.
5. Frédéric Ogée, 'Aesthetics and Empiricism: the Ideological Context of Hogarth's Series of Pictures', and Michel Baridon, 'Hogarth: the Empiricist' in Frédéric Ogée, ed., *The Dumb Show: Image and Society in the Works of William Hogarth* (Oxford, 1997).
6. Roy Porter, 'Enlightenment and Pleasure' in Roy Porter and Marie Mulvey Roberts, eds, *Pleasure in the Eighteenth Century* (Basingstoke, 1996), p. 4.
7. Jerome Stolnitz, ' "Beauty": Some Stages in the History of an Idea', *Journal of the History of Ideas*, vol. 22 (1961), pp. 185–204.
8. See Lawrence E. Klein, *Shaftesbury and the Culture of Politeness: Moral Discourse and Cultural Politics in Early Eighteenth-century England* (Cambridge, 1994).
9. Bernard Mandeville, *Fable of the Bees*, 1705, 1714, 1723, edited by F.B. Kaye (Oxford, 1924).
10. Christopher Berry, *The Idea of Luxury: a Conceptual and Historical Investigation* (Cambridge, 1994), pp. 130–2.
11. Hutcheson, *Inquiry*, pp. 12 and 78.
12. *Ibid.*, pp. 93–4. On Hutcheson's *Inquiry* as the rehabilitation of luxury, see Preben Mortensen, 'Francis Hutcheson and the Problem of Conspicuous Consumption', *The Journal of Aesthetics and Art Criticism*, vol. 53, n 2 (Spring 1995), pp. 155–65.
13. Alexander Gerard, *An Essay on Taste*, 1759 (Menston, 1971).
14. *Ibid.*, p. 198.
15. *Ibid.*, pp. 192 and 203.
16. Hogarth, *Analysis*, p. 33.
17. Gerard, *Essay*, pp. 35 and 36.

18. Hogarth, *Analysis*, p. 32.
19. Paulson's footnote refers to Locke's *Essay*, Nidditch, p. 7; *Analysis*, p. 32.
20. Hutcheson, *Inquiry*, pp. 99–103.
21. Hogarth, *Analysis*, p. 34.
22. See B.R. Hergenhahn, *An Introduction to the History of Psychology*, fourth edition (Belmont, CA, 2001) on mid-nineteenth-century psychophysical parallelism, p. 223, and late nineteenth-century Russian Objective Psychology on social and emotional events as stimuli, pp. 342–5.
23. Hogarth, *Analysis*, p. 34. Italics in original.
24. John Weaver, *Anatomical and Mechanical Lectures upon Dancing* (London, 1721).
25. *Ibid.*, p. 108. Throughout this text Weaver stresses the parallels between the psychological need for variety and the body's constant alternating movement.
26. Joseph Addison, 'Pleasures of the Imagination', *The Spectator*, Nos 411–21, 1712, in *The Spectator* edited by Donald F. Bond, 5 vols, vol. III (Oxford, 1965).
27. *Ibid.*, pp. 411, 539, 412, 542, 413, 546.
28. The correspondence between Hogarth's beauty and Addison's novel has been noted by Paulson. See introduction to *Analysis*, pp. xvi–xvii.
29. Gerard, *Essay*, pp. 34 and 38.
30. Hogarth, *Analysis*, p. 46.
31. See, for example, David Hume, 'Of Commerce', in *Selected Essays*, ed. Stephen Copley and Andrew Edgar (Oxford, Worlds Classics, 1993), p. 163.
32. Hogarth, *Analysis*, p. 33.
33. See Act 2 scene 1 of Sir George Etherege's *She Would if She Could* in *The Plays of Sir George Etherege*, edited by Michael Cordner (Cambridge, 1982). Two spirited young women about town decide to play the rakes at their own game without loss of honour by tempting them to pursuit. Stage directions have them passing 'nimbly' across the stage as they lead the rakes on in a London park, p. 129. Highly excited, a rake declares the women's 'tongues are as nimble as their heels', p. 130. When finally caught the women racily tell the men they may 'entreat them to hear a fiddle or to mingle in a country dance', p. 133.
34. Hogarth, *Analysis*, pp. 17 and 50.
35. *Ibid.*, p. 107, see figure 120 in the left margin of plate 2.
36. Tom Sorrell, 'Thomas Hobbes', in Edward Craig, general editor, *Routledge Encyclopedia of Philosophy* (London, 1998), vol. 4, pp. 459–76.
37. Hogarth, *Analysis*, p. 116.
38. The likely influence of Hogarth's editors and other friends, and as far as science is concerned, particularly Benjamin Hoadly physician and artist Benjamin Wilson who published his experiments on electricity, is discussed in detail by Ronald Paulson in *Hogarth, Volume 3: Art and Politics 1750–1764* (Cambridge, 1993), pp. 59–64.
39. Hogarth, *Analysis*, p. 116.
40. Hutcheson, *Inquiry*, p. 101.
41. Addison, 'Pleasures of the Imagination', pp. 420 and 575.
42. See Robert E. Schofield, *Mechanism and Materialism: British Natural Philosophy in an Age of Reason* (Princeton, 1970).
43. *Ibid.*, pp. 72–8.
44. C.U.M. Smith, 'David Hartley's Newtonian Neuropsychology', *Journal of the History of the Behavioural Sciences*, 23 (April 1987), pp. 123–36.
45. Schofield, *Mechanism and Materialism*, p. 162 on the speculators' dream of being able to explain a whole range of phenomena through electricity, a dream shared by Hogarth's friend Benjamin Wilson.
46. Hogarth, *Analysis*, pp. 98–9 and 96.
47. Klein, *Shaftesbury*, pp. 94–5; Hogarth, *Analysis*, p. 107.
48. John Weaver, *An Essay Towards a History of Dancing* (London, 1712), pp. 21–6, gives self-presentation and exercise as the 'Rationale of the Art', quotes John Locke's *Thoughts on*

Education on the self-confidence given by graceful motion and suggests that this makes a man the 'framer of his own fortune' and aids his advances in marriage since women's fancy is appealed to by the lightness of dancing. Kellom Tomlinson's *The Art of Dancing* (London, 1735), p. 3, began with the injunction to readers, given the importance of grace in company, to consider themselves as 'so many living Pictures drawn by the most excellent Masters'.

49. Weaver (1721), *History of Dancing*, suggests that no bone is actually perpendicular because of the situation of the joints for articulated motion (p. 98), thus the most graceful positions are those of moderate and medium reflection which reflected this natural situation of the joints as 'a little bent' (p. 103).
50. Hutcheson, *Inquiry*, p. 26.
51. Hogarth, *Analysis*, p. 67.
52. Nicolas Barbon, *A Discourse of Trade* (London, 1690), p. 14, cited by Berry, *The Idea of Luxury*, p. 112.
53. 'An Inquiry into the Origin of Moral Virtue', Mandeville, *Fable of the Bees*, p. 39.
54. Preface to 'Fable of the Bees', *ibid.*, p. 3.
55. 'Remark (L)', *ibid.*, p. 119, and pp. 120–3.
56. Nicolas Barbon, *An Apology for the Builder: or a Discourse shewing the Cause and Effects of the Increase of Building* (1685), cited in Berry, *The Idea of Luxury*, p. 116.
57. 'Remark (C)', p. 70.
58. Berry, *The Idea of Luxury*, p. 113.
59. *Ibid.*, p. 112.
60. Bernard Mandeville, *The Female Tatler*, vol. 107 (20 March, 1710), cited in M. M. Goldsmith, *Private Vices: Public Benefits. Bernard Mandeville's Social and Political Thought* (Cambridge, 1985), p. 139. Goldsmith argues that Mandeville's writing is a contribution to the establishment of the mentalité of capitalism.
61. Hogarth, *Analysis*, p. 32.
62. Daniel Defoe, *A Plan of the English Commerce* (London, 1728), p. 51, cited in John Sekora, *Luxury: the Concept in Western Thought, Eden to Smollett* (Baltimore and London, 1977).
63. David Hume, 'Of Refinement in the Arts' entitled 'Of Luxury' in some editions, in *Selected Essays*, pp. 168–9.
64. Hogarth, *Analysis*, pp. 102 and 53.
65. Ogée, 'Aesthetics and Empiricism'.
66. *Analysis*, epigraph to frontispiece, 'So vary'd he [i.e. Satan], and of his tortuous train/ Curl'd many a wanton wreath, in sight of Eve/ To lure her Eye'. (*Paradise Lost*, 9. 516–18). Explicated by Paulson as linked to Milton's prelapsarian variety in Eden. 'all the earth yields/Variety without End.' (7.541–2), *Analysis*, pp. 144–5.
67. Sekora, *Luxury*, pp. 44–5.
68. *Ibid.*, p. 69.
69. Samuel Fawconer, *Essay on Modern Luxury* (1765), cited in *ibid.*, p. 99.
70. Berry, *The Idea of Luxury*, p. 121, and Goldsmith, *Private Vices*, pp. 65–70.
71. Sekora, *Luxury*, p. 70.
72. 'Remark C, Fable of the Bees', Mandeville, *Fable of the Bees*, p. 68.

Plates

12. 'The Third State', plate 1 of William Hogarth, *The Analysis of Beauty*, March 1753.
13. 'The First State', plate 2 of William Hogarth, *The Analysis of Beauty*, March 1753.

9

From Luxury to Comfort and Back Again: Landscape Architecture and the Cottage in Britain and America

John Crowley

In *Sense and Sensibility* the egregious Robert Ferrars expressed his envy for the new cottage life of the Miss Dashwoods:

> I am excessively fond of a cottage; there is always so much *comfort*, so much elegance about them. And I protest, if I had any money to spare, I should buy a little land and build one myself within a short distance of London, where I might drive myself down at any time and collect a few friends about me and be happy.

Jane Austen's satire marked a recent fashion for cottages. Ferrars' 'cottage' referred to a house whose acceptability depended on its modesty and physical comfort. This usage not only gave a new meaning to cottages; it employed a new concept in talking about any house, namely comfort.[1]

Physical comfort – self-conscious satisfaction with the relationship between one's body and its immediate physical environment – was an innovative aspect of eighteenth-century Anglo-American culture, one that had to be taught and learned. During the eighteenth century Britons and Americans used the word *comfort* with increasing frequency to express their satisfaction and enjoyment with immediate physical circumstances. This usage indicated a disposition to criticise traditional material culture and to improve it.[2]

Comfort drew the attention of political economists, moral philosophers, scientists, humanitarian reformers, even novelists. These commentators gave the term *comfort* a new physical emphasis as they reconceptualised values, redesigned material environments, and urged the relearning of behaviours. For centuries previously *comfort* had primarily meant moral, emotional, spiritual and political support in difficult circumstances. To be '*comfort*less' had meant being 'without anything to allay misfortune', and 'discomfort' involved feelings of 'sorrow', 'melancholy' and 'gloom' rather than physical irritation.[3]

Language and concepts emphasising a physical meaning of *comfort* developed initially in nascent political economy around 1700, as it analysed the differences between *luxury* and *necessity*. Luxury had long been the subject of political and social thought, but it was defined by an antonym, necessity, which had been taken for granted as having a natural definition. Luxury was what people desired beyond necessities. When eighteenth-century political economists began to analyse necessity as well as luxury, they effectively deconstructed luxury by showing how luxury in one context could be necessity in another.[4]

In *The Grumbling Hive* (1705) and its notorious prose commentary, *The Fable of the Bees* (1714), Bernard Mandeville not only defended luxury for its unintended social benefits, he used the distinction between necessity and luxury to show that *all* supposed 'necessities' were social constructions and therefore 'luxuries'. It made no difference whether every material need was considered as a luxury or as a necessity, because the distinction between them broke down when applied to specific items in specific societies. *Luxury* simply measured the extent to which 'Thought, Experience, and some Labour' had made 'Life more *comfortable*' than an animal-like 'primitive Simplicity'.[5]

Mandeville had set the agenda for political economists to analyse how demand shaped economic development. Adam Smith concluded the *Wealth of Nations'* celebrated first chapter, on the division of labour, with a paean to the 'universal opulence which extends itself to the lowest ranks of the people'. Among the items composing this opulence were a woollen coat, a linen shirt, shoes, a bed, a kitchen-grate and its coals, 'all the other utensils of his kitchen, all the furniture of his table, the knives and forks, the earthen or pewter plates upon which he serves up and divides his victuals, bread, beer', and 'the glass window which lets in the heat and the light, and keeps out the wind and the rain . . . without which these northern parts of the world would scarce have afforded a very *comfortable* habitation'. The diversity of production possible with a high degree of division of labor had allowed the 'accommodation' of 'an industrious and frugal peasant' to exceed that of a ruler in savage societies.[6] Smith was talking about comfortable cottages.

Before 1750 it was unlikely that anyone would *design* a cottage, much less have *comfort* among its architectural priorities. No British architectural publication had the word 'cottage' in its title before 1780; in the next two decades at least 17 did. Historically, cottages and cottagers were synonymous with poverty and misery. In the middle of the eighteenth century Samuel Johnson still defined a cottage as 'a hut; a mean habitation; a cot; a little house'. Over the next few decades, however, architecturally designed cottages became synonymous with comfort, the first house type to have this equivalence.[7]

The association of the cottage with physical comfort originated after 1750 from fashions in an archetypal domain of luxury – landscape architecture.[8] Two sets of architectural pattern books mark the new association of the cottage with comfort: the first for garden buildings, published largely from the 1750s through the 1780s, and a second set from the 1790s through the 1820s, when British architectural writers produced dozens of pattern books with designs for cottages. These architectural pattern books provide crucial evidence for the invention of the cottage as a comfortable house. For the first time, at the end of the eighteenth century, architectural publications carried the term 'comfort' in their titles, and then only in association with cottages. Humphry Repton, then Britain's leading landscape architect, identified a new priority among the classical principles of 'convenience, duration and beauty': 'in architecture and gardening, the present era furnishes more examples of attention to *comfort* and convenience than are to be found in the plans of Palladio, Vitruvius or Le Nôtre, who, in the display of useless symmetry, often forget the requisites of habitation.'[9]

British landscape design allowed experimentation with garden buildings because learned architecture had largely ignored them. In the first half of the eighteenth century, British landscape architects claimed to have repudiated luxurious artificiality – as associated with the formal garden and identified with the straight lines, topiary and parterres attributed to French and Dutch influences. But the types and use of garden buildings actually proliferated across the eighteenth-century British landscape. Capability Brown included numerous highly stylised garden buildings in his supposedly natural landscapes.[10]

During the period of Brown's career, from 1749 when he began to work independently, until his death in 1783, pattern books for garden buildings flourished as never before. Such buildings manifested the stylistic avant-garde in the eighteenth century, especially in its neoclassical varieties. Their relatively small size and low demands for durability allowed experimentation on a manageable scale at relatively low costs, both in money and design failures. Doric, Palladian, Gothic, rustic and grotesque styles all were revived for garden buildings. 'Grotesque architecture' for 'rural amusement' now included an extraordinary variety of types to which the customary generic terms – 'pavilion' and 'folly' – hardly do justice since they were specific types themselves. A far from exhaustive list, taken from title-pages alone, would include 'garden-seats, banqueting houses, summerhouses, lodges, terminies, piers', 'huts, retreats, summer and winter hermitages, terminaries, Chinese, gothic, and natural grottos, cascades, rustic seats, baths, mosques, moresque pavilions, grotesque seats, green houses', 'a bath, a dog-kennel, pavilions, farm-yards, fishing-houses, sporting-boxes, shooting-lodges, single and double cottages'.[11]

The cottage became the object of architectural design as just one type among a plethora of garden buildings. Its deliberate rusticity mirrored that of vernacular cottages, but the so-called cottage was not a frequent type of building in landscape architecture until the 1760s. Its predecessor among garden buildings was the yet meaner *hut*. As garden buildings, huts were studies in rusticity, either as hermitages or as neoclassically primitive dwellings. Hermitages made use of elementary materials to experiment with the minimal necessities for comfort: floors 'paved with sheep marrow-bones placed upright' but provided with a 'couch' and 'seats of retirement', walls 'lined with wool or other warm substance intermixed with moss' for winter use, seats 'composed of large irregular stones, roots of trees', interior lighting by a 'gazebo, supported by trunks of trees twined about ivy' (Plate 14).[12]

Architectural primitivism focused on the design of huts and cottages as antitypes to luxury. Robert Morris, the foremost architectural theorist in mid-eighteenth-century Britain, epitomised this linkage in *Rural Architecture*. Confronted with 'the Gaiety, Magnificence, the rude Gothic, or the Chinese unmeaning

Stile' studied by 'our modern Architects', Morris urged a return to 'Grecian and Roman Purity and Simplicity': 'in every Structure, in every Climate, Nature had dictated the Architect to the Disposal of it, for Use and Convenience'. According to such primitivism, houses were initially made with materials at hand – tree branches, moss and turf. Reminders of such primitive houses could be seen in the 'thousands of Mudwall, and Thatched buildings' in England and Wales, where 'we see Huts and Cottages built in the same Manner, just as if the Inhabitants had newly started into Being, and were led, by Nature and Necessity, to form a Fabric, for their own preservation, from the Inclemencies of the Season'. Neoclassical primitivism virtually required that experimental and innovative styles be brought to bear on architecture in the countryside. Columns of tree trunks supporting overhangs of thatched roofs reminded viewers to consider how the luxurious excesses of Baroque style had distorted classical architecture from the pure forms of the Greeks.[13]

The hut's exploration of the elementary necessities of comfort made sense in the garden, where buildings were by definition for 'pleasure and recreation'. Such garden and park buildings as lodges, gatehouses, keepers' houses and summerhouses allowed experimentation with plans and designs that provided full-fledged residential accommodation for dining, entertaining and sleeping. Many garden buildings incorporated more sophisticated hygiene in relation to water than was likely to be found in permanent dwellings. John Plaw designed a 'Wood Pile House' to serve as a water closet 'intended for a convenience in a park or plantation where the walks or rides are extensive'. As so often with garden buildings, rustic ornament gave a counterpoint to the basic comfort of this water closet: 'built with the arms and boughs of oak trees, not too large, cut into regular lengths, and bedded in tempered clay, mixed up with straw; the roof is thatched, and the inside, above the lining, is stuck with moss.' Similarly, fashionable people were more likely to take a bath in the garden than in the house. Garden-bathhouses advertised a closeness to elemental nature, but actually had far more careful designs for the control of air and water temperature than in most luxurious houses.[14]

The deliberately unconventional setting of the landscape garden suited the development and application of the new value of comfort. Dairies, in particular, exquisitely combined fashionable naturalness with careful control over environmental insults. On farms, dairies were the province of women and were separated against contamination from the rest of the farmyard. But when located in a garden or park as a highly decorated leisure space, their premium on cleanliness and temperature control presented new standards for comfort. Genteel women designed and supervised dairies that integrated function with ornament. Extensive tinted glazing provided a diffuse bright light by which to gauge the stages of processing. Dairies were tiled for coolness and cleanliness, and the emphasis on clean utensils allowed for lavish display of porcelain and other ceramics. The most desirable porcelain was Chinese, and dairies often had correspondingly exotic designs. In the 1760s Josiah Wedgwood developed cream-coloured Queen's Ware, which was ideal for garden-dairies because they often had tea rooms for entertaining.

Wedgwood expected that 'the consumption [of cream-coloured ware] will be great for Dairys, Baths, Summer Houses, Temples'. Genteel dairies virtually cried out on functional grounds for picturesque handling. Verandah-like sheds shielded interiors from glare while complementing thatched roofs in moderating temperature changes outside.[15] With such vernacular elements, plus accommodation for a milkmaid, the designs of dairies merged with those for cottages.

Sentimental associations with the cottage also developed in the context of landscape design. Oliver Goldsmith's poem *The Deserted Village* (1770), so often cited as a condemnation of the social injustices of enclosure, actually dealt with the removal of villagers to improve Lord Harcourt's *view* at Nuneham Courtney. The poem related to landscape gardening, not intensive agriculture, and condemned the enclosure of *park*land, not fields.

> Thus fares the land, by luxury betrayed,
> In nature's simplest charms at first arrayed,
> But verging to decline, its splendours rise,
> Its vistas strike, its palaces surprize;
> While scourged by famine from the smiling land,
> The mournful peasant leads his humble band;
> And while he sinks without one arm to save,
> The country blooms – a garden, and a grave.

In the 1770s cottages and their sentimentalised occupants began to proliferate on the cultural landscape. They figured importantly in genre scenes, as cottagers displaced livestock, pets and genteel conversations as privileged subjects in English landscape painting.[16]

Sentimentality towards the cottager was simultaneous with the development of architectural interest in cottages, first in landscape architecture, then in philanthropic designs, and finally in residential architecture for the propertied. In the last quarter of the eighteenth century, humanitarian reform for the first time gave priority to standards of architectural comfort and applied them to model cottages. While it might be taken for granted that humanitarian reformers would want to enable the poor to have comfortable housing, this assumption mistakenly begs the question that comfort was a pre-existing architectural priority.

Nathaniel Kent and John Wood established the genre for the philanthropic model cottage, and their designs acquired a generic quality that allowed frequent imitations and borrowings. As the King's bailiff at Windsor and the estate surveyor for Thomas William Coke, the pre-eminent agricultural improver, Kent spoke authoritatively on cottagers' physical conditions. Since Wood had designed Bath's Royal Crescent and New Assembly Rooms, his credentials were unassailable when he called for the application of architectural expertise to ordinary buildings. He capitalised on neoclassical awareness to assert the need for attention to cottages: 'no architect had, as yet, thought it worth his while to offer to the publick any well constructed plans for cottages', but they should, 'considering the regular gradation between the plan of the most simple hut and that of the most superb palace; that a palace is nothing more than a cottage improved; and that the plan of the latter is the basis as it were of plans for the former'. His book, *A Series of Plans for Cottages or Habitations of the Labourer*, put the cottage in the architectural mainstream and established the model cottage as a generic design (see Plate 15).[17]

The design of model cottages took place as public attention focused on cottagers' social and economic plights. Philanthropists advised enlightened landlords to build model cottages for their own best interest as well as charity. With crushing condescension, reformers argued that well-designed cottages harmonised aesthetic, social and economic priorities:

> As a number of labourers constitutes one of the requisites of grandeur, *comfortable* habitations for its poor dependents ought to be provided. It is not more necessary that these inhabitants should be seen immediately near the palace than that their inhabitants should dine at the same table, but if their humble dwelling can be made a subordinate part of the general scenery, they will, so far from disgracing it, add to the dignity that wealth can derive from the exercise of benevolence.[18]

The assertion of basic architectural needs for physical comfort was one of the ways humanitarians identified a common humanity across social gulfs. In presenting model cottages as tests in the efficient design of minimal comfort, housing reformers urged magnanimous landlords to consider comfort to be a right: 'it is as necessary to provide plain and comfortable habitations for the poor as it is to provide *comfortable* and convenient buildings for cattle. . . . we bestow considerable attention upon our stables and kennels, but we are apt to look upon cottages as incumbrances, and clogs to our property.' Kent, Wood, and other agricultural reformers interested in housing tested their readers' sensitivity by challenging them to enter imaginatively into 'the shattered hovels which half the poor of this kingdom are obliged to put up with . . . those who condescend to visit these miserable tenements, can testify, that neither health or decency can be preserved in them'.[19]

The design of philanthropic model cottages defined comfortable housing, at least minimally. In 1793 Parliament established the Board of Agriculture and charged it with proposing ways of reducing rural disturbances. In 1797 the Board published the results of its national inquiry concerning the best designs for cottages. As a result of this inquiry, the design of cottages for labouring and poor families acquired generic characteristics. Many were two-storeyed, because 'upper apartments are more wholesome to sleep in than ground floor', but they seldom had a full two storeys in elevation. The basic plan was two rooms, with floor plans generally 12 by 16 feet. The main downstairs room was multi-purpose, with a variety of names, such as 'living', 'dwelling' and 'working' room – seldom 'kitchen' – and usually included space for a bed. The second storey might have a fireplace, but if there were two chambers upstairs, one would be unheated because cottages seldom had more than one chimney. There was only one window per room, with about 10 square feet of glazing. Roofs were thatched, and floors were sometimes earthen. At a time when house plans for the wealthy usually failed to include sanitary facilities, plans for cottages often identified privies, albeit outside (Plate 16).[20]

As a public issue, the miserably *un*comfortable housing of the mass of the rural population was a new historical phenomenon. In the 1780s and 1790s reports on vernacular architecture became a convention in travel literature from all locales in Britain as well as abroad. Arthur Young, the pre-eminent authority on agricultural reform in late eighteenth-century Britain, included the adequacy of peasant housing in his inventory of questions when assessing a region. When touring Catalonia, for example, he noted repeatedly how the houses lacked chimneys and glazed windows. Young was perplexed to explain 'a poverty which hurt our feelings', among people whom he found highly industrious in their use of agricultural resources. He tentatively attributed the disparity to absentee landlords who neglected their social responsibilities. In England, Young thought, the apparent comfort of cottages contributed to the beauty of the landscape that kept the landed class on the land:

> To the taste of a man that is fond of a country in a northern climate, there are few objects more pleasing to the eye, or more refreshing to the imagination, than the natural landscape scenes of a well-cultivated and well-peopled country. These have, in England, features that charm and instruct. Inequalities of country, not too abrupt, woods that present rich masses of shade, rivers that offer the contrast of their silver bosoms, gliding gently through vales of constant verdure, which are neither hurt by their rapidity, nor rendered marshy by their sluggishness; inclosures, which mark the value and the culture of the soil; and scattered habitations of the poor, clean and *comfortable*, mixed with the houses of farmers, in a state of ease and prosperity; and with the seats of gentlemen, who find society and liberal pleasures, without deserting the fields, which give them their support, for the profusion and taste of a capital.[21]

Young was describing the English landscape as a landscape garden, with comfortable cottages prominent among its picturesque features.

British humanitarian concern with model cottages reinforced the potential in landscape architecture for the design of comfortable cottages. The same architects – Humphry Repton, John Plaw, John Soane, Charles Middleton, James Malton and John Claudius Loudon – designed model cottages for labouring families as well as picturesque cottages for propertied people. Some of the best known among them were primarily landscape architects. After all, model cottages might not have much ornament themselves, but they enhanced the appearance of the estate. In criticising the transposition of rustic style from the garden to domestic architecture in the last quarter of the eighteenth century, Richard Payne Knight, arch-theorist of the picturesque aesthetic, deftly noted the style's influence: 'Rustic lodges to parks, dressed cottages, pastoral seats, gates and gateways, made of unhewn branches and stems of trees, have all necessarily a still stronger character of affectation. . . . for to adapt the genuine style of a herdsman's hut or a ploughman's cottage to the dwellings of opulence and luxury, is as utterly impossible, as it is to adapt their language, dress, and manners to the refined usages of polished society.' Knight's snobbish comment emphasised how garden buildings ran the architectural liability of being victims of their own stylistic success, and indeed there was a fashionable reaction against the proliferation of temples, rotundas, ruins, and pagodas. But he erred about the adaptability of the cottage to polite taste. Cottages enjoyed stylistic privilege because they were both exotic and authentically British.[22]

The cottage made the transition from garden to residential architecture at the same time that housing became an object of social reform. Architectural pattern books of the 1790s and early 1800s identified the cottage's irregularity with the newly fashionable picturesque aesthetic. In his *Essay on British Cottage Architecture*, Malton confidently presented a verbal image to guide aesthetic responses to the cottage's physical appearance:

> When mention is made of the kind of dwelling called a Cottage, I figure in my imagination a small house in the country; of odd, irregular form, with various, harmonious colouring, the effect of weather, time, and accident; the whole environed with smiling verdure, having a contented, cheerful, inviting aspect, and the door on the latch, ready to receive the gossipy neighbour, or weary, exhausted traveler. There are many indescribable somethings that must necessarily combine to give a dwelling this distinguishing character. A porch at entrance; irregular breaks in the direction of the walls; one part higher than another; various roofing of different materials, thatch particularly, boldly projecting; fronts partly built of walls of brick, partly weather boarded, and partly brick-noggin dashed; casement window lights are all conducive, and constitute its features. (Plate 16)

How could genteel people imagine living in houses of a type previously identified with rural poverty? Ann Bermingham has shown how the picturesque aesthetic eulogised a landscape that was disappearing with agricultural development: the aesthetic simultaneously admired a landscape and put it at a safe distance socially and historically. Once stylised by this aesthetic, architectural irregularity and crude materials could be used as signs that rural necessity had been transcended while its traditional virtues had been maintained. Designedly picturesque cottages for the propertied complemented the generic architecture of cottages now intended for laboring households.[23]

The picturesque cottage could take shape quickly because of the preceding half-century of rustic architecture in landscape design. By the time that Malton published his essay, he could take for granted that the harmony of nominal cottages with the landscape made them a housing option for virtually all social groups: 'These [designs] are humbly presented as hints to those Noblemen and Gentlemen of taste, who build retreats for themselves, with desire to have them appear as cottages, or erect habitations for their peasantry or other tenants: And to the Farmer, as a guide in the construction of his dwelling, that it may agree and correspond with the surrounding scenery.' Malton criticised the prevailing use of cottages as garden buildings, and sought to make domesticity the priority in their design: 'With reference to its decay, or with regard to its moveables, any dwelling may be rendered mean; but where *comfort*, plenty, and hospitality reign; or where cleanliness, content, and smiles appear meanness must necessarily be excluded.'[24]

In comparison with philanthropic model cottages, cottages for families of property had more privacy and specialised spaces. They had many more bedrooms and additional types of rooms such as halls, parlours, kitchens and water closets. A spectrum of leisure spaces – studies, dining rooms, withdrawing rooms, conservatories – provided both psychological and physical comforts to 'a family with a small independent fortune, or a retreat occasionally to relax from the bustle of business'. Not bound by regularity, the cottage particularly lent itself to convenient designs. Neoclassical sensibilities encouraged an evolutionary perspective on household amenities in the 'graduation of buildings, from the primitive Hut, to the superb Mansion'.[25]

Repton carried this evolutionary perspective on comfort forward from its neoclassical context: 'The present style of living in the country is so different from that of former times, that there are few houses of ancient date which would be habitable, without great alterations and additions': '[The] Eating room . . . library . . . drawing-room . . . music room . . . billiard room . . . conservatory . . . boudoirs, wardrobes, hot and cold baths . . . are all modern appendages unknown in Queen Elizabeth's days. Under these circumstances, it is difficult to preserve the ancient style of a mansion without considerable additions.' If comfort had a history, then it could still be changing in contemporary Britain. If comfort were changing, and it was an architectural priority, then, Repton argued, the picturesque style was peculiarly suited to the design of dwellings, not just on grounds of appearance but because of its functional adaptability:

> When we look back a few centuries, and compare the habits of former times with those of the present, we shall be apt to wonder at the presumption of any person who shall propose to build a house that may suit the next generation. Who, in the reign of Queen Elizabeth, would have planned a library, a music-room, a billiard-room, or a conservatory? Yet these are now deemed essential to *comfort* and magnificence: perhaps, in future days, new rooms for new purposes will be deemed equally necessary. But to a house of perfect symmetry these can never be added.[26]

No sooner had convenience and comfort gained priority over picturesqueness in the design of cottages than cottages gained potential for a new virtue, elegance. Use of the term 'elegance' increased dramatically in the 1790s. (It will be recalled that Robert Ferrars admired cottages for their elegance as well as their comfort.) Elegance had connotations of unpretentious, tasteful beauty. It implied neatness rather than extravagance. Particularly as a standard for interior finish and plan, elegance could complement the cottage's exterior rusticity: 'Elegance is a term applied to such objects as show a degree of refinement, or smoothness of surface, a delicacy of proportion, when compared with the general appearances of such objects.' By the first decade of the nineteenth century assertions of elegant design cautioned against building *only* with a concern for comfort. The 'ornamented cottage' – also referred to as the 'cabâne ornée' and 'cottage orné' – met this test, but still gave priority to comfort:

> [it is] a building that owes its origin to the taste of the present day, and though humble in its appearance affords the necessary conveniences for persons of refined manners and habits, and is, perhaps, more calculated than any other description of building for the enjoyment of the true pleasures of domestic life, unincumbered with the forms of state and troublesome appendages. The leading feature of this style of building is to appear in every respect a dwelling calculated for *comfort* and convenience, without minute attention to the rules of art; every part having its uses apparent, and this appearance not in any case sacrificed to regularity.

Ornamented cottages could be elegant if they looked manifestly comfortable.[27]

By 1800, villas and ornamented cottages were suburban cousins. Many pattern books presented both types of buildings on a continuum of design along the axis of comfort and elegance – from labourers' cottages through ornamented cottages to villas. Villas should have an identifiable style, but the choices were eclectic. They could be Roman, Greek, Gothic, Italianate, neoclassical, even 'cottage', as long as 'an elegant simplicity reign[ed] throughout the whole, and the general forms and construction be such, as plainly demonstrate at the first view, that nothing grand and magnificent is attempted'. Cottages were intimate, whether for entertainment or domestic life. Villas provided space for elaborate entertainment, while maintaining opportunities for domestic retreat through a range of rooms implying fine gradations between privacy and interaction with outsiders. A specific plan for a villa would have some, though not necessarily all, of these rooms: vestibule, ante-room, drawing room, parlour, music room, billiard room, dining room, breakfast parlour, library, cabinet, study and dressing room. The manifest elegance of villas set them between the rusticity of cottages and 'the magnificence and extensive range of the country seats of our nobility and opulent gentry'. Their supposed lack of pretension implied their comfort, as underlined by their frequent associations with cottages.[28]

*

The American story of the comfortable cottage provides a contrasting illustration of how architectural comfort was a construction of eighteenth-century British culture. In the initial phase of English colonisation, Governor William Bradford readily employed the historical association of 'cottage' with substandard housing when he referred to the early houses of Plymouth Colony as 'small cottages'. After all they lacked foundations, and had wooden chimneys, thatched roofs, earthen floors, unglazed or small-paned casement windows and wattle-and-daub walls. The plans, amenities and finish of the houses in which most Americans at the end of the eighteenth century still lived would have signified them as cottages in England – room and loft house plans, wood and clay chimneys, few and small windows, and construction from local raw materials. The first American publication, in 1798, of a design for a 'cottage' had a 14 by 10 foot floor plan, a masonry or brick chimney with fireplaces on both floors, one window each for the living room and pantry on the first floor, and three beds in the two rooms in the loft (one of the rooms was windowless). It derived from the model cottages of improving landlords.[29]

In contemporary Britain, cottages marked people as lacking sufficient landholdings to support a household, but in colonial and early national America there were many more cottages than cottagers. Most American households held sufficient land to provide livelihoods for their members, so they were not cottagers in social status. The usual terms for American cottagers' houses were 'tenant house', 'tenement', 'house' and 'home', not 'cottage'. When, in 1799, John Beale Bordley, an American agricultural reformer, advocated that American farmers follow the English practice of providing their waged labourers with houses, he assumed that the terminology was unfamiliar to his American readers: 'It is deemed advantageous for the farmer to have some number of *labourers* on his estate at a rent, in a small very confined house called a *cottage*; and the *labourer* taking it is called a *cottager.*'[30]

In early nineteenth-century Anglo-America, the houses of a large proportion of the rural population looked like cottages, but belonged to propertied families. Spending on the newly fashionable architectural comforts of heating, lighting, privacy and hygiene still had a relatively low priority. It did not correlate so strongly with wealth as did consumer spending on luxurious furnishings and other durables. In the initial decades of the American republic, the pursuit of happiness began to give a higher priority to housing. More spending, particularly by merchants and artisans in towns and cities, went into permanence of construction, stylish exteriors and refined interior spaces for entertaining. This 'transformation of living standards' took place during a period not noted for increases in per capita wealth, which by some estimates may even have fallen. The priority of housing in household spending had increased, but still remained generally low: 'most Americans were still living in small, mean, vernacular houses'. Two-room houses were the modal plan. The size of houses need not have increased to meet the new standards of decoration and finish, because those standards focused largely on the front parts of the house, particularly the areas for entertaining, while the areas for everyday domestic activity – the kitchen and chambers – changed little in their degree of finish. In the early nineteenth century household comfort had not yet become so popular a need as refinement and gentility.[31]

American architects waited more than a generation to borrow from British developments in articulating architectural comfort, particularly as represented by the cottage. The apparent precondition for this borrowing was a broadening of American interest in landscape architecture, beginning in the 1830s. The writings of the British landscape architect, John Claudius Loudon, especially his *Encyclopaedia of Cottage, Farm and Villa Architecture and Furniture* (first published in 1833), served as the acknowledged intermediary between American architects and British authorities on the comfortable cottage. In 1838, in an effort to improve the 'bald and uninteresting aspect of our houses . . . to those who are familiar with the picturesque Cottages and Villas of England', Alexander Jackson Davis published the first cottage in an American architectural pattern book. His design's bucolic landscape setting, columns of unhewn logs, and open porch signified harmonious relations between the inhabitants of the cottage and their immediate physical environment. With Davis's assistance in an extraordinarily successful series of publications over the next decade, Andrew Jackson Downing made the cottage an American byword for comfort, and he made comfort the crucial consideration in the design of houses (Plate 17). No American manifested the links among improvements in horticulture, landscape architecture, and cottage architecture more clearly than Downing, and he forthrightly acknowledged his inspiration from British landscape architecture and theory.[32]

By the turn of the nineteenth century British social thought had naturalised the desire for physical comfort. The mature work of Thomas Malthus represented and synthesised the invention of comfort in material culture and social thought: the impossibility of precise distinctions between necessity and luxury, the acceptance of popular consumption patterns, the philanthropic impulse to establish minimal entitlements to comfort, and the demonstrability of respectable family life by comfortable domestic environments. Between the first edition of the *Essay on the Principle of Population* in 1798 and the second edition in 1803, largely as a result of his travels comparing British living conditions with ones elsewhere in Europe, Malthus came to the realisation that desires for comfort and convenience were crucial to the 'moral restraint' that allowed sufficient control over the principle of population to maintain happiness in a society: 'throughout a very large class of people [in Britain], a decided taste for the conveniences and *comforts* of life, a strong desire of bettering their condition, that master-spring of public prosperity, and, in consequence, a most laudable spirit of industry and foresight, are observed to prevail.' Malthus's image of the comforts of British life came straight out of genre representations of happy cottagers: 'a good meal, a warm house, and a *comfortable* fireside in the evening'. What was minimally comfortable for the propertied was needed by the poor as well, and it was reasonable and desirable that the poor should want those 'luxuries' of the propertied that were really comfortable: 'It is the spread of luxury therefore among the mass of the people, and not an excess of it in a few, that seems to be most advantageous, both with regard to national wealth and national happiness[,] . . . if it be observed that a taste for the *comforts* and conveniences of life will prevent people from marrying, under the certainty of being deprived of these advantages.'[33]

The design of cottages had created a single type of house with a wide social range of acceptability, from the working poor to people who were wealthy but not landlords. The basis for this acceptability was comfort. Three aspects of eighteenth-century British culture – architectural primitivism, sympathetic humanitarianism, and the picturesque aesthetic – had dealt with physical comfort in ways that could be explored in the design of cottages. Each movement addressed markedly different architectural contexts – landscape gardens, farms and suburbs. In landscape gardens comfort gained associations with leisure in small groups; on improved farms comfort redressed poverty; and in the suburbs comfort expressed elegant taste. In each of these contexts cottages represented how the realisation of comfort tested sensibility as well as technology.

Notes

1. J. Austen, *Sense and Sensibility* (1811; reprint, New York, 1995) chapter 14, pp. 213–14. 'Comfort' has been italicised in all quotations.
2. J.E. Crowley, *The Invention of Comfort: Sensibilities and Design in Early Modern Britain and Early America* (Baltimore, 2001).
3. *The Oxford English Dictionary* (Oxford, 1989) s.v. 'comfort'; S. Johnson, *A Dictionary of the English Language*, 2 vols. (London, 1785) s.v. 'comfort', 'comfortless', 'discomfort'.
4. *Comfort* in English derived from the medieval French *conforter/confort* (= *soutenir/encouragement*); A.J. Greimas, *Dictionnaire de l'ancien français jusqu'au milieu du XIVe siècle* (2nd edn, Paris, 1977) s.v. 'conforter'. But in the seventeenth and eighteenth centuries the usual French term to assess satisfactory physical circumstance was *commodité*. Only in the early nineteenth century did French usage of the term *confort* take on such connotations, having borrowed the term back from English with a new meaning; *Le Grand Robert de la langue française: dictionnaire alphabétique de la langue française*, edited by A. Rey, 9 vols. (2nd edn, Paris, 1985), s.v. 'confort'; P. Perrot, *Le luxe: Une richesse entre faste et confort XVIIIe–XIXe siècle* (Paris, 1995) pp. 65–90; A. Pardailhé-Galabrun, *La naissance de l'intime: 3,000 foyers parisiens XVIIème–XVIIIème siècles* (Paris, 1988) p. 331; J.-P. Goubert, *Du luxe au confort* (Paris, 1988) pp. 21–9; Jean Fourastié, *Histoire du confort* (Paris, 1973) pp. 86–9.
5. B. Mandeville, *The Fable of the Bees: Or Private Vices, Publick Benefits* (6th edn, 1732), edited by F.B. Kaye, 2 vols. (1924; reprint, Indianapolis, 1988) I: 25–6, 107–8, 169, 183.
6. A. Smith, *An Inquiry into the Nature and Causes of the Wealth of Nations* (1776), edited by R.H. Campbell and A.S. Skinner, 2 vols. (Oxford, 1976; reprint, Indianapolis, 1981) p. 23; for Smith's usage of 'necessaries and conveniencies of life', see pp. 10, 47, 51, 95, 176, 927.
7. Studies of early architecturally designed cottages include: S. Blutman, 'Books of Designs for Country Houses, 1780–1815', *Architectural History*, XI (1968) 25–33; S. Lyall, 'Minor Domestic Architecture in Britain and the Pattern Books' (PhD diss., University of London, 1974); M. McMordie, 'Picturesque Pattern Books and Pre-Victorian Designers', *Architectural History*, XVIII (1975) 43–59; D.P. Schuyler, 'English and American Cottages, 1795–1855: A Study in Architectural Theory and the Social Order' (MA thesis, University of Delaware, 1976); M. McMordie, 'The Cottage Idea', *RACAR: Revue d'art canadienne Canadian Art Review*, VI (1979) 17–27; J.D. Hunt, 'The Cult of the Cottage', *The Lake District: A Sort of National Property* (London, 1985) pp. 71–83; S. Lyall, *Dream Cottages: From Cottage Ornée to Stockbroker Tudor, Two Hundred Years of the Cult of the Vernacular* (London, 1988); J.S. Ackerman, *The Villa: Form and Ideology of Country Houses* (Princeton, 1990) pp. 212–27.
8. S. Taylor-Leduc, 'Luxury in the Garden: *La Nouvelle Héloïse* Reconsidered', *Studies in the History of Gardens and Designed Landscapes*, XIX (1999) 74–85.
9. H. Repton, *Observations on the Theory and Practice of Landscape Gardening* (London, 1803) p. 11. Some publications including the term *comfort* in their titles are: J. Wood, *Series of Plans for Cottages or Habitations of the Labourer . . . Tending to the Comfort of the Poor and Advantage of the Builder* (1781; reprint, London, 1806); J. Plaw, *Sketches for Country Houses, Villas, and Rural Dwellings; Calculated for Persons of Moderate Income, and for Comfortable Retirement* (London, 1800); E. Gyfford, *Designs for Elegant Cottages and Small Villas,*

Calculated for the Comfort and Convenience of Persons of Moderate and of Ample Fortune (1806; reprint, Westmead, 1972). On architectural pattern books, see J. Archer, *The Literature of British Domestic Architecture 1715–1842* (Cambridge, Mass., 1985) pp. 21, 28–30, 56–71, 78–83.

10. B. Langley, *New Principles of Gardening* (London, 1728) pp. x–xi, 193–5; W. Chambers, *A Dissertation on Oriental Gardening* (2nd edn, London, 1773) pp. 16, 21; *idem, Plans, Elevations, Sections and Perspective Views of the Gardens and Buildings at Kew* (London, 1763); L. Fleming and A. Gore, *The English Garden* (London, 1979) pp. 18, 24, 27–9, 32, 34, 38, 60, 62, 92; H.F. Clark, 'Eighteenth-Century Elysiums: The Role of "Association" in the Landscape Movement', *Journal of the Warburg and Courtauld Institute*, VI (1943) 165–89; M. Jourdain, *The Work of William Kent, Artist, Painter, Designer, and Landscape Gardener* (New York, 1948) p. 79; D. Stroud, *Capability Brown* (London, 1950) pp. 87, 161, 180, 208–9; S. Lang, 'The Genesis of the English Landscape Garden', in *The Picturesque Garden and its Influence outside the British Isles*, ed. N. Pevsner (Washington, D.C., 1974) pp. 22–9; R. Turner, *Capability Brown and the Eighteenth-Century English Landscape* (New York, 1985) pp. 86, 145–6, 181, 187; T. Hinde, *Capability Brown: The Story of a Master Gardener* (New York, 1987) pp. 134, 139; M. Saudan, S. Saudan-Skira and F. Crouzet, *From Folly to Follies: Discovering the World of Gardens* (New York, 1988) p. viii; G. Mott, S.S. Aall and G. Jackson-Stops, *Follies and Pleasure Pavilions: England, Ireland, Scotland, Wales* (New York, 1989) p. 9; T. Williamson, *Polite Landscapes: Gardens and Society in Eighteenth-Century England* (Baltimore, 1995).

11. W. and J. Halfpenny, *Rural Architecture in the Gothick Taste* (London, 1752); W. Wrighte, *Grotesque Architecture, or, Rural Amusement* (London, 1790); J. Plaw, *Ferme Ornée; or Rural Improvements* (London, 1795); *Ideas for Rustic Furniture Proper for Garden Seats, Summer Houses, Hermitages, Cottages* (London, ca. 1790); T.C. Overton, *Original Designs of Temples, and Other Ornamental Buildings for Parks and Gardens in the Greek, Roman, and Gothic Taste* (London, 1766), pl. 34 [misprinted as 43]. For early examples of cottages as part of landscape architecture, see N. Temple, *John Nash and the Village Picturesque* (London, 1979) pp. 5–7; M. McCarthy, 'Eighteenth Century Amateur Architects and Their Gardens', in *Picturesque Garden* p. 51; T. Mowl, 'The Evolution of the Park Gate Lodge as a Building Type', *Architectural History*, XXVII (1984) 468.

12. Wrighte, *Grotesque Architecture* pp. 3–5, pl. 1; W. and J. Halfpenny, *The Country Gentleman's Pocket Companion, and Builder's Assistant, for Rural Decorative Architecture* (London, 1753) p. 9; Plaw, *Ferme Ornée*, p. 6, pl. 12.

13. R. Morris, *Rural Architecture* (1750; reprint, Westmead, 1971), preface and introduction; M.-A. Laugier, *An Essay on Architecture; in which its True Principles are Explained, and Invariable Rules Proposed* (London, 1755) pp. 11–12; *idem, Essai sur l'architecture* (2nd edn, Paris, 1755) p. 9.

14. T.C. Overton, *The Temple Builder's Most Useful Companion* (London, 1774); W. Halfpenny and J. Halfpenny, *Rural Architecture in the Chinese Taste* (3rd edn, 1755; reprint, New York, 1968) pls. 9–13; Halfpenny and Halfpenny, *Rural Architecture in the Gothick Taste* pp. 10–11, pls. 14, 15, 18; J.-F. Blondel, *De la distribution des maisons de plaisance*, 2 vols. (Paris, 1737) I: 71–2, II: 129, pl. 10; Plaw, *Ferme Ornée*, pp. 2–3, 7; C. Over, *Ornamental Architecture in the Gothic, Chinese and Modern Taste* (London, 1758) p. 4, pl. 16; J. Soan[e], *Designs in Architecture . . . for Temples, Baths, Cassines, Pavilions, Garden-Seats, Obelisks, and other Buildings; for Decorating Pleasure-Grounds, Parks, Forests* (1778; reprint, Westmead, 1968) pls. 9–10, 34; P. de la Ruffinière du Prey, *John Soane: The Making of an Architect* (Chicago, 1982) pp. 124–8; J. Colton, 'Kent's Hermitage for Queen Caroline at Richmond', *Architectura*, II (1974) 181–91.

15. J. Malton, *A Collection of Designs for Rural Retreats* (London, 1802) pp. 33–4, pls. 27–8; J. Langner, 'Architecture pastorale sous Louis XVI', *Art de France*, III (1963) 170–86; Wedgwood quoted in A. Kelly, *Decorative Wedgwood in Architecture and Furniture* (London, 1965) pp. 119–23, pls. 58–61; A. Kelly, *The Story of Wedgwood* (London, 1975) pp. 21–2; J.M. Robinson, *Georgian Model Farms: A Study of the Decorative and Model Farm Buildings*

of the Age of Improvement, 1700–1846 (Oxford, 1983) pp. 82–96, pls. 84–96; du Prey, *John Soane*, pp. 245–55, 377; M. Willes, 'Country House Dairies', *Apollo*, CIL, no. 446 (1999) 29–32.

16. O. Goldsmith, 'The Deserted Village', in *Collected Works of Oliver Goldsmith*, edited by A. Friedman, 5 vols. (Oxford, 1966) IV: 298, lines 295–302; H.J. Bell, ' "The Deserted Village" and Goldsmith's Social Doctrines', *Proceedings of the Modern Language Association*, LIX (1944) 747–72; J. Barrell, *The Dark Side of the Landscape: The Rural Poor in English Painting, 1730–1840* (Cambridge, 1980) pp. 35–88; A. Bermingham, *Landscape and Ideology: The English Rustic Tradition, 1740–1860* (Berkeley, 1986) pp. 14–54; C. Payne, *Toil and Plenty: Images of the Agricultural Landscape in England, 1780–1890* (New Haven, 1993) pp. 23–66.

17. N. Kent, 'Reflections on the Great Importance of Cottages', *Hints to Gentlemen of Landed Property* (London, 1775); Wood, *Series of Plans for Cottages.*

18. Repton, *Observations*, pp. 137–8.

19. N. Kent to Coke of Norfolk, 1789, as quoted in Robinson, *Georgian Model Farms* p. 109; Kent, *Hints to Gentlemen* pp. 229, 230, 237; Wood, *Series of Plans*, p. 3.

20. *Communications to the Board of Agriculture on Subjects Relative to the Husbandry and Internal Improvement of the Country*, 7 vols. (London, 1797) I, part 2, *Cottages:* 89, 96–8, 103–17, pls. 34–5; J. Miller, *The Country Gentleman's Architect* (London, 1791); J. Malton, *An Essay on British Cottage Architecture* (London, 1798) pp. 17–18; Wood, *Series of Plans*, pp. 5, 22, pls. 1–28.

21. A. Young, 'Tour in Catalonia', *Annals of Agriculture and Other Useful Arts* (Bury St. Edmunds, 1787) VIII: 202, 207, 210, 263, 273; G.E. Fussell, *The English Rural Labourer: His Home, Furniture, Clothing & Food from Tudor to Victorian Times* (London, 1949) pp. 50–67.

22. Kent, *Hints to Gentlemen*, p. 238; R.P. Knight, *An Analytical Inquiry into the Principles of Taste* (2nd edn, London, 1805) p. 222.

23. Malton, *Essays on British Cottage Architecture*, pp. 2, 4–5; Bermingham, *Landscape and Ideology*, pp. 40–1, 69–75.

24. C.T. Middleton, *Picturesque and Architectural Views for Cottages, Farm Houses, and Country Villas* (London, 1793) p. 2; *idem, The Architect and Builder's Miscellany* (1795; reprint, London, 1979) pls. 1–15; Malton, *Essay on British Cottage Architecture* pp. 4–5, 22, pls. 10–12, 14.

25. Middleton, *Picturesque and Architectural Views* p. 1, pls. 1–12; Gyfford, *Designs for Elegant Cottages and Small Villas* pp. 1–3, pls. 1–6; Plaw, *Sketches for Country Houses*, pp. 11–12, pls. 8, 13; Malton, *Essays on British Cottage Architecture*, p. 27.

26. Repton, *Observations*, pp. 177–9; J. Loudon, *A Treatise on Forming, Improving, and Managing Country Residences*, 2 vols. (London, 1806) I: 69–71; H. Repton and J.A. Repton, *Fragments on the Theory and Practice of Landscape Gardening* (London, 1816) p. 15; S. Daniels, *Humphry Repton: Landscape Gardening and the Geography of Georgian England* (New Haven and London, 1999) pp. 103–48.

27. Johnson, *Dictionary*, s.v. 'elegance, elegant'; T. Dyche and W. Pardon, *New General English Dictionary* (London, 1765) s.v. 'elegance, elegant'; N. Bailey, *An Universal Etymological English Dictionary* (London, 1794), s.v. 'elegance, elegant'; W.F. Pocock, *Architectural Designs for Rustic Cottages, Picturesque Dwellings, Villas* (London, 1807) pp. 1, 8–9; E. Bartell, *Hints for Picturesque Improvements in Ornamental Cottages* (London, 1804).

28. J. Randall, *A Collection of Architectural Designs for Mansions, Casinos, Villas, Lodges, and Cottages* (London, 1806) pp. iv–v; E. Gyfford, *Designs for Small Picturesque Cottages* (London, 1807) pp. v–vii; Plaw, *Sketches for Country Houses*, pls. 15–17, 21; Daniels, *Humphry Repton* pp. 207–54; T.R. Slater, 'Family, Society and the Ornamental Villa on the Fringes of English Country Towns', *Journal of Historical Geography* IV (1978) 129–44; J. Summerson, 'The Classical Country House in 18th-Century England', *Journal of the Royal Society of Arts*, CVII (1959) 139–87.

29. W. Bradford, *Of Plymouth Plantation 1620–1647*, ed. S.E. Morison (New York, 1952) pp. 76, 136; C.R. Lounsbury, *An Illustrated Glossary of Early Southern Architecture and*

Landscape (New York, 1994) p. 97. The design was first published in J.B. Bordley, *Country Habitations* (Philadelphia, 1793) and subsequently appeared in J.B. Bordley, *Essays and Notes on Husbandry and Rural Affairs* (2nd edn, Philadelphia, 1801) p. 5, fig. 2.

30. Bordley, 'Thoughts on Hired Labourers and Servants, Cottages and Cottagers', in *Essays and Notes on Husbandry* p. 389; L. Simler, 'The Landless Worker: An Index of Economic and Social Change in Chester County, Pennsylvania, 1750–1820', *Pennsylvania Magazine of History and Biography*, CXIV (1990) 168–9, 175–6, 179, 187; *idem*, 'Tenancy in Colonial Pennsylvania: The Case of Chester County, Pennsylvania', *William and Mary Quarterly*, 3rd ser., XLIII (1986) pp. 562–8.

31. T. Jefferson, *Notes on the State of Virginia* (1785; reprint, Gloucester, Mass., 1976) pp. 145–8; E.A. Chappell, 'Housing a Nation: The Transformation of Living Standards in Early America', in *Of Consuming Interests: The Style of Life in the Eighteenth Century*, edited by C. Carson, R. Hoffman, and P.J. Albert (Charlottesville, 1994) pp. 167–233; J. Larkin, 'From "Country Mediocrity" to "Rural Improvement": Transforming the Slovenly Countryside in Central Massachusetts, 1775–1840', in *Everyday Life in the Early Republic*, edited by C.E. Hutchins (Winterthur, 1994) pp. 175–201; L. Soltow, *Distribution of Wealth and Income in the United States in 1798* (Pittsburgh, 1989) p. 57; B. Herman, *Architecture and Rural Life in Central Delaware, 1700–1900* (Knoxville, Tenn., 1987) pp. 14–41, 109–4; *idem*, *The Stolen House* (Charlottesville, 1992) pp. 183–95, 206–10, 217–22; D. Upton, 'The Traditional House and its Enemies', *Traditional Dwellings and Settlement Review*, I (1990) 71–84.

32. A.J. Davis, *Rural Residences* (New York, 1837–38); A.J. Downing, *Treatise on the Theory and Practice of Landscape Gardening* (New York, 1841); *idem*, *Cottage Residences* (New York, 1842); *idem*, *The Architecture of Country Houses* (New York, 1850); D. Schuyler, *'Apostle of Taste': Andrew Jackson Downing 1815–1852* (Baltimore, 1996).

33. T. Malthus, 'An Essay on the Principle of Population: The Sixth Edition (1826) with Variant Readings from the Second Edition (1803)', in *The Works of Thomas Robert Malthus*, edited by E.A. Wrigley and D. Souden, 9 vols. (London, 1986) III: 466–8, 520.

Plates

10
Vase Mania

Jenny Uglow

Vase mania hit Britain in the late 1760s, peaking from 1771–2. It was a time of great unrest – of growing tension with the American colonies after the Stamp Act of 1765, of 'Wilkes and Liberty' riots after John Wilkes's election as MP for Middlesex in 1768; of disturbances among silkworkers, coal-heavers, farmworkers across the country. Yet amid all these upheavals the polite world was obsessed with classical vases. Perhaps the uncertainty of the time added to their appeal: the image of the Greek urn already carried with it the aura of timeless serenity that Keats would later celebrate. Such vases evoked the birth of European civilisation, the Golden Age, and the urns bore too an aura of dignity transcending death, just as they had physically survived the tombs in which they were found. Ironically, perhaps, far from being precious at the time when they were made, the decorated pottery urns found amid the bones were themselves copies of silver vessels – and soon eighteenth-century British manufacturers were providing their own copies of these copies to meet the demand of the public.

Vases, of course, had been popular luxury objects for many years – they are there among the other auction trash on the crowded mantelpieces of Hogarth's engravings in the 1740s satirising life *à la mode* – but over the past two decades a whole set of influences had come into play to raise this particular classical form to the height of fashion. The fashion also provided an opportunity for particular British manufacturers to capture elite markets, chief among them Josiah Wedgwood, currently planning to expand his pottery in Staffordshire, and Matthew Boulton, the 'toy maker', who with his partner John Fothergill was developing the most advanced metal-working 'manufactory' of the day at Soho, just outside Birmingham. In using new materials to reproduce ancient art-works these two men provided novel, piquant luxury goods for eager purchasers. And as they leapt at the chance, so the white heat of the vase craze sharpened their manufacturing, their design and particularly their marketing, and catapulted them on to a new stage. The rhetoric that accompanied their triumph was patriotic, heard often in arguments about raising the national taste, but just as often in terms of bald competition, particularly with France. At the same time, the mass production of fine objects raised issues about the nature of art, craft and originality. Although my narrative is one of production rather than consumption, from either perspective a simple vase could carry complex meanings.

From the mid-century on, knowledge of the classical world – of its buildings, its art and its artefacts – had been deepening and broadening. Rome had always been open to British travellers, but Athens, under Turkish rule, was inaccessible, and Greek ornament was far less well known. In 1748, a group of English enthusiasts working in Rome decided that this must be remedied. They included the Scottish artist, James Stuart, and in 1751, funded by the Society of Dilettanti, he and his friend Nicholas Revett had set out for Greece. After two years in Athens they travelled to Salonica, Smyrna and the Aegean islands, returning in 1755. They eventually published their influential *Antiquities of Athens* in 1762, but as soon as they returned, Stuart was in demand as an interior designer, creating vigorous, attractive ensembles for rooms in which every detail had its place – including vases. A drawing of 1758 for Sir Nathaniel Curzon's Kedleston Hall in Derbyshire, for example, shows a Gainsborough painting above a table sheltering a recently acquired Sicilian urn, flanked by other urns, below a niche ornamented with swagwork.[1]

Another leader in the introduction of the antique taste was William Chambers, later architect to the king, but Stuart's real rival – who adhered, like Chambers, to the 'Roman' rather than 'Greek' style – was the young Scottish architect, Robert Adam. In the mid-1750s Adam spent two years in Rome, perfecting his drawing technique with Piranesi. On his return, determined to 'blind the world', he set himself up in St James' and then in Grosvenor Street, and immediately won influential clients – among them Sir Nathaniel Curzon.[2] Stuart's new interiors for Kedleston were decried as 'pityfulissimo', and Adam took over as designer with his dazzling, colourful, neoclassical designs. He too was concerned with every detail from ceilings to candlesticks and his commissions inevitably involved other trades: at one point, Adam Smith reckoned 3,000 people were dependent on the Adam brothers for work. He was constantly in demand: Elizabeth Montagu, writing to Lord Kames, said that if his wife really wanted to be in fashion, and 'would have anything *en meubles*, extremely beautiful, she must employ my friend Mr Adam here. He has made me a ceiling and a chimney-piece, and doors, which are pretty enough to make me a thousand enemies: Envy turns livid at the first glimpse of them.'[3]

The antique craze was fuelled by news of the finds at Herculaneum and Pompeii. Although the two sites were excavated from 1738 and 1748 respectively, it was not until the early 1760s that major work at Pompeii began. And while some early collections of engravings from classical sites had been published, like Bernard de Montfaucon's *Antiquitee Expliquee* (1719), a host of new publications appeared in Britain and France in the 1750s and 60s: these included Robert Wood and James Dawkin, *The Ruins of Palmyra* (1753); the Comte de Caylus, *Receuil d'Antiquites Egyptiennes, Etrusques, Grecques et Romaines* (1752–67); J. F. Neuff, orges's *Receuil Elementaire d'Architecture* (1757–68) and J. C. Delafosse's *Nouvelle Iconologie Historique*.[4] Winckelmann's immensely influential *History of Ancient Art* appeared in 1764, and Robert Adam published his own *Ruins of the Palace of the Emperor Diocletian at Spalatro* soon afterwards. In addition, there were specific folios of vases, including those made by J.-F. Saly (1746), C. de Wailly (1760) and E. A.

Petitot (1764). Some, like Joseph-Marie Vien's *Suite de Vases* (1760), with engravings 'in the taste of the antique', were unashamedly pattern books, eagerly ransacked by craftsmen and designers.

Genuine vases were much sought after by dedicated collectors. One such was Sir William Hamilton, ambassador to Naples. As soon as he arrived, in 1764, he collected vases unearthed in nearby tombs, buying them from dealers or other collectors and even opening tombs himself.[5] Like everyone at the time, he called his vases 'Etruscan', believing them to come from the ancient pre-Roman culture, while in fact they were Greek, many made in Athens in the fifth and sixth centuries BC and imported into Italy – although Hamilton himself later worked to correct his error, the Etruscan name stuck.[6] Hamilton employed the brilliant, eccentric Baron d'Hancarville to write a commentary on his collection, with over 450 engravings. The complete set of *Antiquites, Etrusques, Grecques et Romaines* was not published until 1776, but the first volume appeared in late 1767.

Wedgwood and Boulton were keenly alert to this burgeoning classicism. In 1765 an order for gilt brass door-furniture for Kedleston Hall came to Soho, and Lord Shelburne ordered girandoles when Adam remodelled rooms at his house at Bowood in Wiltshire.[7] Wedgwood, too, noted the taste of patrons who bought his fashionable creamware (for which he had been given the title 'Queen's Potter' in 1764). Through Lord Cathcart, who was married to Hamilton's sister, he acquired prints from the first volume of the *Antiquites*, and soon received the complete volume from another patron, Sir Watkins William Wynn. Poring over these and other prints, he wrote to his friend and partner Thomas Bentley:

> The colours of the Earthen vases, the paintings, the substances used by the Ancient Potters, with their method of working, burning &c ... Who knows what you may hit upon, or what we may strike out betwixt us. ...'[8]

Hamilton had wanted exactly this response. His writing had a complex note of 'patriotism', a determination to raise British taste and design. In his preface he declared:

> We think also, that we make an agreeable present to our manufacturers of earthenware and china, and to those who make vases in silver, copper, glass, marble etc. Having employed much more time in working than in reflexion, and being besides in great want of models, they will be very glad to find here more than two hundred forms, the greatest part of which are absolutely new to them; there, as in a plentiful stream, they may draw ideas which their ability and taste will know how to improve to their advantage, and to that of the public.[9]

This could hardly have been more direct, and the hint was quickly followed by Boulton as well as Wedgwood. In 1767, an agent travelling in Italy for Boulton subscribed to Hamilton's *Antiquites* on his behalf, telling him that he thought this would be a good source of designs for Soho.[10] In the summer of 1767, Boulton decided that for a metalworker like himself, the way to target the market for vases was to mount them in ormolu. Defined strictly, ormolu was the gilding of metal with ground gold, *'or moulu'*, mixed with mercury: so far the French bronziers had led the field but Boulton now decided to challenge them. Two years earlier, in Paris, he had noted the fashion for mounting vases in gilt metal and had since been busy finding out about gilding. He could see that the use of vases could easily extend beyond mere ornament: with metal branches added they could become candelabra and candle-holders; with a clock or watch fitted they were lavish time-pieces; with perforated lids they turned into 'cassoulets' or perfume burners. (Inviting Boulton to her London house in 1771, Elizabeth Montagu told him '& then you will be sensible how agreeable the aromatick gales are from these Cassolettes when they drive away the vapour of soup and all the fulsome savour of Dinner.'[11]) Soon Boulton looked to other products, planning ormolu tripods and girandoles, ice-pails and tea-urns.

Wedgwood's vases inevitably caught his eye as suitable for mounting, and in the spring of 1768 he broached the subject of collaboration. During a weekend at Soho, Wedgwood told Bentley: 'we settled many important matters & laid the foundation for improving our manufacture, & extending the sale of it to every corner of Europe.'[12] The main idea was that Boulton would set Wedgwood's vases in metal but he stirred the potter's competitive spirit by telling him that French artists were coming over to England and picking up 'all the whimsical ugly old things they could meet with', taking them back to Paris, ornamenting them and then selling them back as great rarities to 'Millords d'Anglise'. To Wedgwood, the prospect of expanding in this direction was alluring: 'This alone (the combination of Clay & Metals) is a field, to the farther end of which we shall never be able to travel'.

Later that year, the two men met in London to go 'curiosity-hunting' together, with their wives in tow. Sarah Wedgwood's only complaint during this trip was that,

> my good man is upon the ramble continually and I am almost affraid he will lay out the price of his estate in Vases he makes nothing of giving 5 or 6 guineas for . . . if we do but lay out half the money in ribband or lace there is such an uproar as you never heard.[13]

Wedgwood and Boulton raided Harrache's exclusive shop, and Boulton sent for an artist from Soho to draw the 'pretty things' he saw. He was aiming for the top, as Wedgwood saw, ignoring the court of St James and 'scheming to be sent for by his Majesty! I wish him success. He has a fine spirit, and I think by going hand in hand we may in many respects be useful to each other.'[14]

By the end of the year Boulton had ordered several Wedgwood vases, including mottled ware, resembling 'the green blood stone that hath a few red specks in it', to match a French vase sent him from London. 'I would have some of the little ones to be of the black Etruscan clay,' he added, 'some green, some blew, or any other simple colour you think proper'.[15] But the scheme petered out, with Boulton complaining that orders had not been filled, and hinting that he was thinking of a deal with the Chelsea factory. In fact, china turned out to be far too fragile to bear the heavy ornaments, especially for big pieces like candle-holders. Instead Boulton explored the possibility of glass and gilt, lacquered and japanned metal and turned to Derbyshire marble and 'Blue John', the beautiful banded purple fluorspar found only in Treak Cliff, near Castleton. Although it had been known since the beginning of the century, the mining of Blue John had only begun in earnest around 1765 and it was thus an intriguing, extremely novel material. (A local sculptor, John Brown, made a fireplace from it at nearby Kedleston.) In early 1769 Boulton bought an amazing 14 tons of this rare mineral, and although he failed in gaining a monopoly, he always cannily pretended to have one.[16]

Wedgwood also had the perfect vase material. Two years earlier, in 1766, he had perfected a richer, smoother form of the old Staffordshire 'Egyptian Black' ceramic body, which he called 'black basalt' (perhaps influenced by the controversy over the volcanic origins of basalt rock, in which Hamilton was also involved). Next, to imitate the red designs on Greek vases, he developed a matt red 'encaustic' enamel, the only process for which he ever took out a patent. In addition to his 'Useful Works' at Burslem, where his creamware was produced, he also soon had a new 'Ornamental Works', which he called Etruria, and which was opened with a great feast in June 1769. Wedgwood himself threw six perfect copies of a black 'Etruscan' vase, which were fired and sent to London to be hand painted with encaustic enamel in the decorating studio at Chelsea. On one side were three figures from what was considered the most beautiful vase in Hamilton's *Antiquites*, the 'Meidias Hydra'. Below was an inscription: *Artes Etruriae Renascuntur* – the Etruscan arts reborn (Plate 18).

*

The previous September Bentley had inspired Wedgwood with the notion that they could, with effort, outshine their rivals abroad as well as at home. 'And do you really think that we may make a complete conquest of France?' a delighted Wedgwood asked:

Conquer France in Burslem? My blood moves quicker, I feel my strength increase for the contest. Assist me, my friends, and the victorie is our own. We will make them (now I must say Potts, and how vulgar it sounds), I won't though, I say we will fashion our Porcelain after their own hearts, and captivate them with the Elegance and simplicitie of the Ancients. But do they love simplicitie?[17]

Boulton too vowed to make his ormolu simpler than the ornate French ware. He too saw his trade as a patriotic battle and so did his patrons, like Elizabeth Montagu, who declared she took greater pleasure in victories over the French in arts in arms: 'Go on then Sir,' she told him, 'to triumph over the French in taste & to embellish your country with useful inventions & elegant productions.'[18]

Boulton made no pretence to originality. 'Fashion hath much to do with these things & the present age has distinguished itself by adopting the most Elegant ornaments of the most refined Grecian artists,' he declared: 'I am satisfyd in conforming thereto, & humbly copying their style, & making new combinations of old ornaments without presuming to invent new ones.'[19] But copying was not so easy. Once he and Wedgwood had established a demand, both quickly had to increase the range of their designs and raise their rate of production. Sometimes a note of panic sounds through their letters and – particularly on Boulton's part – a string of ingenious excuses (Mrs Montagu had to wait about three years for a 'plaited tea-vase') (Plate 19).

The first problem was design. The two manufacturers borrowed works of art from rich clients and from friends and rivals, shopkeepers and sculptors. They obtained introductions to the British Museum, and Wedgwood saw collections at the Oxford colleges and at Blenheim. Woodcarvers like John Coward and sculptors like John Bacon made models for them and they bought plastercasts from John Flaxman in Covent Garden, father of the more famous sculptor, whose precocious talent Wedgwood was quick to spot.[20] They also begged models from architects: lion's heads and tritons and gryffins, winged figures and sphinxes, Caryatids and Persian Slaves. This last – used by both manufacturers – was based on a design by the King's architect, Chambers: when Boulton breakfasted with him in 1770, Chambers gave him 'a present of some valuable, usefull and acceptable models'.[21]

A second problem was finding craftsmen.[22] Wedgwood's letters are full of troubles with modellers and painters, and he looked for men and women from the porcelain works in Derby, Worcester and Liverpool, from among the fan painters with their talent for miniatures, and from the coach and fresco painters.[23] Boulton faced similar problems. For some time, on his trips to London he had been noting down the names of both French and English ormolu workers in his diary. But most were not to be poached, so in 1770 he told Robert Adam proudly that he was training up 'plain Country Lads, all of which that betray any genius are taught to draw, from whom I derive many advantages that are not to be found in any manufacture that is or can be established in a great & Debauch'd Capital'.[24]

Once the designs were obtained and models made, Wedgwood and Boulton reduced costs by having an interchangeable range of ornaments and designs, varying them to provide customised articles. They sent drawings to clients who could supposedly choose what they wanted, but if a commission meant new designs or special tools Boulton often managed to 'delay' to the point of non-delivery, while Wedgwood told Bentley to avoid orders for 'any *particular kind* of Vases . . . at least till we are got into a more methodicall way of *making the same sorts over again*'.[25] Sighing over one such order, he added, 'It is this sort of *time loseing* with *Uniques* which keeps ingenious Artists who are connected with Great men of taste poor'.[26] Good business worked against originality.

Far from downplaying their modern industrial processes, both Wedgwood and Boulton made much of them. They were certainly copying the antique – Soho, they joked, could be the new Corinth, the classical city of metal, just as Burslem was the new Etruria – but their machines were part of their cachet. 'It was always in Mr Boulton's mind,' noted Boulton's friend James Keir, 'to convert such trades as were usually carried on by individuals into great manufactures by the help of machinery, which might enable the articles to be made with greater precision and cheaper than those commonly sold.'[27] Etruria had a waterwheel and a windmill for grinding flint and enamels; Soho was powered by water and, increasingly, steam. Boulton was the first to use a watermill to turn laps for grinding and polishing, while Wedgwood developed an improved engine-turning lathe (first seen at Soho), which cut patterns on a fired clay vase, and he later acquired a rosette lathe to cut curving shapes.

Although ultimately it was skilled hands, not new technology, that made the difference in their vase-making, the machines made their factories into showplaces. 'I must again thank you for the most agreeable day I pass'd at the Soho Manufactory,' wrote Mrs Montagu:

> The pleasure I received there, was not of the idle & transient kind which arises from merely seeing beautiful objects. Nobler Tastes are gratified in seeing Mr Bolton & all his admirable inventions. To behold the secrets of Chymistry, & the mechanick powers, so employ'd, & exerted, is very delightful. I consider the Machines you have at work as so many useful subjects to great Britain of your own Creation: the exquisite Taste in the forms which you give them to work upon, is another national advantage.[28]

Mechanisation, Boulton told Lord Warwick in 1773, made it possible to defeat continental competitors. The other key factor, he insisted, was the separation of processes. Foreign visitors always remarked on the division of labour, although specialisation had been applied in different British trades for some time and in fact at Soho each workshop still operated independently: the only rough move towards a 'production-line' was in trying (not always successfully) to orchestrate the making so that it proceeded stage by stage. Similarly, although Wedgwood, notoriously, wanted perfection and saw it in mechanical terms ('I have been turning models,' he told Bentley in October 1769, '& preparing to make such *Machines* of the *Men* as cannot err'), it would be quite wrong to talk of 'assembly-lines' or 'mass production' at Etruria.[29] Wedgwood had, however, looked carefully at the Soho organisation and had learnt from the Worcester factory, where the workroom spaces were laid out in an order that reflected the steps in the manufacturing process.[30] Under the pressure of producing vases to meet an expanding market, Wedgwood also undertook a pioneering analysis of the costs of his methods of production.[31] In negotiations with his workers he explained that if overheads could be spread over more products by '*making the greatest quantity possible in a given time*', the cost of each individual article, and consequently the selling price, could be reduced.[32] So although the pay per piece might be lower, theoretically the higher productivity meant that overall wages would rise. It was a pivotal moment: from now on accounting and 'calculating' were applied to industry with increasing care.

The combination of machines, cost-accounting and paternalist discipline was a pattern Boulton and Wedgwood shared with other leading manufacturers, a model for the century ahead.[33] But if the vase craze accelerated the drive towards sharper work practices, the key issue was still command of the market. Here patronage remained vital and Boulton's letters to his wife in 1770 show how hard he worked to get it. Hearing that Lady Shelburne had a 'putrid sore throat' and 'wished that she could have a few of my pretty things to amuse her', he dashed off and brought back a load, 'and sat with her Ladyship two hours explaining and hearing her criticisms'.[34] He breakfasted with William Chambers, had an audience with the Duke and Duchess of Northumberland, visited the Earl of Dartmouth and the Dowager Princess of Wales. Then came the visit to the palace. The Queen, he decided, was 'extremely sensible, very affable, and a great patroness of English manufactorys'. After she and the King talked to him for nearly three hours, 'the Queen sent for me into her bedchamber, shewed me her chymney piece and asked my opinion how many vases it would take to furnish it, for says she all that china shall be taken away.' His manager, John Scale, must send a set of Blue John vases within the fortnight. (There is still a Boulton perfume burner at Windsor.)

The Midlands manufacturers also organised exclusive public sales in the capital. Wedgwood had always been concerned to find a showroom that would suit his smart customers, 'for you well know they will not mix with the rest of the World any farther than their amusements, or conveniencys make it necessary to do', he told Bentley in 1767. It had to be chic and private but also 'Large', as vases would decorate the walls and a full display of at least six or eight complete dinner services was essential 'in order *to do the needful* with the ladys in the neatest, genteelest & best method'.[35] In August 1768 his showroom moved from Charles Street to Great Newport Street, and six years later would move again, to the grand Portland House in Greek Street, Soho. The display changed constantly so that visitors always had something new to see: the black basalts were shown off by yellow backgrounds, the Queensware by blue or green, the rarest vases kept enticingly in a locked room for private view.[36]

The sales of vases and ormolu were deliberately planned as spectacles, rivalling the shows at the Royal Academy or the Society of Artists (Plate 20). Writing in May 1770, in between news of Wilkes's stint as Lord Mayor, and parliamentary factions and ominous reports from Boston, Horace Walpole gossiped about sales of the day, like an auction of expensive stuffed birds and three simultaneous exhibitions of pictures, 'it is incredible what sums are raised by mere exhibitions of anything; a new fashion'. Another rage, he noted, was for English portraits:

> Then we have Etruscan vases, made of earthen ware in Staffordshire, from two to five guineas; and *or moulu*, never made here before, which succeeds so well, that a tea-kettle which the inventor offered for 100 guineas, sold by auction for 130. In short we are at the height of extravagance and improvements, for we do improve rapidly in taste as well as in the former.[37]

In 1770, 1771 and 1772, Boulton held grand week-long sales at Christie's and Ansell's showrooms in Pall Mall. In 1771 there were three days of viewing, the first for the nobility alone, so that they could place orders in comfort. Christie's room glittered with 265 lots, with over 400 pieces, ranging from candlesticks at four guineas to a Persian candelabra at £200, a staggering price. His show was the talk of the town, but in this world of spectacle, just as in manufacture, there was competition. This year Duesbury was displaying his Derby china, and James Cox, maker of fabulously expensive bejewelled automata, was opening what he called his 'Museum'. Wedgwood rightly foresaw that Boulton might be outshone, or even eclipsed:

> for what with the fine things in Gold, Silver & Steel from Soho, the almost miraculous magnificence of Mr Coxes Exhibition, & the Glare of the Derby & other China shews – What heads or Eyes could stand all this dazzling profusion of riches & ornament if something was not provided for their relief.[38]

That much needed relief, he hoped, might just be provided by his own black, Etruscan and Grecian vases.

By 1772, however, the ormolu craze had peaked, as had the vogue for vases as a whole, and Boulton was left with cart-loads of beautiful, unsold stock. (He was only saved by shipping tons of ormolu to an admiring Catherine the Great.) Wedgwood, meanwhile, saw that the loss of elite trade could be offset by addressing a different market.

> The Great People have had these Vases in their Palaces long enough for them to be seen and admired by the *Middling Class* of People, which Class we know are vastly, I had almost said, infinitely superior, in number to the great, and though a *great price* was, I believe, at first necessary to make the vases esteemed *Ornament for Palaces*, that reason no longer exists. Their character is established, and the middling People would probably buy quantitys of them at a reduced price.[39]

Another response was to diversify. Increasingly, in 1772 and 1773 Wedgwood and Bentley worked on a different line, the production of seals in *cameo* and *intaglio* form, serving another current craze, the collecting of carved antique gems. And soon Wedgwood was supplying an even wider taste, making portrait medallions of Popes and Kings and Queens, and the 'Heads of Illustrious Moderns from Chaucer to the Present Time'. Among the first of his 'Etruscan Portraits', made in April 1771, was one of Sir William Hamilton. Two months earlier Hamilton had sold his collection to the British Museum for £8,400, but Wedgwood later calculated that Etruria had made three times that sum in profits from the vases which Hamilton had inspired.[40]

Boulton's answer to slipping sales was also to try something different. In 1773, Hamilton urged him to try to make glassware in the antique style, but Boulton was more realistic: he now intensified his attention on silverware, on the basis that unlike ormolu silver was never out of fashion. His fine craftsmen, new techniques and classical moulds could all be adapted to make expensive ornaments for the gentry and cheaper versions in plate for the 'middling classes'. In this connection his successful fight to establish a local Assay Office in Birmingham in 1773 proved yet another provincial victory over a virtual London monopoly.

Boulton went on to make his fortune in the next decade, not from vases and toys, ormolu or silver, but from his partnership with James Watt in developing steam power. Wedgwood, however, always stuck to ceramics, his great passion as well as the trade he had grown up in. Vases remained a staple of his ornamental ware; in 'Etruscan' style, in plain black basalt and in the new ceramic body 'jasper', which he perfected in late 1777 after 5000 experiments.[41] This unglazed vitreous fine stoneware was coloured in many 'Adam' shades – green, lilac, yellow, maroon or black – as well as the famous 'Wedgwood blue' and provided a superb background for white bas-reliefs, with delicate undercutting. Large sets of vases were made from 1780 until the end of the century. One of the most beautiful was decorated with a relief designed by John Flaxman (used as a plaque from 1778), of 'The Apotheosis of Homer', adapted from one of Hamilton's vases (Plate 21). Wedgwood gave a Homer vase to Hamilton and in 1786 presented another to the British Museum – an extraordinary gesture, in which the manufacturer presented his 'new' product, as a work of art, to the institution which held the originals on which his work was based.

Equally evocative was the Portland Vase, the supreme production of Wedgwood's later years, perfected twenty years after the first heady vase mania. This copy of the famous first century BC Alexandrian 'Barberini' vase, originally made in deep blue glass, quickly became an icon. In 1787, when Benjamin West was commissioned to design paintings for the ceiling of the Queen's Lodge at Windsor, he made ceramics the principal subject of the scene representing 'British Manufactory' (Plate 22). In West's vaguely 'classical' workshop, a naked boy in the foreground holds a copy of the Portland Vase, which Wedgwood was currently creating.[42] The classical vase, and all it represented, thus grew from being the object of a fashionable craze into a symbol of British craftsmanship as a whole – a proud boast that the nation's modern industry and culture could rival the greatest achievements of the ancient world.

General note

The Wedgwood-Bentley correspondence can be found in K.E. Farrer, ed., *Letters of Josiah Wedgwood* (3 vols, Manchester, 1903–6) but in a highly edited form. I have therefore quoted the originals from the Wedgwood Archives at Keele University, by kind permission of The Wedgwood Trust; many, however, can also be found in Ann Finer and George Savage, eds, *The Selected Letters of Josiah Wedgwood* (London, 1965).

References to the Matthew Boulton papers in Birmingham City Archives are given in the form used in 2001. The whole labyrinthine archive is currently being re-catalogued, but to assist future researchers, cross-references will be made from the old to the new system.

1. Illustrated as Plate 125 in Charles Saumarez Smith, *Eighteenth-Century Decoration* (London, 1993).

2. John Fleming, *Robert Adam and his Circle* (London, John Murray, 1962), pp. 246–7.
3. A.F. Tytler, *Memoirs of the Life and Writings of the Hon. Henry Home of Kames* (Edinburgh, 1814) II, pp. 63–4.
4. See Nicholas Goodison, *Ormolu: The Work of Matthew Boulton* (London, 1974: new edition due, 2002), pp. 49 and 51.
5. See David Constantine, *Field of Fire: A Life of Sir William Hamilton* (London, 2001), p. 32.
6. Ian Jenkins and Kim Sloan, *Vases and Volcanoes: Sir William Hamilton and his Collection* (London, 1996), p. 51. See also Constantine, *Field of Fire*, pp. 32–45.
7. *Ormolu*, p. 26.
8. Josiah Wedgwood to Thomas Bentley, 16 February 1767, Wedgwood Archive, Keele University: E25-18163.
9. [Sir William Hamilton], D'Hancarville, *Collection of Etruscan, Greek and Roman Antiquities* (1766–76) I, p. viii, quoted in *Ormolu*, p. 55.
10. P.J. Wendler to Matthew Boulton, 1767, Matthew Boulton Papers, Birmingham City Archive: MBP 261.35–9.
11. Elizabeth Montagu to Matthew Boulton, 31 October 1771, MBP 330.1.
12. Josiah Wedgwood to Thomas Bentley, 15 March 1768, W.E25-18193. (Wedgwood reminded Bentley that they had seen these at Lord Bolingbroke's, and he had spotted 'two or three old China bowles, for want of better things, stuct rim to rim which had no bad effect but look whimsical and droll enough.')
13. William Cox, Sarah Wedgwood and Catherine Willett, joint letter to Thomas Bentley, 29 November 1768, Keele University W.M2.
14. Josiah Wedgwood to Thomas Bentley, 21 November 1768, W.E25-18215.
15. Matthew Boulton to Josiah Wedgwood, 30 December 1768 (also 17 January 1769), quoted in *Ormolu*, p. 28.
16. *Ormolu*, p. 30.
17. Josiah Wedgwood to Thomas Bentley [13 September 1769], W.E25-18252.
18. Elizabeth Montagu to Matthew Boulton, 31 October 1771, MBP 330.1.
19. Matthew Boulton to Elizabeth Montagu, 16 January 1772, draft, MBP 330.3.
20. Josiah Wedgwood to Thomas Bentley, 7 September 1771, W. LHP. In 1770 Boulton bought a lion, a ram's head, a deer's head, a sleeping Bacchus and a 'Group of Hercules and Atlas', *Ormolu*, pp. 57–8.
21. Matthew Boulton to Anne Boulton, 6 March 1770, MBP 279.
22. For this as a general issue in ceramics, see Hilary Young, *English Porcelain, 1745–95* (London, 1999), pp. 94–154.
23. See, for example, Josiah Wedgwood to Thomas Bentley, 25 June 1769, W.E25-18245, and 17 September 1769, W.E25-18255.
24. Matthew Boulton to James Adam, 1 October 1770, MBP 136, Letter Book (1768–1830), p. 29. For drawing and design generally, see Charles Saumarez Smith, 'Eighteenth-century Man', *Designer* (March 1987), pp. 19–21. For Birmingham, see Young, p. 100.
25. Josiah Wedgwood to Thomas Bentley, 1 October 1769, W.E25-18264.
26. Josiah Wedgwood to Thomas Bentley, 19 November 1769, W.E25-18269.
27. James Keir, Memorandum on Matthew Boulton, sent to Matthew Robinson Boulton, 3 December 1809, MBP 290.112.
28. Elizabeth Montagu to Matthew Boulton, 31 October 1771, MBP 330.1.
29. Josiah Wedgwood to Thomas Bentley, 9 September 1769, W.E25-18265.
30. Young, p. 23.
31. See Neil McKendrick, 'Josiah Wedgwood and Cost Accounting in the Industrial Revolution', *English Historical Review* XXIII (1970), pp. 45–67.
32. Josiah Wedgwood to Thomas Bentley, 22 July 1772, W.E25-18381.
33. For factory discipline generally in Britain and France, see Paul Mantoux, *The Industrial Revolution in the Eighteenth Century* (1983 edn.), pp. 375–6. For Wedgwood, see N. McKendrick, 'Josiah Wedgwood and Factory Discipline', *Historical Journal*, IV (1961), pp. 30–55.

34. Matthew Boulton to Anne Boulton, 6 March 1770, MBP 279.
35. Josiah Wedgwood to Thomas Bentley, 31 May 1767, W.E25-18141.
36. On Wedgwood's showroom practice in the 1770s, see Malcolm Baker, 'A Rage for Exhibitions: The Display and Viewing of Wedgwood's Frog Service', in Hilary Young, ed., *The Genius of Wedgwood* (London, 1995).
37. Horace Walpole to Sir Horace Mann, 6 May 1770, *Horace Walpole's Correspondence*, ed. W.S. Lewis, 44 vols (New Haven, 1937–83), vol. 20, pp. 211–12.
38. Josiah Wedgwood to Thomas Bentley, 11 April 1772, W.E25-18365.
39. Josiah Wedgwood to Thomas Bentley, 23 August 1772, W.E25-18392.
40. Constantine, *Field of Fire*, p. 65.
41. Josiah Wedgwood to Thomas Bentley, 3 November 1777, W.E25-18790.
42. See David Irwin, *Neoclassicism* (London, 1997), pp. 172–3. Benjamin West, *British Manufactory, A Sketch, 1791* (Cleveland Museum of Art).

Plates

18. Wedgwood, 'First Day Vase', 1769.
19. Boulton and Fothergill, Pattern Book I, p. 129.
20. Boulton and Fothergill, Pair of ewers, ormolu and Blue-John, *c.* 1772.
21. Wedgwood, Vase with relief of 'The Apotheosis of Homer', designed by John Flaxman, 1786.
22. Benjamin West, preparatory design for a ceiling painting. 'British Manufactory Giving Support to Industry', 1791.

Part IV
The Female Vice? Women and Luxury

Part IV addresses the gender politics of the luxury debates. From classical times, woman functioned as a 'sign' of dangerous excess. Luxury was associated with weakness, effeminacy and perilous female desire. Over the course of the eighteenth century, however, women gradually became associated with a move to re-moralise luxury as a socially progressive force. Ballaster, Jones and Eger share an interest in considering the tension between women's cultural power as both the subjects and objects of representation in the luxury debates.

In Chapter 11, 'Performing *Roxane*: the Oriental Woman as the Sign of Luxury in Eighteenth-Century Fictions', Ros Ballaster explores the recurrence of a composite figure of Orientalised femininity in dramatic and prose fictions of the late seventeenth and eighteenth century. She argues that the Oriental woman became an overdetermined signifier of ambivalent attitudes towards luxury in England. She emphasises the class mobility and ideological flexibility of the Oriental woman in Enlightenment culture, contrasting Lady Mary Wortley Montagu's appearance in Turkish dress with the exotic fiction of Daniel Defoe's *Roxana*. Ballaster's essay links the genre of Oriental fiction with the more overt economic and social emphasis of debates over luxury in eighteenth-century literature.

In Chapter 12, 'Luxury, Satire and Prostitute Narratives', Vivien Jones addresses a more explicit economy of desire, using the figure of the prostitute to examine models of exchange and luxury. Throughout the eighteenth century, the prostitute figures as sign of luxury and excess. Typified by Bernard Mandeville's justification of brothels on the grounds of their social and commercial utility, the much older morality figure of Lady Luxury is in this period given renewed energy as the whore of commerce. Whether urban streetwalker or expensive courtesan, Moll Flanders or Roxana, the prostitute seduces consumers away from productive labour into un(re)productive spending, mocking authentic exchange through the renewable, but indivisible, capital resource of her body. Jones demonstrates how the satirical and pornographic figure of the trickster-whore lends itself to the paradoxes of desire and commercial expansion analysed by Mandeville. Whether real or fictional, the prostitute memoirist is both admired and vilified; like commerce itself, her resourceful adaptability refuses the containment of a simple moral narrative.

Finally in this part, we consider the role of luxury at the opposite end of the contemporary moral spectrum. In Chapter 13, 'Luxury, Industry and Charity: Bluestocking Culture Displayed', Elizabeth Eger explores the sexual politics of commercial culture in the salons of Europe's capital cities. Women took an active part in contemporary moves to re-moralise luxury as the positive sign of social progress, vital to the progress of civilisation, and inevitably bound to emerging notions of national pride. Elizabeth Montagu self-consciously defined her salon as morally superior to those of eighteenth-century Paris. Eger considers the role of patronage, charity and the art of conversation in her argument that women made innovative contributions to the practice and theory of taste in the Enlightenment.

11

Performing *Roxane*: the Oriental Woman as the Sign of Luxury in Eighteenth-Century Fictions

Ros Ballaster

The figure of woman functions as a 'sign' of a dangerous excess in the earliest representations of luxury. John Sekora points out that the original topos of the discourse on luxury is the garden of Eden, its victim being Adam lured by Eve into a fall, noting that 'almost all personifications of luxury are feminine'.[1] The term 'luxury' has two classical roots: *luxus* meaning sensuality, splendour or pomp, and *luxuria* meaning riot, excess or extravagance. This double meaning coheres in the figure of the excessively beautiful and tempting female object of lust who also stands as a 'sign' of the power and authority of the man who enjoys and/or displays her. Early modern English representations of a feminine luxury also associate her with 'foreignness', most often French or Ottoman, the two cultures of the period with powerful and magnificent courts, extensive imperial powers and a reputation for gallantry. Sekora notes a turn of meaning over the course of the eighteenth century, toward a positive revaluation of luxury as a social and economic benefit, propelled by imperial and commercial expansion and voiced most powerfully by Bernard Mandeville's *Fable of the Bees* (1714) and David Hume's 'Of Luxury' (1752). Did one popular figure for luxury, that of the Oriental woman, undergo a similar re-evaluation through the century, acquiring new and positive connotations? Like the category of 'luxury' itself, older and newer connotations co-existed, sometimes openly in conflict, sometimes articulated independently in different contexts and registers.

Not all spokespersons for the new trading and commercial institutions of early eighteenth-century England understood 'luxury' in unequivocally positive terms and many continued to personify luxury negatively in the shape of a woman, not least Daniel Defoe. Honest trading labour had to be differentiated from personal greed to ensure a moral high-ground and political authority. Sekora comments that Defoe's 'major nonfictional works are defenses of the commercial interests against the prevailing attack upon luxury'.[2] Defoe in his novels and prose repeatedly contrasts aristocratic pleasure or parasitism, masquerade, feminine forms of display and indulgence with masculine plain-dealing, frugality and self-control. In *The Complete English Tradesman* he tells us:

TRADE is not a ball, where people appear in masque, and act a part to make sport; where they strive to seem what they really are not, and to think themselves best drest when they are least known; but 'tis a plain visible scene of honest life, shewn best in its native appearance, without disguise; supported by prudence and frugality; and, like strong, stiff, clay land, grows fruitful only by good husbandry, culture and manuring.[3]

The metaphor of the masked performance is an important one which had surfaced earlier in Defoe's most sustained representation of an excessive and self-absorbed form of trade in the figure of *Roxana: or, The Fortunate Mistress* (1724) (see Plate 23). The French-born heroine acquires the sobriquet Roxana after she becomes celebrated for the performance of a dance in Turkish dress which attract the attention of King Charles II at a series of balls she hosts at her Pall-Mall apartments; she unites in her person the twin sources of foreign luxury, France and Turkey. Roxana tells her readers that her dancing 'had the French Behaviour under the Mahometan Dress'.[4] The inconsistent chronology of Defoe's novel has often been noted: in her opening paragraph, the heroine informs us she fled to England as a child with her Protestant parents under Catholic persecution in 1683, yet in her mature years she is dancing for a monarch who died in 1685. If this inconsistency produces a rent in the realist fabric of the text, on another level, that of ideology, it serves to bring together two periods of ostentatious luxury with very different class associations: the expansion in trade, markets and colonial activity embodied in the new financial institutions of the Bank of England, the City, etc. of the early eighteenth century and the late Stuart Court of Charles II (1660–85), repeatedly presented in fiction, poetry and drama of the period as a mirror of the Ottoman seraglio with a decadent pleasure-loving monarch at its centre.

Taking the figure of Defoe's Roxana as its starting point, this essay explores the recurrence of a composite figure of Orientalised femininity in dramatic and prose fictions of the late seventeenth and eighteenth century as an overdetermined signifier of the ambivalent attitudes toward luxury in England. This figure demon-strates enormous class mobility (hers is a role 'performed' by whores, actresses and aristocratic women alike) and ideological flexibility (she can stand for suffering virtue, moral and political duplicity, economic agency and economic exploitation). When the working-class woman, particularly the prostitute or actress, adopts Turkish dress she does so to turn a profit from male voyeurs; when the aristocratic woman such as Lady Mary Wortley Montagu adopts Turkish dress she does so to express her freedom from the constraints of western marriage and government. Contrast Lady Mary Wortley Montagu's description of her Turkish habit to her sister Lady Mar from Adrianople on 1 April 1717 with the description by a prostitute named Mary who tells her story in the second part of the popular picaresque series entitled *The English Rogue* by Richard Head and Francis Kirkman of 1668. Mary adopts Turkish dress to keep the attention of her young lover, a country gentleman who is enamoured of the image of Roxolana, Suleyman the Magnificent's wife (see Plate 24) as portrayed in William Davenant's play *The Siege of Rhodes* (first performed in 1656, and extensively revised in 1661):

I so ordered the matter, that I got a Taylor, and other persons who were used to make habits for the Players, to make me a habit in all things like to that of Roxolana; this being done, I acquainted my young Gentleman, and told him that for his better satisfaction, he should see the famed Princess at our quarters, where he might have more freedom then at any other place; he was herewith very well contented; he habiting himself in the richest garbs he had, and a Colation was provided to treat his expected Mistris; all things being thus fitted on his part, I put on the provided habit; and instead of the expected Roxolana, I entred the Room where he was, attending by two or three, who bore up my train, and had set my self out with so many Jewels, both good, and counterfeit; and was indeed in all things so like the Roxolana he had seen, that he doubted not but I was the very same, and was much surprised at the matter: and although my face was as lovely as hers, yet I had added somewhat thereto to appear more beautiful.[5]

Lady Mary has also obtained a tailor and she too stresses the luxury of the garb; the jewels she describes are, however, all genuine and she provides a minute account of materials used and their treatment. She calls particular attention to the 'modesty' of her clothing, as well as its comfort, strangeness and value:

The first piece of my dress is a pair of drawers, very full, that reach to my shoes, and conceal the legs more modestly than your petticoats. They are of a thin rose colour damask, brocaded with silver flowers, my shoes of white kid leather embroidered with gold. Over this hangs my smock of a fine white silk gauze, edged with embroidery. This smock has wide sleeves hanging half way down the arm and is closed at the neck with a diamond button; but the shape and colour of the bosom is very well to be distinguished through it. The *entari* is a waistcoat made close to the shape, of white and gold damask with very long sleeves falling back and fringed with deep gold fringe, and should have diamond or pearl buttons. My caftan of the same stuff with my drawers, is a robe exactly fitted to my shape and reaching to my feet, with very long straight-falling sleeves. Over this is the girdle of about four fingers broad which all that can afford have entirely of diamonds and of other precious stones; those that will not be at that expense have it of exquisite embroidery on satin, but it must be fastened before with a clasp of diamonds. The *cüppe* is a loose robe they throw off, or put on, according to the weather, being of a rich brocade (mine is green and gold) either lined with ermine or sables. The sleeves reach very little below the shoulders. The headdress is composed of a cap, called kalpak which is in winter of fine velvet embroidered with pearls or diamonds and in summer of a light shining silver stuff. This is fixed on one side of the head, hanging a little way down with a gold tassel, and bound on either with a circle of diamonds (as I have seen several) or a rich embroidered handkerchief. On the other side of the head the hair is laid flat and here the ladies are at liberty to show their fancies, some putting flowers, others a plume of heron's feathers and, in short, what they please; but the most general fashion is a large bouquet of jewels made like natural flowers; that is, the buds of pearl, the roses of different coloured rubies, the jessamines of diamonds, the jonquils of topazes, etc, so well set and enamelled 'tis hard to imagine anything of that kind so beautiful.[6] (See Plate 25.)

The contrast is not between the natural and the artificial so much as different kinds of performance on the part of the two Marys. The working-class Mary puts together a show that successfully passes in the dim evening light for an authentic imitation of an imitation (she is copying an English actress playing the part of a Turkish sultana). Lady Mary, by contrast, is concerned with calling attention to a sophisticated performance of beauty and ornamentation, finishing on the image of jewels carved into the shape of flowers, thus making the connection between her own aristocratic status and the luxury indulged in by Ottoman women of an equivalent class.

The performance of Defoe's Roxana, the representation of which was no doubt influenced by Kirkman's earlier fiction although Montagu's letters would not have been available to Defoe (they were not published until 1763), is ambiguously placed between these two class-determined positions. Defoe's appears to be performing one role, that of the aristocratic lady flirting with Oriental dress and practice as a sign of her wealth and intellect, where the readers are aware of the economic imperatives which drive the heroine's performances of a host of identities and the history of selling sexual services prior to the adoption of this role. So too her performance is poised between the authentic and the inauthentic. Defoe's heroine has learnt Turkish and Moorish dances and smatterings of language and song from a female Turkish slave acquired for her at Leghorn by her lover the Prince whom she has joined on his Grand Tour. Her Turkish dress was obtained from the same Maltese man of war which had seized a Turkish vessel going from Constantinople to Alesandria with a cargo of ladies bound for Grand Cairo in Egypt:

> and with this Turkish Slave, I brought the rich Cloaths too. The Dress was extraordinary fine indeed, I had bought it as a Curiosity, having never seen the like; the Robe was a fine *Persian*, or *India* Damask; the Ground white, and the Flowers blue and gold, and the Train held five Yards; the Dress under it, was a Vest of the same, embroider'd with Gold, and set with some Pearl in the Work, and some *Turquois* Stones; to the Vest, was a Girdle five or six Inches wide, after the *Turkish* Mode; and on both ends where it join'd, or hook'd, was set with Diamonds for eight Inches either way, only they were not true Diamonds; but no-body knew that but myself. The Turban, or Head-Dress, had a Pinacle on the top, but not about five Inches, with a piece of loose Sarcanet hanging from it; and on the Front, just over the Forehead, was a good Jewel, which I had added to it.[7]

On her second appearance at the king's request as Roxana at a ball at her lodgings, Defoe's heroine faces competition in the shape of two bare-headed, unmasked, richly attired 'authentic' Turkish ladies, one from Georgia the other from Armenia. Significantly, they wear no jewels and the heroine informs us complacently that their dancing pleased with its novelty 'yet there was something wild and Bizarre in it, because they really acted to the Life the barbarous Country whence they came; but as mine had the French Behaviour under the Mahometan Dress, it was every way as new, and pleas'd much better, indeed'.[8] The authentic 'barbarous' (derived, of course, from the 'barbary' coast of West Africa) Turkish femaleness is understood to be beyond western comprehension. More familiar is the image of the aristocratic slaves of the Grand Sultan's seraglio at Constantinople, a role made familiar by the drama and art of the period. The inauthentic performance of the Roxana role is closer to the Western construction of the luxurious East than those 'real' representatives conjured up in the novel to rival the western European woman's dominance.

Class ambivalence was recognised as a characteristic associated with the historical figure of Roxolana who is the primary 'source' for early eighteenth-century English Roxanes. Roxolana or Hurrem ('the laughing one') Sultana, was a slave of Russian, probably Ukrainian ('Russelana'), extraction who became the favourite of Suleyman the Magnificent in the mid-sixteenth century. She confined herself in her apartments and refused Suleyman sexual access until he had legally married her, making her the first legal 'wife' of an Ottoman Sultan. In 1541 when the Old Palace, in which the courtesans and children of the Sultan were housed, burnt down, Roxolana moved to the Grand Seraglio with her entourage of odalisques and eunuchs marking the beginning of what was referred to as 'The Reign of Women', a long period in Ottoman history when the Sultans were ostensibly under the sway of their mothers, mistresses and daughters, more interested in sexual and luxurious pleasures than military glory and imperial expansion. In the late 1540s Roxolana plotted to turn Suleyman against his eldest male child by another courtesan, Mustafa, resulting in Mustafa's death by his father's hand. She died in 1557 two years after she had given her support to an attempt on the part of her younger son, Bajazet, to displace his older brother, Selymus, as Suleyman's heir. Richard Knolles stresses the class contradictions in his 1603 description of Roxolana at the height of her power as 'of late a Slave, but now become the greatest empresse of the East'; Knolles provides a handsome engraved image of Roxolana and also a poem which warns 'Too fairest lookes trust not too farre, nor yet to beautie brave: / For hateful thoughts so finely maskt, their deadly poisons have.'[9]

This same Roxolana also appears in a French romance by the influential Madeleine de Scudéry entitled *Ibrahim, or the Illustrious Bassa* (first translated in 1652 from the 1641 original). Scudéry's *Ibrahim* is presented as a secret history in which the famous Grand Vizier of the reign of Suleiman the Magnificent, Ibrahim, is revealed to be a Genoan hero. The real Ibrahim's death by strangling in March 1536 probably at the instigation of Roxolana is, in Scudéry's fiction, explained as a device which enabled Ibrahim (really Justiniano) to leave Turkey with his Genoan beloved, Isabella, for whom Soliman had developed an unfortunate passion. The narrative's apparently simple opposition between Occident (Isabella and Justiniano share an elevated and courteous love) and Orient (Soliman and Roxelana are driven by powerful passions of desire and ambition) is complicated by class hierarchies. Roxelana is the daughter of a low-born Grand Vizier and a slave girl who has been educated to use her sexual attraction as a lever in the attainment of political power. Soliman's refined aristocratic sensibilities about loyalty to his friend, Ibrahim, mean that he struggles to overcome his feelings for Isabella. However, rationalism, the tempering and deferral of desire, remain firmly on the side of the European races. When Soliman determines to declare his love to Isabella, he opens by asking her whether 'an error, which is not voluntary, merits as much chastisement, as a premeditated malice?'[10] Isabella responds that 'all persons that have great Souls like thy Highness can never commit faults but voluntarily. There is nothing that can force Reason when one will make use of it; and the most violent passions without doubt are but the pretext of weak ones . . .'[11]

However, although the Oriental woman is imagined in the examples above as the source of violent and excessive passions, these are not on her part simply sexual; the performance of Roxolana's role is also understood as an important model for women who wish to secure political and marital power. In the story of Charlot in Delarivier Manley's scandal fiction, *The New Atalantis* (1709), the unfortunate Charlot is seduced (largely through the introduction of erotic classical material to her reading) and then neglected by her guardian, the Duke. She is befriended by an older Countess who 'advised her to bestow no more favours, till he paid her price; made her read the history of Roxelana who, by her wise address brought an imperious sultan, contrary to the established rules of the seraglio, to divide with her the royal throne.'[12] Charlot's resolution wavers and she is cast off in favour of the Countess who wisely refuses the Duke sexual gratification until after marriage.

The Roxolana of Davenant's popular tragi-comedy *The Siege of Rhodes* also serves as a role-model for European court women. Like Scudéry, Davenant concerns himself with the contrast between an Occidental couple, Alphonso and Ianthe (Neapolitans who are in Rhodes when Suleiman lays siege to it) and Suleiman and Roxolana. However, the Oriental couple, after appearing at first to conform to the stereotype of bloody, vengeful and passion-driven Eastern autocrats, are revealed at the play's close to be truly courtly and gallant. Suleiman has put Ianthe in Roxolana's power to test his wife's restraint while Roxolana threatens to kill Alphonso to test the strength of Ianthe's love. The play closes on reconciliation and a celebration of the mutual chastity and devotion of the two couples. Perhaps unsurprisingly, it is female dress that becomes a key metaphor for a luxurious departure from state business, but it is also, Roxolana reveals, only a performance, a dress adopted to conceal her aspiration to political agency. Roxolana after an exchange with the court favourite Bassa Rustan comments that mistakenly he thinks her simply an ornament without political power:

> These are Court-Monsters, Corm'rants of the Crown:
> They feed on Favour till th'are over-grown;
> Then sawcily believe, we Monarchs Wives
> Were made but to be Dress't

> For a continu'd Feast;
> To hear soft Sounds, and play away our Lives.
> They think our Fulness is to wane so soon
> As if our Sexes Governess, the Moon,
> Had plac'd us, but for Sport on Fortunes lap;
> They with bold Pencils, by the changing shape
> Of our frail Beauty, have our Fortune drawn;
> And judge our Breasts transparent as our Lawn;
> Our hearts as loose, and soft, and slight
> As are our Summer Vests of Silk;
> Our brains, like to our Feathers light;
> Our blood, as sweet as is our Milk:
> And think, when Fav'rites rise, we are to fall
> Meekly as Doves, whose Livers have no Gall.
> But they shall find, I'm no European Queen,
> Who in a Throne does sit but to be seen;
> And lives in Peace with such State-Thieves as these
> Who rob us of our business for our ease.[13]

Roxolana both invokes and revokes the parallel between Occident and Orient, recalling the expected role of vengeful queen associated with her name only ultimately to play a different part in the drama, that of facilitator of harmony and reconciliation.

Behind these versions of Roxolana, lie other Roxanes and Roxanas associated with the Orient. Perhaps most famous is the Roxana of Nathaniel Lee's *The Rival Queens* (1677), first wife of Alexander the Great who murders her rival, the virtuous Persian princess and newly made second wife, Statira.[14] An over-blown caricature of Oriental excess, Lee's Roxana practises her art in order to hold the most powerful ruler of the globe. When the feeble Cassander offers her his affections in place of Alexander who has returned to Statira's arms, she mocks:

> You thought, perhaps, because I practis'd charms
> To gain the King, that I had loose desires:
> No, 'tis my pride that gives me height of pleasure,
> To see the man by all the world admir'd,
> Bow'd to my bosom, and my Captive there:
> Then my veins swell, and my arms grasp the Poles,
> My breasts grow bigger with the vast delight,
> 'Tis length of Rapture, and an age of Fury.
> No, if I were a wanton I wou'd make
> Princes the Victims of my raging fires:
> I, like the changing Moon, wou'd have the Stars
> My followers, and mantled Kings by night
> Shou'd wait my call; fine Slaves to quench my flame,
> Who lest in Dreams they should reveal the deed,
> Still as they came, successively shou'd bleed.[15]

Lee's Roxana deploys the same range of allusion as Roxolana (moon, milk, blood), but fulfils the role of the vengeful queen rather than revoking it. However, for both Oriental queens it is ambition rather than lust, social, economic and political influence rather than excessive sexual desire, that drives their behaviour and leads them to exercise their arts and charms. The rivalry between Statira and Roxana is also the key narrative in Gauthier de Costes de la Calprenède's romance, *Cassandra* (1652), although here it is their mutual passion for the Scythian Oroondates that leads them into conflict. Here, too, duplicity and splendid dress are the twin characteristics of Roxana; at her first meeting with Oroondates she is 'exceeding handsome, and very sumptuous apparelled'; when she realises his devotion to Statira she uses 'a thousand malitious tricks' and 'little inventions' to cause a breach between the lovers, yet later in the story all her 'beauty and subtilty' are not enough to prevent Alexander returning to his first passion for Statira and taking her as his second wife.[16] Two other influential French Roxanes act from frustrated sexual desire rather than political ambition, throwing away their political power and finally losing their lives in the pursuit of romantic or sexual fulfilment. The Roxane of Racine's *Bajazet* (1672) and the Roxane of Charles Montesquieu's *Lettres Persanes* (1721). Racine's *Bajazet* again deploys the contrast between the virtuous and the violent Oriental woman; Roxane, violent and sensual chief courtesan of Sultan Morad IV (1623–40) lusts after his brother, Bajazet, and tries to persuade him to marry her and usurp his brother's Sultanate in Amurat's absence. Bajazet, however, loves the intelligent and virtuous Ottoman aristocrat, Atalide, who persuades him to go along with Roxane in order to save his own life. The play concludes with the deaths of all three protagonists.[17] Montesquieu's Roxana is the most virtuous courtesan in the seraglio of Usbek, the Turkish traveller whose ironic observations on the French court make up the bulk of the novel. Roxana, we are told, like her namesake Roxolana, refused her sexual favours for some time, refusing to give up her chastity for two months. However, the novel concludes with the discovery by Usbek's chief eunuch that 'her stern virtue was all a cheat; it was only a Veil to her perfidiousness.'[18] The novel closes on a letter from Roxana to Usbek which she writes as the poison she has taken works through her body after she has been discovered with her young lover:

> How could'st thou think me so credulous, as to fancy my self sent into the world for no other purpose than to adore your Caprices? that at the same time thou allowed'st thy self all manner of liberties, thou hadst a right to confine all my desires? No: I lived indeed in servitude, but still I was free. . . . [T]hou hast had a long time the advantage of believing a heart like mine was a slave to thee: we were both of us happy: you fancy'd you cheated me, and I all the while actually cheated you.[19]

There can be little doubt of the importance of this Roxana as a model for Defoe's heroine, who discusses the relative merits of concubinage over marriage in the retention of women's freedom and contemplates suicide toward the close of her own narrative.

However, the links between these versions of Roxane/Roxana/Roxelana lie in the association of the Oriental woman with a kind of verbal agility which wins her political influence, the performance of luxury (the indulgence of sexual passion, the display of a voluptuous body to the desiring male) which conceals political ambition, astuteness and in some cases moral agency. Katie Trumpener concludes that by the early eighteenth century Roxane 'the literary character, [was] an oriental queen who always, no matter what the plot in which she appeared, embodied ambition, sexuality, revenge, exoticism; in fact, in the eighteenth century she came to personify womanhood itself: mysterious, sensual, resentful.'[20] The figure of the Oriental woman in European narrative is, above all else as the examples discussed above indicate, associated with the practice of plotting, whether for positive or negative ends. Bacon cites Roxolana as a 'cruel' example along with Livia and Isabella, queen to Edward II, of the kind of danger to empire posed 'when the Wives have Plots, for the Raising of their owne Children; Or else that they be Advoutresses [i.e. adulteresses]'.[21] Roxolana manages male sexual passion in order to gratify her own (for political sway). The Oriental woman as an expert manipulator of fictions is not always however presented in this negative light, as the exploiter of a masculine weakness for luxurious pleasure in order to advance her own interests at the expense of the state. She can also exercise a profitable indulgence of luxury in her use of stories to curtail and control masculine excess. The figure of Roxana, or the violent and transgressive Oriental queen, is often contrasted with a figure of virtuous but equally articulate and performative Oriental femininity: Atalide in Racine's play, Statira in Lee's and in *Cassandra*. The best-known female Oriental figure of the period is the fictional Scheherazade who can also be classed in this tradition. Translations into French from Arabic by the Orientalist Antoine Galland appeared in his native country in twelve volumes under the title *Mille et Une Nuit* from 1704 to 1717 and as each volume appeared it was almost immediately translated into English. *Turkish Tales*, translated into English from his fellow Orientalist François Pétis de la Croix's French text based on a pre-Islamic Persian cycle of tales known as the Sindibad-nama, appeared in England in 1708. The frame narratives of Galland's and Petis de la Croix's collections present a power struggle between male autocrats and female speakers and usefully stage the contrast between positive and negative uses of plotting by women. Galland's frame is the best known: the vizier's daughter, Scheherazade volunteers to marry the Sultan Schahriar, who has vowed to execute each new wife the day after the wedding night to ensure he can never be cuck-olded. She persuades her younger sister Dinarzade to prompt her each morning to begin a new tale which she then leaves in suspense so that her husband delays her execution to hear its conclusion. Many of the tales, particularly those told at the start of the collection when the frame is still in place, are tales about the withholding of arbitrary and tyrannical punishment in exchange for further storytelling, so that narrative content parallels narrative frame. Pétis de la Croix's *Turkish Tales* also involve a female story-teller, but in this case the tales 'which the Turks call in Derision The Malice of Women' are tales told by a sultana about tyrannous sons to counter stories of deceitful women told by his visiers to a sultan who has to decide whether to execute his son, the latter sworn to a vow of silence, for an alleged sexual assault on the sultaness.[22]

The contrast between these two models of dangerous and virtuous Oriental female story-tellers might be paralleled with that between the older idea of luxury as a wasteful entropic decadence and new formulations of it as a productive source of power, indeed vehicle for the advancement of civic virtue. These popular narratives also connect in a different way to the luxury debates as themselves products of an expanding market in foreign imports. The narrative content of fiction, particularly French versions of the Oriental tales, can be viewed as one among other exotic foreign imports such as tea and chocolate that provided pleasurable, sometimes cast as dangerous, stimulation to an expanding English consumer culture. Like Roxana's dance, these tales are all the more attractive because they have been tailored by their translators French and English to Occidental tastes and preconceptions of the Orient; their inauthenticity/performativity is the guarantor of their affect. The performance of Oriental womanhood continues throughout the century to be associated with luxuriant pleasures and empty display. Ottoman courtesans in the Grand Seraglio stand as the signs of the wasteful pursuit of empire for the adornment of the female body and the empty display of power. Imitation of this kind of folly by the expanding English empire can only lead to similar degeneracy and eventual decline (the indulgence of luxury is seen as the cause of the fall of both the Roman and the Ottoman empires). A late example of the association of feminine luxury with the degeneracy of a ruling power, can be seen in Mary Robinson's 1797 novel *Walsingham* in which the narrator gives a scathing description of Lady Emily Devlin entering a gathering in Turkish dress:

> The music had long been interrupted by the trifling gabble of the company, when a new object of attraction entered the room: it was a fashionable female, dressed like the high-priestess of a Turkish haram. the perfumes of Arabia scented the air as she fluttered through the room, and the general display of complaisance which she manifested to all, excluded every one present from the vanity of individual attention. She walked in a mincing step; prattled in a small and affected tone; smiled without meaning, and was grave without being thoughtful.[23]

However, if the image of the aristocratic European woman donning Oriental dress and manners is now a source for mockery, the image of the bourgeois English girl indulging a taste for the marvellous in reading the Oriental tale retains through the century a certain moral currency. The Oriental woman can stand for both political absolutism (Roxolana) and for resistance to it (Scheherazade) and women writers of the late eighteenth century advocate the positive benefits to the growing imagination of girls of reading oriental stories. Hannah More, a writer rarely associated with female rebellion, provides an instructional cameo in her *Coelebs in Search of a Wife* (1809). Mr Stanley's children organise a fairy party for the eight-year-old Kate, who is to give up her 'little story books' for grown-up books. Her father comments that the story books are an incentive to reading, but must be abandoned or she will not move on to full-length novels and histories.

> even story books should not be founded on a principle totally contradictory to [serious doctrines], nay totally subversive of them. The Arabian Nights, and other oriental books of fable, though loose and faulty in many respects, yet have always a reference to the religion of the country. Nothing is introduced against the law of Mahomet; nothing subversive of the opinions of a Mussulman. I do not quarrel with books for having no religion, but for having a false religion. A book which in nothing opposes the principles of the Bible I would be far from calling a bad book, though the Bible was never named in it.[24]

Mary Hays' passionate heroine, Emma Courtney, is a young aficionado of the tales, significantly here too presented as a form of early education. They are told to her at the age of four or five by her aunt who has adopted the young Emma in place of a girl who died in infancy:

> When myself and my little cousins had wearied ourselves with play, their mother, to keep us quiet in an evening, while her husband wrote letters in an adjoining apartment, was accustomed to relate (for our entertainment) stories from the Arabian Nights, Turkish Tales, and other works of like marvellous import. She recited them circumstantially, and these I listened to with ever new delight: the more they excited vivid emotions, the more wonderful they were, the greater was my transport: they became my favourite amusement, and produced, in my young mind, a strong desire of learning to read the books which contained such enchanting stores of entertainment.[25]

Charlotte Smith, perhaps the most ardent of the women advocates of the French Revolution of the period, makes a reference to the mutual pleasure of reading such tales in young people as a means of resisting the stultifying seraglio-like incarceration of her young hero and heroine in the home of a tyrannical spinster aunt in *The Old Manor House* (1794). When Orlando is sent away to school he says to Monimia, the fourteen-year-old orphan who has been his playmate: 'promise me then, Monimia . . . that when I come home from school entirely, which I shall do at Christmas, we shall contrive to meet sometimes, and to read together, as we used to do, the Fairy Tales and the Arabian Nights last year, and the year before. – Will you promise me, Monimia?'[26]

Performing Roxane, then, serves multiple purposes in the early eighteenth century, and works on many different registers, not confined simply or solely to the representation of woman as the vicious source of an incitement to luxury that wastes the manly powers of a nation. The idea of the female speaker of moral tales which curb the absolutist luxurious tendencies of male authorities is also associated with the figure of the Oriental woman and especially with the moral agency of the eighteenth-century novel. Both images, like the doubled discourse of luxury as both beneficial and wasteful, co-exist; the former however acquired increasing authority, as did the vehicle for its representation, the novel, through the course of the eighteenth century.

Notes

1. John Sekora, *Luxury: The Concept in Western Thought, Eden to Smollett* (Baltimore and London, 1977), p. 44.
2. *Ibid.*, p. 117.
3. Daniel Defoe, *The Complete English Tradesman* (Dublin, 1726) volume 1, p. 93.
4. Daniel Defoe, *Roxana The Fortunate Mistress, or, a History of the Life and Vast Variety of Fortunes of Mademoiselle de Beleau, afterwards called the Countess de Wintselsheim in Germany, Being the Person known by the Name of the Lady Roxana in the time of Charles II*, ed. Jane Jack (Oxford, 1964), p. 179.
5. Francis Kirkman, *The English Rogue Continued in the Life of Meriton Latroon and Other Extravagants Comprehending the Most Eminent Cheats of Most Trades and Professions. The Second Part* (London, 1680), p. 321.
6. Mary Wortley Montagu, *The Turkish Embassy Letters*, ed. Malcolm Jack (London, 1993), pp. 69–70.
7. *Roxana*, p. 174.
8. *Ibid.*, p. 179.
9. Richard Knolles, *The Generall Historie of the Turkes* (London, 1603), pp. 758 and 759. The story of Roxolana was a popular one in the seventeenth century, told also in Painter's *Palace of Pleasure* (no. 10) and Fulke Greville's neo-Senecan drama *Mustapha* (1609, 1633).
10. Madeleine de Scudéry, *Ibrahim, or the Illustrious Brassa, an excellent new romance . . . Englished by H. Logan* (London, 1652), p. 177.
11. *Ibid.*
12. Delarivier Manley, *New Atalantis*, ed. Ros Ballaster (London, 1991), p. 41.
13. William Davenant, *The Siege of Rhodes* (London, 1670), The Second part, Act 2, p. 63.
14. Roxane, the daughter of the Bactrian chief Oxyartes, was captured and married by Alexander in 327 BC during his conquest of Asia. After Alexander's death (323), she had his second wife, Stateria, killed, and gave birth at Babylon to a son (Alexander IV) who was accepted by the Macedonian generals as joint king with Alexander's half-brother, Philip III Arrhidaeus. Roxane was captured in 316 in Macedonia by Cassander, who later took the title of king of Macedonia; he imprisoned her at Amphipolis and then executed her and her son.
15. Nathaniel Lee, *The Rival Queens, or the Death of Alexander the Great* (London, 1677), Act 4, p. 44.
16. Gauthier de Costes de la Calprenède, *Cassandra: the fam'd Romance*, trans. Charles Cotterell (London, 1676), Part 1, book 2, p. 24; part 1, book 4, p. 61 and part 1, book 5, p. 91.
17. Jean Racine, *Bajazet: tragédie* (Paris, 1672). Racine's play was first translated into English in 1717 by Charles Jordan as *The Sultaness: a tragedy, translated with alterations, from the Bajazet of Racine* (London, 1717).
18. Charles Montesquieu, *Persian Letters*, trans. Mr. Ozell (London, 1722), Vol. 2, Letter 149, p. 305.
19. *Ibid.*, pp. 307–9.
20. Katie Trumpener, 'Rewriting Roxane: Orientalism and Intertextuality in Montesquieu's *Lettres Persanes* and Defoe's *The Fortunate Mistress*', *Stanford French Review* 11:2 (Summer 1987), pp. 177–91.
21. Francis Bacon, 'Of Empire', *The Essayes or Counsels, Civill and Morall*, ed. Michael Kiernan (Oxford, 1985), p. 61.

22. *Turkish Tales, Consisting of sevearal Extraordinary Adventures: With the History of the Sultaness of Persia, and the Visiers* (London, 1708). See Preface, p. 2.
23. Mary Robinson, *Walsingham* (London, 1797), Volume 1, p. 187.
24. Hannah More, *Coelebs in Search of a Wife*, 2 vols, second edition (London, 1809), I, p. 383.
25. Mary Hays, *Memoirs of Emma Courtney*, ed. Marilyn L. Brooks (Peterborough, Ontario, 2000), p. 48.
26. Charlotte Smith, *The Old Manor House* (London, 1987), p. 19.

Plates

23. 'The Famous Roxana', frontispiece from Daniel Defoe, *Roxana: or, The Fortunate Mistress*, 1742 edition.
24. 'Roxolana', from Richard Knolles, *General Historie of the Turkes*, 1603.
25. Portrait of Lady Mary Wortley Montagu in Turkish dress, attributed to Jean Baptiste Vanmour.

12
Luxury, Satire and Prostitute Narratives
Vivien Jones

I

In *The Authentick Memoirs of the Life Intrigues and Adventures of the Celebrated Sally Salisbury* by one 'Captain Charles Walker', published in 1723, we find what must be one of the most startlingly graphic representations of sensual, economic and political excess in eighteenth-century writing. Having been rejected by the courtesan Sally Salisbury for two-timing her, the 'Gentleman well known by the Name of *Gambolini*', a holder of high office in Queen Anne's government and '"A most profligate Debauchee"', is invited to join a group of courtiers 'at a Tavern near the Royal Palace of St. *James's*'. Inside, he discovers Sally 'standing upright upon a Bed, but revers'd, her Head being in the Place where her Heels should be, she was honoured with having two PEERS for her *Supporters*, each holding and extending a well-shap'd Leg; thus every Admirer pleas'd with the *Sight*, pull'd out his Gold, and with the greatest Alacrity pursued the agreeable Diversion'.[1] The 'gold' pulled out and tossed by Sally's admirers is to be understood, at least partly, literally: as the bawdy rhyme which follows explains, the courtiers throw golden guineas between Sally's legs, and every coin lodged there '*was* all her own'.[2] Supported by peers of the realm, this iconic woman turns the world upside down to become the sole beneficiary of the courtiers' readiness to throw away their wealth.

Anticipating by some 260 years the performance art of postmodern sexual satirists like Annie Sprinkle, Sally's posture tellingly enacts the precarious mutual dependency engendered in the commerce between prostitute and client. In spite of, or indeed because of, its deceptive passivity, her body both exemplifies and speaks back to the use of the figure of the prostitute as sign of luxury and excess. This identification is pervasive in post-Mandevillian eighteenth-century culture, where the traditional morality figure of Lady Luxury takes on renewed energy as the whore of commerce, both the object and the scourge of new consumerist desires.[3] Whether urban streetwalker or expensive courtesan, Moll Flanders or Roxana, the prostitute seduces consumers away from productive labour into un(re)productive spending, mocking authentic exchange through the renewable, but indivisible, capital resource of her body. For conservative moralists, she represents the most conspicuous case of feminising, debilitating consumption; but as the motivating force of commercial expansion and thus of national ascendancy, her resourceful opportunism is not easily dismissed. (See Plate 26.)

In the Sally Salisbury anecdote, these satirical meanings are put to specific political use. Sally Salisbury – or Sarah Prydden (her real name) – certainly existed. The immediate occasion for Walker's text was Prydden's trial and imprisonment for stabbing the son of the Earl of Nottingham, and the *Authentick Memoirs* was just one of a flurry of life-narratives, broadsheets, and ballads recording her trial and recounting her career as a well-known courtesan for a popular audience.[4] But there is a further opportunistic aspect to the text. The second edition of the *Authentick Memoirs* provides a 'key to the whole', which identifies the figure of 'Gambolini', the 'profligate Debauchee' and former minister of Queen Anne, as 'Lord B-k-e'. Henry St John, Viscount Bolingbroke, leader of the Tory government during Anne's reign, was suspected of Jacobite sympathies and exiled at the accession of George I for his alleged role in secret pro-French negotiations at the time of the Treaty of Utrecht. In 1723, Bolingbroke had just returned to England, having secured a royal pardon by bribing the King's mistress, the Duchess of Kendal.[5] From at least the late seventeenth century, it is impossible to separate any example of prostitution literature from political satire, or to assume that even the most dedicated or apparently inconsequential account of bawds and whores lies outside religious and party faction. The provision of the 'key' makes absolutely explicit the generic relation of the *Authentick Memoirs* to the sexual intrigues and secret histories most famously exemplified by Delarivier Manley's *New Atalantis*.

One way of reading 'Gambolini's' encounter with Sally Salisbury, with its crudely pornographic re-enactment of Zeus's encounter with Danaë in classical myth, would be as a pro-Walpole representation of Tory corruption: as an image of Bolingbroke's bribe to the Duchess or, more generally, his 'profligate' involvement with the whore of Rome, allegedly so beloved by Jacobite sympathisers. Yet 'debauchee' though he is, the Bolingbroke figure watches but does not participate in the performance with Sally, and the text might equally well support an anti-Walpole interpretation which makes Sally the whore not of Rome, but of commerce. In this reading, Bolingbroke arrives back in Britain in the aftermath of the South Sea Bubble to witness – or collude with – the excesses of Whig corruption. The Duchess of Kendal was the recipient, after all, not only of Bolingbroke's money, but of £36,000 of unpaid-for South Sea stock.[6] The ambiguity is perhaps the point, with Sally Salisbury as the clear beneficiary of a general culture of personal excess and political corruption.

Throughout the *Authentick Memoirs*, as these readings suggest, the historical figure of Prydden/Salisbury is inseparable from the conventionalised prostitutes of satirical and scatological discourse. The 'golden shower' scene, representing the slippages of desire which connect sex with money, commerce with prostitution, has its source in classical writings in which the myth of Zeus's appearance to the nymph Danaë in the form of a shower of gold was put to satirical use.[7] But the most interesting effect of the text's conventionality is its celebration of the tantalising, mythic power of Sally Salisbury herself. Walker employs the familiar trope of an edited collection of letters, solicited, it is claimed, from contributors who knew Sally at the height of her success as a courtesan and who therefore guarantee the authenticity of the 'intrigues and adventures' they report. Predictably enough, these 'authentic' anecdotes are made up of more or less formulaic encounters between the prostitute and her clients in which, through her illicit knowledge, social liminality or sheer inventiveness, the prostitute maintains a position of (satirical) dominance. In several of these, their satirical point depends on a vengeful reversal of sexual double standards. On one occasion, for example, Sally is accused of ingratitude when she refuses to reimburse a client who saved her from arrest by lending her money, even though he is now similarly threatened with imprisonment for debt. In her defence, she claims that 'if she once gave Ear to the Cries of her *undone Fellows*, as she call'd them, there would be no end; for, says she, *There is Scarce a Jayl in Town, but what I have made a Present of a Member or two, nor a quarter of the World, but where I have sent some Stripp'd Lover a Grazing*'.[8] Sally's retorts have the gloss of a particularised wit: she neatly transfers 'undone' from herself to her male clients ('her *undone Fellows*, as she call'd them'); and she denies personal responsibility by universalising men's lustful susceptibilities (her '*Stripp'd Lover[s]*' are all over the globe).

The historical Sally Salisbury here becomes inseparable from the traditional figure of the prostitute as irrepressible trickster, familiar from such texts as *The Whore's Rhetorick* (trans. 1683), or Tom Brown's *Letters from the Dead to the Living* (1702), or *The London-Bawd* (various editions, 1705–58), and clearly influential on Defoe's shape-changing protagonist in *Moll Flanders*, published just the year before the *Authentick Memoirs*. The identification is clear from the 'Epistle Dedicatory', addressed to Sally herself, where she is celebrated as standing 'without a *Rival* in *Great Britain* amongst the Professors of *Love's Mysteries*' and as therefore '*ordained* for the Comfort and Refreshment of *Multitudes*'.[9] It is Sally Salisbury who comes out on top here. Again as in *Moll Flanders*, obvious satiric points against her promiscuity, or against a world united in its readiness to pour money away on her charms and tricks, are delivered as an affirmatory fantasy, a celebration of the whore's capacity for adaptability and endless renewal.

A similarly knowing ambivalence structures Bernard Mandeville's analysis of the relationship between private vices and public benefits, pleasure and profit, in *The Fable of the Bees*: 'Luxury / Employ'd a Million of the Poor'. More specifically, Mandeville argues, 'the worst of Women and most profligate of the Sex did contribute to the Consumption of Superfluities, as well as the Necessaries of Life, and consequently were Beneficial to many peaceable Drudges, that work hard to maintain their Families'.[10] And in his pamphlet *A Modest Defence of Public Stews*, written in the persona of a cynical libertine, Sir Harry Mordaunt, Mandeville develops more fully this inscrutably ironic defence of prostitutes and brothels on the grounds of their social and commercial utility.[11] Mandeville's difficult questions about the beneficial status of commerce and luxury become, by extension, questions about the status of prostitution itself.

The ambiguous effects of these paradoxes are evident even in such a schematically anti-Mandevillian satire as the *Tryal of the Lady Allurea Luxury*. Published anonymously in 1757, this is a typical product of the conservative anxiety about a national fighting force debilitated and feminised by the excessive consumption of, usually dangerously foreign, luxury goods, which was prompted by the Seven Years War. In the *Tryal*, Lady Allurea's alleged crime is 'a Conspiracy against the Lives, the Liberties, the Properties, the Virtue, Honour, Peace and Security of all his M[ajesty]'s Subjects' and she is accused, for example, of 'persuading the Sailors to stay at Home, and live at their Ease, and not lie in hard Hammocks, or eat salt Provisions', and of using 'every Stratagem to corrupt, and render effeminate and cowardly, the B[ritish] Soldiery'. Her defenders, in response, offer evidence of her civilising influence: 'She has refined our Taste, enlarged our Commerce, and perfected our Politics and Religion'; without her, they claim, 'Life would be a Burthen – a Scene of Sorrow and Anxiety!'. After a summing-up by the Attorney General which offers a vision of a luxury-free future in which 'Vice will not presume to associate with Opulence – nor Prostitution with Dignity', the prisoner is inevitably found guilty.[12] The figure of Lady Allurea in this text remains comparatively shadowy and largely silent, more passively symbolic and more the fine lady than the resourceful whore, but even here, the attractions of pleasure (*not* lying in 'hard Hammocks' or eating 'salt Provisions', for example) inform against the text's jingoistic moralism, and satiric meaning demands that the representative of luxury and pleasure survive: 'The Prisoner, on her Return from her Tryal, was rescued by a Mob of Nobility and Gentry, who now entertain and caress her, in Defiance of all Law and Justice.'[13]

Both the *Authentick Memoirs of . . . Sally Salisbury* and the *Tryal of the Lady Allurea Luxury* draw heavily on established generic and conceptual structures, putting the satiric resources of whore narratives and the cultural meanings of the prostitute figure to specific use. In spite of obvious differences – the playing with 'secret histories' in the *Memoirs*, the allegorical trial of luxury by an institution of state – those shared structures remain evident in both texts, in which ambivalent desires ensure the survival of the prostitute. What I want to explore now is the generic survival through the eighteenth century of the satirical prostitute narrative, the resources of which were so readily appropriated for use within the luxury debates, and to focus particularly on ways in which the traditional figure of the trickster-whore informs the popular genre of the 'authentic', so-called, prostitute memoir.

II

In studying eighteenth-century representations of the prostitute, I find myself constantly struggling with the question of how to read, and how to represent, the huge number of highly formulaic prostitution narratives produced by the newly deregulated print culture. As I have argued elsewhere, the feminist imperative in analysing this literature must be to resist and supplement, as well as simply to document, processes of marginalisation and silencing; to be wary of repeating narratives of repression; and to effect some kind of mediation between prostitute as sign – of luxury, for example – and prostitutes as working women in conditions often very far from luxurious.[14] In his recent study, *Sex and the Gender Revolution*, Randolph Trumbach provides exhaustive and invaluable documentation of sexual practices and preferences in eighteenth-century London, including a long chapter on the working conditions of (mainly working-class) prostitutes. Using court records, occasionally diaries and letters, but almost no 'literary' texts, Trumbach reaches the provocative conclusion that: 'Women . . . did not in the eighteenth century have heterosexual identities'.[15] My generic approach to prostitute memoirs is in part a response to this claim, an attempt to make the literary historian's case for the relevance of cultural narratives and the mediated nature of all texts (including court records). My aim is to sketch a descriptive taxonomy of this comparatively popular sub-genre, and to begin to speculate on what, if any, model of subjectivity and (hetero)sexuality it might yield.

The *Authentick Memoirs of . . . Sally Salisbury* is a usefully paradigmatic text with which to start since it immediately poses the central question of authenticity. The *Memoirs* are in the third person. They make no attempt to provide any internalised representation of Sally herself. But their blurring mediation of historical figures and events through formulaic devices is characteristic of all prostitute narratives – including those which purport to be, and in some cases undoubtedly are, authored by the women themselves. The representation of the whore as shape-changer, as by definition 'inauthentic', attaches itself to even the most senti-mental of prostitute narratives. In John Gay's ballad opera *Polly* of 1729, for example, one of the characters voices just such an assumption: 'There's not one of these common creatures, but, like common beggars, hath a moving story at her finger's ends, which they tell over, when they are maudlin, to their lovers.'[16] These 'moving stories' of seduction and betrayal which follow the pattern of con-version narratives and spiritual autobiography, are a staple topos in the literature of sensibility and reform later in the century. They constitute a significant sub-genre of prostitute literature and pose different, but related, questions about their strategic and contingent status. According to some accounts, their representation of the prostitute as deserving and redeemable victim takes over around the mid-century from the satirical and theatrical tradition represented by the Sally Salisbury texts – and, of course, by Gay's ballad opera.[17]

But the satirical trickster tradition persists, and its transmutations can be traced in a series of texts spanning the period from the 1720s to at least the 1780s, texts which cast this binary developmental narrative into doubt and in which 'moving stories' of victimised seduction are often simply one item in a picaresque reper-toire of narratives or scenes which are loosely held together by the protagonist whose 'memoirs' they claim to constitute. And these generic characteristics, I suggest, might be seen to construct a female sexual identity defined not in terms of the closed, mutually exclusive categories of domesticity or prostitution, but through strategic responses to change and contingency.

In emphasising generic continuities rather than authenticity, my analysis builds on but qualifies Felicity Nussbaum's discussion of the 'scandalous memoirs' in *The Autobiographical Subject*. Focusing on the memoirs by Teresia Constantia Phillips, Laetitia Pilkington and Anne, Lady Vane, all of which were published between 1748 and 1754, Nussbaum documents the discourses of class and gender which shape their contradictory functions: on the one hand 'to maintain the gender division, confining women to categories of good or bad'; but, on the other, also to 'contradict authorized versions of "woman"'.[18] Implicitly central to her celebration of these texts as 'devis[ing] new tropes for women's lives', however, is the importance of their status as female-authored, as authentic narratives by a verifiable figure, and therefore as demonstrably transgressive.[19] I am less convinced that these are really 'new tropes' and more interested in seeing what happens when we return these texts to what I am defining as their generic tradition.

In the brief but representative survey which follows, then, I have deliberately, but I hope not too violently, yoked together texts which on the face of it might appear heterogeneous – third with first-person narratives; texts which have been categorised as 'scandalous memoirs' with more overtly fictional accounts – precisely because they share significant narrative features. As well as the memoirs discussed by Nussbaum, a (by no means exhaustive) list would include, for example, the (presumably) male-authored *Authentick Memoirs ... of Sally Salisbury*, and *Memoirs of the Celebrated Miss Fanny M[urray]* (1759), both of which are third-person narratives; the first-person *Genuine Memoirs of the Celebrated Miss Maria Brown* (1766), sometimes attributed to John Cleland; first-person, apparently female-authored, texts such as *Clio, or, a Secret History of the Life and Amours of the Late Celebrated Mrs. S[a]n[so]m* (1752), *The Memoirs of Mrs. Catherine Jemmat* (1765), and *The Authentic and Interesting Memoirs of Miss Ann Sheldon* (1787–8); third-person, apparently female-authored, texts such as *The Genuine Memoirs of Miss Faulkner* (1770); and certainly Eliza Haywood's *Anti-Pamela*, published in 1741, in which the heroine's name is Syrena Tricksy.[20]

III

Prostitute memoirs follow a very similar basic pattern in which an initial, formative seduction releases the protagonist into a series of picaresque 'adventures'. These arbitrary, heterogeneous scenes achieve satiric status through their connection with the prostitute's role as the trickster who exposes and castigates excess. They are characteristics already familiar from the *Authentick Memoirs of ... Sally Salisbury*, and they take their initial justification from the reading public's assumed interest in the notoriety, real or imagined, of their protagonists. From time to time, these texts comment on their own generic identity – most often in more or less anxious attempts to distinguish their appeal from that of novels, claiming interest for 'real adventures' over those of 'nobody'.[21] Thus Catherine Jemmat asks in 1765,

> But why may not the true story of Catherine Yeo, who absolutely does exist, divert as much, allowing for the different abilities of the authors, as those of Miss Pamela, Andrews, [*sic*] or Miss Clarissa Harlowe, who never had any local habitation except in the happy fancy of their admirable author, whose characters of virtue and constancy are the narrative children of his truly benevolent soul?[22]

Her claim is echoed the following year at the beginning of *The Genuine Memoirs of the Celebrated Miss Maria Brown*:

> As the reader is not to consider this performance in the light of a novel or a romance, but the real adventures of a person who has made some noise in the gay world; so he must not be surprised if he meets with nothing in these sheets bordering upon the marvellous or surprising. The incidents of my life are not much out of the common road of female seduction, forwarded by the errors of a mistaken genteel education . . .[23]

The apologias are conventional enough – though Brown's disingenuous willingness to be boring or predictable is more knowing than Jemmat's concern to 'divert' her reader. But the juxtaposition suggests a more complicated and extended relationship between satire, scandal, and the novel than the one which Catherine Gallagher posits in *Nobody's Story*, and invites attention to these texts' shared conception of heroinism. In spite of Maria Brown's moralising nod in the direction of the 'common road of female seduction', and in spite of Jemmat's genuflection to Richardson's 'truly benevolent soul', both protagonists are recognisably the offspring of Sally Salisbury.

Jemmat's account of her career includes a good deal of abuse from her unpredictable father (a former Admiral) and a drunken husband, but its interest also depends on tantalisingly unexplained references to possible assignations with other 'lovers', in which she presents herself as mysteriously escaping censure, as well as on anecdotes which demonstrate her wit and spirit. In one near-slapstick scene, for example, she successfully fools an ageing admirer who, she hints, threatened her with violence. Her *Memoirs* stop abruptly at the death of her husband and before she moves to London. They refuse to gratify the curiosity of an audience presumably familiar with a later notoriety; instead, they draw on characteristics of the satirical prostitute-heroine to maintain interest in the little we *are* given.[24]

Towards the end of the *Memoirs of . . . Maria Brown*, as she is about to return to London from Paris, the protagonist again comments on the genre of prostitute narratives, this time in order to claim an exclusivity and originality which, she suggests, is above the kinds of gulling scenarios occasionally imitated even by Jemmat:

> It may be thought that there can be nothing very entertaining or amusing, much less novel, in the adventures of a girl of the town in London, as the histories of so many have already been published, and as they are little more than copies one from the other; the old round of Bob Derry's, Weatherby's, the Shakespeare's-head . . . are now to be sure, think some, to come into play. . . . We are to be informed how a citizen got drunk and was beat at one, was fleeced at another, and p[ox]'d at another; how Lucy C. drank burnt champaign, and danced till five in the morning, if she don't fall asleep before she gets home. All this dull beaten track I shall most cautiously avoid, as I am convinced that

such trite narrations must be unentertaining, if not nauseating: I shall take the reader into politer scenes of action, where his curiosity, added to five guineas, could not gain him admittance.[25]

The 'politer scenes of action' described in *Maria Brown* include the Paris opera and the kinds of high-class brothels in which Fanny Hill works in Cleland's *Memoirs of a Woman of Pleasure*, rather than the 'dull beaten track' of the notorious Shakespeare's-head Tavern in the Covent Garden area, haunt of streetwalkers and, of course, James Boswell.[26] Nevertheless, the pattern of clients getting drunk and being 'beat at one [venue] . . . fleeced at another, and p[ox]'d at another' is not so dissimilar from that in the repetitive lower-class whore narratives she derides in this passage – it is simply that the proceeds are more impressive, and the possibility of a lasting settlement from a particularly rich and besotted client, less completely remote. The resourceful, resilient, and ruthless figure of the whore, the scourge of male susceptibilities, is common to both.

The prostitute in these mid-century memoirs often appears to play a more generalised satiric role than in the texts engendered by the factionalism of the early century. There is always a certain amount of actual name-dropping or hinting at known public figures, but the verbal texture of the narratives tends to target the excesses of sensual indulgence, of luxury and sexual incontinence, rather than of political rivalries or national policies. Thus in the *Memoirs of the Celebrated Miss Fanny M[urray]* (1759), for example, Fanny, newly established in a 'waiting-job' close to the Haymarket, has great hopes of success in this 'emporium of commerce', and plays on her 'credit' with a 'merchant's son', turning the 'trinkets and baubles, which he was charmed to see her accept of . . . into ready money'.[27] And Maria Brown boasts of the employment she creates for milliners and hairdressers when she leads the fashion in Paris.[28] One of several interpolated narratives (another feature of the genre), in *Memoirs of . . . Fanny M[urray]* allegorises this shift of satiric mode. One of the features of this text is a documentary attention to the commercial practices of the London sex trade. Fanny at one point works for Harris, of *Harris's List of Covent Garden Ladies* fame, and Harris gets to tell his story, in which he establishes a connection with the Tory satirical journalism of the 1710s and 1720s. His father, who was one of the 'anti-ministerial writers of those days' and 'a long while a potent antagonist of Sir R[obert] W[alpole]', disgusted by his party's refusal to help him when he is imprisoned for sedition, develops an 'utter detestation' of both parties and advises his son to abandon integrity and learning and pursue corrupt self-interest. The result is Harris's success in the 'insinuating, dissembling, flattering' and 'elegant art' of pimping. And Harris is represented as congratulating himself in terms which explicitly recall Mandeville's commercial approval of the utility of prostitution in *The Fable of the Bees* and *A Modest Defence of Public Stews*: 'I look upon myself to be as useful a member of society . . . as any factor or contractor whatever.'[29] The ironies in this are legion, but here I want simply to point out the way in which this story about the triumph of commerce and corruption over party interest can also be read as a self-conscious acknowledgement of the continuities within the whore narrative: Harris Senior's satiric mantle is taken over by the writers, sometimes also by the protagonists, of these memoirs.

In terms of narrative form, this continuity is in some ways most evident in the latest of the texts I am discussing here: the four-volume *Authentic and Interesting Memoirs of Miss Ann Sheldon*, published in 1787–8. Sheldon's text records a bewildering number of liaisons with peers and / or statesmen, most of whom are explicitly named. Throughout, however, the heroine maintains a sentimental attachment to 'Mr Walsingham', who acts as the voice of restraint to her indulgence in luxurious excess. This gives the text some narrative shape, but the overwhelming experience in reading this memoir is of its relentlessly episodic quality, its adherence to the heterogeneous satirical mode I have been describing. A typical incident involves Ann's concern to keep the use of a carriage lent to her by her lover Sir Peter Lester when he goes into the country: 'This little alarm was very soon communicated to my Privy Counsellors in ordinary . . . who kindly consoled me, by treating it with utmost contempt'. Inevitably, with a brash ease worthy of Sally Salisbury, Ann and her 'counsellors' (her mantua-maker and a fellow prostitute) trick her lover into giving them what they want.[30] The underplayed reference to Ann's 'Privy Counsellors' is a reminder of the satiric political potential which still lurks in such apparently inconsequential, 'private' encounters between prostitute and client.

Ann herself refers to 'the miscellany of my life' and, slightly later, 'the pantomime of my life'.[31] The 'miscellany' includes endlessly repeated incidents of the kind just described, as well as episodes in which she is less successful (narrowly escaping imprisonment for debt, for example), together with examples of her sentimental benevolence, usually involving younger, more vulnerable, and more redeemable prostitutes. 'Pantomime' suggests the theatrical imperative constantly to move on to 'other scenes', and connects her story with the forms of popular culture. Together, they encapsulate the characterising heterogeneity of what I have been claiming is a continuous sub-genre. 'Miscellany' and 'pantomime' might as readily be used to describe the narratives which accumulate around the overtly satirical figure of Sally Salisbury, and 'pantomime' is an accurate term for the iconic dumbshow played out in the scene with which I began. It also, of course, recalls such popular texts as Theophilus Cibber's 'grotesque pantomime entertainment' based on Hogarth's *A Harlot's Progress*.[32] Throughout the century, the narration of female notoriety immediately invokes this popular tradition of heterogeneity, of adaptation and survival, even of comparative inconsequentiality, whether first or third-person, authentic or otherwise.

IV

At one point in the *Genuine Memoirs of . . . Maria Brown*, the protagonist reflects on 'the modest part of the sex': 'I was convinced . . . that every modest woman strove who should most resemble a prostitute. We are upon every occasion the objects of their attention and study. . . . they are only amiable in proportion as they know how to copy us, to tincture their chastity with coquetry'.[33] The memoirist here clearly reveals her identity as Lady Luxury, voicing a version of the satirical commonplace represented in *The Tryal of the Lady Allurea Luxury*, where prosecution witnesses are called to describe what happened when Lady Allurea struck up 'An Acquaintance, or rather Intimacy' with their wives: 'from that Time, I may date the Overthrow of my whole domestic Satisfaction'.[34] The orthodox moral response invited by such claims is shock that 'modest' women should imitate the prostitute's coquettish tactics, performing rather than enacting chastity or allowing a taste for luxury to distort their domestic identity: 'My Wife . . . lolled on a Couch most of the Time that she was not in Bed, at Cards, or at her Toilet'.[35] Such a response assumes an absolute difference between the prostitute and the modest woman, a distinction which Bernard Mandeville knowingly points up in *A Modest Defence of Public Stews*, 'Young Girls are taught to hate a *Whore*, before they know what the Word means'.[36] But Maria's reflections here, as well as her later boasting about the trade she brings to Parisian milliners and hairdressers, make the more difficult Mandevillian point: about the respectable woman's dependency on the whore and the dependency of a successful economy on the excessive desires which the prostitute is used to represent. As Mandeville puts it in *The Fable of the Bees*: 'Chastity may be supported by Incontinence, and the best of Virtues want the Assistance of the worst of Vices.'[37]

At the beginning of this essay, I forged an anachronistic connection between Sally Salisbury and the satirical performance art of Annie Sprinkle.[38] Such a comparison can be only a hopeful, strategic suggestion rather than a firm analogy. Sally Salisbury's performance of excess may or may not have any basis in actuality, and may or may not, therefore, bear the attribution of a self-conscious critical identity. It would be inappropriate to expect to find individualised resistant voices within the formulaic and overdetermined texts which I have been discussing. But at the level of form at least, the analogy retains some suggestive validity. During the eighteenth century, the satirical and pornographic figure of the trickster-whore is given new impetus: her irrepressible, uncomfortable power readily lends itself to the paradoxes of desire and commercial expansion atomised by Mandeville. Whether real or fictional, the prostitute memoirist is both admired and vilified. Like commerce itself, her resourceful adaptability refuses the containment of a simple moral narrative. It is probable that such texts were more widely read by women than we might assume: we know, for example, that one of them was available in a circulating library.[39] In these memoirs, women's sexual lives are shaped by the pressures of contingency and the will to survive. Unlike redemption narratives about penitent Magdalens, this satirical form releases the female subject – as reader, at least – into the right to describe an episodic, shapeless life: into the possibility of variety, rather than choice between predetermined categories of female identity.

Notes

1. Captain Charles Walker, *The Authentick Memoirs of the Life Intrigues and Adventures of the Celebrated Sally Salisbury. With True Characters of her most Considerable Gallants*, 2nd edn (London, 1723), pp. 63, 67, 67–8.

2. *Ibid.*, p. 68.
3. The classic study of the rise of consumerism is Neil McKendrick, John Brewer and J.H. Plumb, *The Birth of a Consumer Society: The Commercialization of Eighteenth-Century England* (London, 1982). See also Ann Bermingham and John Brewer, eds, *The Consumption of Culture 1600–1800: Image, Object, Text* (London and New York, 1995).
4. See, for example, *The Effigies, Parentage, Education, Life, Merry-pranks and Conversation of the Celebrated Mrs. Sally Salisbury* ([London], 1722/3); *An Account of the Tryal of Sally Salisbury, At the Sessions-House in the Old Bailey . . .* ([London?], 1723); *The Genuine History of Mrs. Sarah Prydden, Usually Called Sally Salisbury, and her Gallants* (London, 1723); *Sally Salisbury's Letter to Frank Rig* (Dublin, 1723); *A Compleat History of the Life, Intrigues and Death of that Celebrated Lady of Pleasure, Sally Salisbury. Setting forth her Birth, Parentage and Education; also how she came to be debauch'd* (London, 1734).
5. See Julian Hoppit, *A Land of Liberty? England, 1689–1727* (Oxford, 2000), pp. 391–2, 411–12; Murray G.H. Pittock, *Jacobitism* (Basingstoke, 1998). The key to the second edition of the *Authentick Memoirs* refers to Bolingbroke as the 'late Lord B-k-e' (fol. A1v). Bolingbroke lived until 1751, but the 'late' here refers not to his actual but to his political death and exile. My thanks to John Chartres for pointing me in the right direction on the satirical meanings of this text.
6. Pittock, *Jacobitism*, p. 52.
7. See James N. Davidson, *Courtesans and Fishcakes: The Consuming Passions of Classical Athens* (London, 1997), pp. 119–20. My thanks to Helen Berry for the reference to Davidson's book.
8. *Authentick Memoirs*, p. 90.
9. 'Epistle Dedicatory', *Authentick Memoirs*, fols. B[1]v, [A3]r.
10. [Bernard Mandeville], 'The Grumbling Hive' and 'Remark (T.)', *The Fable of the Bees: or, Private Vices, Publick Benefits*, ed. F.B. Kaye, 2 vols (Oxford, 1924), I, pp. 25, 225.
11. See *A Modest Defence of Public Stews: or, an Essay upon Whoring. As it is now practis'd in these kingdoms. Written by a layman.* (London, 1724; rpt. 1740). The 1740 reprint attributes the text to 'the late Colonel Harry Mordaunt'.
12. *The Tryal of the Lady Allurea Luxury, before the Lord Chief-Justice Upright, on an Information for a Conspiracy* (London, 1757), pp. 6, 18, 22, 36, 49, 89. On anxieties about the effects of consumption on masculinity see: Philip Carter, *Men and the Emergence of Polite Society, Britain 1660–1800* (Harlow, London, New York, 2001), pp. 128–32.
13. *Lady Allurea Luxury*, p. 92.
14. See my 'Eighteenth-century Prostitution: Feminist Debates and the Writing of Histories', in Avril Horner and Angela Keane, eds, *Body Matters: Feminism, Textuality, Corporeality* (Manchester, 2000), pp. 127–42.
15. Randolph Trumbach, *Sex and the Gender Revolution*, Vol. I, *Heterosexuality and the Third Gender in Enlightenment London* (Chicago and London, 1998), p. 49.
16. John Gay, *Polly* (1729) Act I, scene xiv, *Dramatic Works*, ed. John Fuller, 2 vols (Oxford, 1983), II, p. 97.
17. See particularly W.A. Speck, 'The Harlot's Progress in Eighteenth-Century England', *BJECS*, 3 (1980), pp. 127–39.
18. Felicity Nussbaum, *The Autobiographical Subject: Gender and Ideology in Eighteenth-Century England* (Baltimore and London, 1989), p. 181.
19. *Ibid.*, p. 189.
20. My inclusion of Haywood's *Anti-Pamela* makes explicit the interaction between such texts and the novel: most obviously Daniel Defoe's *Moll Flanders* (1722) and *Roxana* (1724), and John Cleland's *Memoirs of a Woman of Pleasure* (1748–9). This important generic relationship is too complex to examine here, but for related discussions, see: William Warner, *Licensing Entertainment: The Elevation of Novel Reading in Britain, 1684–1750* (Berkeley, Los Angeles, London, 1998); Bradford K. Mudge, *The Whore's Story: Women, Pornography, and the British Novel, 1684–1830* (Oxford, 2000).

21. *The Genuine Memoirs of . . . Maria Brown* claims to describe 'real adventures', as compared with Catherine Gallagher's characterisation of the novel as the story of 'nobody'. See: *The Genuine Memoirs of the Celebrated Miss Maria Brown. Establishing the Life of a Courtezan in the most Fashionable Scenes of Dissipation*, 2 vols (London, 1766), I, p. 1; Catherine Gallagher, *Nobody's Story: The Vanishing Acts of Women Writers in the Marketplace 1670–1820* (Oxford, 1994).

22. *The Memoirs of Mrs. Catherine Jemmat, Daughter of The late Admiral Yeo, of* Plymouth, *written by Herself*, 2 vols (London, 1765), I, p. 115.

23. *Maria Brown*, I, pp. 1–2.

24. Jemmat's *Memoirs*, like her *Miscellanies in Prose and Verse* (London, 1766), boasts a huge collection of peers' names in its subscription list, as well as a few blanks indicating subscribers who preferred to remain anonymous. *Miscellanies* includes an 'Essay in Vindication of the Female Sex' which is a defence of prostitutes.

25. *Maria Brown*, II, pp. 115–16.

26. See Tony Henderson, *Disorderly Women in Eighteenth-Century London: Prostitution and Control in the Metropolis, 1730–1830* (London and New York, 1999), p. 33. See also *Memoirs of the Celebrated Miss Fanny M[urray]*, 2nd edn (London, 1759), p. 103.

27. *Fanny M[urray]*, pp. 67–8.

28. *Maria Brown*, II, pp. 75–6.

29. *Fanny M[urray]*, pp. 127–37.

30. *Authentic and Interesting Memoirs of Miss Ann Sheldon (Now Mrs. Archer:) a lady who figured, during several years, in the highest line of public life. Written by Herself*, 4 vols (London, 1787–8), I (1787), 209–10.

31. *Ann Sheldon*, II (1788), 100, 101. On miscellaneity and women's writing more generally, see Clare Brant, 'Varieties of Women's Writing' in Vivien Jones, ed., *Women and Literature in Britain 1700–1800* (Cambridge, 2000), pp. 285–305.

32. Theophilus Cibber, *The Harlot's Progress; or, the Ridotto Al'Fresco: A Grotesque Pantomime Entertainment* (London, 1733), ARS, 181 (1977).

33. *Maria Brown*, II, pp. 25–6.

34. *Lady Allurea Luxury*, p. 13.

35. *Ibid.*

36. *A Modest Defence of Public Stews* (London, 1740), p. 30; rpt. in Vivien Jones, ed., *Women in the Eighteenth Century: Constructions of Femininity* (London and New York, 1990), p. 65.

37. Remark (H.), *Fable of the Bees*, I, p. 100.

38. See, for example, Linda Williams, 'A Provoking Agent: The Pornography and Performance Art of Annie Sprinkle' in Pamela Church Gibson and Roma Gibson, eds, *Dirty Looks: Women, Pornography, Power* (London, 1993), pp. 176–91; Shannon Bell, *Reading, Writing and Rewriting the Prostitute Body* (Bloomington and Indianapolis, 1994), particularly ch. 6, 'Prostitute Performances: Sacred Carnival Theorists of the Female Body', pp. 137–84.

39. There is a bookplate from Humphry's Circulating Library, Chichester, in the British Library's copy of *The Genuine Memoirs of Miss Faulkner; otherwise Mrs. D[one]l[la]n; or Countess of H[alifa]x, in expectancy. Containing, the amours and intrigues of several persons of high distinction, and remarkable characters: with some curious political anecdotes, never before published* (London, 1770).

Plate

26. 'An Evening View on Ludgate Hill', 1749.

13
Luxury, Industry and Charity: Bluestocking Culture Displayed

Elizabeth Eger

Introduction

In 1757 a pamphlet was published, entitled *The Tryal of Lady Allurea Luxury before the Lord Chief-Justice Upright, on an Information for a Conspiracy*.[1] Lady Allurea is depicted as a voluptuous woman in chains, and a foreigner, accused of all manner of evils. The Attorney-General charges his prisoner for having 'maliciously plotted and conspired the Destruction of this Land, by corrupting the Morals of our People, and endeavouring, to the utmost of her Power, to eraze out of their Hearts every Sentiment of Humanity and Religion'.[2] She has encouraged the people to be 'in Love with Sloth and Idleness – to be base, venal, indolent, and cowardly – to give themselves up entirely to empty Amusements – false Pleasures, and the lowest and most unworthy Sensualities'.[3] Lady Allurea is accused of having 'perverted the whole Order of Nature'.[4] She has lured society into believing 'That a short Life is the most eligible, and Self-Murder the best Privilege of a great Soul; and that Gaming, fine Cloaths, Equipage, high and poignant Sauces, Infidelity, soft Beds, Dalliance, midnight Debaucheries, and the letting loose of all our Passions, are the true Springs from whence we are to draw every earthly Felicity.'[5] The Attorney-General concludes that 'Rome fell by the Devices of the Prisoner – so did Greece – and so must every Free State where she is suffered to take up her Residence – She can assume all Shapes – and, by her Blandishments, soften and effeminate the bravest, roughest, and honestest of Mankind – even the *British Sailors!*'[6] As Captain Goodmind declares, Lady Allurea Luxury is 'the Devil in the Form of the Angel'.[7] In the high-blown rhetoric of this satire we can recognise the ancient and negative association of luxury with woman, a tradition in which female desire is a threat and her potential to corrupt and disrupt is without limit. The comfortable furnishings and racey transport devices of a highly advanced society are depicted as effeminating evils that lead swiftly to moral degeneration. London fashions are seen to court disaster and precipitate the fall of civilisation.

However, luxury's disruptive power is not always presented in purely negative terms. From classical times, diatribes against luxury have frequently been ambivalent in tone. Luxury attracts and repels. It has been figured as both plague and medicine, friend and foe of social progress. Mr Bergamot's speech for the defence of Lady Allurea Luxury begins by asking 'Whether the Lady ALLUREA LUXURY is not the Support of all valuable society – or, rather, whether any Society can be rich and flourishing without her immediate Influence and Assistance?'[8] He then lists her achievements, pointing out that her 'daily improvements, as well as Discoveries, in all the great Arcana of Nature, are what give Spirits to all manner of Commerce – . . . she finds Markets for all Sorts of Manufactures – encourages the Arts, and every Branch of ingenious Science – and maintains the Poor and Industrious of every Nation that she takes under her Protection.' For Sergeant Bergamot, Lady Allurea is 'the Life of Every State' who makes the 'Blood' of money 'flow into every Vein of the Body Politic, so as to preserve all the Members in a due State of Salubrity'.[9] If Lady Allurea Luxury is rightfully acknowledged as a necessary support of the national economy, 'the Life of Every State', she must be seen in a very different light.

The eighteenth century witnessed a general movement to remoralise luxury, to defend the role of comfort and pleasure as the source and sign of social progress. Women played a vital role in this movement, as consumers and leaders of fashion and as the manipulators of a new culture of regulated pleasure and opulence.[10] While scholars have focused on aspects of female consumption in the eighteenth century, few have revealed women's more active role in the contemporary economy.[11] Women were aware of their capacity to control and redefine their relation to luxury and morality, and carve a new space in which debates about wealth and virtue could take place. They participated in the remoralisation of luxury through their public involvement in the definition of contemporary culture and the polite arts.

Women were both the subject and object of representation in debates about the relation between commerce and the arts. Like many moral debates of the eighteenth century, discussions about commerce, liberty and luxury both used women as a yardstick for the relative health or degeneracy of the nation and required the idealisation of the female subject as a means of representing the model state. Representations of women as 'liberty', 'justice' or 'virtue', or conversely 'vice' abound in eighteenth-century visual and literary culture.[12] Both the real and symbolic figures of women occupied a visible and active role in the development of a national culture. In contrast to the political realm described by civic humanism, the notion of the public sphere described by writers on taste, such as Addison, Hogarth, Hume and Kames, was constituted by public spaces, locations of polite assembly, commerce and leisure. Women played a formative role in establishing the codes of sociability practised within these spaces, none more so than Elizabeth Montagu.

Elizabeth Montagu's salon: luxurious lyceum

Born Elizabeth Robinson in 1720, Montagu lived until 1800. As the author of an important *Essay on Shakespeare*[13] and as the patron of several well-known writers of the period, she both created and embodied a notion of female taste that contributed to the foundation of contemporary moral virtue and literary criticism.

She also created an opulent yet highly regulated literary salon to rival the most famous salons of Europe's capital cities, self-consciously defining her influence as morally superior to that of her contemporary Parisian hostesses. She represented the epitome of female intellect and taste in her own lifetime, and was heralded in an obituary as 'an ornament to her sex and country'. Her talent for display was frequently praised in such positive terms and while her enthusiasm for exuberant interior decoration appears now to border on unreasonable excess, she seems to have escaped the disdain reserved for the fashionable folly of several of her female contemporaries. She maintained a reputation for moral virtue, despite her conspicuous talent for spending money. While the notion of female display had previously held negative connotations in the context of the luxury debates, Montagu's acts of cultural display were calculated to justify her wealth, to promote what she termed 'the right use of luxury'. Her salon was famous among the men and women of her day for its seemingly perfect balance between culture and commerce, intellect and pleasure.

For Montagu, these spheres were to a certain extent physically demarcated by the contrasting nature and functions of her properties. She divided her time between winters in her London home, the setting for her London assemblies; spring and autumn at Denton near Newcastle, where she managed her collieries; and summers at her country estate at Sandleford in Berkshire, where she retreated from the glare of society and the arduous work of running her mines. She also travelled to Bath, Tunbridge Wells and the country seats of her noble friends. Known as 'Fidget' in her youth, she had unstinting energy for entertaining, whether as a matter of intellectual delight or social duty. Even at Sandleford, she described herself as 'an ambitious farmer' and became minutely involved in the vagaries of the potato trade. As she wrote to her sister on 26 December 1767, Montagu considered herself 'a Critick, a Coal Owner, a Land Steward, a sociable creature'.[14] Her behaviour in all these spheres of activity was integral to her definition of what she termed 'bluestocking philosophy'.

By the time of Montagu's death in 1800, the term 'bluestocking' had become synonymous with women writers and intellectuals, having been used in a gender-specific sense only since the early 1770s. The phrase was originally used to abuse the Puritans of Cromwell's 'Little Parliament' in 1653. It was revived in 1756 when Benjamin Stillingfleet appeared at one of Montagu's assemblies wearing blue worsted stockings, normally the garb of working men.[15] The term came to be applied more generally to all Montagu's visitors, who included Dr Johnson, Elizabeth Carter, James Boswell, Edmund Burke, David Garrick, Sir Joshua and Frances Reynolds, Horace Walpole, Lord Lyttleton, the Earl of Bath and later Frances Burney, Anna Barbauld and Hannah More. Social historians have long remarked on the explosion of societies and clubs at the beginning of the century, which has been interpreted as a sign of cultural optimism and scientific, professional and moral confidence. Women's participation in urban club-life was generally limited.[16] However, the bluestockings did not define themselves as a formal club, but rather promoted a new attitude to manners and intellect, a greater equality between men and women in the realm of conversation, politics and letters. Their assemblies should be seen in the context of the emerging 'cult of sensibility', which critics have defined in terms of a gendered transformation of manners in which feminine attributes, such as softness, sympathy and charity, were adopted by both men and women.[17] While originally aristocratic in formation, the bluestockings admitted members into their circle on merit alone; and although Montagu was not radical in her plans for educational improvement, at her London assemblies she did encourage a new sense of openness, a resituation of knowledge which made participation in literary life more accessible to a greater number of individuals. In 1758, Edward Wilson described Montagu as a 'highly instructive accomplished Woman possessed of great affluence, who indulges herself in a chaste display of fashionable as well as literary Elegance, makes her Drawing Room the Lyceum of the day, maintains a luxurious hospitality for the Votaries of that science which she loves, and patronises learning which she has herself adorned.'[18]

Montagu's guests originally met at her Hill Street home, famous for its 'Chinese room'. It was against the backdrop of pagodas, nodding mandarins, cushions of Japan satin and curtains decorated by Chinese painting on gauze that Montagu's guests were to concentrate on improving their minds. The aspiring author Nathanial Wraxall, who visited the bluestocking assemblies regularly during the 1760s, complained of the brilliance of Montagu's diamonds:

> I used to think these glittering appendages of opulence, sometimes helped to dazzle the disputants, whom her arguments might not always convince, or her literary reputation intimidate. Notwithstanding the defects and weaknesses I have mentioned, she possessed a masculine understanding, enlightened, cultivated, and expanded by the acquaintance of men, as well as of books. . . . She was constantly surrounded by all that was distinguished for attainments or talents, male or female, English or foreign; and it would be almost ungrateful in me not to acknowledge the gratification, derived from the conversation and intercourse of such society.[19]

The gaudiness of Montagu's earrings is seemingly redeemed by her 'masculine understanding'. Wraxall is reluctantly impressed by the conjunction of material and intellectual brilliance that forms the unique quality of Montagu's salon. Hannah More's initial reaction to Montagu is similar in tone. Having arrived in London from the West country, she wrote in a letter of 1775 to her sister of her excitement at meeting Sir Joshua Reynolds and Dr Johnson, Mrs Barbauld and Mrs Carter at Montagu's salon,

> a party that would not have disgraced the table of Laelius, or of Atticus. Mrs Montagu received me with the most encouraging kindness; she is not only the finest genius, but the finest lady I ever saw: she lives in the highest style of magnificence; her apartments and table are in the most splendid taste; but what baubles are these when speaking of a Montagu! her form (for she has no body) is delicate even to fragility; her countenance the most animated in the world;

the sprightly vivacity of fifteen, with the judgement and experience of a Nestor.[20]

After this initial, rather breathless description, More goes on to praise Montagu's assembly, with its 'diversity of opinions' and 'argument and reasoning'. She enjoyed meeting her fellow female writers, and was attracted to those admitted, like herself, for talent rather than rank.[21] Richard Cumberland, who graced Montagu's drawing room on frequent occasions, described her influence thus: 'She can make a mathematician quote Pindar, a master in Chancery write novels, or a Birmingham hardware-man stamp rhimes as fast as buttons'.[22] Cumberland pokes fun at her efficient and mechanical attitude to literary talent, implying that she lacks the true connoisseurship of the gentleman. He also conveys a certain disdain (and perhaps even anxiety) regarding the varied social status of those Montagu attracted to her salon, from young ladies to Birmingham hardware-men. The fashionable attire of Montagu's guests was matched by a self-conscious display of wit and intellect.

Hume, in his essay 'Of the Refinement of the Arts', originally entitled 'Of Luxury', argued that the taste for refinement in the arts creates a community of cultural consumers, of both sexes, who 'flock into cities, love to receive and communicate knowledge; to show their wit or their breeding; their taste in conversation or living, in clothes or furniture'. He emphasised that 'Particular clubs and societies are everywhere formed, . . . where both sexes meet in an easy and sociable manner.'[23] Like Hume, Montagu fostered communication between the sexes, writing that 'no society is completely agreeable if entirely male or female. The masculinisms of men, and the feminalistics of the women, if the first prevail they make conversation too rough, and austere, if the latter, too soft and weak. Discourse led entirely by men is generally pedantick or political.'[24] She was particulary impressed by the level of conversation between the sexes in Paris, where she visited the leading salons in 1776, revelling in the controversy caused by her denunciation of Voltaire in her *Essay on Shakespeare*: 'I am much pleased with the Conversation one finds here, it is equally free from pedantry and ignorance. All the hours I have pass'd in mix'd company I have spent agreeably. The men of letters are well bred and easy, and by their vivacity and politeness shew they have been used to converse with women. The ladies by being well inform'd, and full of those graces we neglect when with each other, shew they have been used to converse with Men.'[25] As Hume observes in his description of mixed urban sociability, there is an inevitably self-confirming pleasure that arises from shared conversation in a suitably tasteful setting, in which people consciously receive pleasure from the process of self-improvement they are enacting: 'besides the improvements which they receive from knowledge and the liberal arts, it is impossible but they must feel an encrease of humanity, and from the very habit of conversing together, and contributing to each other's pleasure and entertainment. Thus *industry*, *knowledge*, and *humanity*, are linked together in an indissoluable chain, and are found, from experience as well as reason, to be peculiar to the more polished, and what are commonly denominated, the more luxurious ages.'[26]

Industry and charity

Montagu practised Hume's categories of industry, knowledge and humanity with equal zeal. She was profoundly self-conscious of the relationship between her material wealth and her interest in the fine arts, especially as she was closely involved in managing and increasing her sizeable income. Montagu's experience of industry was perhaps more practical than Hume's intended meaning here. Her public reputation was made possible by her shrewd head for business. She assumed sole responsibility for the management of her husband's coal mines in Newcastle from 1766, inheriting them on his death in 1775. By the end of her life Montagu had raised her income to £10,000, becoming one of the wealthiest individuals in London. Unusually for a woman, especially an untitled woman, she controlled a personal account at C. Hoare & Co. in a category reserved for the largest property owners, such as Eton College. Bluestocking activity was funded by 'Montagu Main', the second most expensive coal on the market.

Montagu's interest in her coal mines was consistently energetic and ambitious. She matched her attention to technological innovation with a concern for the welfare of her workers, holding regular feasts for her 'black workers'. She reformed the living conditions of her miners at Denton Colliery, taking an active and consistent interest in their children's health and education, and providing a school for the young boys until they were of an age to go down the mines. As the income from her colliery increased she planned to establish a school for girls on her estate, where they would be taught 'spinning, knitting and sewing', qualifications that would be suitable to their rank and might improve their situation.[27] In 1775 she wrote to her brother, from Denton, 'to impart good is enlarging the sphere of enjoyment & I love to think many through my means & on my possessions are made happy. I looked on my happy Tennants with as much pleasure as on the lands they cultivate.'[28] Montagu was similarly concerned for the welfare of her neighbours at Sandleford, as she communicates to her sister in a letter of 1772, 'If rich people do not check their wanton extravagance to enable them to assist the poor I know not what must become of ye labouring people.'[29]

It is apparent from these remarks that Montagu perceived her acts of charity and assistance to the lower classes as a social duty, and perhaps also, more pragmatically, as a matter of good management. Moreover, there is a sense in which her charitable ambitions were inextricably linked to her act of self-fashioning as a woman of society, a bluestocking hostess with cultural and financial capital. Her benevolence was often extremely public, as can be seen in Fanny Burney's description of her gift of an 'annual breakfast in front of her new mansion, of roast beef and plum pudding, to all the chimney sweepers of the Metropolis':

> Not all the lyrics of all the rhymsters, nor all the spring-feathered choristers, could hail the opening smiles of May, like the fragrance of that roasted beef, and the pulpy softness of those puddings of plums, with which Mrs Montagu yearly renovated those sooty little agents to the safety of our most blessing luxury.

Taken for all in all, Mrs Montagu was rare in her attainments; splendid in her conduct; open to the calls of charity; forward to precede those of indigent genius; and unchangeably just and firm in the application of her interest, her principles, and her fortune, to the encouragement of loyalty, and the support of virtue.[30]

Montagu's annual feasts for chimney sweeps were held on the front lawn of her mansion in Portman Square, clearly visible to passers-by. This ostentatious celebration of charity, as Burney suggests, was intended to encourage loyalty from her social inferiors as well as to advertise her own virtue.

The thread of self-interest running through altruism had been laid bare by Mandeville, of course, earlier in the century in his notorious *Essay on Charity and Charity Schools*. By the mid-century however, this link was embraced more positively and often recognised as a vital element of the national economy. As Adam Smith wrote in his chapter 'Of Liscentious Systems',

It is the great fallacy of Dr. Mandeville's book to represent every passion as wholly vicious, which is so in any degree and in any direction. It is thus that he treats every thing as vanity which has any reference, either to what are, or to what ought to be the sentiments of others: and it is by means of this sophistry, that he establishes his favorite conclusion, that private vices are public benefits. If the love of magnificence, a taste for the elegant arts and improvements of human life, for whatever is agreeable in dress, furniture, or equipage, for architecture, statuary and painting, and music, is to be regarded as luxury, sensuality, and ostentation, even in those whose situation allows, without any inconveniency, the indulgence of those passions, it is certain that luxury, sensuality, and ostentation are public benefits: since without the qualities upon which he thinks proper to bestow such opprobrious names, that arts of refinement could never find encouragement, and must languish for want of employment.[31]

One of the most popular and cogent defences of luxury came to lie in the increasing refinement and flourishing vitality of British culture. Adam Smith's work on rhetoric and belles lettres emphasises the civilising effect of culture on the individual, linking intellectual and moral sympathy in his definition of good taste. These virtues were to be cultivated in both sexes, and relied on the interaction between men and women in cementing the civilising process. It is precisely Smith's vocabulary of encouragement, refinement and employment that Elizabeth Montagu made use of throughout her life. She managed to maintain a reputation for virtue and economy while indulging her talent for lavish display.

Women writers of the bluestocking circle frequently acknowledged the explicit link between wealth, charity and the arts. Montagu's friend, Catherine Talbot, exhorted the wealthy to realise their responsibility towards society in her *Essay on the Importance of Riches*:

Thus might the rich, the great, the powerful, consider in like manner: 'This part of my fortune will be nobly employed in relieving the miserable: that, in works of public generosity: so much in procuring the agreeable ornaments of life: in this manner I may encourage the elegant arts: by this way I may set off my own character to the best advantage: and by making myself beloved and respected, I shall consequently gain an honest influence over such as may be bettered by my good example: my advice, my approbation will be useful in such a case: in *this* I may do honour to my country: in *that'* – Up and employ yourselves, you who are lolling in easy chairs, amusing away your lives over French novels, wasting your time in fruitless theory, or your fortunes in riotous excesses. Remember, you have an important part to act.[32]

The part that Montagu preferred to act above all others was that of patron of literature and the fine arts. Her correspondence suggests that she was constantly keeping an eye on the progress of her coal on the stock markets in order to gauge how much money she could spend on her cultural projects in London. As she wrote to the poet James Beattie:

Consider me always in the best light in which you can put me, as the banker of the distressed; and at any time call upon me for such objects; and in all senses of the word, *I will honour your bill.* Vulgar wretchedness one relieves, because it is one's duty to do so; and one has a certain degree of pleasure in it; but to assist merit in distress is an Epicurean feast; and indulge this luxury of taste in me, when any remarkable object offers itself to your acquaintance.[33]

Here Montagu contrasts the different types of charity she exercised, expressing the greater pleasure she receives in helping a particular kind of 'merit', based on talent rather than need. After her husband's death in 1775, she granted annuities to fellow female authors, including Elizabeth Carter, Hester Chapone, Sarah Fielding and her sister, Sarah Scott. While she took a particular interest in helping writers, 'forward to precede those of indigent genius', she was also a keen patron of architecture, landscape design and interior decoration. Perhaps her most cherished act of patronage was her building of Montagu House. Here the virtues of luxury, industry and charity appeared to come together in the form of a resplendent monument to bluestocking culture.

Montagu House

Montagu referred to Montagu House in Portman Square, which took some 20 years to complete, as a 'Temple of virtue and friendship' and a 'a palace of chaste elegance'. (See Plates 27–31)[34] Soon after her husband's death, Montagu purchased from the Portman family a 99-year lease of the land at the north-west corner of Portman Square on which her great house was to be built. She had intended Robert Adam to be her architect, but decided later to employ James Stuart, whose work on the antiquities at Athens has gained him the title 'Athenian Stuart'. She reports, with particular pride, that she paid its costs week by week out of her income:

> between Janry. 1777 and Dec 1777 I paid for my service of plate, and my house [Portman Square] together £4,321: 10s. out of my income and had not then a bill of £20 on my tradesmen's books.

Unlike several of the leading aristocrats of her day, Montagu never went into debt. Her self-justification was bolstered by the pride she took in remaining in credit throughout her life.

The construction of Montagu House became a public event. By 1780 the building supervisor had to issue tickets to limit the number of visitors to a size that would not hamper the workmen or mar the paint. Among the several artists and craftsmen she employed were Angelica Kaufman, Cipriani, Rebecca and Bartoli. While generally using the best solid materials, she also experimented with new decorative techniques that were designed to imitate the most expensive metals, such as ormolu, an alloy that had the appearance of gold. Montagu's network of patronage extended further than ever, as she sought out the best workers in bronze, marble, glass, wood-carving and gilding. James Harris, one of the many writers that Montagu was patron to at this time, wrote to her in 1780, 'I am to inform you I have seen an Edifice, which for the time made me imagine I was at Athens, in a House of Pericles, built by Phidias. Where my reverie ended, I felt a more solid satisfaction of reflecting, that, in my own Country, the Genius of Phidias, could still produce an Architect, and the Genius of Pericles still produce a Patroness.'

Montagu's creation of such an opulent stage for her social gatherings can be seen in the context of Werner Sombart's study of luxury and capitalism, in which he sees the eighteenth century as a significant turning point in the history of luxury, a moment of objectification: 'It was woman who was the guiding spirit in the movement towards objectification, as I wish to term this process. She could derive only scant satisfaction from the display of a resplendent retinue. Rich dresses, comfortable houses, precious jewels were more tangible. This change is exceedingly significant economically.'[35] He characterises the sensualisation and refinement of this period as signalling the triumph of the female who deliberately uses her gender to secure a dominant role. Women's tendency to sensualise luxury is linked to the greater refinement of individual objects, which implies a greater expenditure of human labour on a specific object. The result is a widening of the scope of capitalist industry and, because of the necessity of securing rare materials from foreign countries, also of capitalist commerce. Montagu was aware of her power as a consumer of foreign luxury. In July 1790 she wrote to her sister Sarah Scott,

> I am going to the city end of the town this morning to bespeak 280 yards of white Sattin for the window curtains of my great house, and about 200 for the hangings. I think this order will make me very popular in Spittal Fields.[36]

From the correspondence surrounding the Montagu House, it appears that she kept several hundred people in work over a period of about 15 years.

Among the most impressive sights in her new mansion were her ambitious feather screens, built over a period of ten years (1781–91). Montagu's friends were asked for contributions of feathers to apply to large canvas mounted frames to form decorative collages of landscapes that included flowers, birds and beasts of every variety and shade.[37] Betty Tull, Montagu's forewoman at Sandleford, her country estate, was in charge of creating the screens, which attracted enormous interest and admiration while they were being made. Montagu wrote to Elizabeth Carter in 1781, 'From ye gaudy peocock to ye solemn Raven, we collect whatever we can.'[38] She described Betty Tull's talent in glowing terms: 'Maccoas she has transformed into Tulips, Kings fishers into blue bells by her so potent art.'[39] William Cowper's poem for the *Gentleman's Magazine* conveys the exuberance of the feather-screens, their joyful ostentation:

> The Birds put off their ev'ry hue
> To dress a room for Montagu,
> The Peacock sends his heav'nly dyes,
> His *rainbows* and his *starry eyes*;
> The Pheasant, plumes which now infold
> His mantling neck with downy gold;
> The Cock his arch'd tail's azure show,
> And, river blanch'd, the Swan, his snow.
> All tribes beside of Indian name,
> That glossy shine, or vivid flame
> Where rises and where sets the day,
> Whate'er they boast of rich and gay,
> Contribute to the gorgeous plan,
> Proud to advance it all it they can.[40]

James Barrington wrote to Montagu in a similar spirit of gallantry, 'I will collect all the Peacocks feathers, as well as others for Mrs Montagu; it is the only comfort I have at the death of a beautiful bird, to think that their plumage will have the honour of shining as a Constellation in the exalted situation of Mrs Montagu's Palace at Portman Square.'[41] Montagu received the ultimate accolade in June 1791, when Queen Charlotte and the royal princesses came to do honour to the featherwork.[42]

There is no remaining evidence of the grandeur of Montagu House beyond literary descriptions.[43] The surviving correspondence between Montagu and her guests reveals that Montagu House was a landmark in Britain's capital city, a space in which political and social worlds crossed. Her assemblies were neither strictly private nor public but mediated between the two spheres. Hannah More's poem *Bas Bleu* captures the social world of the bluestocking circle for posterity. In her comparison of material and intellectual brilliance, More asserts the predominance and superiority of the latter over the former. She praises the art of conversation, implying that taste and feeling are nothing to a woman if she cannot discuss them fully and understand their implications. The most impressive sort of display is that of intellect, not dress or jewels. Here she makes clear the high ideals which she and her contemporaries attached to conversation:

> If none behold, ah! wherefore fair?
> Ah! wherefore wise, if none must hear?
> Our intellectual ore must shine,
> Not slumber, idly in the mine.
> Let Education's moral mint
> The noblest images imprint;
> Let taste her curious touchstone hold,
> To try if standard be the gold;
> But 'tis thy commerce, Conversation,
> Must give it use by circulation;
> That noblest commerce of mankind,
> Whose precious merchandise is MIND![44]

More describes a literary community in which the highest value is placed on the exchange of thoughts between equals. Mental and moral profit was central to the bluestocking model of literary community, as can be seen in the correspondence between Elizabeth Carter and Montagu, whose relationship incorporated learning and charity in equal measure. More contrasts the *bas bleu* meetings with the 'tainted affectation and false taste' of the Hotel de Rambouillet, the seventeenth-century Parisian salon, and also with her contemporary society, where 'Cosmetic powers' and 'polish, ton and graces' rule the day. While the bluestocking ideals of conversation and education for women were embedded in the rhetoric of commerce and luxury, they were solidly implanted on a bedrock of morality and concerned to promote learning above luxury.

Montagu House was a material monument to the ephemeral culture of blue-stocking philosophy that took the form of letters, wit and conversation, constantly circulating but never caught. Montagu's contemporaries recognised her achievement in solidifying her virtue. Sir William Pepys wrote to Montagu in 1781, after visiting her mansion, 'while I was surveying the grandeur of the Apartments, & the Exquisite Workmanship of the Ornaments my Mind cou'd not help dwelling upon the whole as a Monument of that judicious Charity for which you have always been so distinguished.'[45] Montagu wrote to her close friend and fellow bluestocking Mrs Vesey:

> We have lived with the wisest, the best, and the most celebrated men of our Times, and with some of the best, most accomplished, most learned Women of any times. These things I consider not merely as pleasures transient, but as permanent blessings; by such Guides and Companions we are set above the low temptations of Vice and folly, and while they were the instructors of our minds they were the Guardians of our Virtue.[46]

Montagu House provides a pertinent example of the way in which one woman could moralise the relationship between wealth and the arts, securing herself a position at the heart of her cultural world.

*

In this essay I hope to have shown how self-conscious and complex was this process of self-positioning, and it is worth noting, finally, that Montagu's interventions in the luxury debates took place on a theoretical as well as a practical level. As a highly intellectual woman, as well as a symbol of learning, she was courted by contemporary philosophers of the Scottish Enlightenment, who believed that the condition of women in society could be taken as an index of the level of civilisation attained.[47] In 1766, Henry Home, Lord Kames, sought out Montagu's opinion on the theory of ornament, asking her to help him in writing his *Elements of Criticism*. She wrote to her close friend George Lyttleton,

> I had a letter the other day from Lord Kames, who tells me he is going to publish a new edition of the Elements of Criticism, & ask'd me about some things in regard to taste in furniture &c., and I assure your Lordship, he told me, he should be glad to have my name join'd with his in his work. See what I have got by going to Scotland! When will you offer to put my name to any of your works? You will imagine I did not avail myself of his proposal.

Montagu did reply to Kames, including a twelve-page epistle on the history, use and theory of ornament from the time of ancient Greece to the present. Kames was evidently impressed by her observations, as he included them in his work, almost verbatim but without acknowledgement.

In his *Elements of Criticism*, Kames associated rationality and good sense with taste:

> We stand therefore engaged in honour, as well as in interest, to second the purposes of nature, by cultivating the pleasures of the eye and ear, those especially that require extraordinary culture, such as are inspired by poetry, painting, sculpture, music, gardening and architecture. This chiefly is the duty of the opulent, who have the leisure to improve their minds and their feelings.[48]

Kames advocates the shared pleasures which good taste encourages, perceiving social intercourse as the antidote to luxuriance. He wrote to Montagu: 'Of the animal Man Some are made for themselves who have no priniciple of sociality because such principle in them would be of no use to others. Such beings of the insect kind, crawling upon the face of the Earth do certainly exist; but my Correspondent is none of these: nay she is the reverse in every respect. Her social connections extend so wide, that it is not easy for her to perform any action or almost to move a step, without affecting others.' Montagu was seen by many of her contemporaries as the ruling planet around which her satellites revolved.

The connections between wealth and virtue, industry and leisure, instruction and pleasure, luxury and charity, were made and lived by Montagu, whom Hannah More described as 'The female Maecenas of Hill Street'.[49] She was widely respected as an arbiter of literary and artistic taste and an icon of moral virtue. Her concern for economic success was propelled by an ambition to celebrate aesthetic excellence in a public fashion. One might say that she was a mistress of conspicuous consumption by the end of her life. How did she manage and manipulate her displays of luxury towards specific, moral ends? How did her identity as a woman affect her role as a patron? Can we talk about a 'right use' of luxury? Is the presence of luxury an expression of social progress or a mechanism of social progress? Can one 'deserve' luxury in life? These broader questions about eighteenth-century culture can be illuminated through a close study of the exact mechanisms of Montagu's economic management of her aesthetic ideals. Kames sensed that she might possess the key to similar questions, asking her in 1772:

> My present work is a general history of the human race in its gradual progress toward maturity; distributed into many articles, Religion, Morality, Manners, arts, commerce with many others. I have in particular one curious chapter viz. Progress of the female Sex from their lowest Savage state to their highest State among refined nations. I want to levy contributions from my friends, such of them as are distinguished by superior taste, that my name may defend to posterity in the same group with theirs. There is variety in plenty for Mrs Montagu's pen; and I would rather her name join'd with mine in such a work, than to have a monument erected for me in Westminster Abbey.

It is, of course, an irony that Kames never did join Montagu's work to his in the publication of either his *Elements of Criticism* or his later *Sketches of the History of Man*. By reinstating her role as a leader and critic of Enlightenment sociability we might come closer to understanding the complex relationship between luxury and taste, industry and charity, a dynamic in which the role of women was crucial.

Notes

1. *The Tryal of Lady Allurea Luxury before the Lord Chief-Justice Upright, on an Information for a Conspiracy* (London, 1757).
2. *Ibid.*, p. 6.
3. *Ibid.*, pp. 6–7.
4. *Ibid.*, p. 7.
5. *Ibid.*, pp. 7–8.
6. *Ibid.*, p. 75.
7. *Ibid.*, p. 25.
8. *Ibid.*, pp. 66–7.
9. *Ibid.*, pp. 67–8.
10. Anna Larpent made the following New Year's Resolution in her diary entry of 1 January 1776, 'I must acquire thought in spending money. An elegant Oeconomy, a proper frugality do nothing from mere spirit of imitation. Every thing with order, nothing giddily – there are: absolute necessities; necessary luxuries.' Anna Larpent, 'A Methodized Journal, 1773–1786' (Huntington Library manuscript, HM 31201), p. 60.

11. See Elizabeth Kowaleski-Wallace, *Consuming Subjects: Women, Shopping, and Business in the Eighteenth Century* (New York, 1997), and Harriet Guest, *Small Change: Woman, Learning and Patriotism* (Chicago, 2000), 'A-Shopping We Will Go'.

12. My previous research has concentrated on the women writers and artists represented in Richard Samuel's painting of *The Nine Living Muses of Great Britain*, exhibited at the Royal Academy in 1779. This impressive act of embodiment conveys the importance of women's contribution to an evolving national culture. The muses are attired as virtuous Roman matrons, both guardians and advertisements of national achievement in the arts. See Eger, Grant, O'Gallchoir & Warburton, eds., *Women, Writing and the Public Sphere, 1700–1830* (Cambridge, 2001), pp. 104–33.

13. Elizabeth Montagu, *An Essay on the writings and Genius of Shakespear, compared with the Greek and French Dramatic Poets. With Some Remarks Upon the Misrepresentations of Mons. de Voltaire* (London, 1769).

14. Elizabeth Montagu to Sarah Scott. 26 December 1767 (MO 5871, Huntington Library Collection).

15. White silk hose was the mark of the gentry, or of a successful London tradesman; blue knitted wool was the dress of the working man. See: Anne Buck, *Dress in Eighteenth-Century England* (New York, 1979), p. 31. For a study of the bluestocking circle, see Sylvia Harcstack Myers, *The Bluestocking Circle* (Oxford, 1990).

16. See Marie Mulvey Roberts, 'Pleasures Engendered by Gender: Homosociality and the Club', *Pleasure in the Eighteenth Century*, eds. Roy Porter and Marie Mulvey Roberts (London, 1996).

17. See G.J. Barker-Benfield, *The Culture of Sensibility: Sex and Society in Eighteenth-Century Britain* (Chicago and London, 1992).

18. Dr Edward Wilson to John Pitt, 2nd Earl of Chatham, 1758 (Huntington Library Manuscript, MO 6780). This manuscript is copied in Elizabeth Montagu's hand and marked 'Extract of a Letter from Doctor Wilson to Mr Pitt when 11 years old.'

19. Sir N. Wraxall, *Historical Memoirs of My Own Time*, 2 vols (London, 1815), vol. I, p. 140.

20. Hannah More, *Selected Writings*, ed. Robert Hole (London: Pickering & Chatto, 1996), pp. 5–6.

21. More, *Selected Writings*, ed. Robert Hole, 8–9.

22. Richard Cumberland, *The Observer: Being a Collection of Moral, Literary and Familiar Essays*. Volume One. London: Printed for C. Dilly in the Poultry, 1786. Essay no. 25. 233–4.

23. Hume, *Essays Moral, Political and Literary*. Edinburgh: Adam Black and Charles Tait, 1826.305.

24. Quoted in Reginald Blunt, ed., *Mrs Montagu, 'Queen of the Blues': Her Letters and Friendships from 1762 to 1800*, 2 vols (London: Constable, 1973), vol. 2, p. 358.

25. MO 671 8 September 1776, Chaillot, Elizabeth Montagu to John Burrow (her nephew's tutor). For printed text see Alice C.C. Gaussen, *A Later Pepys* (London, 1904).

26. Hume, 'Of Refinement in the Arts', *Essays* (Liberty edition), p. 271.

27. John Doran, *A Lady of the Last Century (Mrs Elizabeth Montagu): Illustrated in her unpublished Letters; collected and arranged with a chapter on Blue Stockings* (London, 1873).

28. Elizabeth Montagu to Morris Robinson, 3 July 1775, Denton Hall (Huntington Library Collection, MO 4801).

29. MO 5930 Montagu, Elizabeth (Robinson) to Sarah (Robinson) Scott, 28 July 1772. See Edith Sedgewick Larson, 'A Measure of Power: The Personal Charity of Elizabeth Montagu', *Studies in Eighteenth-Century Culture*. 16 (1986) pp. 197–210.

30. Burney, *Memoirs of Dr. Burney* (1832), p. 273.

31. Adam Smith, *Theory of Moral Sentiments* (Liberty Press edition), p. 313.

32. Catherine Talbot, 'Essay on the Importance of Riches', *The Works of the Late Miss Catherine Talbot*, ed. Montagu Pennington (London, 1809), pp. 116–17.

33. Sir William Forbes, *An Account of the Life and Writings of James Beattie, LL.D.*, 2 vols (Edinburgh, 1806), II: 159–60.

34. Elizabeth Montagu to Leonard Smelt, 22 July 1778 (MO 5019, Huntington Library Collection).
35. Werner Sombart, *Luxury and Capitalism*, trans. Philip Siegelman (Ann Arbor, 1967), p. 94.
36. Elizabeth Montagu to her sister, Sarah Scott, 5 July 1790, Huntington Library Manuscript MO6199.
37. See Reginald Blunt, ed., *Mrs Montagu*, vol. 2, p. 202.
38. Elizabeth Montagu to Elizabeth Carter, 25 September 1781. Huntington Library Manuscript, MO 3517.
39. Elizabeth Montagu to Elizabeth Charlton Montagu, 17 December 1788. Huntington Library Manuscript, MO 2975.
40. Cowper wrote his poem 'On Mrs Montagu's Feather Hangings' in the hope of attracting 'Minerva's' attention. She later supported the publication of his translation of the *Iliad*, adding her name to the list of subscribers and sending the poet a warm letter of encouragement.
41. James Barrington to Elizabeth Montagu, 16 December 1790. Huntington Library Manuscript, MO 156.
42. See Montagu's letter to Elizabeth Carter, June 1791 (Huntington Library Collection, MO 3686).
43. Montagu House was bombed in the Second World War.
44. More, *Selected Writings*, ed. Robert Hole, p. 32.
45. 4 August 1781, Sir William Weller Pepys to Elizabeth Montagu (Huntington Library Collection).
46. MO 6566, 21 September 1781, EM to Vesey.
47. See Sylvana Tomaselli, 'The Enlightenment Debate on Women', *History Workshop Journal*, vol. 20 (1993), pp. 101–23.
48. Henry Home, Lord Kames, *Elements of Criticism*, 3 vols. (London and Edinburgh: A. Millar, and A. Kincaid & J. Hell, 1762), vol. I, p. 6.
49. More, *Selected Writings*, from a letter to her sister, pp. 8–9.

Plates

27. 'Exterior of Montagu House', watercolour.
28. Joseph Bonomi, 'Mrs Montagu's Great Room, Montagu House'.
29. Joseph Bonomi, 'Design for the Great Drawing Room, Montagu House'.
30. Joseph Bonomi, 'Design for a Lampstand for the Staircase, Montagu House'.
31. Joseph Bonomi, 'Design for a Carpet'.

Part V
Luxury and the Exotic

The eighteenth-century discourse on luxury cannot be separated out from responses to the expansion of global trade and the still relatively recent widespread contact of European populations with luxury consumer goods from Asia and the New World. In part luxury was perceived as foreign, and especially exotic, goods.

Was the export ware the East India Companies brought to Europe from China a luxury or a part of everyday life? Just what did the silk and porcelain so sought after in Europe mean to Chinese consumers? Shelagh Vainker, in Chapter 14, 'Luxuries or Not? Consumption of Silk and Porcelain in Eighteenth-Century China', contrasts and compares Chinese markets for ceramics and silk. She contrasts exclusive imperial ware and the inferior export ware, but seeks out an important middle domestic market for individual, high quality and studio-marked ceramics. The consumption of porcelain was otherwise an inconspicuous aspect of everyday life. The consumption of silk, however, increased in eighteenth-century China, reflecting higher incomes and a new reluctance to wear cotton in wider parts of the population. More clothing was purchased ready-made and from shops, and the state attempted to renew sumptuary law on types of garment and colour, though not on the material it was made from.

Rebecca Earle, in Chapter 15, 'Luxury, Clothing and Race in Spanish America', shows that sumptuary legislation on clothing also continued to play a part in the consumption of European luxuries in eighteenth-century South America. The cities of Mexico and Peru, grown rich on the trade in silver and gold to Europe and China, contained diverse populations of Europeans, slaves and free blacks, Indians and mulattoes. There luxury was debated not over consumption of indigenous commodities, but over European imports. Excess expenditure on fashionable clothing and jewellery was perceived to extend across class and race. Clothing in the eighteenth century was a part of racial definition, and sumptuary legislation was resurrected in an attempt to control unsanctioned personal transformations. By the early nineteenth century, 'gaudy' was the epithet to describe luxurious Ibero-American dress.

How goods, especially textiles and ceramics, were produced and consumed in their countries of origin, affected their reception in Europe and inspired new production systems in Europe. Maxine Berg, in Chapter 16, 'Asian Luxuries and the Making of the European Consumer Revolution' shows the enormous impact on European consumption of Indian cottons, especially printed calicoes and Chinese porcelain brought to Europe by the East India Companies. The discovery of sophisticated consumer cultures and technologically advanced production systems in Asia inspired Europe's consumer revolutions. The attempts to imitate, and thus to displace, imports of Indian cotton goods and Chinese porcelain resulted in new consumer goods for a broad middling class market, and generated the industrial revolution which made their large-scale production possible.

14

Luxuries or Not? Consumption of Silk and Porcelain in Eighteenth-Century China

Shelagh Vainker

Silk, porcelain and tea are the three things for which, over the last 300 years, China has been best known in Europe. The fine quality of those goods, and the remoteness of the country that produced them, contributed to a notion of China as exotic and, in the absence of widespread or indeed any profound understanding of China's history, thought or literature, helped define it in the minds of most Europeans.[1] It was never likely, in these circumstances, that these goods should have been similarly regarded in the culture that produced them, and an examination of the consumption of silk and porcelain within China sheds some light on the shift in their values induced by trade.

A sinological view of an eighteenth-century porcelain would define it as a multiple, produced according to manufacturing methods established in the eleventh century AD but relying in some aspects on practices evident in the fourteenth century BC in the production of ritual bronzes, specifically division of processes between separate workshop units.[2] The body and glaze material is essentially the same as the eleventh-century wares, and the techniques of decoration were essentially all current by the twelfth century, though admittedly in the case of overglaze enamels, in the north rather than in the porcelain-producing south.[3] As such, ceramics reinforce the identification of the Song period in general as the premodern peak after which no significant development took place.[4] This situation contributes to the preference among many art historians of China for the rich variety of the early ceramic industry over the monolithic porcelain tradition, that replaced it. In addition, the richly varied kiln complexes of Song dynasty China also anticipated the eighteenth-century production of market-specific wares.[5] If we are to study consumption within the context of ideas current at the time of production, then it is this difference in the intended market, or point of consumption, that informs later as well as contemporary attitudes to the porcelain product. If we take as examples two pieces of commissioned ware, we can say that a piece of eighteenth-century imperial ware, of which there were many thousands, is likely to have been appreciated by its owner in approximately the same measure (or possibly less) as a piece of armorial porcelain (see Plate 32).[6] The imperial piece is of fine body and glaze quality and excellent craftsmanship, is innovative in its technical refinements and is likely even now to be displayed and admired, published and promoted as an object of wonder.[7] The armorial piece is of inferior material, was never ingenious, has lost its novelty and is only likely to be enjoyed with anything approaching its original potency by a few descendants of the person who ordered it, and as a symbol of a moment in trade or international exchange by a somewhat wider audience. All this decreases the interest it might hold for art historians, and explains why it counts for little in the sinological view. Export porcelain is thus as good an example as any commodity, of value gained through physical distance from the place of production, and lost through temporal distance from the point of consumption, and thus represents a fleeting or fickle aspect of the exotic.

None the less, eighteenth-century Chinese porcelain in general continues to be highly regarded by those large numbers of people who are casually interested in the European past, in the exotic invoked by porcelain in that past and particularly in elegant living associated with it. However, the purpose of this essay is not so much to chart the subsequent life of eighteenth-century porcelain, as to identify a third category of porcelain along with its equivalent in silk, neither exclusively imperial nor specifically for export, but produced for the middling domestic market, and to explore how, where and by whom those objects might have been acquired and used, and whether within China, where they could not be exotic, they might yet have been luxuries.

*

The political, intellectual and economic context of eighteenth-century China in which silk and porcelain were produced and circulated in such quantities coincides with the most illustrious period of the Qing dynasty founded by the Manchus in 1644 (and which collapsed in 1911). The period is covered by the reigns of only three emperors: Kangxi (1662–1722), Yongzheng (1723–35) and Qianlong (1736–95) and for the purposes of this essay will comprise a slightly extended eighteenth-century beginning in 1683/4, the 22nd year of Kangxi, in which the ban on maritime trade was lifted and the imperial kilns at Jingdezhen were re-established. It was a time of expansion, notably in the population, which tripled, in the bureaucracy and in the economy, and thus in consumption as well. As a non-Chinese dynasty, the Manchu ruling house depended initially on delegating power to its princelings; however by the mid-eighteenth-century the relationship between conquerors and conquered had deepened sufficiently for the imperial princelings, bondservants and bannermen also to be less necessary: the Chinese intellectual and social elite of the lower Yangzi valley had regained some of their traditional power. They were constrained somewhat, however, by the tightening of imperial control on Manchu aristocrats and on bureaucrats and local elites in general, in a bureaucracy that was patterned on Ming models but with more structures, more layers and more paperwork.[8]

The agricultural basis was extended, and the subsequent growth in the economy saw the beginnings of intraregional trade for bulk goods, including silk. Luxuries too were traded across long distances, providing the trendsetting elites of Beijing, Nanjing, Yangzhou, Hangzhou and Suzhou as well as the urban and mercantile elites of other cities throughout the empire with silk from Nanjing, porcelain from Jingdezhen, ink cakes from Anhui and other fine local products that had acquired nationwide desirability.[9] Intraregional trade and sojourning led to the formation of numerous merchant guilds and societies based usually on common birthplace, some of which became quite significant institutions that came to assume civic responsibilities. This balance between commerce and public life was officially approved, according to the Qianlong Emperor's remark in 1748 regarding the debates on state grain policy: 'With the affairs of the market-place, for the most part one should let the people carry out the circulation for themselves. If once the government begins to manage it, what was originally intended to be beneficial to the people will, with unsatisfactory implementation, turn out full of hindrances.'[10]

The expansion in the bureaucracy that accompanied economic growth was not, however, sufficient to offer the opportunity of an official career – ever the prize of success in China – to all the sons of the traditional elite and those of the newly rich. There were simply not enough official positions to go round, with the result that people from old privileged families turned to employment in the very many scholarly projects sponsored by both the court and wealthy individuals which accompanied the rise of evidential scholarship. The newly rich, who were not necessarily equipped or invited to undertake such work, embarked on the lifestyle of the traditional gentleman *literatus*, and the acquisition of its material attributes. Indeed many successful merchants did the same, though their lack of traditional education contributed eventually to an influential shift in some aspects of this, most notably, painting in Yangzhou.[11] There was thus a substantial group of people in the market for high quality goods. The sorts of goods they desired, the access they had to these, and the uses to which such goods were put, are difficult to identify precisely as the evidence is uneven. In terms of the present discussion, however, it may be noted that ceramics have survived in quantity but are rarely mentioned in texts, whereas silk has mostly perished but is reasonably documented; silk is written of more often in terms of production than consumption, while the large quantities of extant Qing porcelain make it possible to sort the wares according to fineness of body and glaze material, shape, and ornament.

The quality of porcelain produced in the last two decades of the seventeenth century is high, the re-establishment of the imperial kilns in 1683 having had the effect of raising standards at the many private kilns in and around Jingdezhen. Few pieces are designated as imperial, and we cannot be sure that Queen Mary and the Kangxi emperor were not surrounded by very similar pieces indeed, though the former arranged them on furniture and overmantels in her bedchamber and drawing room while the latter used them for eating and drinking. This situation is unique in the history of Chinese export porcelain, which from the eighth century AD had comprised ceramics of middling to low quality, and it was not to last.[12] By the first decade of the eighteenth century porcelain production had diversified, and there was established a category of imperial porcelain that would not have been available outside the court, still less outside the country, so that one might suggest that at this point, what was admired for decoration in the royal palaces of Europe was not fit for the table of the emperor of China.

An indication of the original consumption of a porcelain object is sometimes provided by the use of a mark painted, usually in underglaze blue, on the base of the piece at the time of manufacture. By the mid-Kangxi period in the early 1700s, much porcelain bore the standard six-character imperial mark unchanged since its introduction in the Ming dynasty in the early fifteenth century in its format of two characters for the dynasty followed by two for the emperor's name then two for 'made in the year of'. Since imperial reign marks were copied at private kilns, and imperial pieces did not always bear them, it is actually more instructive to look at the rarer marks giving studio names, commissioned by scholars and the gentry.[13] A piece showing characters from the popular novel *The Water Margin* bears the studio name, Wenxin Zhai, of Sun Chong from Zhejiang province who died in 1702; we know no more about him, from which we might infer he was of middling social status, but what is additionally interesting about this is that dishes of the same size illustrating other characters – usually three – from *The Water Margin*, exist in the Burrell Collection, Glasgow, in the British Museum, in three further examples in the Victoria and Albert Museum and in two more at the Ashmolean (see Plate 33).[14] The extensive porcelain holdings that make up about half of most British public collections of Chinese art were in general acquired from the mid-nineteenth century onwards; some pieces undoubtedly came from China at the turn of the twentieth century but given the rather small number that survives in English country houses, we can assume that some of these were exported from China at the time of their production around 1700.[15] Here, then, is an example of middling quality ware current in both the domestic market, where its literary subject would be instantly recognisable, and the export market, where the same subject would have been simply decoration. The bowl marked *Luyi Tang*, a name used by 18 recorded Qing scholars, is of a type similarly well represented in European collections.[16] Its Kangxi period style, incorporating the overglaze blue enamel introduced around 1700, makes it datable between 1700 and 1722.

This is the period in which specialisation increased, culminating at the very end of Kangxi's reign with the development in about 1720 of a pink enamel glaze that was to become one of the most typical of the eighteenth century as well as giving its name to the 'famille rose' porcelain type, which included some of the finest pieces of the era. These are particularly associated with the reign of Yongzheng (1723–35), which saw the refinement of porcelain types developed under Kangxi and is significant for the appointment in 1728 of Tang Ying to the post of imperial porcelain supervisor. He was responsible for overseeing the increasingly close palace interest in exclusive wares that resulted in the disparity between imperial and export wares outlined above, while the good ordinary pieces produced in large quantities throughout the remainder of the eighteenth century are more easily identified than their earlier equivalents.

The great many examples of general quality ware which make it possible to identify a middle market for porcelain are unfortunately not matched by surviving eighteenth-century silks, for though quite large quantities of Qing dress survive, much of that is loosely dated eighteenth- or nineteenth-century, and the pieces which are reasonably reliably eighteenth-century are considerably fewer, and most of them are imperial. In this they are representative of a prevailing situation in Chinese cultural history: namely, that most cultural survival has been determined to a greater or lesser degree by an imperial agenda. Since the Emperor Taizong formed the first imperial art collection in the seventh century AD, comprising chiefly calligraphy and paintings, a standard has been followed and elaborated by successive dynasts and imitated by scholars and officials. This applies particularly to painting and calligraphy, in which canons were quickly formed, and in antiquities – ritual bronzes, jades and inscription rubbings – which were associated with the authority to rule and began to be particularly collected from the time of the neo-Confucian revival of the eleventh century.[17] It applies also to texts, since the imperial library was always the repository of contemporary writing and earlier works incorporated into collectanea: writings which were not included in imperial book projects had much less chance of surviving, and indeed in the eighteenth century, the Qianlong emperor himself decreed, in 1774, that the officials charged with seeking out texts to be included in the monumental *Siku quanshu* ('Four treasuries') publishing project were equally to track down works that opposed dynastic interests, so that they may be burnt.[18] Such 'seditious' texts encompassed not just historical writing, biographies, local gazetteers, memorials and so forth but also poetry, plays and short stories, and more than 2,000 were ultimately lost in this way.

The same principles of selection, if not necessarily of destruction, apply to high quality objects in a variety of media though here, ceramics provide something of an exception. Ceramics have a sort of democratic durability; they very often survive intact, regardless of the circumstances of their consumption, and even when broken, the sherds yield most of what one would wish to know regarding form and technique, while find context can add more information. This is particularly true of the great period of ceramics production, the Song dynasty, when the first imperial wares were made alongside architectural ceramics and everyday pots in a highly successful industry that covered most of the country. In fact, Song ceramics provide one of the most complete technical and cultural single pictures in all of Chinese art history.

The best source of ordinary grade ceramics is always kiln sites, and though very much less excavation at Jingdezhen has been carried out on the non-imperial kilns, they have yielded some interesting pieces. For example, the Kangxi (1662–1722) period pieces now housed in Jingdezhen Taociguan (Jingdezhen Ceramics Institute) are quite thickly potted and decorated in a sketchy, rapid painting style with somewhat abbreviated pictorial scenes. These include figures with featureless faces seated in a simple pavilion rather than a garden setting, and tall bamboo with birds flying between the branches rather than in a river landscape.[19] The contrast between the soft blue of the painting and the grey-blue tinge of the background lacks the clarity of that between the brilliant blues and sparkling white ground of the Kangxi porcelain known in Europe at the turn of the eighteenth century. The Yongzheng (1723–35) period pieces excavated from private kilns in the vicinity of the imperial ones are brighter, yet the distinction between the wares termed 'folk' (*minjian*) by the archaeologists and those preserved in prestigious collections still applies.[20]

There is evidence of kiln activity across much of southern China for the Qing dynasty, the most notable centre outside Jiangxi being Dehua in the coastal province of Fujian, and known in the West as the producer of Blanc de Chine. Despite their good situation for export, the kilns turned out large quantities of wares for domestic consumption, principally figures of popular gods and goddesses, and vessels for domestic altars and studios. In the nineteenth century, kilns were developed around Canton on the south coast. However, there is practically no evidence of a Qing ceramics industry north of the Yangzi, and for this reason ceramics should be added to the category of bulk goods transported intraregionally.

We can propose this because ceramics were absolutely standard items in everyday life; they were transported north to the court and it is barely conceivable that the rest of north China was eating and drinking from any other material. They are not written about, except as antiques and collectables, because they are a routine and inconspicuous a component of everyday life.[21] As eating and drinking utensils, they were the simplest, as we know from the accounts of grand entertaining in the house of the eighteenth century poet and man of letters Yuan Mei (1715–97): different sizes and shapes of vessels for different dishes, and the use of four or five different wine cups, progressing from small to large, and beginning with porcelain, then jade, then rhinoceros horn and finally glass.[22] At the least, this progression reflects the rarity of the various materials. In the great Qing novel of manners *Hong Lou Meng* or 'Dream of the Red Chamber/Story of the Stone', it is only the precious eleventh-century antiques that are mentioned, otherwise ceramics are described less than tea or jewellery or silk.[23] Indeed, the fine silks mentioned in *Hong Lou Meng* include a robe woven with peacock feathers like the Imperial one that survives in the Palace Museum, and so represent in fact a very rarefied lifestyle.[24] The circulation of novels such as this might possibly be one reason that the literature of elegant living that accompanied the rise of consumerism in the late Ming is apparently absent from, or at least very finely scattered through, the large number of published works in the 18th century. The writings of Li Yu (1611–80) are the closest to the eighteenth century that such texts get, and one should perhaps pose the question (though not for addressing here) of why this body of rather specific texts outlining how to arrange one's furniture and ornaments, what paintings to display at what time of year and so on, was not a significant genre at a time of such increased access to the gentrified lifestyle and its accoutrements.[25]

While literary references to silk goods are somewhat more numerous than those to ceramics, the documentary evidence for silk as a product is far greater. Written evidence of the ceramic industry is scant, particularly before the Ming dynasty, yet silk, as an agricultural product significant both as an export commodity and within the domestic economy, is included in treatises on agriculture and in the dynastic histories from at least as early as the Tang (618–906) dynasty. Such references, albeit to raw or unmade materials rather than artefacts, compensate for the lack of surviving examples, and make it possible to gain some view of the amount produced, the extent of the producing regions and, when added to the references in poetry and literature to its use, also to gain an impression of the contribution of silk to the material world of early China.[26] In the eighteenth century at least 15 dated works on sericulture were published, while dozens more can be attributed to the Qing dynasty as a whole; many of these comprise chapters in longer works on agriculture, and some are illustrated.[27]

Local gazetteers and centrally compiled official records reveal that silk was produced over most of the country, with centres in four places: Jiangsu and Zhejiang provinces in the east (the Jiangnan region); Guangdong in the south; Sichuan in the west; and Shandong on the east coast, north of Jiangsu.[28] The Jiangnan region was the most important of these, the industry having become concentrated there from the late Ming onwards as the silk industry in other parts of the country declined in favour of cotton.[29] Mulberry trees began to replace rice, and silk production remained largely household-based, while its markets increased in complexity. Having been a commodity produced in small quantities to provide peasant households with finished goods to exchange for daily necessities, silk became for increasing numbers of households the principal source of income. This process of specialisation during the early Qing also occurred with paper, tea and sweets as the number of goods available to peasants for cash or exchange increased.[30] It was accompanied by a shift away from producing finished articles as households carried out part-processes, for the countrywide demand for silk from Jiangnan meant that merchants travelled to the region to buy silk, usually in bolts, according to what was desired in their own provinces. The transactions were increasingly carried out through local agents, who in turn placed orders with the Jiangnan workshops.[31] The imperial silk workshops were situated in the region, at Hangzhou, Nanjing and Suzhou and, as with the imperial kilns at Jingdezhen in Jiangxi, had a positive effect on the privately-run workshops.

The dragon robes worn by the emperor for conducting rituals, which were designed by the Board of Rites in Peking and made up in Nanjing or Suzhou, took, it has been calculated, 16 days to accomplish the pattern drawing, one year and one month to complete the groundwork, and one year and four months to complete the embroidery. This excludes time for the weaving of the ground fabric.[32] Regulations for court dress were elaborately formulated in accordance with rank, as indeed were porcelain designs. Imperial rituals were extended to the county level in the eighteenth century, and bureaucratic standards came to permeate most ritual, so that dress at birthdays, marriages, and so on was supposed to be like that of officials, and would therefore presumably have been, wherever possible, of silk. Another use of silk which expanded similarly was for opera costume, as the eighteenth century saw the expansion of performance from private entertainment and touring performances at local festivals, to a more permanent feature of urban life with the establishment of theatres.[33] In daily life too the consumption of silk became more widespread, in that standards of dress in the late seventeenth century had quite changed by the mid-eighteenth century, notably in reluctance to wear cotton, preferences for dragon designs previously exclusive to court dress, and the purchase of clothes in markets and shops rather than making them at home.[34]

In addition to clothing, silk had always been used for ceremonial articles, and indeed textiles associated with Buddhist dress and ritual constitute a considerable proportion of the extant silk from earlier periods, as they have been preserved in monasteries. From the eighteenth century, there are known examples of robes, from miniature to larger than life-size, for clothing images; priests' robes; pictorial hangings depicting Buddhist images, and altar cloths or frontals. Domestic furnishings include table covers, chair covers (see Plate 34) draped over the back to below the seat of high-backed wooden chairs; pictorial hangings, sometimes in sets of six creating a continuous composition, and possibly set in folding screen frames (see Plate 35). Within the palace, silk covers were used for throne cushions and in the palace library, for wrapping books. A type of hanging disseminated down the social scale from grand houses to almost everyone who could afford it was the festive hanging, usually bright red embroidered in gold with auspicious images for good fortune, long life or wedded bliss, with calligraphy according to the occasion.

To what extent are these luxuries? The objects most desired by the most socially ambitious of the newly rich in the eighteenth century would in most cases include paintings, ritual bronzes, jades, calligraphy and other antiques and collectibles associated with a scholar-official elite and the authority to rule. Ceramics and silk were always to some extent functional, and never appeared as categories in catalogues of the imperial collections, for example. A certain amount of exclusivity does however pertain. In porcelain, it was maintained by smashing at the kiln site even slightly imperfect pieces, so there was no circulation of rejects.[35] Silk has a much longer history of imperial control, beginning with the stipulation of official dress in the fourth century BC and the rituals surrounding sericulture and the silk goddess – the only rituals to be conducted by the empress rather than the emperor.[36] Silk had associations, therefore, of its own, whereas porcelain was practically inevitable, and was desirable according to its quality. In this respect increased consumption of silk in the eighteenth century is perhaps a clearer indication of luxury than porcelain consumption.

The dress regulations of the fourth century BC belong to what Arjun Apparudai and Craig Clunas have identified as a method of regulating consumption in a society with stable status and limited commodities.[37] The Chinese tradition that condemned extravagance and despised artisans began some 200 years earlier in the sixth century BC and has persisted through the change to a high consumption society that emerged in the Song (960–1279) dynasty, so that the Han (206 BC–AD 220) dynasty proscriptions of extravagance in funeral expenses, and the ban by the Ming official Zhang Han (1511–93) on elaborate festival lanterns that burnt away in minutes, find resonance in the early twenty-first century condemnation of outsize paper models of cars, mobile phones, and so on that are made for and set alight at the grave-sweeping ceremonies during Qingming festival.[38] Yet the change to a complex consumer society took place as early as the eleventh century, when sumptuary regulations are less evident but the fact that even the servant girls wear gold and silver earrings is lamented.[39] After the Song, the late Ming dynasty and the eighteenth century are periods when consumption also flourished, and porcelain and silk were, as shown above, widely acquired and used.

The regularly renewed sumptuary laws on silk in the late seventeenth century demonstrate an attempt at constraint that is still however politically rather than economically motivated, for they refer to garment type and colour rather than material, while the Qing Code imposes punishments for improper use of orna-mental designs woven or embroidered.[40] Conspicuous consumption was in fact tacitly encouraged by the willing patronage of the throne of some of the most ostentatious of the newly moneyed families, in particular the salt merchants of Yangzhou.[41] Yet though the use of goods of silk, porcelain, lacquer, gold and silver would have been enjoyed by the well-off, it did little to confer social status, and not just because the commodities were widely available. The salt merchants were extremely rich, and one of their aims was to dissociate themselves from the stigma of mercantile activity by using their wealth to educate their sons for official careers and to acquire estates and retinues, which might include resident painters, as well as fine objects. Since at least the Yuan (1279–1368) dynasty 500 years earlier, impoverished scholar-officials had enjoyed some social acceptability, and the mer-chants of Yangzhou were aware of a set of values which they knew could not be represented by wealth. Thus their parties would include officials while excluding fellow businessmen, and their sons received the best schooling in the empire, having had established for them three academies that were staffed by prominent literary figures. In fact, there existed mutual advantage for merchants and officials in the exchange of material wealth for social prestige, and in this way it can be said that taste moderated excess in worldly goods.

While Yangzhou was indeed the scene of some wild extravagances, the whole southern Yangzi region was the wealthiest in the country and was the place of production as well as consumption of many of the finest goods. Silk was manu-factured there, and other materials were transported to the region for carving, with Suzhou in Jiangsu province enjoying the reputation for the most skilled craftsmen. The notion of the exotic, however, did not apply, since almost all came from within the empire, and thus a gulf existed between that which was indeed difficult to obtain and unquestionably luxurious, and the high quality material goods that circulated throughout the population at almost every level, thanks to the combination, exploited so early in China, of fine raw materials and a large well-organised labour force.

The truly foreign and puzzling delights were found only within the very limited sphere of the court, and no discussion of the exotic at this period would be com-plete without some mention of reciprocity. The Qianlong emperor was curious about certain aspects of European art and technology, and had at his court the Jesuit painter Castiglione, known in Chinese as Lang Shining. Porcelain painted in 'Lang Shining' style depicting European figures and pastoral scenes is preserved in the Palace Museum, Taibei and in Beijing, while the emperor was also inter-ested in European clocks, for example.[42] The point has been made that export items never include objects close to a country's nationhood and rituals, yet the adoption of imported exotic materials and techniques to create objects that express ideals and practices can be clearly demonstrated.[43] On the Chinese side, by the commission to Castiglione in 1767 to draft sketches of Qianlong's battle campaigns for subsequent printing in France; on the European, by ecclesiastical robes such as the chasuble embroidered for Jesuits now in the Peabody Museum, Salem, or the cope made up from early nineteenth-century dragon-embroidered silk, possibly originally sewn into cushion covers, formerly in use at Christ Church Cathedral, Oxford and now housed in the Ashmolean Museum (see Plate 36).

Notes

1. The slow development of Chinese studies in Europe from *c.* 1600 onwards is discussed in T. Barrett, *Singular Listlessness: a Short History of Chinese Books and British Scholars* (London, 1989) and M. Wilson and J. Cayley, eds, *Europe Studies China: Papers from an International Conference on The History of European Sinology* (London, 1995). See also A. Reichwein (trans. J. Powell), *China and Europe: Intellectual and Artistic Contacts in the Eighteenth Century* (London, 1925).
2. L. Ledderose, *Ten Thousand Things: Module and Mass Production in Chinese Art*, The A.W. Mellon Lectures in the Fine Arts, 1998, The National Gallery of Art, Washington, D.C., Bollingen Series XXXV:46 (Princeton, 2000), pp. 48–9.
3. The porcelains of south China are distinguished from northern wares partly by the use of the same material for both body and glaze, at least until the fourteenth century when kaolin was first added to the body material. See N. Wood, *Chinese Glazes* (London: A. & C. Black, 1999), pp. 27–73.
4. K.G. Deng, 'Critical Survey of Research in Chinese Economic History', *Economic History Review* 52 (2000), pp. 1–23, in discussing the work of Mark Elvin and G.W. Skinner.
5. Kiln archaeology since the 1980s has revealed that kilns previously thought to have produced only one type of ceramic in fact produced a range. See Henansheng wenwu yanjiusuo, ed., *Ruyao de xin faxian: New Discoveries in Ru Kiln* (Beijing, 1991) for a variety of glaze types from the kiln associated with a rare, blue-green palace ware. Also, the Ding kilns at Quyang in Hebei are recorded as having been used in the imperial palace; some bear the mark 'guan' (official) and others were exported: all are of the same fine white body with ivory-coloured glaze.
6. For example a brushpot with landscape in sepia on a white ground bordered with a glaze imitating wood in the Palace Museum, Beijing. Palace Museum, *Kangxi Yongzheng Qianlong: Qing Porcelain from the Palace Museum Collection* (Beijing and Hong Kong, 1989) pl. 68; a ewer decorated with the arms of Peers, Ashmolean Museum EA 1978.130.
7. A recent example would be the Au Bak Ling collection exhibited at the Royal Academy, London, autumn 1998. See R. Krahl and J. Thompson, *Imperial Chinese ceramics from the Au Bak Ling collection* (Hong Kong, 1998).
8. For Qing social history, see E. Feng and J. Chang, *Qingren shehui shenghuo* (Tianjin, 1990); A. Feuerwerker, *State and Society in Eighteenth-Century China*, Michigan Papers in Chinese Studies no. 27 (Ann Arbor, 1976); D. Johnson, A. Nathan and E. Rawski, eds, *Popular Culture in Late Imperial China* (Berkeley and Los Angeles, 1985); S. Naquin and E. Rawski, *Chinese Society in the Eighteenth Century* (New Haven and London, 1987).
9. Feuerwerker, *State and Society in Eighteenth-Century China*, p. 86.
10. Naquin and Rawski, *Chinese Society in the Eighteenth Century*, p. 26.
11. P. Ho, 'The Salt Merchants of Yang-chou: A Study of Commercial Capitalism in Eighteenth-Century China', *Harvard Journal of Asiatic Studies* vol. 17 (1954), pp. 130–68. G. Hsu, 'Merchant Patronage of Eighteenth Century Yangchou Painting', C. Li, ed.,

Artists and Patrons: Some Social and Economic Aspects of Chinese Painting (Kansas, 1989). G. Hsu, *A Bushel of Pearls: Painting for Sale in Eighteenth-century Yangchow* (Stanford, 2001).

12. The contrast is drawn most clearly by the ceramics in late ninth-century pagodas, which in China include the finest wares available, indeed arguably the most prestigious ever produced, the *mise* secret colour Yue greenwares, and the much rougher wares found in Japan. For greenwares excavated from Japanese temple sites see Tokyo National Museum, *Nihon shutsudo no chugoku toji* (Chinese ceramics excavated in Japan; exhibition catalogue in Chinese and English) (Tokyo, 1978), nos. 3, 4 and 5.

13. A recent, illuminating study of these marks is M. Wilson, *Rare Marks on Chinese Porcelain* (London, 1998).

14. *Ibid.*, no. 34.

15. Those accessible to the public include Burleigh House in Lincolnshire, Long Melford Hall in Suffolk, Hatfield House in Hertfordshire, and Woburn Abbey. The extent that has survived privately is not quantifiable.

16. Wilson, *Rare Marks*, no. 36. An identical bowl and with the same mark is in the Ashmolean Museum EA X.3642, ex Mallett Collection.

17. L. Ledderose, 'Some Observations on the Imperial Art Collection in China', *Transactions of the Oriental Ceramic Society*, 43 (1978–9) pp. 33–46.

18. L. Carrington Goodrich, *The Literary Inquisition of Ch'ien-Lung*, American Council of Learned Societies Studies in Chinese and Related Civilizations Number 1 (Baltimore, 1935). For imperial book collecting and the preservation of texts see G. Dudbridge, *Lost Books of Medieval China*, The Panizzi Lectures 1999 (London, The British Library, 2000).

19. Zhongguo taoci bianji weiyuanhui, ed., *Zhongguo taoci: jingdezhen minjian qinghua ciqi* (Shanghai, 1988), pl. 200, pl. 199.

20. Zhongguo taoci bianji weiyuanhui, nos. 204, 205.

21. The 'secret colour' greenwares produced in the ninth century at the Yue kilns in northern Zhejiang province are the exception, being mentioned in Lu Yu's *Cha jing* (Tea Classic) and the poetry of Lu Guimeng. For Yue ware see Wang Qingzheng, ed., *Yue Ware, Miseci Porcelain* (Shanghai, 1996).

22. Cited in Feng and Chang, *Qingren shehui shenghuo*, p. 86.

23. Cao Xueqin, *Honglou Meng*, chapter 40, Renmin wenxue chubanshe edn. (Beijing, 1973), vol. 2, p. 487 for a reference to Ru ware; the rest of the chapter includes several discussions of silk gauze furnishings, particularly for window and bed curtains. A close discussion of ceramics in this novel is given in S. Naquin, 'Porcelain in *Hongloumeng*', unpublished paper read at University of Pennsylvania, 2001 conference 'Reading Eighteenth Century China Through "Dream of the Red Chamber"'.

24. Zhu Jiajin, *Treasures of the Forbidden City* (Hong Kong, 1987), no. 99.

25. C. Chang and S. Chang, *Crisis and Transformation in Seventeenth-Century China: Society, Culture and Modernity in Li yu's World* (Ann Arbor, 1992). C. Clunas, *Superfluous Things, Material Culture and Social Status in Early Modern China* (Cambridge, 1991).

26. S. Vainker, 'Northern Song Silk: Reconstructing the Evidence', J. Tisdall, ed., *Silk and Stone: the Third Hali Annual* (London, 1996) pp. 160–75 and 196–7.

27. Including Pu Songling, *Nongsen jing* (1705); Yang Shan, *Youfeng guangyi* (1740), in Xuxiu siku quanshu 978:zibu: nongjialei (Shanghai, 1997), also *Xiuji zhihua* (1776).

28. E. Sun, 'Sericulture and Silk Textile Production in Ch'ing China', W. Willmott, ed., *Economic Organization in Chinese Society* (Stanford, 1992) pp. 79–108.

29. J. Fan and W. Jin, *Jiangnan sichou shi yanjiu* (Beijing, 1993); F. Teng et al., *Zhejiang wenhua shi* (Hangzhou, 1992) pp. 331–5; C. Dietrich, 'Cotton Culture and Manufacture in Early Ch'ing China', W. Willmott, ed., *Economic Organization in Chinese Society* (Stanford, 1992) pp. 109–35.

30. Z. Shi, *Qingdai qianqi xiaonong jingji* (Beijing, 1994) pp. 207–8.

31. Fan and Jin, *Jiangnan sichou shi yanjiu*, pp. 239–41.

32. Chen Juanjuan, *Gugong bowuyuan yuankan*, 1984.2 pp. 89–93. Cited in Wilson, *Rare Marks*, p. 98.

33. Surviving eighteenth-century theatre costumes are scarce and difficult to identify. However some late Qing examples, probably acquired at the auction of a Beijing theatrical company's stock in 1929, are now in the Minneapolis Institute of Arts and the Metropolitan Museum of Art. See R. Jacobsen, *Imperial Silks: Ch'ing Dynasty Textiles in the Minneapolis Institute of Arts*, 2 vols (Minneapolis, 2000), p. 433 and nos. 176–93. For the evolution of performance art, see I. Tanaka, 'The Social and Historical Context of Ming – Ch'ing Local Drama', Johnson, Nathan and Rawski, pp. 143–60; Naquin and Rawski, p. 60.
34. Feng and Chang, pp. 182–3.
35. Hong Kong Museum of Art, *Jingdezhen Zhushan chutu Yongle Xuande guanyao ciqi zhanlan: Imperial Porcelain of the Yongle and Xuande Periods Excavated from the Site of the Ming Imperial Factory at Jingdezhen* (Hong Kong, 1989) p. 11.
36. The history of these rituals is intermittent. They began in the pre-Imperial era and were revived periodically, including in the Tang, the Song (both at the end of Northern Song and beginning of Southern Song), and the late Qing.
37. Clunas, *Superfluous Things*, p. 147.
38. *Ibid.*, p. 146. News reports following Qingming festival, 7 April 2002.
39. J. Haeger, ed., *Crisis and Prosperity in Sung China* (Tucson, 1975). S. Vainker, 'Northern Song Silver', *Transactions of the Oriental Ceramic Society* 59 (1994–5), pp. 11–31.
40. In 1672 and again in 1724. See Feng and Chang, p. 186. Article 429. Article 175 on 'violating the use of clothing and houses' prohibits the use of objects designed for one of superior rank. W. Jones, trans., *The Great Qing Code* (Oxford, 1994). Other references to silk are as raw material, and appear in the laws relating to the Board of Revenue rather than to the Board of Rites (Article 175) or the Board of Works (Article 429). For the situation in the Ming dynasty, see C. Clunas, 'Regulation of Consumption and the Institution of Correct Morality by the Ming State', C. Huang and E. Zurcher, eds, *Norms and the State in China*, Sinica Leidensia vol. XXVIII (Leiden, 1993).
41. A focused study of the life-styles of the Yangzhou salt merchants would provide the most acute survey of luxury consumption in eighteenth-century China but has yet to be undertaken. Ho, *Salt Merchants* is an excellent study of their commercial activities and includes a section on lifestyle. Li Dou, *Yangzhou huafang lu* (1795) is a primary source. The example of the Yangzhou merchants acquisition of paintings suggests a loosening of the literati stranglehold on standards of social acceptability, and this in turn may contribute to the lack of 'elegant living' texts referred to above.
42. National Palace Museum, Taipei, *Qingdai hua falang tezhan mulu* (exhibition catalogue in Chinese and English) (Taipei, 1979), nos. 71, 76, 80; Palace Museum, p. 380, no. 61.
43. L. Ledderose, 'Chinese Influence on European Art, Sixteenth to Eighteenth Centuries', T. Lee, ed., *China and Europe: Images and Influences in Sixteenth to Eighteenth Centuries* (Hong Kong, 1991) pp. 221–49 emphasises the distinctions between categories of ritual and export objects.

Plates

32. Ewer with the arms of peers, porcelain with overglaze enamel decoration and gilding, c. 1730.
33. Porcelain dish, depicting characters from the novel *Shuihu zhuan* (*The Water Margin*), c. 1700.
34. Chair cover, silk and gold thread *kesi* tapestry weave, eighteenth century.
35. Silk panel, embroidered in satin stitch, eighteenth century.
36. Cope with dragon embroidery.

15
Luxury, Clothing and Race in Colonial Spanish America

Rebecca Earle

> It may be said without exaggeration, that the finest stuffs made in countries, where industry is always inventing something new, are more generally seen in Lima than in any other place; vanity and ostentation not being restrained by custom or law.[1]

With this grand overstatement the Spanish travellers Jorge Juan and Antonio de Ulloa summed up their account of fashion in 1740s Lima. Dress in the capital of colonial Peru, according to these men, differed from that of Europe only in its extravagance. European goods and clothing, they insisted, were widely available, which allowed the ladies of Lima to indulge their immoderate taste for Flemish lace and pearls, to the ruination of their husbands. Such was these women's passion for finery that they often succumbed to uterine cancer, brought on, the travellers were certain, by 'their excessive use of perfumes'.[2] Moreover, mid-eighteenth-century Lima was, in the eyes of Juan and Ulloa, a city of sartorial democracy:

> Nor is the distinction between the several classes very great, for the use of all sorts of cloth being allowed, everyone wears what he can purchase. So that it is not uncommon to see a mulatto, or any other mechanic, dressed in a tissue equal to anything that can be worn by a more opulent person, they all greatly affect fine clothes.[3]

Juan and Ulloa paint a striking picture of colonial Spanish America as a land awash with European luxury products ('stuffs made in countries where industry is always inventing something new'), and where the use of fine clothing was not controlled by any sort of legal restriction ('vanity and ostentation not being restrained by custom or law'). Neither feature accords very well with current understanding of either eighteenth-century Spanish American trade or Bourbon colonial legislation, and it would be easy to dismiss Juan and Ulloa's account as mere hyperbole.[4] Certainly the extravagance of colonial costume seems for Juan and Ulloa to have served as a metaphor for the unrestrained corruption that they considered typical of creole government in Spain's American colonies.

Readers of this book will by now be familiar with the use of luxurious consumption as a metaphor for political and moral corruption. Nor did the Spanish travellers Juan and Ulloa need to resort to the writings of English and French philosophers to make use of this imagery. In Spain, as elsewhere in eighteenth-century Europe, writers analysed the concept of *lujo*, or 'luxury', and debated whether luxury provided an essential stimulus to the economy, or whether it led to corruption, effemination, and, ultimately, damnation. Works such as Juan Sempere y Guarinos, *Historia del lujo y de las leyes suntuarias en España* (1788) stressed the beneficial aspects of the luxury trades, while others, such as José Cadalso's 1789 imitation of the *Lettres persanes*, worried that excessive consumption, particularly of foreign goods, would weaken the nation. Cadalso's Moroccan traveller Gazel observed, in language not unlike that of Rousseau:

> Examine the history of all nations, and you will see that the authority of each has rested on custom. On this strong base they have grown, from this growth has come abundance, this abundance has produced luxury, from luxury has followed effemination, effemination gives birth to weakness, and from weakness has come ruin.[5]

It would be easy, then, to interpret Juan and Ulloa's description of Limeño luxury as nothing more than an exotic setting for a familiar debate; a Peruvian response to the *Fable of the Bees*. But to do this would be to overlook a further dimension to Juan and Ulloa's account that was largely absent from the European discussion of luxury. This is the role of race. In their account Juan and Ulloa stressed that the uniform use of fine clothing in Lima made it was difficult to distinguish not only between different social classes but also between different races: 'It is not uncommon to see a mulatto, or any other mechanic, dressed in a tissue equal to anything that can be worn by a more opulent person.' The remainder of this chapter will explore the relationship between luxurious clothing and race in colonial Spanish America.

Juan and Ulloa were not alone in viewing Spain's American colonies as a land of widespread sartorial luxury. European travellers from the seventeenth and eighteenth centuries lingered over descriptions of luxurious colonial dress, particularly in Mexico City and Lima, the two most important viceregal capitals in Spanish America. 'Of all the parts of the world, the people here are most expensive in their habit,' reported the British marine captain William Betagh of 1720s Lima.[6] The clothing of the elite was said to be festooned with jewels: the ladies of Lima had 'an insatiable appetite for pearls and jewels, for bracelets, earrings and other paraphernalia, which saps the wealth of husbands and lovers. We have seen ladies who wear sixty thousand pesos worth of jewels on their person,' claimed the French traveller Amédée Frézier.[7] 'Both men and women are excessive in their apparel, using more silks than stuffs and cloth . . . A hatband and rose made of diamonds in a gentleman's hat is common, and a hat-band of pearls is ordinary in a tradesman,' observed the English priest Thomas Gage nearly a century earlier.[8]

As this latter quotation suggests, in these accounts it is not the elite alone who wear such finery. The poor, mixed-race population is also described as dressing with extraordinary elegance and expense:

A blackamoor or tawny young maid and slave will make hard shift, but she will be in fashion with her neck-chain and bracelets of pearls, and her ear-bobs of some considerable jewels . . . The attire of this baser sort of people of black-amoors and mulattoes . . . is so light, and their carriage so enticing, that many Spaniards even of the better sort (who are too prone to venery) disdain their wives for them

sighed an infatuated Gage.[9] The Mexican chronicler Juan de Viera likewise claimed that in Mexico City 'the Indian women who trade in the plaza regard it as fashionable to wear a necklace with six or eight strings of pearls and coral, many reliquaries, and rings of gold, silver and red gold'.[10] The slaves of wealthy women, acting as extensions of the bodies of their owners, display similar finery. Mulata slaves in Chile, claimed English sailor John Byron, 'dressed almost as well . . . excepting jewels' as their mistresses.[11] In Cartagena, slave women strolled through the streets adorned with golden necklaces and earrings, strings of pearls and silken shawls, alleged one eighteenth-century Spanish friar.[12] (See Plate 37.)

Overall, the image presented in such seventeenth- and eighteenth-century accounts is one of luxury, wealth and successful emulation. All races and classes effect elegant garb, as Mexico city's inhabitant Agustín de Vetancurt, noted in 1698:

The beauty of [Mexico City] is in its inhabitants, because of their elegance and cleanliness . . . The poorest woman has her pearls and jewels, and considers herself unhappy if she does not have her gold jewellery to wear on holidays . . . Great is the elegance and lustre . . . it is greatness, but whoever was to see everyone together, not making distinctions between the rich noble or gentle-man, and the artisan, would think it impolitic, but it is the glory of this country, which inspires majesty, aggrandises humble hearts, and annihilates wretched conditions.[13]

Sartorial emulation, such accounts stressed, was neither impractical nor doomed to failure. Instead, dressing luxuriously was presented as both easy and successful. A well-dressed mestiza or mulata might be viewed with moral disapproval, but she was generally acknowledged to be appealing, perhaps all too appealing, as Thomas Gage's remarks suggest. In this these descriptions contrast markedly with the accounts of nineteenth-century European and American travellers. Nineteenth-century travellers generally disdained attempts by the non-white population to dress well as ludicrous failures. The comments of the American abolitionists Thome and Kimball on the costume of Black women in Antigua are typical:

Their dresses were in every colour and style, their hats were of all shapes and sizes, and fillagreed with the most tawdry superfluity of ribbons. Beneath their gaudy bonnets were glossy ringlets, false and real, clustering in tropical luxuriance. This fantastic display was evidently a rude attempt to follow the example set them by the white aristocracy.[14]

For Thome and Kimball these Antiguan women have clearly failed in their 'rude attempt' to emulate white dress, and their fine clothes are certainly not viewed as a sign of 'greatness'. On the contrary, by the 1820s 'gaudy' had become the term most typically used to describe luxurious Ibero-American dress.[15]

Fine clothing, particularly when worn by the non-white population, came in the nineteenth century to signify something quite different from its eighteenth-century meaning. It had ceased to 'inspire majesty, aggrandise humble hearts, and annihilate wretched conditions', as it had in 1698. This change in the meaning of non-white luxury mirrors the significant shift in scientific understandings of the origins of racial difference, and indeed of the very meaning of race. Enlightenment theories such as those of the Comte de Buffon and Johann Friedrich Blumenbach had emphasised that race was the consequence of the effects of climate, food and culture. For eighteenth-century philosophers skin colour was thus in part a function of culture (including dress) and environment.[16] The centrality of clothing, in particular, in designating race is illustrated by Carl Linnaeus's classification of homo sapiens into five racial types:

1. Wild man. Four-footed, mute, hairy.
2. *American.* Copper-coloured, choleric, erect. *Hair* black, straight, thick; *nostrils* wide; *face* harsh; beard, scanty; obstinate, content, free. Paints himself with fine red lines. *Regulated* by customs.
3. *European.* Fair, sanguine, brawny. *Hair* yellow brown, flowing; *eyes* blue; *gentle*, acute, inventive. *Covered* with close vestments. *Governed* by laws.
4. *Asiatic.* Sooty, melancholy, rigid. *Hair* black; eyes dark; severe, haughty, covetous. *Covered* with loose garments. *Governed* by opinions.
5. *African.* Black, phlegmatic, relaxed. *Hair* black, frizzled; *skin* silky; *nose* flat; *lips* tumid; *crafty*, indolent, negligent. Anoints himself with grease. *Governed* by caprice.[17]

Eighteenth-century scientific opinion thus regarded clothing as a racial characteristic. Such views fit well with the concepts of race employed in colonial Spanish America. There, racial categories reflected not only skin colour, but also the level of wealth, and more importantly, the culture with which the individual identified. The transformative potential of emulation was thus an integral part of colonial Spanish American racial classifications.[18] In lawsuits individuals might seek to establish their race by demonstrating that they wore the clothing appropriate to their claimed status; when in 1686 Blas de Horta tried to demonstrate that he was not an Indian, he did not summon his parents. Rather, he produced a witness to affirm that he wore 'Spanish dress'.[19] Thus a mixed-race woman dressed in elegant European clothing truly belonged to a different racial group from the same woman dressed in rags. In fine clothes she might be confirmed in her identity as a mestiza; in rags she might become a *parda*, or another less regarded race.[20] For this reason 'the lowest class of Spaniards are very ambitious of distinguishing themselves from [mestizos], either by the colour or fashion of the clothes,' as Juan and Ulloa observed.[21] This sort of racial self-reclassification through clothing was complemented in the Hispanic world by a complex legal system which allowed individuals to permanently change their race through the acquisition of legal documents confirming the desired racial identity. Processes known as *gracias al sacar* and *autos sobre declaratoria de mestizo*, available throughout the eighteenth century, entitled their owners to alter their racial identity, thereby allowing access to careers and activities open only to legitimately born individuals of 'clean' blood.[22]

It is for this reason that the colonial Americas retained sumptuary legislation for centuries after such laws had been discarded in Europe. Sumptuary laws – legislation designed to control excessive display, particularly through the regulation of clothing – are employed only in cultures which consider it possible to disguise one's status via clothing. In the Americas sumptuary legislation was considered necessary during the seventeenth and eighteenth centuries precisely in order to control the sorts of unsanctioned personal transformation via dress discussed above. Sumptuary legislation had been discarded in most parts of Europe by the seventeenth century, but reached its heyday in the American colonies only in the seventeenth and eighteenth centuries, precisely the period when, as we saw, it was considered possible, even easy, for non-elites to successfully imitate elite dress. The significance of such laws for our purposes thus lies in the attitudes they suggest towards clothing and identity, rather than in their enforcement, which was limited.[23]

Sumptuary legislation in the Americas, as in Europe, attempted to control the clothing worn by different classes of person, but the American codes also tried to preserve distinctions between different races, a feature that was largely absent in the European legislation. In sixteenth-century Mexico, black women were banned from wearing gold, pearls, silk or other luxurious goods, unless they were married to a Spaniard, and were similarly prohibited from wearing Indian garb unless married to an Indian. Most Indian women were at the same time banned from adopting Spanish dress.[24] In seventeenth-century Lima city ordinances banned 'negroes, mulattos and zambos' from carrying swords or other weapons, and black and mulatto women from wearing 'woollen cloth . . . cloth of silk, [or] lace of gold, silver, black or white'.[25] Comparable laws were passed in eighteenth-century Peru aimed at 'moderating the scandalous excesses of the clothing worn by blacks, mulatos, Indians and mestizos'.[26] In eighteenth-century Brazil, white colonials repeatedly asked the Portuguese Crown to legislate against the perceived excesses of coloured dress, while in the French colony of Saint Domingue sumptuary legislation specifically banned free people of colour from the 'reprehensible imitation' of the clothing, jewellery and hairstyles worn by whites. Free people of colour were instead required to dress in accordance with 'the simplicity of their condition'.[27] The eighteenth-century Spanish slave code for Santo Domingo similarly prohibited both slaves and free people of colour from wearing 'pearls, emeralds, and other precious stones', and, equally significantly, prohibited them from wearing the Spanish mantilla in place of the African head-cloth.[28] Comparable legislation was issued for the Dutch Caribbean islands in 1786.[29]

Such laws aimed at preserving the distinctions between white and coloured dress were accompanied by laws intending to preserve class distinctions that survived well into the eighteenth century. Indeed, such legislation first appeared in Britain's American colonies in the 1620s, nearly two decades after all sumptuary laws had been comprehensively revoked in England itself.[30] In Spanish America, legislation aimed at the 'common people who without having sufficient wealth wish to dress like the wealthy' was issued regularly until the end of the eighteenth century.[31] In 1773, for example, the president of Chile's Audiencia ordered that at Carnival 'no person may use a costume that does not correspond to his estate, sex and quality', so as to avoid 'serious inconveniences'.[32]

It was only in the nineteenth century, after the overthrow of Spanish colonialism, that such laws were discarded in Spanish America. They were discarded because they ceased to be necessary: it was no longer considered possible to alter one's race via luxurious dress. On the contrary, as we have seen, attempts by non-whites to dress well were regarded as ludicrous failures. Legislation was no longer necessary to control such transparent deceits. The nineteenth-century abandonment of sumptuary laws thus sheds additional light on the nature of biologised racial theories emphasising the inherited, inflexible, nature of perceived racial characteristics. In Spanish America, changing scientific thinking combined with the official abolition of racial categories, which occurred in many countries after independence from Spain, to make inconceivable the legal alterations of race permitted in the eighteenth century. Racial categories were thus simultaneously abandoned legally and strengthened socially and scientifically in nineteenth-century Spanish America. Mid-nineteenth-century French anthropologist Alcides d'Orbigny's racialised description of 'American Man' contrasts sharply with Linnaeus's eighteenth-century account:

AMERICAN MAN

First Race: ANDO-PERUVIAN: Olive-brown colour, more or less dark. Short stature. Forehead only slightly elevated or receding; horizontal eyes, never narrow at the outer corner.

Second Race: PAMPAS-DWELLER: Olive-brown colour. Stature often of very great. Forehead convex and non-receding; horizontal eyes, sometimes narrow at the outer corner.

Third Race: BRAZILIAN-GUARANI: Yellowish colour. Medium stature. Forehead slightly convex; eyes slanting upwards at the outer corner.[33]

Dress, along with forms of government, has disappeared from this typical nineteenth-century racial classification. Clothing was no longer considered a racial characteristic. As a consequence, a mixed-race woman in fine clothes became simply a jumped-up half-caste. No longer was she the elegant, silk-clad creature of Thomas Gage's account, whose seductive gaze enticed married Spaniards to their doom. The disdain for well-dressed people of colour in the Americas is thus symptomatic of the hardening of racial categories and of the changing meaning of luxury in the nineteenth century. 'Clothes make the man' is not a nineteenth-century sentiment, at least as far as racial identity was concerned.

Acknowledgement

I would like to thank Sheena Boa, John Gilmore, Gad Heuman, Steiner Saether, Guy Thomson and Dror Wahrman, who offered many suggestions and sources, and Maxine Berg for inviting me to speak at the Warwick Luxury Project's winter 2000 workshop.

Notes

1. Jorge Juan and Antonio de Ulloa, *A Voyage to South America* [1806 John Adams translation] (New York, 1964), p. 196.
2. *Ibid.*, pp. 196 and 214.
3. *Ibid.*, p. 196.
4. For eighteenth-century trade, see John Fisher, *Relaciones económicas entre España y América hasta la independencia* (Madrid, 1992); and for Bourbon social legislation, see, *inter alia*, Juan Pedro Viqueira Albán, *Propriety and Permissiveness in Bourbon Mexico*, Sonya Lipsett-Rivera and Sergio Rivera Ayala (trans.) (Wilmington, 1999).
5. See José Cadalso, *Cartas Marruecas* [1789] (Madrid, 1950); and Juan Sempere y Guarinos, *Historia del luxo y de las leyes suntuarias de España*, 2 vols (Madrid, 1788). The quotation is from Cadalso, *Cartas Marruecas*, pp. 168–9. Juan Rico, 'Criptoburgesía y cambio económico en la Ilustración española', *Cuadernos Hispanoamericanos*, vol. 408 (1984), provides an excellent overview of the Spanish luxury debates.
6. William Betagh, *A Voyage Round the World, being an Account of a Remarkable Enterprise begun in the Year 1719* (London, 1728), p. 266.
7. Amadeo Frézìer, *Relación del viaje por el mar del sur* [1716] (Caracas, 1982), p. 191 (see also pp. 219–22).
8. Thomas Gage, *Travels in the New World* [1648] (Norman, 1958), p. 68.
9. *Ibid.*, p. 68 (or see p. 73).
10. Juan de Viera, 'Breve Compendiosa, Narración de la ciudad de Mexico, corte y cabeza de toda la America Meridional' [1778], in Agustín de Vetancurt, Juan Manuel de San Vicente and Juan de Viera, *La ciudad de Mexico en el siglo XVIII (1690–1780): Tres crónicas* (Mexico, 1990), p. 256.
11. John Byron, *Byron's Narrative, containing an Account of the Great Distresses Suffered by Himself, and his Companions on the Coasts of Patagonia from the Year 1740 till their Arrival in England, 1746* (Belfast, 1844), p. 107.
12. Fray Juan de Santa Gertrudis Serra, *Maravillas de la naturaleza*, 2 vols (Bogotá, 1956), vol. 1, p. 43.
13. Agustín de Vetancurt, 'Tratado de la Cuidad de Mexico y las Grandezas que la ilustran despues que la fundaron españoles' [1698], in Vetancurt, San Vicente and Viera, *La ciudad de Mexico en el siglo XVIII*, pp. 46–7.
14. Jas. A. Thome and J. Horace Kimball, *Emancipation in the West Indies. A Six Month's Tour in Antigua, Barbados and Jamaica in the Year 1837* (New York, 1838), p. 8. For other examples, see Charles Stuart Cochrane, *Journal of a Residence and Travels in Colombia during the Years 1823 and 1824* [1825], 2 vols (New York, 1971), vol. 2, pp. 88–9; Captain G.F.

Lyon, *Journal of a Residence and Tour in the Republic of Mexico in the Year 1826* [1828], 2 vols (Port Washington, 1971), vol. 1, pp. 106, 202, vol. 2, pp. 235–6; John Luccock, *Rio de Janeiro and the Southern Parts of Brazil taken during a Residence of Ten Years in that Country from 1808 to 1818* (London, 1820), p. 190; and Isaac Holton, *New Granada: Twenty Months in the Andes* [1856] (Carbondale, 1967), pp. 192–3.

15. For representative examples, see Cochrane, *Journal of a Residence and Travels in Colombia*, vol. 2, pp. 88–9, 119; Joel Roberts Poinsett, *Notes on Mexico Made in the Autumn of 1822* (New York, 1969), pp. 48, 52, 77; Edward Thornton Tayloe, *Mexico, 1825–1828. The Journals and Correspondence of Edward Thornton Tayloe*, C. Harvey Gardiner ed. (Chapel Hill, 1959), p. 40; and Lyon, *Journal of a Residence and Tour in the Republic of Mexico*, vol. 2, p. 235.

16. See Georges Louis Leclerc de Buffon, 'Variétés dans l'Espèce Humaine', *Oeuvres Complètes* [1749+], 6 vols (Paris, 1859), vol. 3, pp. 268–325. For comments on eighteenth-century racial theories, see Stephen Jay Gould, *Ever Since Darwin: Reflections in Natural History* (London, 1973); Londa Schiebinger, *Nature's Body. Sexual Politics and the Making of Modern Science* (London, 1993); Anne McClintock, *Imperial Leather. Race, Gender and Sexuality in the Colonial Contest* (New York, 1995); and Kenan Malik, *The Meaning of Race. Race, History and Culture in Western Society* (London, 1996).

17. Sir Charles Linné, *A General System of Nature through the Three Grand Kingdoms of Animals, Vegetables and Minerals*, 7 vols (London, 1806), vol. 1, p. 9. Linnaeus developed and revised his *Systema Naturae* from 1735 until his death in 1778.

18. A good starting point for exploring the meaning of race in Spanish America is Peter Wade, *Race and Ethnicity in Latin America* (London, 1997).

19. Martin Minchom, *The People of Quito: 1690–1810: Change and Unrest in the Underclass* (Boulder, 1994), pp. 158, 190.

20. For very clear examples, see Jaime Jaramillo Uribe, *Ensayos sobre historia social colombiana* (Bogotá, 1969), pp. 195, 211.

21. Juan and Ulloa, *A Voyage to South America*, p. 137.

22. For *gracias al sacar* and *autos sobre declaratoria de mestizo*, see Minchom, *The People of Quito*, pp. 158–70; and Ann Twinam, *Public Lives, Private Secrets: Gender, Honor, Sexuality and Illegitimacy in Colonial Spanish America* (Stanford, 1999).

23. For discussion of sumptuary laws in Europe, see Francis Elizabeth Baldwin, *Sumptuary Legislation and Personal Regulation in England* (Baltimore, 1926); James Laver, *The Concise History of Costume and Fashion* (New York, 1969), p. 72; Michael and Ariane Batterberry, *Mirror Mirror: A Social History of Fashion* (New York, 1977), pp. 49–50; Alan Hunt, *Governance of the Consuming Passions. A History of Sumptuary Law* (London, 1996); and Daniel Roche, *The Culture of Clothing. Dress and Fashion in the 'Ancien Régime'* (Cambridge, 1996).

Sumptuary laws were retained in Spain and Portugal well into the eighteenth century, far longer than elsewhere in Europe. See Martin A.S. Hume, 'A Fight against Finery (A History of the Sumptuary Laws in Spain)', in *Ten Years after the Armada and Other Historical Studies* (London, 1896); Mary Elizabeth Perry, *Gender and Disorder in Early Modern Spain* (Princeton, 1990), p. 48; Cecelia Salinas, *Las Chilenas de la Colonia. virtud sumisa, amor rebelde* (Santiago, 1994); and Silvia Hunold Lara, 'The Signs of Color: Women's Dress and Racial Relations in Salvador and Rio de Janeiro, ca 1750–1815', *Colonial Latin American Review*, vol. 6:2 (1997).

24. Julia Tuñón Pablos, *Women in Mexico. A Past Unveiled*, Alan Hynds (trans.) (Austin, 1999), pp. 26–8. See also Gonzalo Aquirre Beltrán, 'The Integration of the Negro into the National Society of Mexico', Magnus Mörner, ed., *Race and Class in Latin America* (New York, 1970), p. 24.

25. Josephe and Francisco Mugaburu, *Chronicle of Colonial Lima. The Diary of Josephe and Francisco Mugaburu, 1640–1697*, Robert Miller (trans.) (Norman, 1975), pp. 32, 59, 82–3, 124, 217.

26. R.C. aprobando un bando del Virrey del Peru para moderar el exceso en los trajes que vestían los negros, mulatos, indios y mestizos, San Ildefonso, 7 September 1725, in

Richard Konetzke, ed., *Colección de Documentos para la Historia de la Formación Social de Hispanoamérica, 1493–1810*, 3 vols (Madrid, 1962), vol. 3:1, p. 187. See also R.C. al presidente de la Audiencia de Guadalajara sobre que observe las ordenes y leyes que prohiben traer armas los indios, mestizos, negros y mulatos, Madrid, 30 Dec. 1692; and Pragmática contra el abuso de trajes y otros gastos superfluos, Madrid, 10 Feb. 1716; in Konetzke, ed., *Colección de Documentos*, vol. 3:1, p. 27, pp. 124–34, respectively.

27. Lara, 'The Signs of Colour'; and Réglament provisoire des Administrateurs, concernant le Luxe des Gens de couleur, 9 February 1779, in Médéric-Louis-Élie Moreau de Saint-Méry, *Loix et Constitutions des Colonies Françoises de l'Amérique sous le vent*, 6 vols (Paris, 1784–90), vol. 5, pp. 855–6.

28. Extracto del Código Negro Carolino, Santo Domingo, 14 March 1785, in Konetzke, ed., *Colección de Documentos*, vol. 3:2, p. 562. See also Médéric-Louis-Élie Moreau de Saint-Méry, *Descripción de la parte española de Santo Domingo* [1796] (Ciudad Trujillo, 1944), p. 93.

29. Neville Hall, *Slave Society in the Danish West Indies: St. Thomas, St. John and St. Croix*, ed. B.W. Higman (Baltimore, 1992), pp. 116, 148–9.

30. For comment on this, see Hunt, *Governance of the Consuming Passions*, p. 38.

31. The quotation is from a 1648 appeal by the Audiencia of Chile (Salinas, *Las Chilenas de la Colonia*, p. 114).

32. Salinas, *Las Chilenas de la Colonia*, p. 115. See also pp. 125–6.

33. Alcide D'Orbigny, *L'Homme Américain (de l'Amérique méridionale), considéré sous ses rapports physiologiques et moraux*, 2 vols. (Paris and Strasbourg, 1839), vol. 1, pp. 245–9.

Plate

37. Vicente Albán, 'Distinguished Lady with her Black Slave', Quito School, 1783.

16
Asian Luxuries and the Making of the European Consumer Revolution

Maxine Berg

Introduction

The entry of Asian manufactured goods into Europe in the early modern period takes us to the heart of two debates: the debate during that period on luxury, and the debate during our own recent times on Orientalism. For the products of the East, both foodstuffs and manufactured goods, were desired in Europe because they were 'Oriental', that is to say strange, exotic, other. Trade with the Orient was seen in terms of the senses – colour, texture, smell and taste. Luxury was conflated with sensuality and foreignness.

The exotic East had, however, long been perceived over the course of the medieval and early modern period through seeing objects – fabrics, carpets, ceramics, furnishings, jewels, colours, patterns and ornament. Indeed, back to even earlier periods in other parts of Eurasia, China was called 'Serica' to correspond with the Chinese word 'si' for silk, of 'China' derived from the Chinese word 'ci' for ceramics.[1] Eastern goods retained a sense of luxury and difference. These eastern commodities were, however, prefabricated in much the same way as was discourse. They were a construct of the market, seeming to represent the lives and values of the East, but constructed to meet European preconceptions of eastern art.

Europeans had a long acquaintance with Oriental luxury goods. Fine tableware in ceramics, glass and silver was, in Renaissance Italy, a sign of civility, and princes, aristocrats and wealthy merchants displayed Oriental porcelain among their domestic possessions. The Merchant of Prato in the fourteenth century, though a man of great wealth, had relatively basic domestic possessions, but these included ceramics, glass and silver. By the mid-fifteenth century Cardinal Gonzaga was famed for his collection of treasures and the opulence which marked him as a figure of magnificence and authority; he held in his inventory sumptuous articles of clothing in 'the Turkish style', and damasks, velvets and brocades 'from Alexandria'.[2] Two hundred years later Asian goods were still exotic. Paris shops in 1644 sold 'objects of Lachinage' as a part of collections of curiosities. John Evelyn reported, 'among the Houses is a shop called Noah's Ark, where are to be sold all sorts of Curiositys, naturall & artificial, for the furniture of Cabinets, Pictures and Collections, as of Purcelane, China . . . Shells, Ivory, Ebony: birds, dryed Fishes,

Insects:, etc. of more Luxury than Use.'³ But the trade in Oriental consumer goods was to take on whole new dimensions with the extension of maritime trade and the founding of the East India Companies early in the seventeenth century. This trade was to change the material culture of Europe, bringing with it new objects, colours, patterns and finishes.

Oriental commodities were profoundly attractive; once the possibilities of their possession moved beyond princes and aristocrats, there seemed no stopping the expansion of trade. Apart from the objects themselves, there was enormous fascination with the exotic skills and production processes behind the materials, colours and patterns otherwise undiscovered in Europe. There was a fascination with the refinement and civility of the East, and an admiration for the technical wizardry – the ease in producing materials so precious and objects so finely crafted. For these eastern commodities were not the products of long-accumulated skills and artistic genius of the individual craftsman. They were processes involving large-scale production, division of labour and specialisation, and commercialization and adaptability to the diversity of global markets.

First, the attraction of Oriental goods in Europe was in their perception as luxuries. We thus need to see the objects which reached the West from the seventeenth century onwards as 'constructs'; they formed a part of the European luxury debates. Asian luxury was 'Persian' or 'Oriental'. There was the Enlightenment belief that while the West had progressed, the Islamic world was in decline. Persian luxury and the Orient was associated with excess, the sensual and seduction. The luxury of the East might bring corruption, a loss of identity, falsity and effeminacy. But China was somewhat differently perceived. China was associated not with sensuality and excess, but with ethics, harmony and virtue. China and Confucius inspired Leibniz, then Voltaire and the Encyclopedists to perceive through the prism of Chinese objects their own aspirations to human elegance and refinement. In possessing things Chinese, they sought to access levels of civilisation beyond the market.⁴

The classic ancient luxury import from Asia to Europe was silk, but it was to be the relatively new imports of calicoes, porcelain and lacquered ware whose popularity and extensive trade in the seventeenth and eighteenth centuries was to have the greatest impact of European, and especially British industry. These latter commodities were not perceived to be high luxuries like gold and silver objects or jewellery, or even silk, nor were they base goods for a mass market. They were not like the luxuries which had dominated the old commodities trade in spices, perfumes and groceries. The calicoes, porcelain, lacquerwares and other ornamental goods imported in quantities from Asia in the seventeenth and eighteenth centuries retained the exotic qualities that enhanced their desirability, but as manufactures they were also to have a profound effect on European consumption patterns and production processes.

These were special luxuries – they were part of a group of objects that 'imitated' or mimicked gold and silver in a cross-cultural transmission. It was this quality of 'imitation' which gave rise to the Asian luxury goods trade, and also to the European consumer goods manufacture which succeeded it. An imitative material was a source of wonder, and taste became a new means of displaying prestige. The Portuguese delegate at the Council of Trent in 1562, shocked at the array of gold and silver on the papal table, recommended porcelain from China – 'far superior to silver in elegance and neatness'; 'its lustre surpassing both crystal and alabaster, while its relative low price compensated for its fragility'.[5] Renaissance Italian city states, and especially Venice built on the role of taste in displaying prestige – the consumption of new luxury goods made from relatively inexpensive materials, such as glass and maiolica, opened new markets for consumers. Glass had a special quality in its capacity to imitate other more precious materials such as precious stones and crystal; special value was placed on the beauty, variety and craftsmanship of the object.[6]

The use of these new materials, and their production and trade on a significant level depended on levels of wealth and the possession of some of this wealth in non-elite mercantile and bourgeois groups. Such conditions had previously appeared in Song China, ancient Athens and Renaissance Italy. It depended on customs of civility and taste ranging from the Greek Symposia to the fifteenth-century Italian civility at table with its glass, maiolica, cutlery and silver. These conditions were to reappear again in late seventeenth and eighteenth-century Europe with a parallel context of the English tea table.[7]

These imitative processes at the heart of the cross-cultural transmission of luxury were also the processes that generated product innovation in Europe, and the technological innovation to carry this into an Industrial Revolution. European imitation of Oriental luxury created new products, but also sought to convey the taste for the original.

Oriental luxury, perceived from the perspective of technically advanced and refined consumer objects became incorporated into a new modern luxury. Montesquieu, Hume and Smith wrote of luxury as an aspect of people's desire to better themselves. Luxury could be tamed in refined living and building culture in a well-governed state. Commercial writers were keen to point out what the West could learn from the Orient.

Porcelain, one of the major entries in the Encyclopédie and Postelthwayt's *Universal Dictionary of Trade and Commerce* was based on the Jesuit chronicle of the overseas missions, and the reports of Father d'Entrecolles written in 1712 and on the 'History of Feou-lean'. The entry was revised, translated and reprinted in many of Europe's great commercial dictionaries and encyclopedias. Great admiration was expressed for the secret art, and the huge scale and division of labour on which it was practised.

Postlethwayt's entry on the Mechanical Arts in his *Universal Dictionary of Trade and Commerce* praised those arts of Bengal, China and Japan. Of Bengal he wrote, 'The artizans here have wonderful skill and dexterity; they excel particularly in making linen cloth, which is of such fineness, that very long and broad pieces of it may easily be drawn through a small ring . . .' The Chinese 'gild paper with leaf gold and silver, laid on with a very good sort of varnish they have, which is the same wherewith they varnish their lacquered wares . . . they also gild paper and weave it into their silks.'

'Among the Japanese, they have the art of making lacca in a manner superior to the Europeans . . . The colours wherewith they dye their stuffs never fade . . .'

And finally, 'Upon the whole, in whatever mechanical or manufactured arts other nations may excel Great Britain, our artists should be upon the watch, not only to imitate, but surpass if possible. Those which are imported, and which they can see, handle and minutely examine, they are the most like to imitate or excel. As we have arrived at a great perfection in the China ware, why may we not in divers other eastern arts and manufactures?'[8]

By the time of the arts and crafts movement in Europe in the 1880s this manufacturing superiority came to be perceived as separated off from the market, as the result of a level of civilization beyond the market. It was believed that in China and Japan the skilled workman was respectfully received by a prince, while the richest merchants would be beneath his notice.[9] But in the eighteenth century, it was commerce as well as craft that Europeans sought to replicate.

There is another absolutely vital factor that the new Asian luxuries touched; this was fashion and design styles. The new luxuries came to Europe precisely at the time when styles diffused rapidly across Europe, and indeed became centred on France, and when fashion came to play a major part across the social classes. The new flowered fabric provided surprise and novelty, and were reconfigured and re-elaborated in silk fabrics. Art and design styles shifted from the baroque of Louis XIV towards the lighter, more playful and asymmetrical rococo, or *'le gout moderne'*. The rococo contained all the elements of novelty, surprise and variety so central to contemporary aesthetics. It was developed for interiors, furnishings, ornament, graphic design and art as well as fabric design, and hence had an incredibly wide impact. The Oriental styles were a breath of fresh air, and so easily mixed with other designs, and were so adaptable to innovation as to produce a new chinoiserie.

The *gout moderne* was associated with the new bourgoisie in France. It was an assault on the social and political prerogatives of the nobility; as a new style it brought together commercial and cultural modernity. French furniture makers used exotic woods, and drew on oriental motifs and lacquer techniques to evoke China and Japan. They valorised the novel with a virtuoso display of new world and eastern material along with new fragile and light forms decorated with new techniques in veneers and marquetry.[10]

Asian consumer cultures

Europe discovered Eastern luxury via the Portuguese trade. Lisbon was the centre for Eastern curiosities. The Portuguese and Spanish found contact with China via trade from the Malaccas to the Philippines where Chinese ships came with silk, cotton, porcelain and curios, and on to Mexico and Brazil. And as we know they gained access to Nagasaki in the 1570s. There were Dutch and Portuguese factories on Hirado Island and Nagasaki Harbour by 1609. The Portuguese continued to control direct trade with China until the end of the seventeenth century. Oriental goods, including porcelain was traded from here through the great fairs and cities of Europe, and collected by Europe's elite for their cabinets of curiosities.

Britain gained access to the trade in this luxury through the marriage of Catherine of Braganza and Charles II in 1662. This brought to England the ports of Tangiers and Bombay, and Charles introduced to the English a stylish way of living. This did not include at this stage a widespread taste for Oriental luxury. This taste was spread by the Dutch when the Oriental emporium of Europe shifted from Lisbon to Amsterdam.[11] The ships which brought such vast amounts of exotic luxury goods from across the world opened European eyes to more advanced and elegant ways of living, indeed to consumer cultures just now beginning in Europe. In China, just as in Europe the dynamics of human consumption changed in response to changes in income and shifts in taste. An active consumer culture and highly commercialised economy provided the vital supports for the trade in export wares to Europe.[12]

What were the commercial and manufacturing characteristics of Asian consumer societies? What particular expertise did China, Japan and India acquire in internationally traded consumer and luxury goods? What did western observers, merchants and manufacturers learn from these, and how did they adapt them to their own purposes?

China had long experience of extensive commercialisation and integration into the international economy. It made prodigious technological progress during the Song-Yuan period (960–1368), so much so that Chinese historians have argued for close comparability between eleventh-century China and early eighteenth-century Europe. Ironmakers used coke in blast furnaces for smelting by the eleventh century, and fed a rapidly expanding demand for iron for weapons, farm implements, iron currency and especially for industry. A water-powered spinning machine was invented for use on hemp. State industries developed large workshops alongside a whole range of specialised private manufactures. A wide range of consumer goods, most designed for popular markets, was available to rapidly expanding urban populations.[13]

China and Japan were also highly urbanised societies. By the Ming dynasty (1368–1644) there were 45,000 market towns in China, each of which affected 15–20 villages. Japan under the Tokogawa shogunate in the seventeenth century had 160 places of over 5,000, and a big increase in really large cities – Edo grew from a fishing village to a million by the eighteenth century.

And the market was facilitated by extensive canal development. The merchant and industrial groups grew more prosperous. The state for a short time attempted to curb the extravagance of once humble classes with sumptuary laws, but they proved unenforceable.[14] The extensive urban centres of the Indian Ocean took their life from the substantial presence of merchants, long-distance trade and artisan production.

There was extensive development of the middle market during the Ming and Qing dynasties. There were not enough official positions to go around, and the newly rich patronised the arts. There were a lot of people in the market for high quality goods. This meant product differentiation in products like ceramics and silk which were otherwise either imperial ware, or functional bulk commodities. High quality ceramics were distinguished by studio marks, and would have been made for private consumers in the Chinese middle market. Similarly, silks though functional, were also made in special qualities and designs for this middle market.[15]

In Japan too the domestic market was huge; agricultural productivity growth allowed higher living standards to traders, clerics, warriors and urban producers of goods and services. Cottage industries produced lacquerware, fans parasols, toys, footwear, paper lanterns, and a whole range of small manufactured goods. 'Japan developed a varied, stylish economy, full of clever devices and clever designing, though no machines.'[16]

In India, luxury markets based around the Moghal courts and high degrees of regional differentiation were reflected in a diverse consumer culture. Fashionable clothing was mainly expressed in colour, patterning, embroidery, pleating and various types of adornment and accessories such as sashes, slippers and jewellery. Silk and cotton fabrics were used in an extensive variety of weaves, patterns, colours and degrees of fineness. Urban housing for the wealthy mercantile classes displayed sophisticated architectural design incorporating modular construction, internal courtyards and gardens, wind towers and ventilating rooms.[17]

China, Japan and India provided long-standing models of highly urbanised commercial societies providing for a flowering of consumer culture. Already providing for consumer markets on a vast scale, how were Asian production processes affected by new European markets in the seventeenth and eighteenth centuries?

Asian maritime trade in luxury ware was based on the coexistence of a domestic market of widely differentiated consumer ware. Chinese ceramics sold to 64 foreign destinations, and textiles to 85: it traded metal products, gold, silver, copper and iron to another 134. At the time of the Ming dynasty (1368–1644) China's main imports were horses, materials for Chinese medicines and monetary metals, but throughout the early modern period it was the main supplier of industrial goods. It exported iron goods, textiles (silk and cotton), ceramics and lacquerware, as well as silver, gold and copper and lead products, a whole range of handicrafts, stationery and books.[18] China's main barter good to the Spice Islands was Indian piece goods acquired in its own triangular trade.

There was also an extensive trade to Japan and in the South China Seas. Chinese ships trading to Japan during the Ming period averaged 298.4 tons; those travelling to South and West Asia had loading capacities of 955 tons. During the Ming period 130 Chinese government-registered vessels travelled overseas each year; the return tonnage on these was 1,767,120 tons a year. The China-Manila trade was also extensive, rising to 3,200 metric tons by the end of the Ming period, and was dominated by high-value goods. In Manila the voracious Chinese demand for silver was met by the Spanish trade in South American silver, and Chinese silks and porcelain as well as Asian spices were sent along the American coast and back via Mexico to Europe, or out to other South Asian traders. The Chinese traded great quantities of porcelain to these Asian markets both before and after European markets opened. In 1645 alone 229,000 pieces were sold to the Japanese, and another 300,000 to the Arabs through the Dutch. It was no small wonder that the South China Seas and Indian Ocean are referred to by China's historians as the Asian Mediterranean.[19]

The trade in ceramics was well established by the fifteenth century between China and the South Seas and Japan. In the first half of the seventeenth century more than half the exports from China went to South Seas markets. Most were low-priced coarse ware and medium quality ware. European imports were of higher quality. Europe's share was 31 per cent of the quantity of Chinese ceramic exports in third quarter of the seventeenth century, but its share of value was 50 per cent.[20] Japanese sources of supply of ceramics were important from the mid seventeenth century, and came to compete with the Chinese. There was a prior internal Japanese market for high quality expensive blue and white porcelain; but higher quality Japanese ware was exported in South Seas markets and to Europe, largely through Chinese merchants and through a small trading factory at Deshima on Hirado Island. Kakiemon ware was exported first – then Imari – enamelled red and green decoration. The bulk of the Japanese trade also went to the South Seas, and only 10 per cent to Europe.[21] The Dutch traded Asian silks brought to Batavia for Japanese porcelain bought in Deshima or in other South Asian ports. China shipped silk to Batavia for re-export to Japan along with silk arrived from Bengal. In return China imported cotton textiles from India, some for re-export, spices, sandalwood and other timber for ships or ships themselves from South-East Asia, and silver from everywhere.

A new Asian–European direct trade in manufactured goods was also erected on a longstanding intra-Asian trade in textiles and ceramics. The Indian cotton textile trade faced a stable and continuous demand in Asian foreign trade. There was an enormous degree of product differentiation finely tuned to the specialised tastes of highly diversified markets. Interregional trade was based on fine textiles supplied from special centres – muslins from the Dacca districts of East Bengal, silks and taffetas from Kasimbazar, fine chintzes and transparent muslins from the towns of West and Central India, Ahmedabad and Sironj. A much more extensive trade in cheaper and coarser cotton textiles as well as basic foodstuffs was exported from Gujarat to the Red Sea area as well as to Indonesia. When Indian merchants lost the carrying trade in spices in the Indian Ocean in the seventeenth century, textiles came to be even more important. Until the early eighteenth century with the decline of the port of Surat and the Indian fleet there, the mass of trade in the Indian Ocean was in Indian hands.[22]

The trade in textiles and ceramics between Asia and Europe was based on trade routes and trade organization already marked out for the spice trade, and subsequently for colonial groceries, notably tea. The trade in high-quality luxury manufactures was based in the long-standing emporia trade. But the extensive production and marketing throughout the Asian world of coarse low quality wares was also well developed by the fifteenth century. This was not a 'mass' production since products were finely adapted to fit the specialised tastes of different markets throughout southern Asia. These pre-existing conditions allowed to Europeans the opportunity to develop a new scale of marketing for what came to be seen as semi-luxury ware. These goods were both differentiated to suit the demands for distinctive identities and novelty in the markets of the middling classes. They were also produced and traded in sufficient volumes to make them affordable. And they were still foreign, 'Oriental', and so endowed with the qualities of luxury ware.

European imports of Asian luxuries in the seventeenth and eighteenth centuries were thus added to large pre-existing domestic markets and a highly developed Asian trade. There was, nevertheless, a demand shock. In the case of China, the Dutch traded a million pieces of porcelain at the end of the seventeenth century. The effect of this European trade for China was a shift from a more broadly-based consumer goods trade to one based in silk and porcelain. The axis of trade shifted from the south to the north, and from the interior to the coastal trade. This was accompanied by a shift in population. But even greater changes were to come with the shift in the East India Company trade in the late eighteenth century away from luxury goods to tea – tea increased to over 90 per cent of imports of the British East India Company in the 1790s.[23]

European markets for Asian luxuries

The growth in European demand for Indian textiles was fostered by the East India Companies, and subsequently curtailed by European governments. As early as 1609 the English East India Company was investigating types of cotton cloth available in Western India which were deemed suitable for European and Middle Eastern markets. It sought 12,000 pieces of fine white fabrics and the painted calicoes of Gujarat; the VOC ordered 7,000 similar pieces in 1617 (see Plate 38). Imports also focused on the coarser cottons of the inter-Asian trade, imported both for the African slave trade and for the cheaper ends of the European market, but at this stage, for clothing, there was little displacement of European linens and fustians for common use. In the 1620s the Court of the English East India Company reported 'calicoes are a commodity whereof the use is not generally known, the vent must be forced and trial made into all parts . . . much of it is very useful and vended in England whereby the price of Lawns, Cambricks and other linen cloth are brought down.'[24]

The Company was clearly testing the market for its textile imports, and frequently expressed concerns about overstocking the market. It imported velvets, coverlets, quilts, damasks, taffetas and pile carpets from Persia; it tried out cotton piece goods, gave up on some, but did well with white baftas from Gujarat used for bed and table linens. It used the terminology of the European linen trade, for example, calico lawns, to sell the new cloth. It imported coarse strong calicoes usually dyed blue or brown and used for packing and making sails. Its greatest successes were with chintzes, pintadoes and striped calicoes, used initially for curtains or hangings.[25]

By the latter half of the seventeenth century the main increase in demand was for clothing fabric. The Company emphasised luxury and semi-luxury markets. It asked the Surat Factory in 1683 for chintz printed on fine cloth desirable to upper-class women: 'in Holland the Indian chintzes were already the ware of Gentle-women', but in England 'of the meaner sort'. Four years later it reported that chintz had become 'the ware of ladyes of the greatest quality, which they wear on the outside of Gowns and Mantuas which they line with velvet and cloth of gold'.[26] By the later seventeenth century, the Dutch and English companies were importing over a million pieces each of Indian cotton goods. By the eighteenth century Bengal muslins and Coromandel chintz were the new luxury textiles.[27] (See Plates 38 and 39.)

The companies forged their successes not on mass market textiles, but on more expensive, differentiated fabrics for a discerning class conscious market. The key to the market was in identifying a wide range of semi-luxury and luxury fabrics, colours and patterns suited to a broad middling class attuned to distinctiveness, fashion and novelty, as well as a clear divide between ornamental and useful ware. These fabrics were clearly seen by their consumers and by contemporary moral-ists as luxuries partly because they were Oriental imports, but more because they were coloured, patterned and fine fabrics. The Dutch moralists who condemned the vainglorious cloth harmful to the nation's interests did not stand a chance against a public which liked the cloth. Swedish Puritans who associated the cloth with Eastern luxuries and the decline of morals could not hinder the prosperity of the Swedish East India Company.[28]

The importance of porcelain exports in Europe cannot be underestimated. They arrested the development of tin-glazed earthenware which had diffused from Italy to Holland in the early sixteenth century. The universal appeal of the Chinese blue and white which ranged from Japan to Istanbul to Amsterdam went with the urbanised, commercial cultures of these places. The very receptive markets in Europe were connected with changes in food conventions and etiquette, and espe-cially in Northern Europe with the growth of increasingly prosperous middling ranks. The Dutch East India Company imported 43 million pieces from the begin-ning of the seventeenth century to the end of the eighteenth century. The English, French, Swedish and Danish Companies shipped another 30 million.[29]

Chinese imports thus dominated the ceramics trade in Europe for approxi-mately 200 years. It was not until the mid-eighteenth century that the rise in Chinese porcelain prices combined with a new phase of ceramics innovation in Europe contributed to a relative decline in the trade. Just as in Indian textiles, the same luxury and semi-luxury markets lay behind the rise of porcelain imports in the same period. But in this case the companies needed to make no effort to create a vent for a desirable product for which no substitute existed. Porcelain always constituted a relatively small proportion of the Companies' total trade, but it was important in very different ways. It was porcelain, to a much greater degree than textiles, which defined the 'Orient' to European consumers. The early pieces to reach Europe were high luxury goods, esteemed for their translucence, durability and fine distinctive blue and white decoration. There was nothing in Europe at the time to match these (hard paste porcelain was not made there until 1709). Most English families ate from pewter plates, wooden trenchers or coarse earth-enwares which were still clay or brick-coloured. Tin glazed earthenwares of the

Delft type were owned first by the elites then later the middling households of Holland from the early seventeenth century, but the white glaze was easily chipped, and the earthenware was unsuitable for teawares. Oriental porcelain was thus not just an ornamental novelty, but a useful decency.[30]

Porcelain, however, had other qualities which lifted it beyond elite luxury markets. It could be produced in China and Japan in large quantities, and even the most basic Chinese ware was still more attractive than what was available in Europe. It was also heavy, and if not used as ballast (more commonly copper or saltpetre was used for this), it went deep into the holds just on top of the true ballast of ships carrying valuable cargoes of spices and silk, and later of tea. It was an ideal semi-luxury good; the highest quality ornamental pieces graced the porcelain cabinets of the palaces and chateaux of Europe's monarchs and nobility. But equally, upwardly mobile tradespeople in European towns could afford the pieces of useful ware distributed by local 'china men'.

Asian production processes

Asian success stories in providing consumer markets in Europe go back to the special features of luxury commodities, and the trade established in these throughout Asia. Luxury objects produced by specialised non-local craftsmen were universally desired by most societies. The reasons for this lie not just in aesthetic sensibilities, but in art, religion and magical transformation. The appeal of such objects dictated the continuity of trade even in times of political conflict. But an active trade also developed across Asia in ordinary domestic commodities – coarse cloth, earthenware, iron implements and brass utensils. Product variations even in very ordinary goods were closely associated with locality, along with a sense of the markets such goods were intended for. Regional specialization and extensive product differentiation were the key to production processes.[31]

There are celebrated descriptions of the porcelain city, Jingdezhen during the late Yuan period (1279–1368) as the largest industrial operation in the world, with over 1,000 kilns, 70,000 workers and production processes that anticipated modern assembly-line manufacture.[32] 'Tens of thousands of pestles shake the ground with their noise. The heavens are alight with the glare from the fires, so that one cannot sleep at night. The place has been called in jest "The Town of Year-Round Thunder and Lightning."'[33] The kiln technologies developed as far back as the Han period (206 BC–220 AD) surpassed European techniques until the nineteenth century. By the Song period multi-chamber 'dragon kilns' stretched up hillsides as much as 60 metres. They could fire more than 50,000 pieces at a time over several days. They also provided for temperature differences of as much as 600 degrees Celsius between the firebox in the lower area and the chimney in the upper, so that in a single operation a whole range of wares could be produced from high-fired porcelain in the lower chambers to earthenware in the top.[34]

Textile production was equally finely tuned to large-scale output combined with diversity. Indian industrial districts added production for Europe to longstanding production cycles for the pan-Asian trading ring. As we have seen production had long been honed to diverse tastes across social, religious and national groups from the Middle East to Japan. These export-oriented textile regions quickly assimilated and adapted European styles and motifs to a new kind of Oriental design for European markets.

The key point about these regions was their capacity to produce an enormous range of types, qualities, patterns, lengths and widths of cloth, a diversity we usually think of as available only in the global markets of the twentieth century.[35] The link between the Company and the weavers was achieved through Indian merchants at the ports who used an advance contract system, that is they employed agents who advanced money to weavers specialising in the kinds of fabrics needed. The whole system relied on a close network of information town to town, village to village of skilled and reliable weavers able to deliver the qualities and patterns desired on time, and agents travelled the textile regions seeking these out.[36]

Porcelain production was more concentrated, but flexibly accommodated the diverse demands of Asian and European markets. Much of the European ware was produced in one centre, Jingdezhen, a whole city of porcelain production, with a small amount, as well as decoration, available in Canton. Another centre, Tehua, produced the *blanc-de-chine* also admired in Europe. Jingdezhen had been rebuilt after a fire in 1683; a series of innovative directors reorganised its factories, promoted the invention of new glazes, and increased productivity. Factories were departmentalised even down to a high degree of division of labour in the decorating studios. Painters specialised in particular motifs, flowers, birds and animals or mountains and rivers, and no one piece of porcelain was a personal creation.[37]

Most of the porcelain was bought through a Hong Merchant who took European merchants out to some of the hundred or so shops in Canton where they bought their goods, and placed orders for others. The production system was flexible enough to absorb the increase in demand for goods in the seventeenth and eighteenth centuries, and also adept at copying the shapes and designs sought in European markets. In 1777–8 well over 800 tons of chinaware was carried by European East India Company vessels.[38] (see Plates 40–41.)

Imitation and the creation of chinoiserie

Adaptation of designs and shapes to European tastes required a complex interaction of responses to market demand and technique. A process of imitation was put in train, and a form of chinoiserie created in the process. This imitation was frequently commented on by western observers who admired the ease with which Asian craftsmen accommodated to the alien shapes, colour schemes and flora preferred in Europe. In the early Coromandel chintzes the subject matter was derived from Persian or Deccani miniature paintings and from Chinese ceramics, as well as from Jesuit engravings. But from the third quarter of the seventeenth century artisans were increasingly dependent on pattern books or musters sent from England, Holland and France. The effect of this international market orientation was to reinforce the specialization of producers to specific export zones. High risks, born by the merchants, attached to experimentation with designs.[39] The East India Company merchants, by the eighteenth century however, attempted to break through to a more adaptive form of imitation. The Court of Directors wrote:

> We send you some patterns, which may govern you so far as to see thereby that we want some new Works...endeavour to send us every year New Patterns, as well of the Flowers as Stripes, at least five or six in a bale, and let the Indians Work their own Fancys, which is always preferable before any Patterns we can send from Europe.[40]

This example from India was similar to practices in China and Japan. European shapes were sent out to China for basic tea and chocolate cups, saucers, plates, bowls, but also for more specialist candlesticks, goblet-shaped flower pots, punch bowls, small tea kettles in a whole range of stoneware, silver, pewter and glass as models for ceramic imitations. Key innovations adapting Chinese and Japanese eating and tea settings to European tastes were the tea and dinner services. The dinner service with complete setting for each person was an invention of the VOC and EIC which started importing porcelain dinner services in early eighteenth century. During the eighteenth century, English families commissioned from China 4,000 services with coats of arms. Each setting cost ten times that of ordinary settings.

These oriental imitations of European culture were not a new departure for Chinese and Japanese producers, for their design and production processes had long accommodated the variety of forms and decorative style demanded in a wide range of cultures across South-East Asia and India, as well as the Middle East.

To go even further back, porcelain was the principal material vehicle for assimilation and transmission of cultural themes across great distances. Chinese porcelain artists adapting alien forms & decoration, and exported these to foreign places, including some where these forms had originated generations before.[41] The adaptive product innovation arising from this practice of 'imitation' was an integral part of production for world markets. The Asian imitation of European forms and designs was combined with Oriental themes in a product design for world markets. A further development on these imitative principles was to come with European responses.

European responses

What impact did these Asian luxury goods have on Europe? The three areas which I have identified are:

1. The design and style of luxury and semi-luxury consumer goods for a civilised way of life.
2. Production and mercantile systems able to make a rapid transition to a demand shock – to be able to produce and distribute a highly diverse range of goods for large urban and middling class markets right across the world. This was

production was production on an industrial scale which had never before been seen in the West.
3. The imitative processes involved in product development for Western markets. If China, Japan and India could do this, why could not the West? What part did 'imitation' play in the development of European consumer goods?

If imitation was part of the design aesthetic of oriental commodities, it was also central to western aesthetic traditions. Certainly, during the eighteenth century artists and moral philosophers from Hogarth and Reynolds to Smith and Hume made imitation a central part of their theories of taste and aesthetics.

Imitation was, of course, central to policies of import substitution, and it was also important to technology. If we look first to import substitution. Imports of Asian luxuries were perceived to cause an imbalance of trade. There were no comparable markets for European exports in Asia. While there seemed no possibility of finding substitutes for the raw materials and foodstuffs imported from Asia, especially tea, in the eighteenth century, it was seen as possible to stem the tide of Asian manufactures. Could not Europeans produce similar goods in the Asian style? Thus it was that these desirable consumer goods soon faced heavy tariffs and prohibitions in Europe. In Britain from the late 1680s a series of restrictions, duties and excise taxes were imposed, followed by outright prohibition of imported printed calicoes in 1700.

The restrictions in England reached not just to imported wares, but to home-produced calicoes. Vested interests in the woollen, linen and silk industries succeeded in another prohibition in 1721 on the sale, purchase or wearing of all printed cloth containing cotton; printers instead exercised their talents on linens, fustians and calicoes for export. The French acted earlier, banning the import, production and use of painted calicoes in 1686, but retracted the prohibition in 1759. The Spanish waited until the Peace of Utrecht, then in 1717 banned silks and other textiles from Asia and China, and the next year extended this to the use of all these materials.

The Dutch as well as the German states and the Swiss took a more liberal stance. A liberal policy on imports also spawned a local printing industry. Local textile producers protested in the Netherlands, but the Republic did not intervene, and as well as importing from Asia, there was a proliferation of calico-printing shops around Amsterdam, as well as in the German towns of Bremen, Frankfurt, and Hamburg. The French printers took refuge in the Swiss towns establishing a French industry in exile in Neufchâtel, Lausanne, Geneva and Basel.[42]

The printing of cotton in England started in the seventeenth century. In 1676 Will Sherwin was granted a patent to print on broad cloth. But polychromy in fast bright colours was not possible until 1740. There were large numbers of patents in England for printing technologies, and the London base of the industry from the mid-eighteenth century was facing competition from Lancashire. This import substituting semi-luxury industry, basing its markets in the demand for printed fabrics of fine counts inspired by the Asian imports, sparked the growth of the cotton industry and the rapidly mechanising processes which accompanied it.

There were no corresponding prohibitions on the import of ceramics from Asia, but European rulers and princes patronising their own early porcelain works imposed strict controls on competing factories. In the case of France, Louis XV and XVI kept excise duties high and issued prohibitory edicts to protect the royal manufactory at Sèvres from competition.[43] Though there were no prohibitions in England on the importation of Far Eastern ceramics, the goods nevertheless faced tariffs which rose rapidly over the course of the eighteenth century. These started in 1704 at 12.5 per cent of the value at wholesale auction prices; the duty rate was approximately one third of the sale value for sample years during the 1770s, and by the early 1790s was charged at half the auction value. The East India Company faced high tariffs, but its returns on imported porcelain were further restricted by an oligopoly of London china dealers, operating a ring to keep prices artificially low. The discovery prompted its decision to discontinue its bulk importation of porcelain.[44]

These protectionist measures on some of the most rapidly growing manufactured imports did indeed foster the rapid growth of import-substituting industries. The markets for these industries had been prepared by Asian imports: a huge re-export trade (40 per cent of British exports by 1750) now absorbed high proportions of colonial imports, and new domestically-produced substitutes swelled exports.

The effect of Asian imports of ceramics was to inspire the rise of Europe's great porcelain works, and indigenous pottery industries. Tin-glazed approximations were available in various forms from the end of the sixteenth century. There was the Spanish and Islamic then Italian faience and maiolica distinguished by its white glaze and sparse decoration. There was delftware, and there was Dutch and English majolica.

Other ceramics works were royal manufactories or high luxury producers of European porcelain. Meissen first produced a hard red unglazed stoneware close the red stoneware of Yi Hsing. These were imitated in Bayreuth, Delft and in Staffordshire. The Meissen factory, the royal works of Saxony, made the breakthrough to produce hard-paste porcelain in 1709, and produced expensive goods in Chinese and Japanese designs. Likewise, France's Chantilly factory which produced a soft-paste porcelain before the end of the seventeenth century was the project of an aristocrat who owned a large collection of Japanese original decorative pieces. Rouen, Vienna, St Cloud and Mennecy all followed suit. During the eighteenth century there were porcelain factories under the patronage and control of rulers and princelings at Sèvres, Paris, Berlin, Vienna, Naples, Florence and Vicenza. The English porcelain works, Chelsea and Bow both took their patterns from aristocratic collections of Japanese originals. Bow called itself the 'New Canton'. Worcester copied the Imari patterns and colours.[45]

European porcelain may have been an import substitute, but it did not meet the market demand of Chinese porcelain. Indeed Postlethwayt set out the key difference between this European porcelain and that of Asia.

'What render the Oriental porcelain so universally estimable is, not only is general delicacy, but its general greater cheapness compared to that of Dresden, or any other nation: and 'till England, France, Holland or Saxony, can afford this manufacture at as reasonable rates as the Eastern nations do, it can never be expected that any, or indeed all the united European porcelain manufactures, will vend so large a quantity as is done by the Asiatics in general.'

The real substitute was provided by another imitation of Asian ware, fine earthenware. This drew on cheaper indigenous materials, was developed in Britain's own pottery region, and set in train an extensive product innovation in eating and drinking utensils. The substitute was not provided by Europe's porcelain works, but by European earthenware manufacturers who worked to perfect a 'creamware' or 'pearlware' alternative to porcelain. This fine lead-glazed earthenware was first made in Staffordshire between 1730 and 1740, and quickly demonstrated its advantages over the softer, easily chipped continental tin-glazed faience and delftware. Wedgwood was one of a number of earthenware manufacturers in Staffordshire, Liverpool, Leeds and elsewhere now turning their attention to creamware. In 1763 he described this as 'a species of earthenware for the table quite new in its appearance, covered with a rich and brilliant glaze bearing sudden alterations of heat and cold, manufactured with ease and expedition, and consequently cheap'.

He established a prosperous export trade, and saw himself turning the tables on the Chinese when he wrote to Bentley in 1767: 'Don't you think we shall have some Chinese Missionaries come here soon to learn the art of making Creamcolour.'[46]

Conclusion

Imitation was the means by which a quality consumer goods manufacture was introduced to Europe, and especially to Britain during the later seventeenth and eighteenth centuries. This was a process of creating an 'economy of quality' in response to Asian luxury. It was a policy of using the arts, including the fine arts and design in combination with modern manufacturing technique. This was the lesson that merchants and manufacturers had learned from Asia.

The great Asian manufactures which entered Europe on a large scale between the later sixteenth century and the eighteenth century brought a new kind of semi-luxury to world trade. These were novelty consumer goods, exotic in provenance and style, but domestic and endowed with the variety to display taste and individuality. They were also produced and traded at a level which made them available, not just to traditional elites, but to the rapidly expanding middling and urban populations of Europe.

Notes

1. Gang Deng, *Chinese Maritime Activities and Socioeconomic Development c. 2100 B.C.–1900 A.D.* (Westport, Conn. and London, 1997), p. 113.
2. R.A. Goldthwaite, *Wealth and the Demand for Art in Italy 1300–1600* (Baltimore, 1993), pp. 224–50; Lisa Jardine, *Worldly Goods. A New History of the Renaissance* (London, 1996), p. 69.

3. Carolyn Sargentson, *Merchants and Luxury Markets* (London, 1996), p. 66.
4. P.J. Marshall, 'Taming the Exotic: the British and India in the Seventeenth and Eighteenth Centuries', in G.S. Rousseau, R. Porter, eds, *Exoticism in the Enlightenment* (Manchester, 1990), pp. 46–65, 57; Chandra Mukerji, *From Graven Images: Patterns of Modern Materialism* (New York, 1983); A. Reichwein, *China and Europe. Intellectual and Artistic Contacts in the Eighteenth Century* (London, 1925), p. 89.
5. J. Raby and M. Vickers, 'Puritanism and Positivism', in M. Vickers, ed., *Pots and Pans: A Colloquium on Precious Metals and Ceramics in the Muslim, Chinese and Graeco-Roman Worlds* (Oxford, 1985), pp. 217–23, at 217–19.
6. Patrick McCray, *The Fragile Craft Glass in Renaissance Venice* (Aldershot, 1999).
7. Andrew Sherratt, 'Silver and Skeuomorphism in the Ancient World: the Social and Economic Context of Greek Pottery Production', Unpublished paper; Michael Vickers and D. Gill, *Artful Crafts. Ancient Greek Silverware and Pottery* (Oxford, 1994).
8. Malachy Postlethwayt, *J. Savary des Bruslons, The Universal Dictionary of Trade and Commerce*, I, fourth edition (London, 1774), entry on Mechanical Arts.
9. Cited in J.M. MacKenzie, *Orientalism, History, Theory and the Arts* (Manchester, 1995), p. 127.
10. Linda Colley, 'The English Rococo. Historical Background', in M. Snodin, ed., *Rococo Art and Design in Hogarth's England* (London, 1984), pp. 10–17; Kate Scott, *The Rococo Interior* (New Haven and London, 1995).
11. E.L. Jones, 'The Fashion Manipulators: Consumer Tastes and British Industries 1660–1800', in L.P. Cain and P.J. Uselding, eds, *Business Enterprise and Economic Change* (Ohio, 1973).
12. On the significance of this Chinese and Japanese consumer culture, and a sophisticated intra-Asian trade in luxury goods, see John E. Willis, 'European Consumption and Asian Production in the Seventeenth and Eighteenth Centuries', in John Brewer and Roy Porter, eds, *Consumption and the World of Goods* (London and New York, 1973), pp. 133–47; Peter Burke, 'Rex et verba: Conspicuous Consumption in the Early Modern World', in Brewer and Porter, *Consumption and the World of Goods*, pp. 148–61; Craig Clunas, *Superfluous Things. Material Culture and Social Status in Early Modern China* (Cambridge, 1991), and his 'Modernity Global and Local: Consumption and the Rise of the West', *American Historical Review*, 104 (1999), pp. 1497–511.
13. E.L. Jones, *Growth Recurring: Economic Change in World History* (Oxford, 1988), and Kenneth Pomeranz, *The Great Divergence. China, Europe and the Making of the Modern World Economy* (Princeton, 2000).
14. Kent Deng, 'A Critical Survey of Research in Chinese Economic History', *Economic History Review*, 52 (2000), pp. 1–23; Jones, *Growth Recurring*, pp. 80–2.
15. See Shelagh Vainker, 'Luxury or Not: Silk and Porcelain in Early Modern China', this volume.
16. Jones, *Growth Recurring*, p. 158; Eric Jones, Lionel Frost and Colin White, *Coming Full Circle. An Economic History of the Pacific Rim* (Boulder, Colorado, San Francisco, Oxford, 1993), p. 35.
17. K.N. Chaudhuri, *Asia before Europe* (Cambridge, 1990), pp. 186–90, 200–20.
18. Deng, *Chinese Maritime Activities*, p. 134. Kent Deng, 'Critical Survey of Research in Chinese Economic History', *Economic History Review*, 53 (2000), pp. 1–28, 4–5.
19. Gang Deng, 'The Foreign Staple Trade of China in the Pre-Modern Era', *The International History Review*, 19 (1997), pp. 253–83, 264–5, 276.
20. C. Ho, 'The Ceramic Trade in Asia, 1602–82', in A.J.H. Latham and H. Kawakatsu, *Japanese Industrialization and the Asian Economy* (London, 1994), pp. 35–70, 36–49, 43, 47.
21. Oliver Impey, 'Japanese Export Porcelain', in J. Ayers, O. Impey, J.V.G. Mallet, *Porcelain for Palaces* (London, 1990), pp. 25–36; H. Nishida, 'Japanese Export Porcelain during the 17th and 18th Centuries', D. Phil Thesis (Oxford, 1975), pp. 65–70; C. Ho, 'The Ceramic Trade in Asia, 1602–82', pp. 43 and 47.

22. K.N. Chaudhuri, *The Trading World of Asia and the English East India Company 1660–1760* (Cambridge, 1978), pp. 205 and 242; A. Dasgupta, 'Indian Merchants and the Trade in the Indian Ocean', in T. Raychaudhuri and I. Habib, *The Cambridge Economic History of India*, I (Cambridge, 1982), pp. 407–33, 415–16 and 428–33.
23. Kent Deng, 'Critical Survey of Research in Chinese Economic History' and [Gang] Deng, 'The Foreign Staple Trade of China in the Pre-Modern Era', 253–83, 264–5 and 276.
24. K.N. Chaudhuri, *The English East India Company. A Study of an Early Joint Stock Company 1600–1640* (London, 1965), p. 195.
25. *Ibid.* For further detail on adapting these imports to European taste see Maxine Berg, 'Manufacturing the Orient: Asian Commodities and European Industry', Proceedings of the Istituto 'Francesco Datini', Prato, vol. 29, 1998, pp. 385–419; John Styles, 'Product Innovation in Early Modern London', *Past and Present*, 168, 2000, pp. 124–69; and especially Beverley Lemire, *Fashion's Favourite. The Cotton Trade and The Consumer in Britain 1600–1800* (Oxford, 1991).
26. Chaudhuri, *The Trading World*, p. 282.
27. Chaudhuri, 'European Trade with India', in T. Raychaudhuri and I. Habib, *The Cambridge Economic History of India*, pp. 382–406 and 402.
28. *Ibid*, p. 401; M. Beurdley, *Porcelain of the East India Companies* (London, 1962), pp. 117–18.
29. Robert Finlay, 'The Pilgrim Art: the Culture of Porcelain in World History', *Journal of World History*, 9 (1998), pp. 141–88 and 168.
30. G.A. Godden, *Oriental Export Market Porcelain and its Influence on European Wares* (London, 1979), p. 114.
31. K.N. Chaudhuri, *Asia Before Europe. Economy and Civilisation of the Indian Ocean from the Rise of Islam to 1750* (Cambridge, 1990), pp. 304–9.
32. Finlay, 'The Pilgrim Art', p. 148.
33. Elvin, *The Pattern of the Chinese Past*, p. 285.
34. Finlay, 'The Pilgrim Art', p. 148.
35. Lemire, *Fashion's Favourite*, p. 18.
36. K.N. Chaudhuri, *Trade and Civilization in the Indian Ocean* (Cambridge, 1985), pp. 200–2.
37. Godden, *Oriental Export Market Porcelain*, p. 113; D.F. Lunsingh-Scheuleer, *Chinese Export Porcelain* (London, 1974), pp. 24–8.
38. *Ibid.*, p. 47.
39. Chaudhuri, *Asia Before Europe*, pp. 302–3 and 312.
40. Cited in Chaudhuri, *Asia Before Europe*, p. 303.
41. Finlay, 'The Pilgrim Art'; Jessica Rawson, *Ancient China*, pp. 206–12.
42. J.K.J. Thomson, 'State Intervention in the Catalan Calico-Printing Industry in the Eighteenth Century', in M. Berg, ed., *Markets and Manufacture in Early Industrial Europe* (London, 1991), pp. 57–89 and 61.
43. Robin Reilly, *Wedgewood*, I (London, 1989), p. 76.
44. Hilary Young, *English Porcelain*, p. 74.
45. J. Mallet, 'European Ceramics and Influence of Japan', in U. Ayers, O. Impey, J. Mallet, eds., *Porcelain for Palaces* (London, 1990), pp. 35–55; W. Bemrose, *Bow, Chelsea and Derby Porcelain* (London, 1989), p. 35.
46. Robin Reilly, *Wedgwood*, I, p. 184. For a broader treatment see Maxine Berg, 'From Imitation to Invention: Creating Commodities in Eighteenth-centery Britain', *Economic History Review*, 55, 2002, pp. 1–30.

Plates

38. Skirt and frock of cotton, handpainted in India.
39. Chintz overdress, painted and dyed cotton.
40. Chinese octagonal plate, *c.* 1736, with European Delft tile, used as a pattern, *c.* 1745.
41. Saucer and cup with handle, *c.* 1720.

Index

Adam, Robert 152, 156, 197
 Ruins of the Palace of Emperor Diocletian 152
Addison, Joseph 191
 'Pleasures of the Imagination' 123, 129
aesthetics 3, 85*n*, 132*n*
 debate 19
 and human body Plate *12*, 119, 126–7, 130
 moral-sense paradigm 121–2
 picturesque 141–2, 146
 serpentine (Hogarth) 120, 124–5, 130–1
 see also taste
agricultural reform 139–40, 142, 147
 America 145
agriculture
 balance with manufacturing 22
 threatened by urban consumption 33–4
 see also cottage(s)
Agriculture, Board of 140
Alexander the Great, and Roxane 176*n*
amber 8
American colonies 151
 architectural comfort (cottages) 144–6
Amsterdam 50, 51–2, 232, 240
 silk industry 52
Anglomania, in Europe 19
Anhui, Chinese ink production 209
Anti-Gallican Society 14
Antigua 221–2
antiques, classical 152
Apparudai, Arjun 214
appearances, culture of 46–7, 48
appetite (desire)
 for esteem 128, 131
 indulgence 2, 129–30
 male 128
 in materialist psychology 119, 120–1, 127–8, 131
 see also moral-sense paradigm
Appleby, Joyce 48
Arabia, cultivation of 11, 76
archaeology 152
architecture
 Baroque 138
 for basic comfort 140–1
 'Chinese' 137
 classical style 137, 138, 152

garden buildings Plate *14*, 136, 137, 138–9
 Montagu House 197–201
 picturesque 141–2, 146
 primitivism 137–8, 146
 rusticity 137, 138
 villas 144
 see also cottages; landscape architecture
Aristotle 45
 Nicomachean Ethics 8
artisans *see* craftsmen
arts and crafts movement (1880s) 231
Asia
 interregional trade 232, 233–4
 moral debate on luxury in 7–8
 see also China; India; Japan
aspiration(s)
 and economic development 44, 55*n*
 and luxury 9
 in modern consumer society 23
 plebeian 103, 105, 111–12
 social 128
assemblies 1, 7
Athens, classical 152, 230
Auslander, Leora 72
Austen, Jane, *Sense and Sensibility* 135
Authentic and Interesting Memoirs of Miss Ann Sheldon 183, 186
authenticity
 Christian 46, 47
 and performance 168, 169
 prostitute memoirs 181, 182
Authentick Memoirs . . . of the Celebrated Sally Salisbury 178–80, 181, 182, 183–4, 187
Avant Coureur (Parisian weekly) 80, 82
avarice, Mandeville on 30, 32–3, 45

Bacon, Francis 173
Bacon, John, sculptor 156
Bamford, Samuel 112–13
banks and banking
 Paris pawnshop 98–100, 102*n*
 role of pedlars 91, 93
Barbauld, Anna 192, 193
Barbon, Nicholas 9, 31, 127
baroque style 85*n*, 138, 231
Barrington, James 199
Batavia (Indonesia) 234